SOCIOLOGY:
A Christian Approach for Changing the World

SOCIOLOGY:
A Christian Approach for Changing the World

Cynthia Benn Tweedell
General Editor

Triangle Publishing
Marion, Indiana

This book
is dedicated to the memory
of
Charles DeSanto,
who devoted his career to promoting
a Christian perspective in sociology.
He was a world changer.

Sociology: A Christian Approach for Changing the World
Cynthia Benn Tweedell, General Editor

Direct correspondence and permission requests to one of the following:
E-mail: info@trianglepublishing.com
Web site: www.trianglepublishing.com
Mail: Triangle Publishing
        4301 South Washington Street
        Marion, Indiana 46953
        USA

Unless otherwise noted, all scriptural quotations are from the NRSV, *The Holy Bible: New Revised Standard Version,* copyright, 1989, by the Division of Christian Education of the National Council of the Churches of Christ in the U.S.A. Used by permission. All rights reserved.

Scripture quotations marked NIV are taken from *The Holy Bible: New International Version®.* NIV®. Copyright © 1973, 1978, 1984 by International Bible Society. Used by permission of Zondervan Publishing House. All rights reserved.

Scripture quotations marked RSV are taken from *The Holy Bible: Revised Standard Version,* copyright © 1946, 1952, 1971 by the Division of Christian Education of the National Council of the Churches of Christ in the U.S.A.

Scripture quotations marked KJV are from *The Holy Bible, the Authorized King James Version, 1611.*

Tweedell, Cynthia Benn, General Editor
Sociology: A Christian Approach for Changing the World
ISBN 1-931283-02-8

Copyright ©2003 by Triangle Publishing. All rights reserved. No part of this publication may be reproduced, stored in a retrieval system, distributed or transmitted in any form or by any means: electronic, mechanical, photocopy, recording or any other, except for brief quotations in printed reviews and as permitted under the United States Copyright Act of 1976, without prior written permission of the publisher.

Printed in the United States of America
by Evangel Press, Nappanee, Indiana

CONTRIBUTORS

Sarah Anders, Ph.D., Professor Emerita, Dept. of Sociology, Louisiana College. A long-time supporter of Baptist Women in Ministry, she is one of the energizing forces behind its creation.

Lori J. Anderson, Ph.D., Professor of Sociology and Department Head for Social Work, Sociology, and Criminal Justice, Tarleton State University. Her areas of expertise include theory, family, social psychology, and aging.

Steven Bird, Ph.D., Associate Professor of Sociology, Taylor University. His primary professional interests are statistical, methodological, and organizational issues, as well as the sociological study of religion.

Julian Bridges, Ph.D., Professor of Sociology and Chair of the Sociology Department, Hardin-Simmons University. He is the general editor of the widely used *Sociology: A Pragmatic Approach* (Hunter, 1986).

Charles DeSanto, Ph.D., served for many years as Professor of Sociology at Lock Haven State University and edited several Christian sociology texts. Before his death in 2000, he coordinated an earlier version of this text.

Murl O. Dirksen, Ph.D., Professor of Anthropology and Sociology; Chair of the Department of Behavioral and Social Sciences, Lee University. Centered in Asia, Central America, and the Middle East, his research has focused on nomadism-pastoralism, modern and social change, and religious movements.

John Eby, Ph.D., Professor of Sociology and Chair of the Department of Sociology and Social Work, Messiah College. His field of expertise includes development, social policy and social change, service-learning, faith and culture, and the scholarship of teaching and learning.

Donald Gray, Ph.D., Professor of Sociology, Eastern College. His areas of interest include research methods, family, and social change.

Kenneth F. Ferraro, Ph.D., Professor of Sociology and Director of the Gerontology Program, Purdue University. His research, supported by the National Institute on Aging, focuses on health inequality across the life course, minority health, and the link between religion and health.

Pati K. Hendrickson, M.A., Assistant Professor of Criminology, Tarleton State University. Her interests include criminology, research methods, theory, and corrections.

Thomas C. Hood, Ph.D., Professor of Sociology, University of Tennessee, Knoxville. In addition to focusing on collective behavior/social movements, he writes and teaches about the work of Erving Goffman, environmental sociology, research methods, and popular religion.

Larry Ingram, Ph.D., Professor of Sociology, University of Tennessee at Martin. Active in organizing and serving on the Steering Committee of the Christian Sociological Society, his research interest was the sociology of religion. Dr. Ingram died in 2001, shortly after completing his chapter for this text.

R. Boyd Johnson, Ph.D., Assistant Professor of International Studies, Indiana Wesleyan University. His areas of interest include foreign missions, international business, and cultural anthropology.

Michael M. Jessup, Ph.D., Professor of Sociology, Taylor University. His academic interests include social movements, social theory, and sociology of the family.

Aubrey Keller, Ph.D., Professor in the Department of Sociology, Social Work, Criminal Justice, and Anthropology, University of Tennessee at Martin. His interests include general sociology and the sociology of knowledge.

Brenda King, M.A., Associate Professor of Sociology, Cornerstone University. Her areas of expertise include family, social problems, social psychology, and research.

Jerome R. Koch, Ph.D., Associate Professor of Sociology, Texas Tech University. His primary areas of research interest include sociology of religion, sociology of medicine, deviance, organizations, drugs/alcohol, and bio-ethics.

Barbara Carr Matchette, M.S.W., Assistant Professor of Social Work, Indiana Wesleyan University. Her academic interests include gender issues, social problems, and social work.

Harold Osborne, Ph.D., Professor and Chair of the Sociology Department, Baylor University. His area of expertise includes criminology, juvenile delinquency, and social change.

Donald Ratcliff, Ph.D., Associate Professor of Education, Biola University. He teaches educational psychology and research methods classes, primarily at the graduate level. His key academic interests are child and school culture theory, qualitative research, and children's spiritual development and experience.

William Smith-Hinds, Ph.D., Professor of Sociology, Lock Haven State University. His area of expertise is race relations. He helped to edit *A Reader in Sociology: A Christian Perspective* (Herald Press, 1980), a widely read volume of Christian sociology.

Cynthia Benn Tweedell, Ph.D., Assistant Dean of Accreditation and Assessment, Indiana Wesleyan University. She has taught introductory sociology for twenty-five years. Among her interests are social inequality issues, including removing the barriers conventional education systems create for women and minorities.

Michael L. Yoder, Ph.D., Professor of Sociology, Northwestern College, Iowa. His primary interest areas are sociology of religion, ethnicity, demography, and Latin American society.

PREFACE

This text has a long and interesting history filled with the grace of God. It is based on a text written in the mid-1980s by Julian Bridges, published by Hunter Textbooks. In his third edition, Dr. Bridges asked several colleagues, all Christian sociologists, to contribute chapters. When a fourth updated edition was needed, Charles DeSanto, who had edited several other Christian sociology textbooks, was asked by Dr. Bridges to coordinate the work. He contacted many Christian sociologists, including those in the earlier work, and compiled a text. However, the publisher was concerned about the market for such a text, so DeSanto's edition was never released.

In 2000, Triangle Publishing asked me to consider writing a sociology text. I knew that it had been several years since Charles DeSanto had produced a text for Christian sociology students and that such a book was long overdue. I contacted my friends and colleagues at the Association of Christians Teaching Sociology. They informed me about the text that had been edited and never published. Thomas Hood provided me with a copy of the unpublished work. I spoke with Charles DeSanto, who was very pleased that I was continuing his work. A few days later, dear Charlie went to be with the Lord.

This text is quite different from the unpublished work edited by Charles DeSanto. It also differs dramatically from the original text edited by Julian Bridges. Those books were not overtly Christian textbooks and did not have a world-changing focus. Statistics and references are updated. Several new authors have been added. There are new sections on Biblical Reflections and How Christians Can Change the World. While inspired by the work of Bridges and DeSanto, it is quite different in its focus and content.

In 2000, Indiana Wesleyan University launched a new mission to change the world by "developing students in character, scholarship, and leadership." This book's focus articulates that mission by using principles of sociology to change the world. It also reflects Indiana Wesleyan's commitment to promote excellence in adult education by giving real-world examples that are meaningful to adults struggling with careers and family. The brevity of the text is designed for the accelerated adult education format. However, this book will also be useful for all sociology students at Christian colleges that take seriously the integration of faith and learning.

This text would not be possible if it were not for the support of Indiana Wesleyan University's Triangle Publishing and particularly Nathan Birky, Publisher. The work was enthusiastically encouraged by Dr. David Wright, former Vice President of Adult and Graduate Studies, and Dr. Mark Smith, former dean and current Vice President of Adult and Graduate Studies. Bobbie Sease, technical editor for Triangle, put in many hours ensuring that all the different authors would speak in one unified voice. Vanetta Bratcher, Juli Knutson, Aimee Williams, and Janice Miller assisted with proofreading. R B Kuhn reviewed the entire manuscript and made many valuable editorial contributions. Gary Phillips contributed the graphic design. Andy Inskeep gave technical assistance.

More than fifty people have been involved in writing chapters and test questions, as well as reviewing and inspiring this project. Together we changed the world by producing a sociology text that does not insult a student's Christian faith. We pray that the students receiving this gift of Christian sociology will use it to change the world for Christ.

Cynthia Benn Tweedell
March 2002

TABLE OF CONTENTS

CHAPTER ONE	The Sociological Perspective *Cynthia B. Tweedell*	1
CHAPTER TWO	Sociological Theory and Methods *Cynthia B. Tweedell and Donald Gray*	11
CHAPTER THREE	Human Culture *Murl O. Dirksen*	27
CHAPTER FOUR	Social Structure, Groups, and Organizations *Donald Ratcliff, with contributions by Julian Bridges*	47
CHAPTER FIVE	Socialization *Barbara C. Matchette and Sarah Anders*	63
CHAPTER SIX	Deviance, Crime, and Social Control *Brenda King*	81
CHAPTER SEVEN	Social Stratification *Harold Osborne, Cynthia B. Tweedell, and R. Boyd Johnson*	103
CHAPTER EIGHT	Race and Ethnic Stratification *William Smith-Hinds and Cynthia B. Tweedell*	121
CHAPTER NINE	Gender and Society *Lori J. Anderson, Pati K. Hendrickson, Sarah Anders, and Cynthia B. Tweedell*	137
CHAPTER TEN	Aging *Kenneth F. Ferraro*	155
CHAPTER ELEVEN	Marriage and Family *Michael M. Jessup, with contributions by Charles DeSanto and Cynthia B. Tweedell*	175
CHAPTER TWELVE	Religion *Larry Ingram and Aubrey Keller*	195

CHAPTER THIRTEEN	Education *Steven Bird, with contributions by Charles DeSanto and Cynthia B. Tweedell*	215
CHAPTER FOURTEEN	Health and Society *Jerome R. Koch*	233
CHAPTER FIFTEEN	Economic Life *Michael L. Yoder*	247
CHAPTER SIXTEEN	Politics and Government *John Eby, with contributions by Julian Bridges*	267
CHAPTER SEVENTEEN	Collective Behavior and Social Movements *Thomas C. Hood*	287
CHAPTER EIGHTEEN	Social Change *Cynthia B. Tweedell*	299

CHAPTER ONE

The Sociological Perspective

chapter outline

I. What is sociology?
    A. Where did sociology come from?
    B. Where does sociology fit in the world of knowledge?
    C. Why study sociology?

II. The assumptions of a sociological perspective
    A. Human beings are social in nature
    B. Society changes people
    C. People change society

biblical reflection

"You are the light of the world."

—Matthew 5:14

You are about to embark on an interesting journey. We hope you will enjoy the ride. But be careful—it gets bumpy and may be hazardous to your mental health. We are going to challenge you to think critically about the world around you and to rethink your personal faith. Accepting this challenge means thinking "Christian-ly" about your taken-for-granted world. As we demonstrate ways to act out your faith in a world struggling for stability, we hope you will find that **sociology** is an indispensable tool in helping you become a world changer.

PLAN OF THIS TEXT

We have gathered Christian sociologists from across North America to contribute their best efforts to this textbook. It is our consensus that *sociology* and the *Christian faith* are intertwined. Our faith informs our thinking about sociology. Sociology has changed the way we look at the Christian church. As we share some of those insights in this text, we invite you to draw your own conclusions. We do not claim to have a single, united Christian theory of society. Rather, we represent many *Christian perspectives* on society. It is our hope that you will add your own Christian perspective as you consider the social world around you.

Although different authors have written each chapter, you will find some common threads throughout. Of particular interest is how three basic sociological theories can apply to almost all social phenomena. You will also see examples of how Christians can use sociology to change the world.

WHAT IS SOCIOLOGY?

Sociology is the science of society. It explores the influences and consequences of social behavior.

We view much of our behavior as the result of our own personal choices. But is it really? (We warned you that sociology was potentially hazardous to your mental health!) Did you ever get the feeling that a lot of things in your life are just beyond your control? For example, was your college choice really your own independent decision, or was it the product of a myriad of social forces: family, high school, work, friends, government, etc.? Sociology uncovers the many layers of social forces that impinge upon our personal freedoms. We really don't have many choices about our social behavior because there are a host of social forces pushing us in different directions.

Your social behavior has consequences as well. Every *social interaction*—face-to-face or E-mail to E-mail—changes someone's life a little. When people get together, things happen! Sociology studies the effects of your behavior—and everyone else's.

So sociology takes a second look at the "world taken for granted."[1] Think of the world as that chair across from you. Right now you see the chair from one particular perspective, but cannot see the whole chair. You have all kinds of assumptions about what the other side, the top, and the bottom of the chair look like. But you will never truly know until you get up, walk around it, and closely examine it from a variety of viewpoints. Right now you may only see two legs of the chair (though you may assume, based on your previous experience with chairs, that there are two more legs). Your friend across the room may see three legs and another friend may see four. Who is right?

Likewise, sociology is *one* perspective on the world. It will supplement the perspective you have been given by your parents, your in-laws,

Industrialization created new challenges for societies that were organized around farming and small-town living. New social problems required a new perspective on the social world: sociology.

your high school teacher, your pastor, your supervisor, etc. Based on scientific data rather than on Grandma's "wisdom," a sociological perspective will help you have a more complete view of the world.

WHERE DID SOCIOLOGY COME FROM?

Curiously, sociology did not emerge as a discipline until well after the scientific revolution of the 1700s. It is one of the most recent of the sciences. In the Dark Ages, if one needed to know about society, one would consult the local church, which was the protector (and censor) of all knowledge. As the influence of the church waned in Europe, there arose a need for an alternative source of knowledge about the social world. The Industrial Revolution produced social problems such as homelessness, urban blight, and crime that the church could not (or would not) address. It was out of this need for social change that sociology was born.

Most of the earliest sociologists had philosophic roots in Judeo-Christian theology. As we shall see in coming chapters, many sociologists come from religious families, so they have a great appreciation for the role of religion in stabilizing a chaotic society. When the influence of the church wanes, there is a need for alternate patterns of religious thought. For some, science has become a pseudo-religion.

French social philosopher **Auguste Comte** (1789-1857) coined the term "sociology" as "the science of society." Dubbing sociology the "queen of the sciences," he reasoned that if we can measure the physical world by using scientific methods, then we ought to be able to measure the social world in the same way. In his understanding, sociology was a higher form of science, since the social world is more complex and more important than the physical world. The sociologist was a "new priesthood" that would use science to improve society.

As North America encountered its own social crises at the turn of the twentieth century, sociology was imported from Europe to solve problems of urban decay, crime, and poverty. Early American sociologists were likewise interested in using this new science to change the world for the better.

As sociology has developed in North America over the past century, it has continued to attract people with religious roots. While many contemporary sociologists are not overtly religious, most have great appreciation for the role of religious ideas combined with sociological insights to change the world.

WHAT SOCIOLOGY IS NOT

Sociology is not *theology* or *philosophy*. Theology tells us about the nature of God and humankind. Philosophy informs us about the way things "ought to be." Theologians and philosophers comb through "sacred" texts (like the Bible) and use logic to explain the nature of the world. Sociology uses *science* to describe the way things are—not what ought to be. Every educated person should have some insights from philosophy and theology to formulate an image of an ideal world. Then we can use insights from sociology to understand the details about the current state of the world (its "fallen-ness") and where we need to work to bring it back to its ideal state (how we can be Christ's hands and feet to redeem the world).

Sociology is not *psychology*. Both sociology and psychology are *sciences*—using scientific data to understand human behavior. However, psychology emphasizes the human mind (the *intra*-personal)—feelings, emotions, self-image, etc. Sociology emphasizes *inter*-personal behavior—what happens between individuals. The two fields are closely related. In fact, there is an interesting field called *social psychology* that looks at the impact of interpersonal behavior on one's attitudes and vice versa. We will be taking a look at some of these interesting insights later in this text. Generally speaking, psychologists use slightly different methods of collecting data—favoring experiments over surveys—and are more focused on unusual behavior (the neurotic or psychotic) rather than the norm. Sociologists focus on the everyday, typical behavior of large groups of people rather than on one specific unusual case.

Sociology is not *socialism*. It is not a political philosophy advocating a particular economic or power structure. Because it is a science, sociologists try to be objective in gathering data and truthful in presenting information. There are sociologists who are politically conservative, and those who are politically liberal. But in the practice of sociology, we try to be neutral and honest in our methods of studying and understanding the social world.

WHERE DOES SOCIOLOGY FIT IN THE WORLD OF KNOWLEDGE?

One of the presumptions of this text is that all truth is God's Truth. Christians believe that biblical truth is the core of all knowledge. Christian philosophers apply biblical wisdom to understand the nature of the world around them. Artists express these inner truths on canvas or in other creative media. Sociology is one of many social and natural sciences that use *empirical* data (facts) to understand the current (and sometimes past) state of the world. The applied scientist uses these insights to act in the world. So while Christian sociologists try to maintain neu-

FIGURE 1:1
Where Sociology Fits in the Map of Christian Knowledge

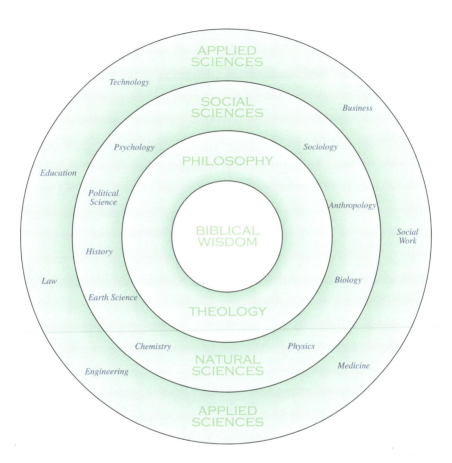

trality in studying the world, our responses to our discoveries are seldom neutral. As Christians we are obligated to help change the world.

WHY STUDY SOCIOLOGY?

As you can see from the figure above, a truly educated person needs a variety of insights in order to live and work in the world. Sociology complements the other disciplines so one may more fully understand the world. The Bible can tell us about the sinful nature of human beings, but sociology can help us understand the details of this sinful state. Sociologists use terms like "deviance" and "dysfunction" to systematize our understanding of what the Bible refers to as "sin."

By studying sociology you will gain a **sociological imagination**[2] which will liberate you to see yourself within a social context. Most of us go through life falsely believing we are the center of the universe. A majority of the time you probably see your personal troubles as isolated problems, unconnected to society as a whole.

Sociology helps you take the blinders off so that you may broaden your vision and see your world as you've never seen it before. What we often see as "private troubles"—poverty, unemployment, anorexia, drug use, divorce—are really public issues. For example, while we often see people caught in poverty as just "lazy individuals," sociology sees poverty as the product of a malfunctioning social system.

Likewise the Bible informs us that Jesus Christ died to cancel out *sin: individual sin and social sin*. Sinful individuals create **social sin** —structures and institutions built on sin. "For our struggle is not against enemies of blood and flesh, but against the rulers [principalities], against the authorities, against the cosmic powers . . ." (Eph. 6:12). Sociologists focus on the social sins deriving from these "principalities and powers." We see examples of how Jesus interacted with His social world in radical ways: healing on the Sabbath (Matt. 12); affirming the worth of women and children (Mark 10; Mark 14; John 4; Matt. 19); denouncing material wealth (Mark 10). Sociology helps us understand what this means in the twenty-first century. What areas of our social world need radical transformation? How can we act as Christ's hands and feet to help cancel the social sins around us?

If you are interested in working in any of the applied areas shown above, you need a sociological perspective. If you need help in your everyday interactions with people, you need a sociological perspective. If you want to understand the power structure at your office in order to do God's work there, you need a sociological perspective. If you want to understand why your mother or father, husband or wife, son or daughter act as they do, you need a sociological perspective. If you want to understand why things are the way they are, you need a sociological perspective.

THE ASSUMPTIONS OF A SOCIOLOGICAL PERSPECTIVE

Remember the chair analogy? Sociology is one platform from which to view the chair (the world). As humans we cannot see the whole world at once (only God can see all), so we must take a position in order to view the chair. This stance is based on certain assumptions. Assumptions are statements that predispose you to see the world in a certain way. An assumption is not a point to debate; it is just where you are standing to view the world. In order to "do" sociology, we are asking that you see the world from a certain stance. This stance is based on three assumptions. You don't have to walk away from this course accepting them all. But consider, just for the time being perhaps, these three assumptions of the sociological perspective[3]:

1. HUMAN BEINGS ARE SOCIAL IN NATURE.

"Then the Lord God said, 'It is not good that the man should be alone'" (Gen. 2:18). And so God created other people to love and care for us. God created people to need other people. It is not part of our nature to be alone. Psychological research shows that when a person is left alone for an extended period of time, abnormalities ensue: anxiety, hallucinations, and insanity. We quite naturally seek the company of others. Since we are created in God's image, we seek the same intimacy with others that God seeks with us. We need close relationships with at least a few people in order to survive. And other people need us to love and care for them. Jesus said, "By this everyone will know that you are my disciples, if you have love for one another" (John 13:35).

Can you think of some people without whom you could not survive? Start with your earliest caregivers. Aren't you glad they didn't abandon you at the hospital to fend for yourself? You needed people to feed you and give you warmth and lots of hugs. As you grew up, you needed family, teachers, and friends to help you learn about the world.

Now that you are older, you still need people, though often you would prefer to be left alone. People help us to navigate the world: They sell us food and clothing, give us jobs, and buy our products. As adults we still need lots of hugs. We thrive as individuals when we have healthy relationships with other people. It's just the way God created us.

2. SOCIETY CHANGES PEOPLE.

We need people, but people create problems for us. Sometimes they interfere with our personal freedom, intimidate, exploit, and alienate us. When people organize into a thing called "society," the social forces can be very far from God's command to "Love one another." Society has rules (**norms**) and no-nonsense ways of enforcing those rules (**sanctions**). Sometimes these norms seem rather arbitrary and inane. For instance, why are North American women expected to shave their legs while men can have hairy legs? There's no biblical mandate or logic to it: It's just the way society is. Society can make us do things we would not ordinarily do just by making us feel guilty or inferior. This book will explore the ways in which people, organized into a society, change other people.

Some of these changes are good. For example, aren't you glad your high school English teacher kept nagging you about your grammar and punctuation? You need those skills now to survive your sociology class! Chances are, other people encouraged you to consider this college, this class, and even to consider Jesus Christ! These are things you probably would not have done on your own.

Some changes are vexing. For example, did other kids affect your self-image by calling you names in school? Do certain elements of society make you feel guilty for juggling career and homemaking? Are you weighed down with the extra baggage of disappointments, making it more difficult for you to succeed in college? Social forces can affect the way we feel about ourselves and change the way we behave.

3. PEOPLE CHANGE SOCIETY.

But let's not blame society for all the bad things that happen to us. Who is society? ***We are society!*** People, by organizing themselves, create a society. And ***people, by working together, change society.***

You don't have to go on a mission trip or demonstrate in the streets to change society. You are in the process of changing society right now. Think about people whose lives are different because you are here. Do you remember the movie *It's a Wonderful Life*? George Bailey (played by Jimmy Stewart) discovers the world would be radically different if he were not alive. What about *your* parents, spouse, children, coworkers, and friends—would their lives be much different if you were not here? With each interaction, you are changing the world. Didn't you change the world for that woman at the checkout counter when you smiled at her? Didn't you change the world when you told your sick friend you would pray?

You can change the world for better or for worse. You decide. If you don't get control and change things for the better, society may come along and change you for the worse. This book will help you understand the way society works so that you can be pro-active instead of re-active. You can be part of some positive change instead of being taken in by other social forces seeking to gain at your expense.

CONCLUSION

Sociology explores the relationship between society and the individual. God creates the individual with the need for loving interactions with others. God seeks a loving interaction with the individual; the individual, having been made in the image of God, seeks God. As well, individuals made in the image of God create a society—however flawed—in which to have relationships with others. This society becomes a nemesis for us. It changes the individual by shaping attitudes and behaviors. But the individual, in turn, changes society by creating and sustaining culture, social structure, and social institutions. Sociology explores the details of this dyad in detail.

We are intricately connected to our social world. Sometimes we would like to escape, and often we do escape for a brief vacation, but we are called to social interaction. So interact we must.

We are like puppets on a string. The strings connect us to society. Society is pulling the strings and we are always moving in response to those tugs of society. But what would happen if we cut those strings to society? What would happen if we disconnected ourselves from our society? . . . THUD! We would fall to the ground, lifeless.

So we are puppets on a string, connected to society and tugged upon by social forces: family, school, media, and church. Is that it? Of course not! We can look up and say, "Hey, who's tugging those strings?" And occasionally we can tug back. That is what sociology is all about. We are investigating the puppet-master: the society that is tugging on our strings. We will examine what those tugs are all about and who is doing the tugging. And, having understood society, we will gain courage and skill to TUG BACK . . . maybe just a little. And so we will change the world!

FIGURE 1:2
The Individual is in Society—Society is in the Individual (adapted from Berger, 1963)

overview

- Sociology is one of many perspectives on the world. It takes a second look at everyday social interactions. But the perspective of sociology is unique in that it is the science of society. It studies the antecedents and consequences of social behavior.

- The roots of sociology are in the social philosophy of nineteenth-century Europe. Auguste Comte and others tried to use scientific principles to understand social changes precipitated by the Industrial Revolution. From the beginning, sociologists have sought to change the world by understanding the social forces that act upon human behavior.

- Sociology is a unique discipline, but it often overlaps with other disciplines. Though its subject matter is similar to philosophy and theology, it uses scientific methods to gather and analyze data. It is a social science, similar to other social sciences like economics, history, anthropology, psychology, and political science. But the focus of sociology is on interpersonal behavior and how these behaviors contribute to a social system.

- Sociologists operate from three basic assumptions about the world:

    1. Human beings are social in nature.
    2. Society changes people.
    3. People change society.

- We study sociology to understand the social world around us. By becoming aware of social forces and the way in which these forces affect individual behavior, we can better understand ourselves and others. By understanding the way in which society works, we can become agents of change to improve our world.

key concepts

Comte, Auguste
Nineteenth-century French social philosopher who is seen as the "father of sociology."

norms
The social behavior expected of people within a society.

sanctions
Positive and negative behaviors used to enforce a norm.

social sin
Social structures and institutions that are built on individual sin.

sociological imagination
The ability to take a second look at the "world taken for granted," enabling an individual to see him/herself within a social context.

sociology
The scientific study of society that explores the antecedents and consequences of social behavior.

endnotes

1. Peter L. Berger, *Invitation to Sociology: A Humanistic Perspective* (Garden City, NY: Doubleday & Co./Anchor Books, 1963).
2. C. Wright Mills, *The Sociological Imagination* (New York: Oxford University Press, 1956).
3. D. Stanley Eitzen and Maxine B. Zinn, *In Conflict and Order: Understanding Society* (Boston: Allyn & Bacon, 1998).

CHAPTER TWO

Sociological Theory and Methods

chapter outline

I. Three theoretical perspectives in sociology
    A. Structural-functional perspective
    B. Social conflict perspective
    C. Interactionist perspective

II. Doing Sociology
    A. Selecting a researchable problem
    B. Formulating testable hypotheses
    C. Choosing a data collection method
    D. Collecting data
    E. Preparing and analyzing data
    F. Interpreting results

III. A Christian perspective on social research

biblical reflection

"The eye is the lamp of the body. So, if your eye is sound, your whole body will be full of light."

—Matthew 6:22 RSV

In the previous chapter we defined sociology and looked at its possibilities for understanding and initiating social change. Sociology is a way of looking at the world. It challenges the "world taken for granted" and enables us to see the world as we have never seen it before. But what does a sociologist DO? This is not a profession you frequently see listed in the "want ads." This chapter will discuss the different tools sociologists use to "do" sociology. Different theories and methods are tools the sociologist uses to look at the social world.

When you choose to change the world, you must decide where to start. Where are you going to place yourself? What values and beliefs will become your presuppositions? What is your world and life view? This is the place from which you will launch effective change. Lasting social change starts from deep theoretical roots. For the Christian, these roots are primarily anchored in the Gospel of Jesus Christ. The foundation of Christ gives Christians the inspiration to be the salt and light of the earth (Matt. 5:13-14). But not all Christians take the same position from which to effect social change. Some identify themselves as politically liberal, some politically conservative, some fundamentalist, some reformed, etc. All are legitimate Christian positions from which to view the world. By taking different stands, Christians complement one another in doing God's work (1 Cor. 12). Where do you stand?

THREE THEORETICAL PERSPECTIVES IN SOCIOLOGY

Sociology is a perspective—a way of seeing the world. There is nothing "unchristian" about taking a sociological perspective on the world. In fact, it can illumine vital aspects of God's creation and human sin. But even within sociology there are different perspectives on the social world. Each complements the other. Taken together we get a more complete view of the social world.

This book uses three theoretical perspectives as an underlying framework from which to analyze a variety of sociological topics. These perspectives are all consistent with a Christian view of the world, though some Christians may favor one perspective over another. All three perspectives rest on presuppositions about the nature of society. They are places from which to view the world. Before a sociologist can make inquiries to understand the world, the sociologist must choose a perspective from which to view the world.

Remember the chair analogy in the last chapter? The chair looks different depending on where you are standing. Some may see three legs; some two; some see none. It all depends on where you are standing. But you must choose to stand somewhere in order to see the chair. It is the same with sociology: You may choose any one of the three perspectives from which to view the world. Each perspective gives a different view of the world. Taken together the three theoretical perspectives in sociology can give us a more complete view of the social world.

THE STRUCTURAL-FUNCTIONAL PERSPECTIVE: SOCIETY AS A WELL-OILED MACHINE

How does society hold together? Why are we not constantly at war with one another, in a state of anarchy? This thought was the passion of early sociologists like **Emile Durkheim** (1858-1917) and **Max Weber** (pronounced VAYber) (1864-1920). In post World War II America, this perspective fueled sociologists like **Talcott Parsons** (1902-1980) and **Robert Merton** (1910 -).

Durkheim was a Frenchman who searched for "social facts"—basic forms of behavior which he saw as the building blocks of a society. Curious as to how these basic forms of social behavior contributed to the solidarity of a society, he wanted to know how society held together. He concluded that these elementary forms of behavior, often religious in nature, *functioned* to create a *collective conscience* among the people.[1] In a well-functioning society, people cooperate and get along because they believe it is the "right thing to do."

Weber, a German sociologist from the same historical era as Durkheim, was also fascinated by the secret to social solidarity. He was particularly interested in how social institutions adapt to the social changes of the Industrial Revolution. The Europe about which he was writing was caught in economic and political turmoil, which eventually would spark World War I. Weber tried to sort it all out in order to help his society cope with the changes. He was generally optimistic about society's ability to organize itself around a core set of beliefs. His most famous work, *Protestant Ethic and the Spirit of Capitalism* (translated in 1930), explores the relationship between the Protestant founders of America and the new capitalism that was developing in the early twentieth century. Here he demonstrates that a religious belief system can *function* to change an economic system.

These early sociologists saw the development of a social structure as an important prerequisite to a healthy society. They were optimistic that humans would naturally work toward building a stable social system in order to survive. The increasing complexity of the twentieth century magnified the importance of building a society to integrate different segments and promote stability.

These ideas were taken up by twentieth-century American sociologists **Merton** and **Parsons**. Parsons was particularly interested in the ways in which social institutions functioned to meet basic social needs and promote a stable *social system*. Merton suggested that we analyze a system in terms of its interdependent parts and their *functions*. Such functions may be *manifest* (intended) or *latent* (unintended). For example, a school has as one of its manifest functions the preparation of future citizens. At the same time, the school has a latent function of providing friends and activities for young people. Merton also notes the presence of *dysfunctions*.

Contemporary **structural-functionalists** generally see the world from the following presuppositions:

1. **Society is a system of interconnected parts**. For example, a church may consist of a senior pastor, associate pastor, youth pastor, financial officer, Christian education director, administrator, and many people with many skills and talents to contribute to a stable organization. The people often form specialized committees interconnecting with one another and with the larger community.

The functionalist sees society as a system of interconnected parts, each with its own function.

2. **Each part has a function.** For example, in the church each leader and committee

Chapter Two: Sociological Theory and Methods

has a specific function to promote stability in the organization. Together all the people, committees, and leaders work like a well-oiled machine, humming and functioning to promote faith in the larger community.

3. **Society orders itself to promote a balance (equilibrium) among the various components.** For example, a church may have a leader or an activity that is *dysfunctional* to the overall mission of the organization. In such a case, the system will restructure itself to eliminate this dysfunctional element and so promote equilibrium.

The structural-functional perspective, then, focuses on how society survives by building a social structure of interconnecting social units. The sociologist who takes this perspective will examine the functions (manifest or latent) of the elements of a social structure. Any dysfunctional elements must be eliminated so that the social order is preserved.

THE SOCIAL CONFLICT PERSPECTIVE: SOCIETY AS A PRODUCT OF TENSIONS AND POWER STRUGGLES

In contrast to the structural-functional perspective, the **social conflict perspective** focuses on the tensions and power struggles in a society. Sociologists working from a conflict perspective gain inspiration from *Karl Marx* (1798-1857), who theorized that all social change is a product of tension and struggles for power.

Marx, like other early social theorists, puzzled over the impact of industrialization in Europe. He saw a society in which the owners of the means of production *(the bourgeoisie)* oppressed those who lacked money and property *(the proletariat)*. As a result of this oppression, the poor felt loss of pride in their work and consequently felt alienated, unlikely to contribute constructively to their society. Such *alienation* was only changed when the poor recognized that through united action they could change their world. For Marx, no change came without struggle and tension. He traced all of human history as a series of revolts against oppressive rulers.

Karl Marx saw society as a series of struggles for power.

Contemporary conflict theorists uncover ways in which people are oppressed and exploited by the ruling forces in a society. They generally use the following presuppositions in their perspective on the world:

1. **Conflict is more prevalent than order in a society.** For example, by preaching a Gospel that de-emphasizes material wealth, a church may create conflict in a community that measures success by one's economic clout. A church may create social conflict by challenging the gender and racial segregation of a community. At the same time, there is probably conflict within the church over theological issues and how to best implement ministry.

2. **Conflict is necessary to produce social change.** For example, a church can change a community by promoting racial harmony and social justice. However, there will probably be opposition to these ideas from certain people in the commu-

Sociology: A Christian Approach for Changing the World

nity and even within the church. When opposed, people will often work harder to produce the change they desire. While a social change group may not attain everything it works for, it will inevitably make a mark on its community just by raising consciousness.

3. **When disadvantaged people work together, change can happen.** A church need not consist of many wealthy members in order to change the community. All that is really necessary is for people to work together against social injustice.

Conflict can be very destructive to a society when it is not effectively managed. But constructively channeled conflict is a positive force for change within a society. A sociologist viewing the world from the social conflict perspective will examine tensions between individuals, within social organizations, and within society as a whole. Such conflict is often produced when powerful forces wish to maintain control by making less powerful people feel they are unimportant. A conflict theorist will assume that such conflict is not necessarily bad, but constructively channeled can be redemptive to the individual, the organization, and the society.

THE INTERACTIONIST PERSPECTIVE: UP CLOSE AND PERSONAL

The structural-functionalist and conflict perspectives are **macro-theories** or "big picture" views of the world. They focus on larger social forces that work to create order or produce conflict. Such a macro-sociological perspective seeks to understand the world from a broad, comprehensive level. In contrast, there are **micro-theories**, which look at individual social interactions. Such a perspective focuses on the

The interactionist perspective looks at how individual interactions shape our social identity.

individual's words, gestures, actions, and the meanings they create. This perspective is inspired by the work of American sociologists such as *George Herbert Mead* (1863-1931).

Mead was interested in meaning created by manipulating symbols such as language, gestures, and dress. In his book, *Mind, Self, and Society* (1934), he posited that at birth an infant is only a bundle of potentiality with an undeveloped identity. It is only through interactions with our society that we become fully human. *Significant others*, such as family and close friends, interact with us using language, gestures, and other symbols. We also interact with *generalized others*, the society as a whole. These forces, significant and generalized, affect our self-perception and produce for us a very real self-concept. This self-concept changes the way we interact with others.

Sociologists who see the world from an **interactionist perspective** make the following assumptions about the social world:

1. **Individual social interactions define how we see ourselves and others.** When someone calls you a "man," it creates quite a different perception in your mind than when someone calls you "boy" or "girl." Some women may feel very confused when they are called "girl" or "man" because it doesn't fit with their view of themselves. Using the words "Lord" or "Father" to describe God creates a different image than words like "Shepherd" or "Friend."

2. **Our perception of a social situation changes the way we behave.** We become different people in different social situations. In a church setting or with Christian friends, we may think and act very differently than we would in a nonchurch setting with nonreligious friends.

3. **Individuals interact to create, maintain, and change society.** While individual interactions are often confusing or stressful, they are the building blocks of a society. Jesus changed individuals by utilizing the power of social interactions. Using powerful symbols such as parables, Jesus worked one-on-one with people.

The interactionist perspective can enable people to better understand themselves and others. It takes a second look at the everyday interactions of individuals with a particular interest in the meanings that are created. A sociologist looking at the world from an interactionist perspective would take note of the symbols that humans use to create meaning. A word, a look, a gesture, a piece of clothing, all can communicate something about who we are.

The chair (the world) looks different depending on where you're standing (your perspective).

THREE WAYS OF LOOKING AT THE WORLD

The three perspectives in sociology—structural-functionalist, conflict, and interactionist—complement one another to enable us to see the social world more completely. All three perspectives are legitimate points from which to view the world. Each perspective produces a different image: sometimes the chair looks like it has two legs, sometimes three or four. It all depends on where you are standing.

The two macro-level theories appear to contradict one another but actually enable us to see a more complete view of the social world. The *structural-functionalist* looks at how the social world is held together. The *conflict theorist* looks at how the world is falling apart. Both order and conflict are happening simultaneously. Tensions and power struggles in the world are always acting to recreate the social order.

The micro-level *interactionist theory* gives us a completely different view of the social world. By focusing on individual interactions and the meanings they create, we can understand more about ourselves and others. Symbols such as language or dress become powerful elements in social analysis.

These three perspectives will be applied throughout this book. Each one will shed new light on topics such as deviance, family, and religion. By seeing society in new ways, you

FIGURE 2:1

Steps in Doing Sociological Research

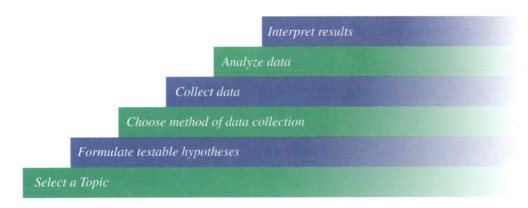

will become liberated to make the kinds of changes God calls you to make.

DOING SOCIOLOGY

How do we know anything about society? How can we possibly predict what people will do? How can we know the impact of a proposed social change? How can we tell if the changes we are making are effective? We could guess and use a trial-and-error method of social change. However, that could be a bit costly in terms of time, money, and human lives. A better approach—the sociological approach—is to use *scientific methods* to systematically determine the causes and effects of human social behavior. Sociologists have very distinctive steps in approaching research.

STEP 1: SELECTING A RESEARCHABLE SUBJECT

What is important to you? What do you think needs to be changed? In order to convince others of the need for change, it helps to have some data on the current situation. What is currently happening and why is it in need of change? It also is helpful to have some data to substantiate your claim that the change will be effective.

The types of questions sociologists address are not basically different from the kinds the rest of us have. Among these are the questions a journalist typically asks—who, what, where, and when? *Who* is ahead in this year's congressional elections? *What* do college students feel about abortion? *Where* do homeless people sleep at night? *When* will the job market improve? These questions give rise to *descriptive* studies, which attempt to provide accurate information about the way things are. Often such studies provide useful baseline information that has practical implications. If you are managing an election campaign, it is helpful to know whether your candidate is ahead or behind in the polls, and by how much. If you are going to graduate next year, you may want to estimate what your chances are of getting the kind of job you want.

While sociologists are interested in accurately describing social life, they are usually more interested in explaining it. Knowing several months before election day why your candidate is behind in the polls may help you develop a more effective campaign strategy. *Explanatory* studies usually include elements of description as well.[2]

STEP 2: FORMULATING TESTABLE HYPOTHESES

The major concepts of scientific research are *variables* capable of having two or more constant states or values.[3] Explanatory studies propose one or more **hypotheses**, statements about expected relationships between two or more variables. This relationship is positive when the two variables increase or decrease together, and negative when one variable decreases as the other increases. Some examples of two-variable relationships (the most common kind) might be:

1. Women will have higher rates of church attendance than men.

2. Adolescents who enjoy school will be less likely to be delinquent than those who do not enjoy school.

3. As the dress types of a music group conform more closely to emerging fashion norms, the popularity of the group will increase.

Note the variables in each statement—gender and church attendance, school enjoyment and delinquency, dress types and popularity. Also, each **hypothesis** has an **independent variable** which is mentioned first (e.g., dress styles) and is typically assumed to influence or "cause" a change in the **dependent variable** (e.g., popularity) that follows.

Hypotheses are especially informative if they can be derived from a general theory. Durkheim suggested that suicide rates are related to the level of social integration and regulation in a society. From this, he concluded that since married people are more integrated and regulated than single people, marrieds would be less likely to commit suicide. By the same logic, Catholics should have lower rates than Protestants, and women lower rates than men. Let us modify Durkheim's theory slightly to contend that persons who are more integrated and regulated will be more likely to participate in important social rituals. Let us assume that women tend to be more socially integrated and regulated than men. Let us further assume that church services are important social rituals. The first hypothesis above follows by logical deduction.

However, deduction alone is not sufficient to support a hypothesis. Its predictions must be tested against real-world events. This requires that the variables of the hypotheses be measured. The **reliability** of a hypothesis will depend on the consistency with which a measure can be reproduced. The hypothesis must also demonstrate **validity**, the degree to which a measurement of a variable accurately reflects what it claims to measure.

Measurement involves a three-step process. First, a variable is given a *conceptual* definition using other familiar concepts. Second, specific events or indicators that are concrete instances of the variable are identified. This is followed by an *operational* definition that details what steps must be taken in order to make the desired measurement.

Applying these steps to a concept like school enjoyment, mentioned in the second hypothesis above, we might develop a conceptual definition like "having a positive evaluation of various aspects of the school experience." This definition could then be operationalized in terms of a series of questions whose indicators are how well a person likes his or her classes, teachers, fellow students, extracurricular activities, etc. The results could be combined into an index that would reflect overall satisfaction with school.

STEP 3: CHOOSING A DATA COLLECTION METHOD

Sociologists use a variety of methods to collect the data they need to test their hypotheses.

Here we will touch on three major methods: surveys, observation, and using secondary data.

SURVEYS

Surveys are employed in all kinds of research — scientific, pseudoscientific, and otherwise. Sharply dressed women approach us in shopping malls in order to find out our clothing preferences. Our congressional representatives send us brief questionnaires with loaded questions (Should I oppose gun control or leave the ordinary person defenseless?) in order to justify their special interest voting patterns. We get telephone calls from someone wanting a few minutes of our time, often as a pretext to sell us something.

Despite these questionable uses, a survey can be a very efficient tool for scientific research. A survey gathers information from a relatively small portion of a population in order to draw conclusions about the whole population. *Interviews* are probably the most common type of survey. An interview is simply a conversation in which one person asks questions and records information, while another provides answers. Interviews can be highly *structured*—all respondents are asked exactly the same questions in the same order and are required to choose from one of several predetermined responses. More *unstructured* interviews are almost like ordinary conversations—lines of questioning are more flexible and open-ended; respondents are allowed to answer in their own words. While most interviews are still done face-to-face, a growing number are being done by telephone in order to reach a wider variety of people more inexpensively.

Questionnaires are like structured interviews, except that they are a written form of communication. In a questionnaire the researcher poses a set of questions, usually with fixed answer categories, for the respondent to answer at leisure. Since the researcher is usually not present to clarify the meaning of the questions, it is important that these questions be stated in a clear, unbiased manner. Guidelines for asking questions include the following:[4]

1. Avoid asking loaded questions that encourage respondents to answer in a certain way.

2. Avoid questions with theoretical concepts that will be confusing to respondents.

3. Avoid "double-barreled" questions that are really two questions in one. For example, "Do you believe we should spend less money on welfare and more to control crime?" is a question that should be broken down into separate questions on crime and welfare.

4. Avoid questions that your respondents are not prepared to answer because they lack appropriate information or simply have not bothered to develop an opinion. Many respondents will have an opinion about abortion, but few have thought much about such issues as whether TV cameras should be allowed in courtrooms.

Those who do questionnaire surveys with a vested interest in the results (industry reps, politicians, etc.) will often play "fast and loose" with these guidelines. A good rule of thumb is never to trust the reported results of a survey unless you know how the questions were asked.

OBSERVATION

Direct observation is an important way to do social science research. For anyone who believes strongly in the old adage "seeing is believing," the arguments for using observation can be quite convincing. How do we know that the people we interview are telling us "the whole truth and nothing but the truth"? How do we get beyond the tendency of well-intentioned people to idealize their own behavior patterns, especially when strong norms prevail concerning how they *should* behave? How do we avoid the tendency to misinterpret and apply stereotypes in unfamiliar settings?

To deal with problems like these, it can be very helpful to observe behavior directly rather than rely on the reports people give us, or even on sociological stereotypes (heaven forbid!). There was a time when sociologists tended to believe that all poor communities were "socially disorganized." This is no longer a prevailing view, due in large part to observational studies of poor neighborhoods that have uncovered many strong and enduring social ties among their residents.[5]

While observational research is less structured than either experimental or survey research, general guidelines for its practice have been gradually emerging. Two of these involve important decisions the researcher must make regarding how to relate to subjects. First, will the researcher participate in the activities of the group he or she is studying, or observe those activities in a detached manner? Second, will the researcher's identity be made known to the people being studied?[6] One can sometimes choose to observe subject behavior at a distance without people knowing they are being observed. For example, one might pretend to be window-shopping but really be watching whether people who park their cars along the street put money in the parking meter. One might even take note of certain features such as each subject's gender and approximate age, as well as the make of the subject's car. An advantage of this type of *detached observation* is that the observer probably does not influence subjects' behavior. On the other hand, one is also unable to interview subjects as to why they "feed" the meter or not.

In most observational studies, the researcher both participates in group activities and makes her/his identity as a researcher known. Such **participant observation** is considered by many to be the best strategy. It allows the researcher the most latitude for movement within the group and for supplementing pure observation with other methods, especially unstructured interviewing. The latter can be especially important for gaining insights into the meaning that various activities have for group members.

SECONDARY DATA

Some people like to cook their own meals, while others prefer to eat out. Similarly, some researchers find it rewarding to collect their own data while others would just as soon let others do it for them. There are good reasons for the latter approach. Prepared data are relatively inexpensive. For around one hundred dollars or less, you can have access to computerized survey data from multimillion-dollar studies using national samples. Research institutes around the world now reproduce and sell them. Also, in contrast to fast food, "fast data" are often of higher quality and larger quantity than is feasible for you as a novice researcher to produce.

Secondary data collected by others come in varying degrees of preparation. Statistics from government agencies such as the Census Bureau and the FBI are sometimes computerized, sometimes summarized in various written documents.[7] Sometimes such data are other people's trash. Archaeologists spend their lives unearthing fragments from antique garbage dumps that they dignify with such titles as "ancient ruins." Modern garbage piles can also provide useful data. You could do a study of drinking patterns on a college campus simply by observing the beer cans and liquor bottles in dormitory and fraternity dumpsters.

The most common form of secondary data is in the form of written and visual communication—books, newspapers, movies, works of art, and the like. Such data require some "cooking." This involves *content analysis*, a systematic examination of the properties of messages.

Content analysis is employed to measure variables that are indicated in the message and are assumed to reflect some characteristic of the message producer or receiver. Among other things, content analysis has been used to test hypotheses about value differences between the conventional and the underground press.

STEP 4: COLLECTING DATA

Well-stated hypotheses and an appropriate data collection method are certainly essential to the success of social research. But so is attention to detail in the actual implementation of your method. To use the analogy of meal preparation, you may have the finest ingredients, but the details of cooking are still crucial.

ACCESSING A POPULATION

Before you begin to collect data, you must identify an appropriate population. While we tend to think of a population as people, sociologists use this term for other units as well—geographic areas like cities or states, articles in newspapers or magazines, or any other objects that might be sources of information. You must also select your population so that its elements are accessible. In doing an interview survey, you will not want to designate your population to be all U.S. citizens eighteen years or older unless you are ready to travel extensively or have a generous research grant to hire interviewers. Even if your population consists of the adult members of a local church, you may want to obtain permission to make contacts at a congregational meeting. Often an organization can facilitate access to a population, provided its leaders are not overly concerned about their members' privacy or are otherwise threatened by the content of your survey.

SAMPLING

Researchers usually study large populations by selecting samples. This is best achieved by representative sampling procedures, which means that every unit in the population has the same chance of being selected. Representative sampling is especially important when you want to estimate certain characteristics of the total population. If you want an accurate estimate of how the voting public feels about various candidates in an upcoming election, you will probably not want to limit your sample to members of a local country club or labor union.

Representative sampling may be achieved by either simple random sampling or more systematic sampling. If you wanted to do a survey on your campus and could obtain the cooperation of your Registrar's office, it would be possible to select a **simple random sample** using student identification numbers. **Systematic sampling**[8] frequently involves the use of a phone book for telephone surveys. It is also used to sample portions of documents when conducting content analysis. In a systematic sample, every "kth" element is selected from a list in which a random number from 1 to k is chosen. For example, if your directory has five thousand names and you wanted a sample of five hundred, you could choose every tenth student.

Many researchers who test hypotheses rely on convenience samples, segments of a population that happen to be readily available. They may pass out a questionnaire to a large lecture class in order to get a sample of college students. Since such a sample is not randomly selected, it is likely to produce biased results when estimating, say, the religious beliefs of the entire student population. Still, it may be useful for testing a hypothesis about how religious beliefs affect the choice of a major, especially when one is concerned merely with whether such a relationship exists, not with the relative strength of the relationship.

RESPONSE RATES

When human populations are involved, researchers must be concerned with motivating subjects to participate. Typically, people respond positively to a personal contact. If the time required is brief, response rates for interviews run over 90 percent. By contrast, mailed questionnaires often produce rates as low as 15 to 20 percent. Timing is also crucial for some populations. Launching a campus survey during midsemester exams is usually deadly.

Various techniques have been devised to improve response rates.[9] Follow-up requests will produce some improvement in responses to mailed questionnaires. Modest payments will increase respondents' willingness to participate in longer interviews. With a student population, you might get away with a slice of pizza at a time when everyone is tapped out by their book bills.

STEP 5: PREPARING AND ANALYZING DATA

We are finding applications for computers in virtually every facet of social life, and social research is no exception. Field researchers who type their notes on laptop computers are finding them to be ideal tools for reorganizing their information according to various topical schemes. The analysis of survey data is also greatly facilitated by the use of a *statistical package*. This software contains various routines that allow you to enter your data and analyze it. These packages also produce tables and graphs, sometimes of a quality that can be directly incorporated into a report. Most colleges and universities are making statistical packages available to their students in computer labs around the campus.

TABLE 2:1
Ages of Entering Freshmen at Inclusive Tech

AGE	PERCENT
Under 18	7
18	38
19	31
20	15
Over 20	9
Total	100
N	(1,537)

Source: hypothetical

DESCRIPTIVE ANALYSIS

Once your data have been computerized, the next step is to use the analytical routines of the statistical package to organize the data so that it addresses your research questions. Descriptive questions can be answered using *univariate analysis* of single variables. Sometimes frequency distributions are appropriate. Table 2:1 provides an illustration of an age distribution for first-year students at the hypothetical Inclusive Tech. Distributions can be summarized by a single value with a **measure of central tendency**. One such measure is a *mean* or arithmetic average. To compute a mean, simply find the sum of everyone's age and divide by the number of persons (in this case 1,537). Other summaries involving a single value are a *median* and a *mode*. The median is the value in which the middle element of the distribution is located (19 in Table 2:1); the mode is the most popular value (18 in Table 2:1).

Suppose we had hypothesized: "The more urban the state, the higher its murder rate will be." We can then measure urbanization by the percent of persons in a state living in metropolitan areas and the murder rate by FBI statistics.

STEP 6: INTERPRETING THE RESULTS

When we said earlier that a hypothesis states a relationship between two variables, we did not say whether the relationship was a causal one. Unless otherwise stated, a hypothesis implies that the independent variable is a cause of variation in the dependent variable. Besides a statistical relationship of the kind described above, two other criteria must be met in order to demonstrate that a causal relationship is present.

First, the independent variable must operate prior in time to the dependent variable. One way to test time order is to do a *longitudinal* study, where the dependent variable is measured at a later point in time than the independent variable. Since it is usually very difficult to find the same subjects at a later date, most survey research is *cross-sectional* —all variables being measured at the same time. For this reason, time order remains inconclusive in many explanatory studies.

Second, a causal relationship must not be spurious. A spurious relationship is one in which two variables are related simply because a third variable is simultaneously causing changes in both of them. A humorous illustration is the old wives' tale that storks bring babies. If you did a survey in the Netherlands, you might find that people who see more storks have more children, establishing a statistical relationship. But if you take into account where people live, you would probably discover that living in a rural area is related to both how many storks one sees and how many children people have. Storks nest in rural areas. Rural families have historically had more children, probably because children can be an economic asset in an agricultural society. There is probably no direct causal connection between storks and babies. Too bad. Unplanned pregnancies would probably be a lot easier to control if all you had to do was avoid the stork!

A CHRISTIAN PERSPECTIVE ON SOCIAL RESEARCH

When Christians do social research, they approach it with a different perspective than secular researchers. Because Christians believe that all people are created in the image of God, they ought to be careful not to diminish the dignity of the individual by reducing research subjects to numbers in a database. Above all, the spiritual welfare of the individual needs to be tended and preserved. For example, if in the course of an interview a research subject becomes distraught and obviously in need of spiritual care, the Christian should probably discontinue the interview and seek to minister to the individual. This means the interview process will take longer because some subjects will be disqualified from the data pool. However, shouldn't one's duty as a Christian take precedence over one's duty as a scientist? To paraphrase Luke 9:25: For what does it profit a sociologist if he/she gains excellent data and loses a soul?

Ethical issues in research first became prominent in the 1960s after Milgram did a laboratory experiment in which subjects were led to believe they were administering severe electrical shocks to fellow subjects as part of a learning experiment. In fact, no shocks were administered and the experiment was a test of how far subjects would go in violating normal behavioral restrictions when told to do so under the authority of science. Because Milgram's subjects showed many signs of severe stress, other researchers were quite critical of his work.

Reactions to these and other controversial studies have resulted in the development of ethical codes by professional societies, federal agencies that sponsor research, and almost all research universities. These codes share a common set of ethical principles regarding the treatment of human subjects.

> Three widely recognized ethical principles are:
>
> 1. *Protection from harm.* Care should be taken to avoid physical and psychological damage to subjects.
>
> 2. *Avoiding deception.* Normally, subjects should not be deceived concerning the nature or purpose of the research.
>
> 3. *Privacy protection.* Information the subject reveals should not be connected with the subject's name in any research report.

While these principles may seem to be unambiguous, their application can be subject to a variety of interpretations. For this reason most universities now have rules which require that all research on human subjects receive the approval of an ethics committee. If you are interested in doing research on your campus, you should check to see what the approval process requires.

Often in our zeal to change the world, we bypass both good science and ethics. As Christians, it is imperative that our investigations be honest, valid, and uplifting to humans. In short, may our science be glorifying to God!

overview

- What does a sociologist do? In this chapter we have given you an overview of the theory and methods of a sociologist. These theories will be applied throughout this textbook. While you obviously will not master these principles right away, some understanding of research methods will help inform your reading.

- Sociologists have a very systematic way of viewing the world. Their understanding starts with theory and is tested by scientific methods. Three major schools of thought inform sociology:

1. Structural-functional theory looks at how order is created by the interconnection of social elements, each functioning to promote social stability. A structural-functionalist looks at the functions of each part in promoting order within the social system. To a structural-functionalist, social problems arise when social elements are dysfunctional to the system. Social change needs to be focused on these dysfunctional elements, eliminating or correcting them so that the social order is maintained.

2. A sociologist viewing the world from the

social conflict perspective will examine tensions between individuals, within social organizations, and within society as a whole. Such conflict is often produced when powerful forces wish to maintain control by making less powerful people feel they are unimportant. A conflict theorist will assume that such conflict is not necessarily bad, but can be redemptive to the individual, the organization, and the society.

3. The interactionist perspective can enable people to better understand themselves and others. It takes a second look at the everyday interactions of individuals, with a particular interest in the meanings that are created. A sociologist looking at the world from an interactionist perspective would take note of the symbols that humans use to create meaning. A word, a look, a gesture, a piece of clothing—all can communicate something about who we are.

- Sociologists use these three perspectives to do social research. Theory will inform hypotheses, which are predictions about the relationship between variables. Collecting and analyzing data will test these hypotheses.

- The primary means that sociologists use to collect data are surveys, observation, and secondary data. Care must be taken to identify the population from which data is collected, and insure that sampling procedures are scientific. Data are usually analyzed using computerized statistical methods. Sociologists take care not to jump to hasty conclusions regarding the causes of social behavior.

- By using scientific methods in an ethical manner, sociologists can understand a lot about social behavior. Such an understanding is important in formulating plans to become a world changer.

key concepts

conflict theory
A macro-theory that focuses on the tensions and power struggles in a society.

dependent variable
A variable that is influenced by another (independent) variable.

Durkheim, Emile
Nineteenth-century French sociologist who sought to understand how social elements function to promote social stability.

hypothesis
A statement about how two or more variables are related to each other.

independent variable
A variable that causes change in another (dependent) variable.

interactionist theory
A micro-theory that focuses on the meanings created by the interpersonal exchange of symbols such as words, gestures, and other actions.

macro-level theory
Large-scale analysis of society such as structural-functional theory or conflict theory.

measure of central tendency
A single typical value that characterizes a distribution of values. Three types of such a measure are mean, median, and mode.

Merton, Robert
Twentieth-century American sociologist who analyzed social structures in terms of manifest and latent functions or consequences.

micro-level theory
Small-scale analysis of interpersonal social behavior such as interactionist theory.

Parsons, Talcott
Twentieth-century American sociologist whose writings form the basis for structural-functional theory.

participant observation
A data collection method in which the researcher observes subject behavior while interacting with the subject(s) and making his or her identity as a researcher known.

reliability
The consistency with which a measure can be reproduced.

secondary data
Information used by a researcher after it has been collected by another researcher.

simple random sample
A sample in which every combination of elements in a population has an equal chance of being selected.

structural-functionalism
A macro-theory that views society as a system of interconnected parts that depend on each other for proper functioning to maintain stability and equilibrium.

survey
A data collection method that elicits information by way of an interview or questionnaire.

systematic sample
A sample in which every kth element is selected from a list after a start in which a random number between 1 and k is chosen.

validity
The degree to which a measurement of a variable accurately reflects what it claims to measure.

Weber, Max
Nineteenth-century German sociologist who sought to understand social structure.

endnotes

1. Emile Durkheim, *The Division of Labor in Society* (Glencoe, IL: Free Press, 1933).
2. Earl R. Babbie, *The Practice of Social Research*, 6th ed. (Belmont, CA: Wadsworth Publishing Co., 1992), 92.
3. Ibid., 32-33.
4. Ibid., 147-151.
5. William H. Whyte, *Street Corner Society* (Chicago: University of Chicago Press, 1943); Herbert J. Gans, *The Urban Villagers* (New York: Free Press, 1962).
6. Raymond L. Gold, "Roles in Sociological Field Observations," *Social Forces* 36 (1958): 217-23.
7. For example, see U.S. Bureau of Census, *Statistical Abstract of the United States* (Washington, D.C.: U.S. Government Printing Office, published annually).
8. For further discussion of sampling techniques, see Royce A. Singleton, Jr., Bruce C. Straits, and Margaret Miller Straits, *Approaches to Social Research* (New York: Oxford University Press, 1993).
9. For a discussion of techniques for increasing response rates, see Kenneth D. Bailey, *Methods of Social Research* (New York: Free Press, 1982).

CHAPTER THREE

Human Culture

chapter outline

I. Culture as an abstract concept
   A. Cultural universals
   B. Symbolic qualities of culture

II. Elements of culture
   A. Language
   B. Cognitive components
   C. Normative components
   D. Cultural material

III. Theoretical perspectives for understanding culture
   A. Structural-functional perspective
   B. Conflict perspective
   C. Interactionist perspective

IV. Subcultures and countercultures

V. Cultural diversity
   A. Ethnocentrism
   B. Stereotyping
   C. Cultural relativism

VI. Christians challenging culture

biblical reflection

"Let us therefore make every effort to do what leads to peace and to mutual edification."

—Romans 14:19

Murl Dirksen's personal anecdote begins this adventure into discovering the meaning of the concept of "culture" and examining the diversity of human cultures:

> I was playing with my Hopi friends outside my family's adobe pueblo in the village of Kykotsmovi, Arizona, when my mother came bursting outside yelling, "Where's my broom?" She was obviously disturbed because she could not find the broom she used daily to sweep the hard-packed dirt floor of our village home. The tone of her voice and the suddenness of her appearance stunned not only me but also my half-dozen friends who vanished in many different directions. Realizing the rudeness of her request, my mother asked me to come inside where she apologized to me for her emotional outburst that had frightened off my playmates. Not more than five minutes later there was a knock at the door and my mother went to answer. Standing there were all my village friends, each holding a broom. And each in turn said, "Mother, here is your broom." Not yet understanding what was happening, she looked over the array of brooms being extended towards her by this small group of village lads and responded, "No, none of those is mine." Again, almost in chorus, the boys uttered, "Mother, here is your broom."
>
> At that point she realized what was happening. She remembered that she was not living in a farmhouse in central Kansas in the middle of a Mennonite community. Her family was now residing in a collective village on the high desert of Arizona among the Hopi. To the Hopi, personal property was almost nonexistent; therefore, we had no need for locks on doors. There was nothing to be stolen. Things were not coveted because everything was available to the person needing it. My mother and I immediately understood that my Hopi friends had not been frightened off; they had gone to get a broom. My mother was also their mother. Hopi society being communal, mother had asked her sons to help her find a broom, and they had obliged. This incident was also a lesson for me. It made me understand that all mothers in Kykotsmovi were my mother. All homes were my home. All brooms were my broom. However, I was a bit confused because I could not figure out what "mother" meant.

CULTURE AS AN ABSTRACT CONCEPT: DEFINITIONS OF CULTURE

Referring to a people's unique customs and beliefs, social scientists often speak of culture when describing a group's way of life. Hopi culture in the anecdote above included social values, family life, economic concepts, customary ways of acting, and so on. Ralph Linton defined culture as "the sum total of knowledge, attitudes and habitual behavior patterns shared and transmitted by members of a particular society."[1] This definition includes both cognitive characteristics—knowledge and attitudes—and observable behavior. We can only know what a person is thinking and feeling by observing actions, although all behavior is ultimately the result of mental activity. In the most general sense, we can conceptualize the term **culture** as the way of life of a group of people, what they are thinking, feeling, and doing.

Many contemporary sociologists and anthropologists prefer a more specific and exclusive definition of culture that emphasizes the information and ideas that people in a group share rather than the way they behave. The **ideational definition of culture** is useful because it distinguishes the ideal from the real, culture from behavior. In this conceptualization, culture is the knowledge of guidelines to which a person's behavior may or may not correspond, as in American marriages. According to Ward Goodenough, culture sets "standards for deciding what is . . . what can be . . . how one should feel about it . . . what to do about it . . . how to go about doing it."[2] This definition focuses on culture as a cognitive phenomenon and not as behavioral or material. The ideational definition considers behavior and artifacts to be products of culture since culture is the mental mapping that determines the form of social interaction and material and nonmaterial objects.

James Peoples and Garrick Bailey recommend a very useful clarification of the concept of culture that focuses on the nonmaterial basis of culture: "Culture is the socially transmitted knowledge and behavior shared by some group of people."[3] The utility of this definition is that it contains *four* essential characteristics.

1. Culture is *socially transmitted* from one generation to the next generation, from people in one community to those in another community. While we use the trial-and-error method of learning, it has a high risk factor, and it is much safer to learn from others' mistakes.

2. Cultural knowledge is composed of *shared ideas, beliefs, values*, and *worldviews* that have been shown to be meaningful and adaptive. Hopi snake dances are supposed to bring summer rains for the corn to grow. If it doesn't rain, it is because of a failure in the skill of the dancers or because of a malevolent spirit in the village. Failure does not stifle Hopi belief that dances send messages to *kachinas,* the ancestral spirits, to produce rain.

3. Despite individual differences, every culture has rules of appropriate conduct, *shared behavioral patterns*. Physical aggression occurs in every culture, but each culture decides under what circumstances and in what ways it can be expressed. The Semai of Malaysia refuse to behave in any way that might be interpreted as anger or hostility. They teach their young never to strike anyone. Also, parents never spank their children.

4. And finally, a culture is *shared by members of a society*. They collectively agree on basic cultural knowledge, although small groups within a culture might have specialized views and rules. Culture is taught and learned in the context of group interaction and is systematic in that it integrates all the elements of a social order into a single comprehensive system of understanding.

Members of a culture generally affirm similar behavioral standards and values. They possess knowledge that binds them together as a culture. We know that North America is in the center of a world map because our culture places our country in the middle of the maps it makes. We know that a tall slender body with a mouth full of straight white teeth is beautiful. We know how to speak and write English, so we agree that it must be the best language for communication, and that Romanized letters are the only real way to write. Every culture has a reservoir of knowledge that specifies what is good and bad, taboo and sacred, appropriate and inappropriate, and has both a verbal as well as a nonverbal communication system. One feels comfortable in his/her culture because members generally agree what shape the world is, what one's teeth should look like, and what language we should use for clear communication.

With so much diversity in religious beliefs, rituals, standards of conduct, and social organization, we might ask if there is any such thing as a Christian culture. One would tend to think not when we include all the various American forms of Christianity, as well as those found throughout the world. Yet, if you have ever fellowshipped with a group of Christian believers in another country—where you did not understand a word of the language and their worship forms were unfamiliar—you would know what I mean when I say that one can still feel a real sense of unity with fellow believers, a sense of involvement with what is occurring, and a sense of God's presence. This has happened to me personally in a government-controlled church in China, in St. Stephan's Cathedral in Vienna, and in a snake-handling church in Alabama. A cognitive, ideational definition of culture can help to explain the common community and communion that all Christians can have in spite of vast differences in worship forms and theological views.

CULTURAL UNIVERSALS

It is a bit risky to suggest that all people share certain cultural elements and to claim that humans are more similar to each other than they are different. A common approach to the study of culture is to show the variety in human responses to one another and to the natural environments but, in fact, human beings are very much alike in our general nature. An explanation of cultural universals illustrates these commonalities along with specific adaptations. Every culture must respond to the questions of shelter, clothing, food, reproduction, family, religion, affection, aggression, and many other social and psychological needs. There are universal requirements for individual human survival, as well as for the continual existence of the groups they form.

Human subsistence requires food: finding, preparing, and partaking. Nourishment is an obvious requirement for physical survival, but what, when, where, how, and with whom people should eat is a precise adaptation that culture makes. Humans can in fact eat anything that is digestible and nontoxic. Because people from one culture find some things to be disgusting to consume does not exclude these things from the category of edible items. North American culture consumes the meat and the dairy products of cows. Mongolians enlarge this group of dairy animals to include goats, sheep, horses, and yaks. Cheese, milk, yogurt and meat are more desired and available from their horses than from their cows. After his conversion to Christianity, the Apostle Paul found that the old food taboos no longer applied.

> "I know and am persuaded in the Lord Jesus that nothing is unclean in itself; but it is unclean for anyone who thinks it unclean. If your brother or sister is being injured by what you eat, you are no longer walking in love. Do not let what you eat cause the ruin of one for whom Christ died. So do not let your good be spoken of as evil. For the kingdom of God is not food and drink but righteousness and peace and joy in the Holy Spirit. The one who thus serves Christ is acceptable to God and has human approval."
> Romans 14:14-18

Paul was establishing his approach in dealing with cultural differences and the essence of Christian living.

What utensils one uses to eat the food is also open to variation. North Americans use forks and spoons, Chinese use chopsticks, and Mexicans use spoons and tortillas. Touching food with their hands is barbaric to the Chinese, but we have a whole genre of foods called fast foods that we eat with our hands. Not only the manner in which one eats but also how food is prepared is relative to culture. Some people eat a lot of raw foods, while others must cook everything. Americans consume something they call salad, a variety of raw vegetables mixed together. The Chinese find the eating of raw food disgusting and terrible for one's health.

Body covering is another universal. How much of the body should be covered for one to be appropriately dressed is based on cultural values. What clothing is fitting for various occasions is a normative question. Materials used for clothing are dependent on the animals, plants, and technology available to the group. An illustration of a cultural response to clothing comes from a tribal group in Papua, New Guinea, where the men traditionally wore only gourds, or what could be described as this tribal group's interpretation of an athletic cup. When asked by an American missionary about the people on the other side of the mountain, a local tribal Christian described them as a group of "naked barbarians" that needed to be converted. Questioned further as to why he was so negative and prejudiced toward his neighboring tribe, he responded by saying it was because the men of the neighboring tribe didn't wear gourds—they wore only woven vine belts. Small variations in clothing can identify different cultural groups and give people a sense of belonging when wearing a particular type, color, and design of clothing. But garb can give group members a basis for making value judgments about what body covering is proper for other groups as well. Thus, a garment is not only for body warmth, but also a cultural symbol that expresses the wearer's identity.

Might we include in a list of cultural universals the idea that God has placed in each person a sense of Himself (a "High God concept," as some refer to it), and the need to communicate with Him? In their quest for ultimate meaning, people in every culture strive to find the infinite source of all creation, although they will do so in a variety of ways. The rituals associated with such quests vary tremendously and that is the reason the Apostle Paul reminds us, "Some judge one day to be better than another, while others judge all days to be alike. Let all be fully convinced in their own minds. Those who observe the day, observe it in honor of the Lord" (Rom. 14:5, 6a). The Old Testament had a lot of ceremonial days that were not relevant for Christianity and Paul is asking that all days be dedicated to holy living and service no matter what one's preference. "Let us therefore no longer pass judgment on one another, but resolve instead never to put a stumbling block or hindrance in the way of another" (v. 13).

SYMBOLIC QUALITIES OF CULTURE

All culture consists of shared patterns of meaning expressed through symbols. Spradley explains how this process occurs. Information about the material world comes through sensory experiences and these personal experiences form our knowledge. Knowledge is composed of concepts that have been selected, abstracted, and arranged from the empirical world. "But the most significant transformation comes when we employ objects and events to act as signs which refer to other phenomena, including those that have no physical reality. Symbols—those signs which are arbitrarily attached to referents—open up a myriad of possibilities for man."[4] Thus, **symbols** are objects that are given an arbitrary meaning that members of a culture generally agree on, and all communication is based on the ability to symbolize. All written language uses symbols to represent selective sounds. The sounds of a language, referred to as phonemes, are vocalizations that carry meaning to the speakers of that language. Likewise, nonverbal communication is symbolic in that it is composed of gestures, body position, and spacing whose meaning is closely attached to the emotions or feelings of the communicator. While symbols and signs are both ways of representing something else, symbols are more arbitrary, abstract, and versatile.

Human communication, on the other hand, is

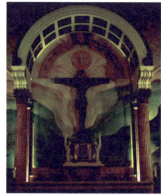

Every culture fashions symbols for that which is ultimately meaningful to them.

an elaborate system of abstract associations combining ideas and objects into categories that indicate their similarities as well as differences. The symbol of the cross is fundamental to western civilization. One can make the sign of the cross in the air with the hand upon entering a chapel. A cross can be made out of gold and hung around the neck of a devout believer or worn by a style-conscious person. Hoping it will protect them from evil, citizens might make a gigantic cross out of concrete and place it on a prominent hill overlooking their community. The essence of the cross is not in the tangible, physical material from which it is constructed but in the associated emotions, beliefs, and activities it represents. People have died for it and killed others over it; they have laughed at it and cried on it; they have worshiped it and burned it.

A material object or concrete action becomes a symbol with an abstract meaning that elicits an emotional reaction by persons in a culture. Can you imagine a novice to Christianity walking into one of our churches and hearing us sing, "I'm washed in the blood, in the soul-cleansing blood of the Lamb"? If taken literally, the newcomer would be frightened at the barbaric practices espoused by the worshipers. But the members of the congregation are referring symbolically to the forgiveness of sins through the death of Jesus Christ. Christian culture has made this referential association between the concepts of blood, death, and sacrifice and the concepts of cleansing, forgiveness, and restoration.

Christian symbolism comes from both a pastoral way of life that has existed for centuries in the Middle East and still continues today among the Arab Bedouins, and the agrarian life of farmers in the same arid environment. The symbol of water for ritual cleansing is significant to Christianity, originating in the importance of water that is such a scarce commodity to the people of the Arabian desert areas. The bread and wine used during the Communion service are the grain and fruits of the Middle Eastern farmers' labor. Religious symbolism takes us beyond the everyday and the mundane and accentuates the sacred. In this way, the twenty-first-century American Christian living in suburbia can continue to use religious symbols originated by pastoral and agrarian people in a far-away desert place.

Proxemics is the social space between people and is another area of real concern for foreign visitors. In friendly conversation, guests from the Middle East are accustomed to much less physical space between participants. A close personal relationship is symbolized by physical nearness. One's face should be near the other's while talking. In Asia, holding the hand of your best friend of the same sex is totally appropriate. Communication comes through what is being said as well as from what is being felt during personal discourse.

Cross-cultural proxemics is evident in the North American's way of standing in line. We have developed a variety of line forms, but normally we stand with our faces to another person's back, and we teach our children that cutting in line is bad. Many cultures see no need for so much social ordering and leave it to the biggest and most aggressive person to get served first. Drivers in many cultures follow this same general rule. The fastest, most aggressive chauffeur is first to arrive at a destination and is even more likely to arrive alive than the hesitant motorist. Hand gesturing and body space are salient features of intercultural communication.

ELEMENTS OF CULTURE

LANGUAGE AND CULTURE

Language, the ability to symbolically communicate with one another, makes human culture possible. A limited number of arbitrary sounds are combined in an infinite number of ways to symbolize ideas. It is what sets humankind apart from animals. God created us with the ability and necessity to use language. "In the beginning was the Word, and the Word was with God, and the Word was God" (John 1:1). The Greeks used the term "Word" for both spoken and unspoken words, the reasoning of the mind. On the other hand, the Jews used it to refer to God, so the Apostle John is using a term that was meaningful to both cultures. If we use the Greek meaning, we might say that in the beginning was *reasoning* that made possible the capacity for humans to create language, allowing for human survival.

Noam Chomsky asserts that although human language is not instinctive like the communication systems of animals, the ability to acquire language is innate. He posits the existence of a language acquisition device present in all normal human brains, which is comparable to a computer program for language learning.[5] When a child is exposed to language data, this program performs the phenomenal task of sorting, classifying, and processing the data so that the normal child has complete command of the rudiments of language by about age six. Children are not taught language in the same way formal education teaches math and writing, by imitation and memorization. If exposed to several languages, they acquire more than one grammar and usually do not confuse them. All normal children learn language deductively, without formal instruction, in a remarkably short period of time, and regardless of how competent they are in other cognitive tasks.

The mind organizes cultural knowledge in much the same way it does grammatical knowledge. Cultural understanding is as basic to customary behavior as grammatical knowledge is to speech. In trying to understand how culture is organized, *ethnoscientists* have applied linguistic methods for studying the classification systems of language. Humans classify reality by perceiving different features of things and recognizing these differences as important. An illustration of this is the difference between a hamburger and a cheeseburger. These two words describe basically the same food item except for the presence of cheese. A hamburger may or may not have pickles, lettuce, mustard, ketchup, mayonnaise, and a sesame seed bun. If any of these minor condiments are excluded, the food item's terminology does not change—it is still called a hamburger. But if cheese is added, the object receives its own categorical term, cheeseburger. Cheese becomes the salient characteristic that distinguishes it from a hamburger. Classification systems are hierarchical with specific things included under the next higher level of abstraction. Thus cheeseburgers and bacon burgers are members of the more generalized category of "burger," of which fish sandwiches are not members. However, fish sandwiches belong to a more general level of classification referred to as "fast foods," which do include hamburgers and cheeseburgers. Cultures divide the world differently by classifying and categorizing the physical and social environment, and these differences are reflected in the terminology of the language.

Language shapes the perceptions and the worldview of a culture, but it does not define the worldview of its speaker. Language is a mirror of the culture; it does not create the culture. For example, Christians around the world probably speak thousands of different languages but can hold a similar worldview based on the teachings of Jesus Christ. An extensive lexicon develops around those things important to the culture. The Yaqui of northern Mexico have a complex vocabulary of desert plant terms. They gather the fruit from cacti and make edible foods. The Netsilik Eskimo people have an elaborate terminology system for snow. North American ranchers and farmers classify and categorize animals, and mechanics have words for their specialized tools and parts. Speakers of the same language may have very different worldviews. While English has become an international language, it is spoken by people in cultures with very different views of reality. International business and political negotiations, however, prove difficult even when participants speak the same language. In fact, people who speak very different languages may support a single worldview. Christianity has adherents from around the world who gather to engage in common worship. Finally, while the human capability to produce language makes culture possible, it is the thing that distinguishes us from animals.

COGNITIVE COMPONENTS OF CULTURE

Every culture has a **worldview**, a cosmological order that provides a picture of what the universe is like. Members of a group share a mental map that organizes all of the salient natural and supernatural elements of a culture. For example, many cultures are dualistic—their universe is divided into two opposing yet interacting parts. The visual representation of Chinese dualism is the *yin yang* symbol, a circle with one half shaded and the other half unshaded. Each half has within its section a small circle with the shade of the opposing half, signifying that while there are dichotomous elements in the world, the total cosmos is ultimately balanced and united. All Chinese cultural elements must be placed into this positive and negative order, including wind and water, male and female, cool foods and hot foods, and sky and earth.

Western culture has tended to use three segments to indicate completeness. For instance, Christians believe in a triune God, speeches are

What is beautiful? Cultural agreement varies on defining the ideal.

to elucidate three points, and the rules of baseball dictate "three strikes and you're out."

Native Americans often have a cosmology that uses four segments to represent wholeness. In this cosmology, the four worlds of the Hopi are the locales of their mythological history. The four cardinal directions are correlated with red, blue, yellow, and white corn. Animals and birds are also included in this cosmic order with the mountain lion and oriole corresponding to yellow and north. The Hopi tribal organization is divided into four groups of clans for ceremonial and administrative functions. Cultural worldviews provide generalized categories that help fit experiences and acquired knowledge into a comprehensible order.

Values are the shared ideas of those things that members of a culture think are good and desirable. The lifestyles we pursue are influenced by our values, and the quality of life we desire is based on generally agreed upon **beliefs** about what is enjoyable and satisfying. On the other hand, Americans value freedom and personal rights in property and speech, education and religion, dress and residence. Sociologist Robin Williams composed a list of twenty core values of American culture with the basic ones condensed into four general categories: success, progress, efficiency and practicality, and freedom.[6]

Americans believe that hard work, achievement, and material wealth are all part of the great success story. Positive about the future, North Americans have great faith in the ability of science and technology to bring them the good life. Saving time, energy, and money are essential to our daily lives. And finally, Americans vehemently affirm the right to freedom, of which individualism, equality, and patriotism are all corollaries. Chinese culture, on the other hand, values such things as conformity to the group, family and ancestral locality, friendship, and devotion to authority. Changes in values will be reflected in modifications to the standards and rules that reinforce the behaviors. Thus, as the Chinese become more individualistic, their loyalty to work groups and kin groups will gradually diminish and their cultural values will adjust.

Values are guidelines for human behavior and do not necessarily reflect what people in the culture actually do. There are both the *ideal cultural values* and *real cultural behaviors*. Americans place a high value on being healthy by exercising and eating right. They buy all sorts of exercise equipment, are constantly embarking on a better diet, and spend a tremendous amount of money on health club memberships; yet, as a whole, they are more overweight, are less physically active, and eat more junk food than ever before. Americans value marriage and marry at very high rates, but fail to maintain solid marriages. Americans value personal material wealth, but are probably the most philanthropic people in the world. At times cultural values conflict, as in the case of individualism and equality. American public education is designed to give each child a chance at success, but makes it a highly competitive process where some individuals must fail.

NORMATIVE COMPONENTS OF CULTURE

William Graham Sumner, an American sociologist and anthropologist, created the term **folkways** to refer to the customary ways people do things, the acceptable and approved ways that normal folks act.[7] Slurping one's soup in an American restaurant will bring about disapproving glances from patrons, but soup slurping in a southern European pub will go unnoticed. Lifting your bowl and drinking from it is acceptable etiquette in Southeast Asia, where no distinction is made between cups and bowls. But blowing one's nose into a piece of cloth, putting the cloth in the pocket, and carrying the wet cloth around all day, as North Americans do, is thought to be a filthy, unhygienic act. Traditional Asians prefer to spit the nasal mucus onto the ground or floor and walk away from it, not carry it with them all day. However, behavioral modifications are being made as modern Asians adopt the western handkerchief.

Normative culture is concerned with the limits that a culture imposes upon its members' behavior, limits that are referred to by sociologists as **norms**, rules, and standards of the culture. Some of these cultural rules are very informal, with weak sanctions imposed for violations. On the other hand, informal norms that incur mild disapproval are called *folkways*. These have to do with such things as table manners and dress. To belch at the dinner table in American culture probably means that others

What is normative in one culture seems quite unusual in another: an Irian Jaya ritual dance.

will think of you as uncouth. On the other hand, there are informal norms that might elicit strong disapproval, as in the case of sexual promiscuity. These are known as **mores**, norms that a group feels are essential to the survival of society. When formalized, they become its code of moral and civil law. **Law** is a type of **social control** that intentionally structures authority, application, obligation, and punishment. Laws and punishments that apply to less serious offenses, such as truancy and traffic violations, are generally scaled to suit the severity of the offense. Murderers, rapists, and child molesters not only violate formal norms, but in most cultures their behavior is considered so reprehensible that imprisonment or death is thought necessary.

Violations of informal and formal norms may produce mild or severe **sanctions**. *Positive* *sanctions* reward cultural conformity while *negative sanctions* chastise violations. Punishment may be to socially isolate the violator, as in the Amish community where shunning is practiced. No one is to speak to the disobedient Amish member for a period of time deemed appropriate for the offense committed. In Japanese schools, where group cohesion and work are so much encouraged, punishment means being sent out of the class away from one's peers. Hopi villagers will ban a person from residing in that village if he or she refuses to abide by the village code of conduct. In earlier times the code included abstinence from alcoholic beverages. Sanctions can also be institutionalized under the auspices of an organization that tries, convicts, imprisons, paroles, and rehabilitates. The judicial system in North American culture performs all these functions. The degree of punishment is dependent on the perceived threat of the violation to the continuance of the culture. In American society the value of individual rights diminishes the number of rules and, thus, the quality and quantity of punishment. Singapore fines its residents for chewing gum and not flushing the public toilets. People with even small amounts of illegal drugs are executed in this city. Sanctions are relative to the perceived seriousness of the violation, and seriousness is based on how much the infraction disrupts the sociocultural order.

Cultures have always found very cruel ways of sanctioning those found to be deviant. There were many heroes of the Jewish faith even before the coming of Christ. The unidentified author of Hebrews relates some of these sanctions. They were: flogged, stabbed to death, fed to wild animals, stoned, sawn in two, burned to death, and imprisoned (Heb. 11:32-38).

CULTURAL MATERIAL

Cultural material is actually a tangible expression, an extension of cultural ideas and norms. For example, American culture holds to the idea that knowledge is best transmitted in a specific location over a period of several hours. Thus, a material cultural complex commonly referred to as the school has been arranged to support this educational philosophy. The blackboard and chalk, pictures and maps, tables and chairs, books and pencils, lights and carpet, coats and caps, soft drinks and vending machines are all material artifacts which support the educational process. Added to this list are the more recent educational tools of laptops, Smartboards, wireless modems, compact discs, and a variety of software programs. While these items are not in and of themselves culture, they fulfill perceived cultural needs and thus are expressions of the mental images of these objects.

THEORETICAL PERSPECTIVES FOR UNDERSTANDING CULTURE

STRUCTURAL-FUNCTIONAL PERSPECTIVE

Why does every society develop a culture? Culture allows humans to understand and adapt to their physical and social environment. Our culture gives structure to our lives and allows us to live productive lives without constantly questioning what we should wear, what we should eat, and what we should say. Our culture limits our choices in these areas, making our lives less complicated. When you woke up this morning you were not burdened by the decision of whether or not you should put on clothes. Instead, your culture not only defined the need for clothes, but even limited your clothing choice for today. For instance, you did not consider going to classes or to work in a bathing suit, did you?

Culture also gives us answers to ultimate questions of meaning. "What is the nature of humanity?" "What is our purpose in life?" "What happens to us after death?" Our culture gives us answers to these questions. In North American culture, a funeral is often a ritual that celebrates a cultural agreement that there is life after death. Perhaps your "decision" to be a Christian and the way in which you express your faith has more to do with the culture in which you live than any other factor. Religion—whether Christian-based or not—is a **cultural universal** present in all human societies functioning to meet social needs through community rituals, shared common beliefs, and organizational leadership. Psychological needs are satisfied as well by rites of passage in such Christian ceremonies as baptism, marriage, and funerals.

CONFLICT PERSPECTIVE

While culture gives us structure and makes life easier for us, it also creates conflicts. This is particularly relevant for the Christian who is called not to be "conformed to this world, but [to] be transformed by the renewing of your minds" (Rom. 12:2). Sometimes our culture pressures us to do things that are contrary to our Christian walk. (More about that later when we discuss changing one's culture.)

The conflict perspective takes a hard look at the ways in which culture is used to oppress and dominate people. People who choose to dress differently or live a lifestyle challenging American cultural values of materialism are often made to feel unwelcome or strange. How do certain cultural values become dominant in the first place?

INTERACTIONIST PERSPECTIVE

People behave based on what they believe, on their subjective interpretation of what is going on. The interactionist perspective takes a look at how meanings are created through symbolic cultural rituals. For example, the annual cultural ritual called "The Super Bowl" reflects the cultural values of warfare, domination, and victory. The Super Bowl is symbolic in that it is a "safe" war: No one really gets killed; yet it becomes a rallying point for the public. Thus, cultural events are socially constructed by human interpretation.[8]

Another example is the serpent-handling ritual in which the people of the Appalachian Mountains have taken literally Jesus' words in Mark 16:17-18: "And these signs will accompany those who believe: by using my name they will cast out demons; . . . they will pick up snakes in their hands, and if they drink any deadly thing, it will not hurt them." So what is the symbolic importance of the copperhead and rattlesnake to these mountain people, and why is it central to their worship service? From a symbolic interaction view, one sees the snake as representing the evil of the world: a symbol of the destruction of their mountain culture by the lumber and mining companies; the loss of their land to people from the cities who want summer cabins; and the businessmen who are turning their rivers into attractions for white-water rafting. Ceremonially handling the copperhead and the timber rattler (and living through the experience) is a symbolic way of conquering all the evils of modern society and convincing oneself that the mountain way of life still exists. While others might think of this as crazy, the mountain serpent-handlers are revalidating their culture in ceremonial worship every Friday night in the clapboard church down in the hollow.

SUBCULTURES AND COUNTERCULTURES

Every group must have its own values, norms, and customs in order to function. In modern society an individual participates in a number of groups every day and thus regularly engages in several cultures. Each is a complete culture with specialized language, rules, and attitudes. One's community, clique, company, ethnic group, and church may maintain its own specialized culture. A **subculture** is a portion of the population which, while sharing some of the ways of the dominant culture, has its own distinct norms, values, and symbols. Sociologists often apply the term subculture to ethnic populations within the dominant culture: Cuban Americans, African Americans, Japanese Americans, Italian Americans. New immigrants from Vietnam, Taiwan, Cambodia, and Puerto Rico often relocate to ethnic neighborhoods in Chicago, San Francisco, and New York to maintain their own identities. So, should they be classified as cultures or subcultures? Should Cherokees and Navajos be referred to as cultures, or would it be more accurate to describe these groups as subcultures since they are heavily acculturated to Euro-American ways? The cultural boundaries between groups become very ambiguous because all groups within a country share many common elements, while at the same time maintaining unique customs and traditions.

Occupational subcultures are as equally unique as ethnic subcultures. Truck drivers, farmers, textile workers, waitresses, stockbrokers, college professors, and many other occupational workers maintain unique cultural characteristics. Individuals in these subcultures have a specialized jargon, interact socially in unique ways, hold similar worldviews, and dress in common uniforms. Political subcultures are also present in North American culture. They are distinct in that normally they are fringe groups whose lives are totally consumed with the political activity of either the extreme political right or left. A subcultural designation can also be applied to religious groups such as Pentecostals, Mormons, Muslims, and Christian evangelicals. By affirming supernatural intervention in personal dilemmas, the Pentecostal worldview sets Pentecostals apart from members of the dominant scientific culture. Mormon culture is uniquely American with historical roots and cultural forms that are modifications of American life. Marriage rules and church-centric families are distinct traits of Mormon culture.

Countercultures are alternative groups within the larger society. Many of their values, beliefs, and attitudes are antithetical to those of the dominant culture. A good example comes from the countercultural movement of the 1960s and 1970s. "Hippie culture" was essentially a protest lifestyle poised against the middle-class corporate culture. The hippie culture saw the middle-class culture as both supporting an unjust conflict in Vietnam and spreading capitalism globally. If middle-class people valued cleanliness and hygiene, the hippie culture posited, it was because they were self-centered, self-indulgent hypocrites who did not care about people being killed in war and were unconcerned about the poverty caused by capitalist systems. If members of the dominant culture worked hard in organizational offices and lived in suburbia, counterculture types should move to the country, grow their own food, and make handicrafts in communes. Today there are still groups of artists and musicians, environmentalists and political activists, social dropouts and vagabonds who form alternative communities and challenge the norms and values of the dominant culture.

CULTURAL DIVERSITY

ETHNOCENTRISM

Social scientists employ the term **ethnocentrism** to refer to an attitude asserting that the

Do these expressions of beauty seem ugly to you? You are ethnocentric! Tarahumara Indians painted for power.

values and norms of one's own culture are superior to those of other cultures. This superior-inferior notion is used as a basis for judging and evaluating all other cultures. It is the basis for prejudice against a culture or subculture as well. For example, early European settlers in the New World considered Native Americans to be "uncivilized." Christians are not exempt from ethnocentrism: When early missionaries went to Africa to spread the gospel, some required new African converts (whose cultural dress appeared immodest to American Christians) to change their cultural habits in order to become Christians.

Modern, educated people are as ethnocentric as people in traditional cultures are. An ethnocentric attitude is evident in the way that scientists view and describe early humans. Terms such as illiterate, primitive, Stone Age, and pagan create an image that early humans were barbaric, hairy, violent, proto-human beings. We contrast earlier humans to ourselves and present contemporary people as civilized, modern, and literate.

Conservative American Christians might be considered ethnocentric in their view that there is a single biblical standard by which everyone should live. Some conservative Christians appear to idealize a cultural way of life—including dress, music, and language—as intrinsically "Christian." Some seem to idealize a cultural past (the 1950s are often used as a reference point) when it is believed that people were all morally good, families were all functioning well, everyone went to church, and every American had a three-bedroom home in suburbia. There is a belief that if we return to this past, people could truly be Christians. The dilemma is that this model for life is a cultural product of some Euro-American middle-class folks and does not reflect the great number of non-white, working, and lower-class citizens of the United States. Christianity is not culture specific. Rather, it has proven to be a viable faith for people in a multiplicity of cultural contexts.

STEREOTYPING

A cultural **stereotype** is an idea about an individual based on preconceived, standardized characteristics that have been generalized to a whole category of people. These impressions do not arise from personal experience but rather from the influences and socialization of mass media, peer groups, and parents. Walter Lippmann first suggested the concept of stereotypes and described them as "pictures in our heads" that have not been acquired by personal experience.[9] Martin Marger holds that these mental images serve to support negative beliefs that promote prejudice.[10]

Christian anthropologist Murl Dirksen illustrates how negative stereotypes can be manifested in very odd situations. Basing his report on his experiences at a Hopi reservation, he demonstrates that negative caricatures are sometimes even used by members of the group itself.

> Growing up on the Hopi reservation, like all other normal boys, we played cowboys and Indians, but since I was the only white child, I was always chosen to be the Indian. We all knew from watching westerns on television that the Indians always got slaughtered and lost in the end. Nobody wanted to be an Indian. While I was dancing and chanting around a campfire with a feather sticking out of my headband and holding a bow and arrow, my Hopi friends were riding stick horses and would attack and shoot me. From watching numerous cowboy attack scenes in the movies, we played our stereotypic roles based on the images that white men on horses with guns were stronger than brown men without guns and horses. Hopi boys never thought of themselves as Indians. "Indian" is a negative Anglo caricature of aboriginal Americans.

Cultural stereotypes make people feel they have some familiarity with groups they have not personally experienced. But stereotypes become problematic when they predetermine how we think about people, emphasize the negative characteristics, and define how others ought to be treated. The difference between stereotypes and rational generalizations is that stereotypes are simplistic and exaggerated beliefs that are resistant to change.[11]

To what degree does the mass media affect cultural stereotypes, both positively and negatively? Mass culture has caricatured Italians as pasta-eating, Mafia gangsters. Drug dealers and other criminal types on television and movies are generally Hispanic Americans or African Americans. Arabs and Russians are portrayed in the media as violent, wealthy, and basically uncultured. The images most of the world has of Americans (based on their exposure to American movies) is that they are loud, materialistic, sex-starved maniacs. For children and other individuals with limited experience outside their own communities, the television media provide most of their information and stereotypic images about people in other cultures.

CULTURAL RELATIVISM

The **cultural relativistic perspective** is a view that acknowledges that every culture should be analyzed in its own context and by its own standards. Cultural understanding is best achieved by presenting a cultural group as it views itself and not by imposing some external standard.

Some degree of controversy surrounds the cultural relativism perspective. Some social scientists believe that when members of one culture pass any judgment on another culture's attitudes and behaviors, they violate the cultural relativistic approach. In this thinking, then, everything is culturally relative and to think otherwise shows insensitivity to the people and a lack of comprehension of how culture operates. However, most scientists think that while it is an important attitude to adopt in understanding cultural differences and similarities, it does not mean that one must entirely suspend moral judgment. Sociologists have personal standards that they need not surrender. The holocaust of Nazi Germany can be understood in terms of the racist ideology of the culture of that time, but one need not abdicate judgment on the inhumanness of such activities. Speaking out against and striving for the removal of poverty, injustice, and suffering of all people are our responsibilities. Sociologists must evaluate the moral implications of a culture's norms and values and denounce those they believe are harmful to humans.

CHRISTIANS CHALLENGING CULTURE

What happens when cultural expectations contradict our Christian values? For example, cultural expectations in China support selective abortion and infanticide in order to get an optimal family size and gender distribution. In some African cultures, young females are sexually mutilated ("female circumcision") in order to keep them from pursuing premarital and extramarital sex. In America, the adolescent subculture contains music that promotes sex, drugs, and violence. To what extent do we accept cultural diversity as "relative" and "simply a matter of agreement"? Where do we draw the line and decide we need to challenge and change the culture? Do we dare try to change a culture of which we are not a part?

As Christian sociologists, we want very much to be sensitive to cultural differences, but not at the expense of our biblical principles. The objective in using the relativistic approach is to understand and appreciate diversity, not validate another's cultural patterns. We need to search for Biblical Truth, not in the culture around us, but in the revealed Word of God. And then, knowing that Truth, we need to speak the Truth —with love—to our neighbors. The life we live, which often challenges cultural expectations, speaks volumes to a world we wish to change.

A great example of an effective use of this approach comes from the Apostle Paul in his letter to the church in Rome. The church was very multicultural, mostly Gentiles with a minority of Jews, and Paul was attempting to explain God's overall plan for redemption to a culturally diverse audience. He writes, "Let us then pursue what makes for peace and for mutual upbuilding. Do not, for the sake of food, destroy the work of God. Everything is indeed clean, but it is wrong for you to make others fall by what you eat; it is good not to eat meat or drink wine or do anything that makes your brother or sister stumble" (Rom. 14:19-21).

Culture is a wonderful gift that God has fashioned in us. It gives us the capacity to creatively survive within a complex society. But the sinful nature of humankind has taken cultural differences and created cultural stereotypes, ethnocentric views, and cultural prejudices in order to effectively divide us from one another. Christians are called on to further the kingdom of God through the understanding of one another's cultures, as well as deeply appreciating one's own culture.

We began this chapter with Murl Dirksen's personal anecdote about his childhood experiences in a Hopi village. This is how he concludes:

> So what was "mother"? The broom-sharing experience had taught me the concept of culture and taught me about cultural differences. "Mother" was a semantic category, a way of classifying people in the village by assigning them a specific symbol, a word, and expecting people when using this term to show certain behaviors and emotions. I came to understand I was bicultural and had two classification systems for the same concept, "mother." Anglo motherness was singular in nature while Hopi motherness was a collective image referring to all older females in one's clan. Mothers in the Anglo culture punished and instructed their children, but Hopi mothers never spanked their children. This was the prerogative of the mother's brother, who was responsible for their guidance. Anglo

mothers assigned household tasks to their children, but Hopi boys never had domestic chores and girls worked side by side with their clan mothers. Anglo motherness was based primarily on birth into a nuclear family unit, while one's being mothered among the Hopi came from whose home one was in at a particular time of the day. I came to realize that the mother in the home where I was, whether day or night, was responsible for my feeding, safety, and general welfare. Motherness was culture specific and I happened to have been lucky enough to have both my Anglo mother and Hopi village mothering. Being multicultural was not a handicap but a gift.

overview

- Culture consists of all those things that one needs to know to function as a member of a society.

- Elements of culture include beliefs and values as well as appropriate behaviors (norms). Culture is expressed in a variety of material forms, such as tools and technology. Every human society employs culture to solve universal problems associated with mere existence, including food, shelter, clothing, sex, and emotions.

- Although we have many physical characteristics similar to those of animals, we are specially programmed to share patterns of meaning through the use of symbols. All humans have a complete linguistic system composed of arbitrary symbols and sounds that communicate cultural elements throughout the group.

- Culture creates order and meaning for its members by establishing a cognitive impression of what the world is like, a worldview. Cultural values, those shared ideas of what is desirable and undesirable, form the basis for the normative order of folkways, mores, and sanctions.

- Cultural systems are constantly changing in order to adapt to new environments and social conditions.

- Subcultures and countercultures may form within the larger cultural system, and while they share some characteristics with the dominant culture, they maintain some of their own unique ideas and ways. Prime examples of subcultural groups are those based on ethnicity.

- An understanding of cultural variance can best be achieved by using the perspective of cultural relativism, analyzing every culture in its own context and by its own standards. Analysis does not imply agreement.

- Culture not only makes us human but the variety of cultural responses increases our survival capacity.

key concepts

beliefs
The general agreement by the members of a society that a certain body of knowledge is true or valid.

counterculture
A group's way of thinking and acting that is an alternative to or in opposition to the norms and values of the larger society.

cultural material
Tangible objects that facilitate and express cultural ideas and norms; for example, musical instruments, works of art, religious paraphernalia, currencies, shelter, and clothing.

cultural relativistic perspective
A view that acknowledges that every culture should be analyzed in its own context and by its own standards; an orientation that supports rational, empirical, and comparative analysis of cultures and rejects an ethnocentric view.

cultural universals
Cultural elements that are present in all human societies.

culture
A society's way of life, consisting of beliefs, values, norms, and symbols.

ethnocentrism
Attitudes which support beliefs that values and norms of one's culture are superior to those of another.

folkways
The customary ways people do things.

ideational definition of culture
Knowledge of cultural standards to which a person's behavior may or may not correspond.

language
The means of communication practiced by humans.

law
A type of social control exemplified by intention, authority, obligation, and sanctions.

mores
Cultural rules that are essential for societal survival and have been codified into moral and civil laws.

norms
Cultural rules or standards that are both informal and formal in nature and which occur in all social groups.

proxemics
The physical space between people which is given sociocultural meaning.

sanctions (negative)
Punishments used for violations of cultural rules.

sanctions (positive)
Rewards used for compliance with cultural rules.

stereotype
An idea about an individual based on preconceived, standardized characteristics alleged to a whole category of people.

symbols
Anything—object, gesture, word—that is given arbitrary meaning and about which members of a culture generally agree.

social control
Ways in which individual behavior is directed toward socially acceptable standards.

subculture
A portion of the population having distinctive norms, values, and traits.

values
Shared ideas of things members of a culture think are good and desirable.

worldview
A comprehensible body of beliefs about how the world is organized as represented in a culture's myths, religious ceremonies, social behavior, and value system.

endnotes

1. Ralph Linton, *The Study of Man* (New York: Appleton-Century-Crofts, Inc., 1936), 22.
2. Ward Goodenough, "Comments on Cultural Evolution," *Daedalus* 90 (1961), 521-22.
3. James Peoples and Garrick Bailey, *Humanity* (New York: West Publishing Co., 1994), 23.
4. James P. Spradley, "Foundations of Cultural Knowledge," in *Culture and Cognition*, ed. James Spradley (San Francisco: Chandler Publishing Co., 1972), 34-35.
5. Noam Chomsky, *Aspects of the Theory of Syntax* (Cambridge, MA: M.I.T. Press, 1965), 6.
6. Robin Williams, *American Values—A Sociological Perspective* (New York: Alfred A. Knopf, Inc., 1970), 452-502.
7. William G. Sumner, *Folkways* (Boston: Ginn Publishing Co., 1940), 1-74.
8. Herbert Blumer, *Studies in Symbolic Interaction* (Englewood Cliffs, NJ: Prentice Hall Publishing Co., 1969).
9. Walter Lippmann, *Public Opinion* (New York: Macmillan Publishing Co., 1922), 22. See also John Harding, "Stereotypes," in *International Encyclopedia of Social Sciences*, ed. David Sills, vol. 15 (New York: Macmillan Publishing Co., 1968), 259-261.
10. Martin Marger, *Race and Ethnic Relations* (Belmont, CA: Wadsworth Publishing Co., 1991), 75.
11. Neil Vidnar and Milton Rokeach, "Archie Bunker's Bigotry: A Study in Selective Perception and Exposure," *Journal of Communication* (1974): 46-47.

additional sources

Peter L. Berger and Thomas Luckmann, *The Social Construction of Reality: A Treatise in the Sociology of Knowledge* (Garden City, New York: Anchor Books, 1967).

Rolf Dahrendorf, *Class and Class Conflict in Industrial Society* (Stanford, CA: Stanford University Press, 1959).

Jill Dubisch, "You Are What You Eat: Religious Aspects of the Health Food Movement," in *Applying Cultural Anthropology*, ed. Aaron Podolefsky and Peter J. Brown (Toronto: Mayfield Publishing Co., 1994), 90-97.

Jane V. L. Goodall, "A Preliminary Report on Expressive Movement and Communications in Gombe Stream Chimpanzees," in *Primates: Studies in Adaptation and Variability*, ed. P. Jay (Fort Worth, TX: Holt, Rinehart and Winston, 1968), 22.

Marvin Harris, "India's Sacred Cow," in *Anthropology: Contemporary Perspectives*, ed. Phillip Whitten and David Hunter (London: Scott, Foresman & Co., 1990), 204-05.

Charles D. Hockett, "The Origin of Speech," *Scientific American* (Sept. 1960): 88-90.

Tom Peeler, "Great Moments in Snack Food History," *American Way* (December 1983): 111-14.

Benjamin L. Whorf, "The Relation of Habitual Thought to Behavior," in *Language, Thought and Reality*. ed. J. B. Carroll (Cambridge, MA: M.I.T. Press, 1961), 135.

CHAPTER FOUR

Social Structure, Groups, and Organizations

chapter outline

I. Social structure
   A. Definition
   B. Structural-functional perspective
   C. Conflict perspective
   D. Interactionist perspective

II. Primary and secondary groups

III. Status

IV. Role

V. Social construction of reality

VI. The rise and decline of groups

VII. Formal organization and bureaucracy

VIII. McDonaldization

biblical reflection

"But as it is, God arranged the members in the body, each one of them, as he chose."

—1 Corinthians 12:18

Over a four-month period, Donald Ratcliff observed children in the hallway of an elementary school, interviewing about fifty of the youngsters concerning their views of the hall.[1] One of the things he noticed was that they physically grouped together in three different ways. One way was the school line, where one child followed another single file down the hall, always under the careful scrutiny of a classroom teacher who had required them to group in this manner. In a second kind of grouping, the children walked side by side in groups of two, but often more than two, usually chatting or at least exchanging eye contact as they walked. Because he couldn't find a name for this kind of group, he called it a "phalanx," a military term that designates an array of soldiers going into a battle. A third kind of group was represented by children stopping and forming a circular or semicircular arrangement as they talked about something they considered important. This group can be called a "cluster," because the youngsters usually gathered closely together to hear one another in the conversation.

In contrast, the school around the children was controlled by adults who were given authority to teach the children and to control many of their other activities. That control was obvious not only in the school lines imposed by teachers, but also in the policing and often disbanding of phalanxes and clusters. In the school there was an obvious chain of command, with the principal at the top level in the school, teachers under the principal, and the youngsters below the teachers. There might even have been a chart that showed the level of authority for every employee and student. Not seen were people with even higher levels of power and authority, such as the superintendent of schools, the state board of education, and finally the governor of the state and the society that elected that governor. This is a very different world from that of the children, and yet both clearly existed at the same time and in the same place.

SOCIAL STRUCTURE

DEFINITION

These two views of school life are examples of **social structure**, which refers to the way human activity is organized on a normal, more or less consistent basis. We see patterns of behavior in *every* aspect of **society** and in *all* kinds of groups. Social structure does not describe the people involved, but rather the way they act in group settings. There are two important things about social structure. First, those in the group must *relate* to one another in some way, such as a teacher scolding a student or a student making fun of the principal behind his/her back. Second, there must be an *interdependence* in people's interactions: children depend upon adults to teach them; adults depend upon children to accomplish their task of education; and children depend upon one another for interesting conversations and activities.

It is important to understand social structure because it silently shapes our lives, even though it is invisible to the eye. By studying social structure we can better understand why people act the way they do.

STRUCTURAL-FUNCTIONAL PERSPECTIVE

In Ratcliff's school hallway research, the *manifest (intended) function* of the hallway was to transfer children from one area of the school to another area, or sometimes from the inside of the school to the outside. There were also some hidden or *latent functions*. For example, children could avoid class, be punished, see friends, study, use the drinking fountain or restroom, carry messages, and do many other things in the hallway. A strip of cork lined the entire length of the hallway. The function of the cork strip was for teachers to display the work of students. For most of the semester, there were only a couple of torn posters to be seen in the main section of the hallway; the children may have concluded that nothing they did was worthy of display.

There were also examples of **dysfunction** in the hallway. While in the past schools have generally provided several recess periods a day for children to expend energy and have a change of pace, the school Ratcliff studied—and many others throughout the United States—have limited or eliminated recess altogether. He wondered if some of the fighting and other high-level activities he observed in the hallway were the result of this change. Recess is functional in that it helps children change pace and thus pay more attention in class.[2] Eliminating recess is dysfunctional in that children not only have less concentration in the classroom, but their high energy spills over to the hallway. Thus, the structural-functionalist view of social structure seeks to describe both functional and dysfunctional aspects of groups—from the broadest level of society in general, to the smallest group of the two-person group, the dyad. This perspective asks how groups of every size and variety accomplish their goals and purposes effectively, and what influences keep groups from successfully realizing their purposes and goals.

CONFLICT PERSPECTIVE

This view of social structures emphasizes the struggles between the powerful and less powerful, as well as conflicts that arise from differences in interests, values, and competition. Groups may have conflicts and struggles for control for a wide variety of reasons, and the conflict can be either within a group, between different groups, or both. In the school hallway, Ratcliff was impressed not so much with the conflicts between students—these were relatively rare—but rather with the conflict between teachers and students. Teachers imposed their authority by overt commands and reprimands, and even by paddling. Children, for the most part, negated that authority by passive resistance, such as doing what was asked very slowly or "pushing the limits" by walking very rapidly when scolded for running. Most children view school lines as an oppressive form of imposed authority. Indeed, other research indicates that this kind of line—which has the function of moving people from one place to another—is only found in prisons, mental hospitals, the military, and perhaps concentration camps. Yet children would passively resist line rules by moving out of the single-file formation, playfully punching the person next to them, talking, and making faces when the teacher was not looking. Phalanxes and clusters were additional ways children resisted teacher authority, but these were sometimes tolerated.[3]

INTERACTIONIST PERSPECTIVE

This view emphasizes the symbols, words, and gestures that occur during person-to-person interactions, and the underlying meanings that are conferred to those symbols. While such theorists would rarely analyze society as a whole, they might be impressed with how the religious terminology of politicians results in a variety of meanings being conferred. For example, some people may see those terms as evidence the politician is a Christian; others may interpret them as metaphors that describe political issues in religious ways; and still others may see religious terms as ways to emotionally manipulate people. In the school hallway study, Ratcliff was impressed with some of the symbolic activity of youngsters. He often observed boys pretending to play basketball by jumping and shooting an imaginary ball into a nonexistent basket. Such boys could almost hear the imagined crowd roaring with praise.

One symbolic activity puzzled me for quite a

while: many youngsters would drag their hands or other parts of the body against the walls as they walked. The children could not tell him why they touched the walls, although some offered that it might be due to boredom. After interviewing the children and hearing of the oppressive aspects of classroom life, Ratcliff conjectured that perhaps children saw the walls as welcome dividers between the classroom and the somewhat less controlled hallway. Perhaps the wall rubbing—which probably was a forbidden act—was an affirmation of the comparative freedom of the hallway. Perhaps the rubbing was a "good-bye" to that freedom, with the implication that they would eventually return to touch again.[4]

PRIMARY AND SECONDARY GROUPS

Sociologist Charles Cooley distinguished two basic kinds of groups in any given society.[5] A **primary group** is a small number of people who regularly associate with one another in an intimate, face-to-face, largely cooperative manner. They are called "primary," said Cooley, because everyone belongs to one particular primary group—the family—from the very beginning of life. The family and other early primary groups, such as a child's play group, are primary in importance because they powerfully influence the personality, morality, and ideals of the individual.

Examples of a primary group include a group of friends in a neighborhood, a college roommate, friends on a basketball team, or an engaged couple. In each case the group is small, personal, and involves close, warm relationships. We tend to be open in such groups, we feel free to joke with our friends, and we care what the others think of us—what we say and how we act. There is a sense of belonging in a primary group; we usually talk about such a group as a "we" group because of that feeling of being connected to others in the group. People are valued for themselves in a primary group, rather than for what they can give you or what you can gain from them.

Primary groups tend to be more permanent than other groups. If one loses contact with a friend, often a telephone call quickly reestablishes the relationship and intimacy. In this respect a primary group can be contrasted with an **aggregate**, which is a collection of people who have little or no self-identity and who do not interact with a common goal or purpose. Audiences, crowds, and a gathering of people at a bus stop are common aggregates.

God created us to need primary group relations. Certainly when God declares in Genesis 2:18, "It is not good that the man should be alone," God was affirming the basic need we have for human companionship. God created another human and intended that their relationship be patterned after God's relationship with the first human: close, intimate, and self-fulfilling. It is within our primary group relations that we become more fully human by fulfilling the potential God created in each of us.

In contrast to a primary group (and also an aggregate) is a secondary group. A **secondary group** is marked by relationships that are impersonal, formal, unemotional, partial, and impermanent. Instead of affecting the person's personality, only very specific areas of life are influenced by secondary groups. A college, various workplaces, and even the momentary relationship with a grocery clerk are examples of secondary groups. We often use the word "they" when talking about a secondary group; even if we technically belong to the group—for example, we may be part of a college—we still tend to call the group "they." Sociologists thus make the distinction between "they groups" and "we groups," sometimes substituting the terms "out-group" and "in-group" for these two kinds of groups.

Secondary groups tend to be larger than primary groups, and while a person may make

*The family is a **primary group** because members share themselves completely with one another. The market is an **aggregate** because the people just happen to be at the same place at the same time without necessarily interacting. The office is a **secondary group** because these employees are interacting in a very formal, limited way.*

contact with many people, the contacts are more likely to be impersonal and objective. People in a secondary group are valued for what they can give you; they become a means to an end. For example, checkout clerks are valued for their ability to provide you with a purchase, not for their conversation. There is a strong concern for efficiency in secondary groups, and intimacy can be thought to interfere with efficiency and objectivity. Thus, a military officer is often distant from those under his command, as control and rigorous training are high priorities.

Primary groups can develop within secondary groups. For example, people who work together at a plant may come to like one another and spend time talking around the water cooler. Thus, they form relationships based on friendship—a primary group—even though it was the job that brought them physically together in the first place. Such groups are called **informal organizations**. Sometimes such groups develop for the purpose of self-defense, to counteract the demoralization that can go with a job. People in such informal organizations often eat together, share common problems, and develop strong friendships. While it is possible for such groups to cause difficulties or waste time, they can also increase the organization's morale.

When Christians meet together to sing, pray, and learn, they may do so in either a primary or

Chapter Four: Social Structure, Groups, and Organizations

secondary group setting. It is not just the friendliness of a church that makes the difference—secondary groups can be made up of friendly people who are not interested in being close or intimate. Rather, the size, degree of intimacy, and other differences noted above determine whether a group is primary or secondary.

Many Bible studies, Sunday school classes, midweek fellowships, and some smaller churches can be considered primary groups. In contrast, many churches are secondary groups. This is not to say that they are unfriendly or unpleasant churches; they may be very helpful and mean a great deal to those who attend. When you go to a church that is a secondary group, you can be fairly certain that only certain people will be leading during the service, and that the public address system will enforce that level of control. If those attending have questions, they may not be able to ask them (or have them answered) due to the structured nature of the service. In most churches, the interaction among those attending is limited to a few minutes of "greeting" or perhaps a few minutes before or after the service. The leaders and people who attend are more likely to be a means to some end, such as learning more about the Bible, accomplishing a specific task for the community, or making business contacts. Such a church is unlikely to make significant changes in the attendee's life unless that person becomes involved in a small primary group within the large secondary group.

Thus, any church—regardless of size—can provide opportunities for primary groups to form. Sunday schools, midweek prayer meetings, home Bible studies, and the like can be primary groups that are supported and encour-

God created us for primary group relations: with one another and with God.

aged by a church that is in general more secondary. Some churches deliberately encourage more of a primary group feel for the Sunday evening service, while clearly maintaining Sunday morning as a secondary group. Keep in mind that a secondary group can do some things very well because of the concern for efficiency (and potential to pool funds), but it can also encourage additional primary groups. Most successful mega-churches today have some sort of small group ministry opportunities. As you examine the Bible, you can find God's people assembling in secondary groups, such as the early church conference in Acts 15 or those gathered at Mars Hill in Athens to hear Paul's message (Acts 17). But the "churches" to whom the New Testament was addressed were people who met in homes for worship and study. God uses both kinds of groups for very different purposes.

STATUS

Within primary and secondary groups—indeed within any group, including society in general—an individual tends to have some level of **social status**. This refers to the social position a person has in that group or in society in general. Social status is closely related to prestige and power, but usually carries with it specific responsibilities as well. Consider a medical doctor: in general a doctor has fairly high status, which brings with it the power to write prescriptions for medicine and the benefit of a high income. However, a great deal of responsibility comes with that status and, thus, a doctor is more likely to be sued for any mistake he or she makes. While occupations are related to status, there are also different status levels within a profession. Consider the status of a student: in many respects the status of a freshman is very different from that of a senior. That is, of course, unless the freshman is the daughter of the President of the United States!

Status may be implied by the way one dresses or the car one drives. These are examples of *status symbols*, which are indications of having a certain status. Status is also indicated by the people with whom one associates, the way one speaks, and the mannerisms one uses. While these emphasize the status of the person, *groups* also have status, as reflected in high school students who associate with others who are considered "punks," "jocks," "nerds," and "preppies."

Ascribed status is acquired at birth because of the family into which one is born. In some societies, such as premodern India and medieval Europe, the ascribed status you received at birth almost entirely determined what your life would be like. Even today, if you are born into royalty in England, or to an aristocratic upper-class family in the United States, it is unlikely you will ever become middle- or lower-class within your lifetime.

Achieved status, in contrast, is obtained by what a person accomplishes in life. Obtaining a college degree is an example of an achieved status, as are most occupations, although ascribed status may influence the likelihood a person will achieve a specific status. For example, many people could probably become competent medical doctors, an achieved status. However, the ascribed status that goes with wealth can affect one's ability to be accepted into medical school, as well as influence the assumptions a person holds about whether he or she should even consider medical school.

Sometimes there can be **status inconsistency**. For example, a pastor may be admired and respected by the people in a church, yet may be given an economic status that is inconsistent with a pastor's social status.

How should Christians look at status? The Bible clearly recognizes status, contrasting the status of student and teacher (Matt. 10:24) and describing positions of high and low status at the banquet table (Luke 14:8-10). Yet there is an emphasis in this last passage against taking the high status position because of the possibility of being embarrassed when asked to take a lower

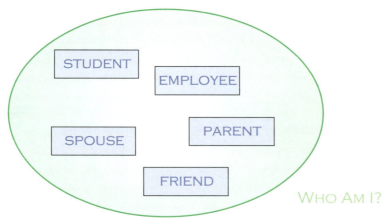

FIGURE 4:1

We have many statuses. Each status determines a role we play. Together they comprise our social identity.

position. We should be impressed with how often the Bible speaks of status inversions, such as Jesus' response to the disciples when they wanted high status in the kingdom. Instead, He told them they must become like children to enter God's kingdom (Matt. 18:1-4).

While the Bible minimizes the status differences in God's eyes (Gal. 3:26-28) and warns that it can be sinful to recognize status differences (James 2:1-9), one might consider being a Christian itself to be a status. Does one achieve the status of being a Christian by accepting Christ, or does God ascribe the status of being a Christian? To some extent, your theology will probably influence your answer to this question. Although most Christians believe God gives salvation without any merit on our part—what Christians call grace, "unmerited favor"—we must also accept what He has freely given. In other words, being a Christian is ascribed once we agree to accept Christ, yet we must also "work out [our] own salvation with fear and trembling" (Phil. 2:12).

ROLE

While status refers to one's *position* in a group or society, **role** refers to the rules or norms for behavior that are expected from someone of a given status. A role involves *rights*; for example, the privilege a teacher may have to a good parking place. It also involves *obligations*, the necessity of calculating grades for students. When people do not follow the socially prescribed role, we will probably be surprised or even shocked. For example, Ratcliff received a phone call one day and the caller said, "Hi, this is Dave."[6] The caller then began to talk about some medical issues. Ratcliff was dumbfounded, trying to figure out who was talking to him, until he realized that "Dave" was the first name of his new doctor. Not only was he fresh out of medical school, but he also tended to ignore status differences. Our society teaches us that medical doctors should identify themselves as "Doctor Jones" rather than "Dave." During certain medical procedures, doctors follow very elaborate rituals to minimize embarrassment, such as during a gynecological exam.[7]

Sometimes a given role may involve expectations that are inconsistent. For example, a wife may be expected to buy a nice present for her husband's birthday, but also make sure there is enough money in the bank to pay the bills. If you are on a tight budget, you may experience **role strain** as you try to decide which of these expectations should be the priority. In contrast, **role conflict** occurs when you have two differ-

FIGURE 4:2

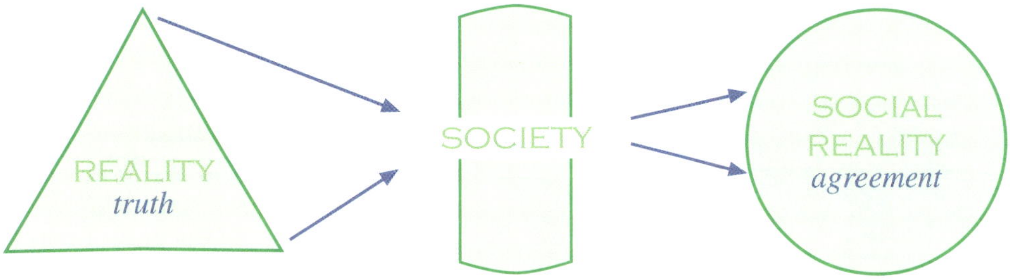

Through the lens of society, reality often looks quite different from what is really there.

ent roles and the expectations of the roles conflict with one another. Married students may try to balance the roles of student, employee, parent, spouse, and friend. Role conflict occurs because there are only so many hours in a day and you find that you cannot meet all of the things expected of your various roles. Yet, with careful time management and a few compromises, you will probably be able to perform each of these roles sufficiently, though perhaps not perfectly or ideally.

From a Christian perspective, roles are important and helpful most of the time, but they can be idealistic and thus encourage inequality in the perceived dispersal of spiritual gifts and duties. For example, some people see their pastor's status in an unrealistic manner: as the ultimate religious authority, who is on call twenty-four hours a day, and whose family is expected to set a good example for everyone. In contrast, the Bible does not demand such perfection. It may be that the role of "superpastor" actually interferes with the way the church should function.[8]

SOCIAL CONSTRUCTION OF REALITY

Our statuses and roles exist as social agreements between others and ourselves. We act as if our social status is real—like we really are what people say we are. We forget, for example, that the only reason we are students is because some people at the university say we are. We have socially constructed this reality that says when you are a student you do not know as much as your instructor. And then we act as if that social reality were the truth: You sit quietly in class, taking notes as if what your instructor says is *really* important. Sound radical? How about this: Isn't Christ the only Truth that is *really* important?

This "socially constructed reality" becomes the foundation for our attitudes and behaviors. To us, this social reality becomes more "real" than the Truth. Thus, we are often responding to a reality that is far from Truth (divine revelation). This becomes important later in this text when we recognize that the idea of social class and race is merely a socially constructed reality. The *reality* is that God values us all, but the *social reality* is that some people are more highly valued than others.

THE RISE AND DECLINE OF GROUPS

Secondary groups, and some primary groups, tend to go through a succession of phases with time. Not every group goes through all of the phases, as some resist progression, and occasionally a group may even go backward a phase or two. But the normal tendency is to move through three phases of development and then on to two additional phases of decline. The end of the process is not always the end of the group; there are plenty of organizations that come to the last phase but continue to exist, even though they are almost completely ineffective.[9]

David Moberg has suggested five phases of church development, although many groups other than churches pass through very similar stages.[10] At the beginning, a new group meets either because of dissatisfaction with an existing church or organization, or sometimes just because of a sense of need. Usually there is a great deal of enthusiasm and excitement, and the leaders of new groups tend to have personal charisma that draws others into the group. Perhaps the most important aspect of this first phase is the **functional base**—the need that is the reason the group exists. In the case of a new church, this need might be fellowship, learning about God, or having more vital worship.

The second phase is marked by a call for commitments to the group, the forming of goals, and sometimes symbols and slogans. At this point **conservation** begins, which means that the group begins doing things to make certain the group will continue. Raising money and establishing positions of leadership with job descriptions often become prominent at this point.

With time, a third phase emerges marked by *maximal efficiency*, says Moberg. There is now more emphasis upon rational thinking and less emotional display. The differences from other groups tend to be minimized, and usually several committees are formed. Rapid growth takes place at this point, as new believers are quickly integrated or socialized into the group. One hears more and more about conservation, such as raising funds and recruiting volunteers for available jobs. Many churches function fairly well at this phase because the "wheels" of church structure are well "greased."

Moberg describes the key aspect of the fourth stage of development as *institutionalization* due to increased formality and more rules in the church. The original need—the functional base—is given less attention, as conservation grows to the point that it is clearly in excess of what is needed for the group to continue. As a result, there is often a conflict between the words and actions of leaders. Even as the functional base—the original need—is still talked about, decisions tend to reflect the growing concern with maintaining the organization as it is—conservation. Symbols and rituals tend to lose their meaning and become an end in themselves, rather than a means to the end of worship and praise. There tends to be little or no fresh thinking, and not much creativity. Leaders tend to disconnect from the average members of the group. The group is definitely in decline.

Finally the church—or other kind of group—becomes more and more of a machine that seems to have little meaning or purpose. There are more and more regulations, and although those who continue to attend halfheartedly hold to the church teachings, they may begin to ignore the ideals that were so strong at the beginning. While many leave the church at this phase, those who remain do so because they feel emotionally attached to the church because of their past experiences there, or because of vested interests.

Tony Campolo once said of these kinds of churches, "If the Holy Spirit wanted to move in some of our churches, He'd have to clear it through three committees, and then He'd only be given a few minutes during the announcements." Perhaps the most important new development at this stage is the emergence of **dysfunction**. As we saw earlier in this chapter, dysfunctions are things done for the sake of conservation that undermine the original functional base. In other words, things are done to keep the group going and keep the machinery moving that directly counteract the purpose for which the church originally began. For example, if the original purpose of the church was to have more vibrant worship, but instead the church finds itself spending a great deal of time trying to raise money at the beginning of a service, by the time worship should begin, people may no longer have an attitude of worship. Likewise, if the church's purpose was to teach people from the Bible, dysfunction might manifest in a large part of the message being given to the need for more volunteers in the church programs. Ironically, a church in Atlanta, Georgia, had accumulated a large amount of money in its savings account, but had lost its membership. The church became focused 100% on conservation and failed to meet individual needs.

FORMAL ORGANIZATION AND BUREAUCRACY

A **formal organization** is a secondary group that is systematically organized to carry out clearly defined goals and purposes, including precise roles for people. Examples include The Ford Motor Company, The United Methodist Church, and The Department of Health and Welfare.

One specific kind of formal organization is the **bureaucracy**. Examples of bureaucracies include corporations, labor unions, the military, colleges and universities, banks, and even farmers' cooperatives. How is a bureaucracy different from other formal organizations? Max Weber, considered one of the founders of sociology, noted several characteristics that set apart bureaucracies.[11] Among these is *division of labor,* which means that people have specific jobs and are expected to know how to do those jobs. The division of labor is arranged in a *chain of command* with a *hierarchy*; in other words, people at any level of the organization have a boss who has authority over them, but each level of authority is also responsible to someone at a higher level. Demands, reprimands, and discipline tend to flow down the hierarchy, while requests and other issues requiring higher-level decisions flow up the hierarchy. The hierarchy includes *centralized authority*—a person or group of people clearly in control, such as a president, a superintendent, or a board of directors—and at each level of the organization, people's authority is related to their appointed positions.

Weber emphasized the importance of written documents that describe a set of *elaborate rules* whose purpose is to make certain each task is accomplished correctly. Relationships between people in the organization—and especially between employers and employees—are based upon *rationality* rather than personality; the basic issue is whether the job is getting done, not who does it. *Efficiency* is of major concern, as is *technical knowledge*; one should have a thorough understanding of job expectations. In an ideal bureaucracy, competent employees cannot be dismissed arbitrarily. Instead, Max Weber suggested, there is the possibility for promotion in a career-centered progression.

Unfortunately, this neat outline of how bureaucracies function is very idealistic, Weber admitted. For example, some jobs—especially higher-level positions in the hierarchy—may have descriptions that are very vague, and when it is not clear what is expected, people tend to "make work" for themselves that may have little to do with their positions. Ratcliff worked for a state government at one point and observed one administrator who was so bored that he would purposefully create misunderstandings between other administrators so he could enjoy the resulting conflict! Someone once said, "Work in a bureaucracy expands to fill the available time," and sometimes that is exactly what happens.

Similarly, relationships that are supposed to be rational, formal, and objective may indeed become very personal—either by the development of a romantic relationship or, at the other extreme, by underlying hostility and distrust. Hierarchies can get in the way of communication. Fearing the loss of power, those in power may restrict the flow of information to those below them. Similarly, those at the lower levels may hide information that may make them look bad to superiors. When people are not treated as human beings, they come to see themselves as meaningless cogs in a wheel. Excessive rules or "red tape" may hamper efficiency. Some jobs can be "dead-end" positions where any kind of advancement is impossible. Bureaucracies may perpetuate themselves long after their original purpose has been fulfilled.

Lawrence Peter also emphasized some of the limitations of bureaucracies and developed the *Peter Principle*. His principle states, "In a hierarchy every employee tends to rise to his level of incompetence."[12] In other words, people tend to be promoted in bureaucracies because they are successful at each level, and when they come to a level where they can no longer do the job, they tend to remain at that level. The net result is that bureaucracies may have people in positions of authority who simply do not know what they are doing and who remain in power until they die or retire. Clearly this is an exaggeration; not every administrator is incompetent. But the principle exaggerates what can and often does occur in bureaucracies.

MCDONALDIZATION

Sociologist George Ritzer describes Weber's emphasis on efficiency, quantification, rules, and control in bureaucracies as helping to bring about a trend he terms McDonaldization.[13] The largest fast-food chain in the country typifies what is occurring in many formal organizations throughout the world, Ritzer claims. The McDonald's restaurant was unique when it initially emphasized the principles of "high speed, large volume, and low price," along with a limited selection of products subjected to precise rules and standards. Food was prepared using assembly-line procedures and sold with the help of stock greetings by cashiers. The resulting efficiency and predictability came at the cost of the dehumanization of employees and customers, as well as mediocrity of product and service. The four primary principles of McDonaldization—efficiency, emphasis upon high quantity of food in a minimal amount of time, predictability, and control of the employees and customers—have infiltrated business practices in every area of society, and indeed have become a worldwide phenomenon. As McDonald's enters a new country, the McDonaldization of that society soon follows.

In contrast to Ritzer's pessimistic view of McDonald's, retired seminary president David McKenna sees McDonald's as a positive model for the church.[14] McKenna emphasizes McDonald's effort to balance *centralized resources*—which reflect a "culture of shared values," such as the requirement that every manager be trained at their "Hamburger University"—and *local management* in task groups so that problems are quickly resolved and the system keeps working smoothly. The company headquarters produces the expensive advertising, highlights heroes of the system, and conducts ceremonies to encourage close connections between the local stores and headquarters. There are also regional supervisors who spot-check quality, build morale, and help in problem solving.

These three levels have their parallels in church ministry. Denominations and other associations of churches provide centralized resources such as education for church leaders, vision for the future, an information system, and communication of shared values. Regional or district superintendents encourage and assist individual churches in troubleshooting and quality control through pastoral evaluation. And the local church is the center for activity by responding to people's needs, being sensitive to the unique aspects of the local context, communicating the values of the church, using centralized resources, acting as a change agent for innovative ministries (including evangelization and discipleship), communicating the concerns, needs, and interests of the church to the larger church organization, and financially supporting the denomination.

overview

- Social structure refers to the way human interaction is organized in groups. The three basic theories of sociology are reflected in the social structure of any given group. Society consists of two basic kinds of groups: primary groups and secondary groups. Primary groups are perhaps the most influential in our lives, while we sense greater distance and formality in secondary groups. In contrast, aggregates are not social groups because they lack a self-identity and common purpose. Informal organizations, primary groups that sometimes form within secondary groups, can increase morale.

- An individual's status is that person's social position in a society or other group. Groups as well as individuals can hold a social status. Status may be ascribed or achieved, and individuals may experience status inconsistency. All statuses have at least one associated role and most have more than one role. Role strain results when one role has inconsistent expectations, while role conflict exists where two or more roles are incompatible.

- Groups often move through a predictable group of stages or phases, marked initially by a functional base, then the rise of conservation, and finally by the presence of dysfunction. Formal organizations are necessary in civilized societies and result in greater productivity and efficiency. However, bureaucracies have distinct disadvantages, such as the Peter Principle and the problems associated with McDonaldization.

key concepts

achieved status
Social position that is acquired because of one's ability to alter one's ascribed status.

aggregate
A number of people gathered in the same place who have no interaction relative to a common goal or purpose.

ascribed status
Social position that is acquired by persons at birth, according to their family background.

bureaucracy
A formal or complex organization characterized by centralization of authority, hierarchical chain

of command, and emphasis on rationality, discipline, and technical knowledge.

conservation
Efforts made by a group or organization that have the goal of self-perpetuation of the organization, as well as related programs and activities.

dysfunction
When a group or organization functions in a manner that hinders the likelihood of accomplishing its original purpose; primarily due to excessive concern for perpetuating the organization and its associated programs and activities.

formal organization
A secondary group particularly organized to carry out explicit objectives, impersonal goals, and defined roles.

functional base
The original need or set of needs a group or organization is intended to address.

informal organization
That social structure which results when individuals interact within formal organizations.

primary group
A small number of people who regularly interact with one another in an intimate, face-to-face, largely cooperative manner.

role
The cluster of behavior norms or rules expected of a person occupying a particular social status or position.

role conflict
What results when two or more roles are contradictory or incompatible.

role strain
What often occurs when a role involves differing, inconsistent expectations.

secondary group
A medium-sized or large number of people who interact in an impersonal, formal, unemotional, partial, and nonpermanent manner.

social structure
The ordered, patterned ways in which persons conduct themselves in social situations and how this organization of behavior relates to the rest of their society.

social status
The social position of an individual in his or her society or smaller group. Groups also possess social status.

society
A distinct group of people who occupy a common territory and live together long enough to organize themselves into a unit different from other similar groups.

status inconsistency
The incompatibility of one status with another.

endnotes

1. Donald Ratcliff, "My Exotic Tribe: Children in a School Hallway," in *Sociology: Concepts and Characteristics*, 11th ed., ed. J. R. Landis (Belmont, CA: Wadsworth, 2001). I also recommend Ratcliff's "Creation, Redemption, and Sociological Theory," in *Christian Views of Sociology*, 2nd ed. (Redding, CA: C.A.T. Publishers, 1999).
2. A. D. Pellegrini, *School Recess and Playground Behavior: Educational and Developmental Roles* (Albany, NY: State University of New York Press, 1995).
3. Interestingly, both girls and boys said that girls were more likely to get by with these in the hallway, and Ratcliff's observations tended to confirm this conclusion.
4. There were dozens of other rituals observed in the hallway, which were the basis of a presentation Ratcliff made at the first International Conference on Children's Spirituality in July 2000. The presentation text is available at http://don.ratcliff.net/childspirit.
5. Charles Cooley, *Human Nature and the Social Order* (New York: Charles Scribner's Sons, 1902) and *Social Organization* (Glencoe, IL: Free Press, 1909, 1956).
6. The name of the caller has been changed.
7. James H. Henslin and Mae Biggs, "Behavior in Public Places: The Sociology of the Vaginal Examination," in *Down to Earth Sociology: Introductory Readings,* 10th ed., ed. J. H. Henslin (New York: Free Press, 1999).
8. See Howard Snyder's description of the "superpastor" role and how this can interfere with how the church should function. Howard Snyder, *The Problem of Wineskins* (Downers Grove, IL: InterVarsity Press, 1975).
9. Some would suggest that some federal and state bureaucracies are examples of this.
10. David Moberg, *The Church as a Social Institution*, 2nd ed. (Grand Rapids, MI: Baker Books, 1984).
11. Max Weber, *The Theory of Social and Economic Organization* (New York: Oxford University Press, 1947).
12. Lawrence Peter and R. Hull, *The Peter Principle* (New York: Morrow Press, 1969).
13. George Ritzer, *The McDonaldization of Society*, 2nd ed. (Thousand Oaks, CA: Pine Forge Press, 2000).
14. David McKenna, *Megatruth: The Church in the Age of Information* (San Bernardino, CA: Here's Life Pub., 1986).

CHAPTER FIVE

Socialization

chapter outline

I. Being and becoming human
   A. "Social" vs. "cultural" in becoming human
   B. Situational isolation
   C. Deviation and social survival

II. Formation of the self: the process of socialization
   A. Cooley and the looking-glass self
   B. Mead and the development of self
      1. Significant others
      2. Generalized others
      3. Play and games
      4. Emergence of self
   C. Goffman and the presentation of self
   D. Other non-interactionist views of self-development
      1. Freud
      2. Erikson
      3. Piaget
      4. Kohlberg

III. Socialization across cultures and the life course
   A. Agents of socialization
      1. Family
      2. School
      3. Peer group
      4. Mass media
      5. Religion and the church
   B. Anticipatory socialization and resocialization

biblical reflection

"Whatever you do, do everything for the glory of God. Give no offense to Jews or to Greeks or to the church of God, just as I try to please everyone in everything I do, not seeking my own advantage, but that of many, so that they may be saved. Be imitators of me, as I am of Christ."

—1 Corinthians 10:31–11:1

This chapter will explore ways in which our self-concept is shaped by our imitation of others. It is certainly important that we anticipate how others will respond so that we do not unwittingly offend them. Our social relationships change us and we, in turn, change other people. Our most important relationship should be our relationship with Christ. By imitating Christ, we become more like God. We begin to think and act as Christ would act. We *become* Christian (are born again). Then we, in turn, change other people for Christ just by the power of Christ's presence in us.

Suppose your professor asked you to do an inventory of your personality traits—where would you begin? Perhaps this inventory would take you back to your birth into a particular family or your entry into the home of adoptive parents. You would probably include what you learned in your neighborhood and from the early childhood playmates that lived there. There would have been "accidents" or unplanned events that helped to redirect your beliefs and behavior. You might look at the people with whom you interacted at school and at church, as well as those in your family. Such an exercise would take some time and might be difficult, but it would make you keenly aware of the process of socialization in your life.

God places us as helpless infants into a society that intends for us to become "fully human." Interacting with other humans in our mini-society, we learn about this process of becoming human beings. We acquire a combination of conforming and unique (perhaps even deviant!) personality traits. We can thank both our social nature and our lifelong dependency on society for this process. God has created us as social beings with the ability to acquire our personality traits from our innate nature and our environment.

BEING AND BECOMING HUMAN

Socialization is the process through which an individual is shaped by the values, customs, and expectations of his or her society. We tend to take this molding process for granted. Its assumption is that to be human is to be social. Beginning in our early months of life, we learn to become unique individuals who seek out interaction with other human beings. It is this process that contributes to our self-awareness and sense of identity.

From conception on, the human depends on social relationships as much as on physical nature. The embryo would promptly die without the umbilical relationship with the mother. If thrust into the outside world, where would an infant be without parental nurture or guidance and protection? None of us would survive physically even through early childhood without depending on other humans. No other creature seems more in need of its own kind for physical survival than the human being.

"SOCIAL" VS. "CULTURAL" IN BECOMING HUMAN

Being social is not enough to guarantee that you will be socialized. An instinctive social relationship occurs among other creatures such as bees, fish, and tigers; however, neither human relationships nor our survival as humans is as prescribed or programmed as is the behavior of lower animals and insects. We are social by nature, learning appropriate ways of behavior by the interaction and relationships we have with the cultural patterns of the group we join by birth or adoption. So we become cultural creatures and we pass on our acquired patterns of believing and behaving to subsequent generations. Therefore, to be socialized is to progress through the process whereby as helpless infants we gradually become self-aware, knowledgeable persons, skilled in the ways of the culture into which we are born.

But what happens to the human who grows up in near-isolation, in almost complete alienation from other persons? And what occurs if he or she resists, rebels, or reacts creatively to the influence of society? Obviously, no humane person could bring up a child away from social influence. However, there are a number of much-discussed cases of children who have spent their early years away from normal human contact. Sociologists ask: If that child should survive physically, will he or she become entirely feral (more beast-animal than human-animal) or will the child inevitably act human? Throughout history, travelers, missionaries, and explorers have reported cases of feral children but without complete validation or documentation. However, several similar cases have been reported and validated in twentieth-century America.

Kingsley Davis reported two of the earliest, best-documented cases of near-feral children in detail.[1] Isabelle and Anna were both about six years old when they were discovered just months apart in different states. Each was born to an unwed mother, hidden from the public, and had received barely minimal maternal care. Both were indifferent to human stimuli and appeared almost deaf. They were undernourished, feeble, with severe physical defects.

Of course, we have to be cautious about interpreting cases of this sort. In each of these examples it is possible that a mental abnormality remained undiagnosed. Alternatively, the experiences to which the children were subjected may have inflicted psychological damage that prevented them from gaining the skills most children acquire at a much earlier age. Yet there is sufficient similarity between these case histories, and others that have been recorded, to suggest how limited our faculties would be in the absence of an extended period of early socialization.

SITUATIONAL ISOLATION

During an individual's normal development process, isolation and deprivation may result from external or social conditions. Kidnap victims, hostages, or prisoners of war frequently report being dehumanized and brutalized by insufficient diets, as well as being housed in lonely, intolerable habitats. The survivors often detail their methods of survival, those means of maintaining their stamina, self-worth, and humanness. In further explaining their adjustment phase upon returning to their former homes and lifestyles, many survivors recount how this causes a form of "culture shock" that leaves them confused and feeling left behind.

These situational isolations often produce a feeling of being tossed around, much like being lost at sea without a compass or moorings. This feeling, referred to as *anomie*, is the lack of enduring relationships that provide guidelines for behavior. Many instances in our historical past involve this concept. Immigrants—whether it is the native Appalachian who moves to the urban north or the Asian who arrives from overseas—have experienced the loss of their close-knit families and communities. Finding that their former rules of behavior no longer apply to their new lives, they experience feelings of disorientation and disconnection. In a sense, we can note a form of positive anomie when an individual becomes a new Christian: the former lifestyle and thinking is changed by God's grace and the individual has to learn new ways of behavior.

Possibly on some large metropolitan campus, Jane Doe arrives from a distant hamlet. Scholarship in hand, she does not know anyone. Shunned by sororities, in awe of aloof and brilliant professors, overwhelmed by mod-styles, cafeteria menus, and campus jargon, she is more alone than she ever expected to be. Any wonder she falters and fails, even in areas of her greatest potential? Embarrassed, defeated, not belonging, she has no help in charting her future.

What happens in such cases? A person may adapt, overachieve, run away, become defiant, or even become depressed and ill. Perhaps you know of such a person, someone who created fantasies or became entangled with the "wrong crowd" or was exploited by some stranger. From a Christian perspective, it is important that we as Christians become aware of these types of anomie in individuals' lives and provide a sense of boundaries and guidelines through God's grace.

DEVIATION AND SOCIAL SURVIVAL

Is it possible for individuals to respond differently to their human environments and still "survive"? The answer lies somewhere between how differently they respond, how much, and why. Most societies distinguish between "different" and "deviant" and how they praise, tolerate, or give special attention to these differences. Certain behaviors and traits may cause a person to be shunned, punished, banished, or even killed.

Many families have experienced polar reactions, as family members react in opposite ways to a strong parental stimulus. For example, two children grow up in a family in which a parent is alcoholic, unusually cruel, unemployed, and abusive. One child reacts with positive identification—drinking and using drugs at an early age, dropping out of school, applying bully tactics. The other child, repulsed by the parental role model, becomes a teetotaler, has high ambitions, and remains highly moral. Admittedly, such polar reactions are more apt to appear under such extreme and ongoing conditions as miserly attitudes, harsh abuse, or overly rigid piety.

FORMATION OF THE SELF: THE PROCESS OF SOCIALIZATION (INTERACTIONIST PERSPECTIVE)

The *symbolic-interaction perspective* looks at self-concept as the major component of personality. It is through language, the symbol system of culture, and in the intimacy of face-to-face interaction that messages about the self are conveyed. How the individual interprets and evaluates this information is central to the social construction of identity. Through our interactions with others, we develop thoughts and attitudes about others and ourselves. This leads to our *self-concept*, an organization of perceptions about who and what kind of person one is. Humans are not born with such knowledge. It is gradually learned and developed through precisely the same socialization experiences by which the culture is internalized.

Only gradually does the infant come to distinguish itself from its nurturer. Of course, it is impossible to question a newborn (or even a young child) about his or her feelings and perceptions. Social scientists can only imagine how it must feel to be an infant. The newborn appears totally absorbed in the nurturer-infant system. But at some point the infant begins to perceive itself as separate from the caregiver. It is at this point that the formation of self begins.

As people talk to you, hold you, and talk to others about you, you learn who you are and become an active agent in creating your self. Our interactions also lead us to act in certain regular ways: we call this *role-playing*. A person may have as many social selves and play as many **roles** as other people—who recognize him or her and carry an image of that person in their minds—will accommodate. Two theorists are relevant here: Charles H. Cooley and George Herbert Mead.

Nonverbal symbols are very important in communication about self.

CHARLES H. COOLEY AND THE LOOKING-GLASS SELF

Charles Cooley (1864-1929) expanded the concept of the social self when he proposed that the **self** is composed of a basic self-feeling that is then shaped and given specific content through interactions with important others, especially within primary groups.

Cooley's concept of the **looking-glass self** demonstrates the development of the self as a reflection of the reaction of others. Just as a mirror reflects a reverse image, one's perception of oneself is never direct but is a reflection.[2] When a person becomes a new creature in Christ, that individual's self becomes a reflection of Christ.

Cooley's theory states that our ideas of self come from imagining: (1) how we appear to other people; (2) how we think they judge our appearance; and (3) how we feel about all this. This process is always developing as we interact with others, whose opinions of us are ever shifting. For example, a child who hears only positive feedback may be confused later when a teacher's reactions indicate a less than satisfactory performance.

Imagine a young woman going out on a first date with a young man. Before the date, they will each spend a lot of time in the "looking glass" trying to see themselves as the other will see them. She may change her sweater because she thinks he may think she is "too easy." He may try out his smile, practice some conversation, and imagine how she will respond. She is trying to be the kind of woman she thinks the kind of man he is will like. He is trying to be the kind of man he thinks the kind of woman she is will like. But this crazy behavior is not just restricted to young lovers. Aren't you trying to "read" your instructor so that you will do the kind of work you think the kind of instructor he or she is will like? When you write a paper for sociology class, you see your behavior through the looking glass of your instructor and try to produce the kind of paper you think will get a good grade. Your instructor sees herself or himself through the looking glass of your behavior and adjusts teaching behaviors to conform to the kind of instructor that will have an impact on you. If the students' eyes reflect boredom, a good instructor will change behavior. If the students' papers indicate they do not understand the material, a good instructor will adjust behavior. You apply this looking-glass technique all day long with your family, your boss, and your friends.

This theory does not imply that an individual is a passive receptor of impressions. Instead, it sees an individual as an active participant in the manipulation of others' reactions, selecting which cues to follow and judging the relative importance of role partners. In general, we tend to accept impressions that reinforce a basic identity and to resist those that do not.

GEORGE HERBERT MEAD AND THE DEVELOPMENT OF SELF

The premise of **George Mead's** (1863-1931) theory was the human ability to use symbols to communicate. He theorized that individuals used symbols, created rules, and adjusted behavior to the expectations of others. A person can do all these things by developing a "self" capable of reflecting on its own behavior while interacting with others. Society is the reflection of all of these activities, despite constant change and redefinition of rules and behaviors. Society is also in our minds through internalized rules, roles, and relationships. Mead's idea is that the self—developing through mind, self, and society—provides a complex link through these three levels of reality.[3]

Taking the role of the **other** is a means of learning who we are by imagining how we appear to other people. In this way the reflexive mind not only sees itself as an object but also can see into the minds of others. Central to the development of self-concept is leaping imaginatively into the mind of another and taking that person's attitude toward oneself.

This process takes place initially during our first socialization experience within a primary group, where we learn the shared meanings of our culture. We are able to guess what others are thinking precisely because we have a common language and shared experiences. The child learns through the process of first being told how to behave, then by applying this information in trial and error, and finally by receiving feedback. The learning happens through language, both verbal and nonverbal. For Mead, the word *gesture* became the means or symbol shared by group members, becoming part of the role performance necessary to internalize the culture. The social structure allows us to take on the role of others, which then leads us to take on society as a part of our "self." Consequently, the self becomes social.

SIGNIFICANT OTHERS

Of particular influence in the formation of self is the interaction of those individuals whose affection and approval are especially desired. Initially parents fulfill this role, followed by peers, role models, and lovers. We refer to these as **significant others**.

GENERALIZED OTHERS

Through **generalized others** we learn the universal norms or expectations of roles within society. These expectations are embedded in role systems, in which a person's status is both different from that of role partners and dependent on them. Anyone in the role must reflect these societal standards of acceptable behavior.

PLAY AND GAMES

According to Mead, it is through *play and games* that the child develops the ability to internalize these expectations. Self and self-consciousness develop when the child experiences situations in which he or she learns both the content of culture and how to understand the attitudes of others.

The first stage in the development of self involves playacting. The very young child takes on the role of parent, doctor, pastor, or some other role model through toys, voice inflections, and attitudes. In the voice of the caregiver, the child carries on an internal conversation between self and other. This child's play is very serious business and becomes the learning ground for language and relationships.

Typically when children enter school and the society of age peers, they are exposed to situations that require internalizing entire role systems. As Mead notes, one must not only take the role of the other, as in play, but must assume the various roles of all participants in the game. This is the skill we carry into adulthood and even to old age.

This system of role-playing is often how we develop as Christians. After conversion and the initial commitment to Christ, individuals must then learn and develop their walk with Christ. This comes by reading the Bible, praying, attending church, and learning the ways of faith and church culture.

EMERGENCE OF SELF

Learning to take the role of the other is only one part in the process of developing self. The self is dynamic, ever capable of change. Mead distinguished two aspects of the self: the "I" and the "me." The **"I"** is the spontaneous and creative element, while the **"me"** is the socialized self, composed of the internalized attitudes of others. The "I" reflects and responds to the "me." This interconnectedness and interaction produces an organization of perceptions that forms the self-concept and guides behavior.

In Christianity the sin nature battle illustrates this conversation between the "I" and "me." Prior to a Christian commitment, the "I" is often the primary motivation for our behavior. However, after conversion the "me" emerges with the desire to follow Christ's teachings.

Mead saw no necessary conflict between "I" and "me," as both are needed to form the social self. Still, there is always the possibility of tension between meaning derived from experience and meaning taken from culture at a particular historical moment. In this view, the relationship between self and society is reciprocal rather than opposing. Society and the self are both simultaneously possible because humans can make the imaginative leap into the mind of others and share their world of meaning—the ultimate triumph of our unique capacity for reflexive thought.

ERVING GOFFMAN AND THE PRESENTATION OF SELF

To Erving Goffman (1922-83), the development of self involves the process of self-presentation, the impression we present to others.[4] In this theory the self always risks being rejected and every encounter becomes one that we "manage," so that we present ourselves as we want others to perceive us. Goffman theorized that we carefully construct a presenting self as the "real me" in order to influence the reactions of role partners and to control the situation.

According to this view, a self exists for every situation. A virtual self (or possible self) awaits us in every role—what society expects of a person in that role. Combined with our innate qualities and individual personalities, each role offers an opportunity to become a particular type of person.

Goffman used the term *role distance* to describe the space that a person can place between the self and the self-in-the-role. People use several distancing techniques to signal others that the *virtual* self implied in the current role is not the *real* self apart from the role. A college student working a temporary job—as a busboy, waitress, cashier, or stock clerk—may bring a college textbook along to the job, a way of signaling to others his or her true aspirations for a career. Role distance protects the self and offers some freedom for the expression of personal style. However, in many situations we have little choice but to become the self-in-the-role.

OTHER NON-INTERACTIONIST VIEWS OF SELF-DEVELOPMENT: NON-INTERACTIONIST VIEWS OF SELF

SIGMUND FREUD

Sigmund Freud (1856-1939), an Austrian physician and the founder of psychoanalysis, contributed to sociology in the area of unconscious motivations. His theories looked at the conflict between the individual and society, the construction of self as a social/psychological process, the role of ego defenses, and the general concept of the unconscious.[5]

Freud postulated that social life is possible only when people can control their behavior. Culture, remember, consists of norms that govern conduct, but humans are also biological organisms with drives and desires. Therefore, a dynamic tension exists between the individual and the society. The individual strives to satisfy basic urges, but cannot survive without the support of others. Social order depends on members of a society being able to forego instant gratification. In other words, as human beings, we are born a bundle of wishes, but if each of us sought to satisfy every need immediately, we could not form the kind of stable groups required for security and well-being. According to Freud, society is based on the control of impulse. Socialization is the process of renouncing (giving up) instant pleasure.

The Freudian psyche involves three aspects: (1) the **id**, consisting of impulsive desires; (2) the **superego**, often called the conscience, consisting of internalized norms; and (3) the **ego** that links the self to the real world, mediating the drives of the id and the control of the superego.

Ego defenses are techniques for dealing with impulses that are unacceptable to the self and that could endanger social solidarity. Defenses include denial, repression, blame, displacement of anger onto socially acceptable objects, and rationalization (finding acceptable reasons for thinking or doing the unacceptable). Because we must depend on one another, loss of self-control would have collective as well as personal consequences. And because the Freudian self is always somewhat discontent—unable completely to satisfy the body's desires—the ego must constantly be protected from our worst impulses and from challenges to one's image of being a good person.

ERIK ERIKSON

The most influential theories of psychosocial and *ego development* are that of Erik Erikson (1902-94). Erikson extended the stages of personality growth and change to cover the entire life course. The life course is composed of a series of challenges or life "crises" that require reorganization of the ego. Erikson suggested the possibility of continual personal change and growth throughout the life cycle. He proposed eight stages in the life cycle, each of which involves a person's ability to adapt to life changes:[6]

> Stage 1. Basic trust vs. mistrust: the infant's experiences with nurturers contribute to the infant's subsequent sense of trust.
>
> Stage 2. Autonomy vs. doubt and shame: during the first three years of life, children learn and practice new kinds of skills that contribute to their level of autonomy.
>
> Stage 3. Initiative vs. guilt: the level of success that four to five year olds experience in exploring the environment and in dealing with peers can lead to a sense of initiative or feelings of guilt resulting from failure.

Stage 4. Industriousness vs. inferiority: school helps children focus on developing self-confidence through educational and peer experiences.

Stage 5. Identity vs. confusion: adolescence is a time when one's sense of self is connected to identity and "who they are." Failure to achieve identity results in role confusion.

Stage 6. Intimacy vs. isolation: the great challenge of adulthood is to establish enduring love relationships; the outcome is intimacy or isolation and loneliness.

Stage 7. Generativity vs. self-absorption: the goal of mature adulthood is to contribute to family, work, and community in order to insure the continuation of society. In contrast, self-absorption or stagnation does not contribute to the well-being of others.

Stage 8. Integrity vs. despair: success in life is not the absence of life changes or challenges. Integrity is finding continuity and meaning in one's life, while despair is the continuation of self-absorption and stagnation.

These eight stages are best understood as ideal types or descriptions of the very best and the very worst in the life course. Few people go through these stages in precisely the same way or according to the same time frame. Most of us meet life's expected and unexpected challenges with only partial success or failure—some self-confidence, a little guilt, general satisfaction, or continued anxiety.

Although Erikson's model is presented as basically psychological, his transition points coincide with major changes in the person's social environment and the sequence of status changes. Each change provides the opportunity for reorganization of the self because the person now interacts with different role partners who have new expectations in a new situation.

JEAN PIAGET

How people understand and organize their personal experiences and relate them over time to societal and other changes is known as *cognitive development*. Swiss psychologist **Jean Piaget** (1896-1980) studied the play of children for many years, seeing the world from their eyes. He concluded that children of different ages have very different ways of processing information and solving problems. The mental tasks emerge as a result of the mind growing and expanding, as well as from the social experiences the child encounters. As children experience situations or receive information that does not fit comfortably into existing structures of thought, they have the opportunity to rearrange their view of the world and produce a new way of thinking. Cognitive growth is a product of the child's active efforts to cope with new information.[7]

Being a psychologist, Piaget focused the growth of the child—within a web of relationships—on individual experience and growth. A more sociological view is suggested by observations of children's peer groups. It is through their shared activities that children collectively create their peer culture and socialize one another. Socialization does not take place privately within an isolated mind, but as part of a creative group process in which the children together confront and cope with the adult world.

LAWRENCE KOHLBERG

Influenced by Piaget's work on cognitive development, Lawrence Kohlberg (1927-87) spent a considerable number of years researching children and the development of their moral character.[8] Kohlberg suggested that children go through a sequence of six stages in their ability to handle moral problems.

Between the ages of four and ten, the child's sense of good or bad is linked to obedience to those in positions of power, based on fear of punishment. In adolescence, conformity to the rules is accompanied by the belief that the existing social order is right and true and deserves to be defended. But with the appropriate moral education, older children and young adults can reach the two highest stages of reasoning. At these stages, considerations of community welfare, general rights, and universal ethical principles—such as justice, equality, and the dignity of individuals—become the guides of action and self-judgment.

The theories discussed in this section of ego development, psychosocial stages, cognition, and moral reasoning are all concerned with processes going on *within* the individual, even though prompted by events in the social environment.

SOCIALIZATION ACROSS CULTURES AND THE LIFE COURSE

Culture is a selection of traits from the range of human possibilities that influence our thinking and behavior. Some cultures, such as the greater American culture, place high value on individualism. Other cultures, even within the American culture, emphasize the sense of community and obligations to the group. Typically, many cultures define personality traits that are desirable for adult females and males, another set of desirable traits for children, and even a third set of acceptable traits for the elderly.

This variety of personality styles is possible because each culture, through its symbol system, creates a particular way of thinking, reinforces certain emotions, and shapes the self-image of its members. The cultural blueprint also determines socialization practices that produce the desired personality types.

AGENTS OF SOCIALIZATION

The continuing and lifelong socialization process in the United States involves many different social forces that influence our lives and alter our self-image. The family is considered the first, primary, and most important socialization agent. Five other agents of socialization and their importance will also be discussed: the school, the peer group, the mass media, the workplace, and the church or religion.

FAMILY

One of the primary functions of the family is the care and rearing of children. As infants and children, our first experience of socialization within the family contributes to our initial sense of self-image. Most parents seek to help their children become competent adolescents and self-sufficient adults, which means socializing them into the norms and values of both the family and the larger society. In this process, adults themselves experience socialization as they adjust to becoming spouses, parents, and in-laws. This lifelong process of learning begins shortly after birth. By giving newborns the ability to hear, see, smell, taste, and feel heat, cold, and pain, God enables them to orient themselves to the surrounding world. Human interaction provided by the human beings in the newborn's life makes up an important part of the baby's social environment. Through feeding, cleansing, and carrying the baby, the primary caretakers, particularly the parents, meet the baby's needs.

This does not imply that infants are asocial. God created humans as social beings, even if babies are not expected to learn social skills

Family is the most powerful agent of socialization. We are more like our family than we are like anyone else.

right away. An infant enters an organized society, becomes part of a generation, and typically enters into a family. Depending on how they are treated, infants can develop strong social attachments and dependency on others.

As both Charles H. Cooley and George H. Mead have indicated, the development of the self is a critical aspect of the early years of one's life. In the United States, such social development includes exposure to cultural assumptions regarding gender and race. African American parents, for example, have learned that children as young as two years of age can absorb negative messages about Blacks in children's books, toys, and television shows—all of which are designed primarily for White consumers.

Children also are influenced by cultural messages regarding gender. The term *gender roles* refers to expectations regarding the proper behavior, attitudes, and activities of males and females. For example, "toughness" traditionally has been seen as masculine—and desirable only in men—while "tenderness" has been viewed as feminine.

Interactionists remind us that socialization concerning not only masculinity and femininity but also marriage and parenthood begins in childhood as a part of family life. Children observe their parents as they express affection, deal with finances, quarrel, complain about in-laws, and so forth. This represents an informal process of anticipatory socialization. The child develops a tentative model of what being married and being a parent are like.

SCHOOL

Like the family, schools play an important role in the socialization of people into the norms and values of a culture. From a conflict perspective, schools provide a latent function of competition through built-in systems of reward and punishment based on grades and evaluations by teachers. Consequently, a child who is working intently to learn a new skill can nevertheless come to feel stupid and unsuccessful. However, the hope is that as the child matures and the self continues to develop, the child will become more capable and realistic about his or her intellectual, physical, and social abilities.

Functionalists point out that, as agents of socialization, schools fulfill the function of teaching students the values and customs of the larger society. Conflict theorists concur with this observation, but add that schools can reinforce the divisive aspects of society, especially those of social class. For example, higher education in the United States is quite costly, despite the existence of financial aid programs. Thus, students from affluent backgrounds have an advantage in gaining access to universities and professional training. At the same time, less affluent young people may never receive the necessary preparation to qualify them for our society's best-paying and most prestigious jobs.

PEER GROUP

As a child grows older, the family becomes somewhat less important in his or her social development. Instead, peer groups increasingly assume the role of George Herbert Mead's significant others. Within the peer group, young people associate with others who are approximately their own age and who often enjoy a similar social status.

Peer groups such as friendship cliques, youth groups, special-interest clubs, and gangs frequently assist adolescents in gaining some degree of independence from parents and other

While family encourages our uniqueness, school emphasizes the importance of being like everyone else.

Sociology: A Christian Approach for Changing the World

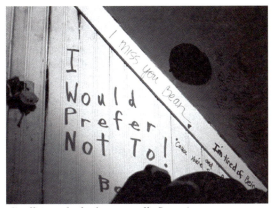
Graffiti on the bathroom stall: Sometimes our agents of socialization make us feel we have no choices.

authority figures. Conforming to a peer's behavior is an example of the socialization process at work. If all of one's friends have successfully battled for the right to stay out until midnight on a Saturday night, it may seem essential to fight for the same privilege. Peer groups also provide for anticipatory socialization into new roles that the young person will later assume. Teenagers imitate their friends in part because the peer group maintains a meaningful system of rewards and punishment. The group may encourage a young person to follow pursuits that society considers admirable, as in a school club engaged in hospital or nursing home volunteer work. On the other hand, the group may encourage someone to violate the culture's norms and values by driving recklessly, shoplifting, engaging in acts of vandalism, and the like.

Gender differences are noteworthy in the social world of adolescents. Males are more likely to spend time in groups of males, while females are more likely to interact with another female. This pattern reflects differences in levels of emotional intimacy: teenage males are less likely to develop strong emotional ties than are females. Instead, males are more inclined to participate in group activities. These patterns are evident among adolescents in many societies besides the United States.

Peer groups serve an important function by assisting the transition to adult responsibilities. At home, parents tend to dominate. At school, the teenager must contend with teachers and administrators. But within the peer group each member can assert himself or herself in a way that may not be possible elsewhere. Nevertheless, almost all adolescents in our culture remain economically dependent on their parents, and most are emotionally dependent as well.

MASS MEDIA

Technology such as radio, motion pictures, recorded music, television, magazines, and the Internet have become important agents of socialization. Television, in particular, is a critical force in the socialization of children in the United States. For some parents the television has become the child's babysitter and favorite playmate. Consequently, children in our society watch an average of three hours of television a day. Apart from sleeping, watching television is the most time-consuming activity in which young people engage.

Television has certain distinctive characteristics when compared to other agents of socialization. It permits imitation and role-playing, but does not encourage more complex forms of learning. Since the expectation is to be entertained, watching television is, above all, a passive experience. Experts generally agree that a great deal of violence is viewed on television. By age sixteen, the average television viewer has witnessed some 200,000 acts of television violence, including 33,000 fictional murders. Indeed, young people around the world are exposed to the violence of television programs produced in the United States.

Like other agents of socialization, television has traditionally portrayed and promoted conventional gender roles. For example, content analysis of television advertising has shown that the best-selling violent and gender-specific children's toys are frequently advertised, whereas the best-selling nonviolent and gender-neutral toys are not.

Lest it be misunderstood, television is not always a negative socializing influence. Creative programming such as *Sesame Street* can assist children in developing basic skills essential for schooling. Television programs as well as commercials can expose young people to lifestyles and cultures of which they are unaware. This is demonstrated through wholesome programs the United States shares with other countries, as well as in the United States itself (e.g., programs in which inner-city children learn about the lives of farm children and vice versa).

While the focus here has been on television, it is important to note similar issues regarding the content of popular music, music videos, motion pictures, and material that can be accessed on the Internet. These forms of entertainment, like television, serve as powerful agents of socialization for many young people in the United States and elsewhere. Controversy continues concerning the content of music, music videos, and films, as certain parents' organizations and religious groups challenge the intrusion of these media into the lives of children and adolescents.

RELIGION AND THE CHURCH

Like the other socialization agents discussed earlier, religion and/or the church profoundly impact not only individuals during their socialization process, but also the norms and culture of the greater society. From the functionalist perspective, religion is an integrative force, providing bonds that often transcend the personal and divisive forces of the society.

Religion, such as Buddhism, Islam, Christianity, or Judaism, offers people meaning and purpose for their lives. It provides certain ultimate values and objectives for people to hold in common. Although subjective and not always fully accepted, these values and objectives help a society to function as an integrated social system. For example, the Christian observance of Communion not only celebrates a historical event in the life of Jesus (the Last Supper), but also represents collective participation in a ceremony with sacred social significance. Similarly, funerals, weddings, bar and bat mitzvahs, and confirmations serve to integrate people into larger communities by providing shared beliefs and values about the ultimate questions of life.

The integrative power of religion can be seen in the role that churches, synagogues, and mosques have traditionally played and continue to play for immigrant groups in the United States. For example, Roman Catholic immigrants may settle near and attend a parish church that offers services in their native language, such as Polish or Spanish. Similarly, Korean immigrants may join a Presbyterian church with a large Korean-American membership and with religious practices similar to the Korean churches they left behind. Like other religious organizations, these Roman Catholic and Presbyterian churches will help integrate immigrants into their new homeland.

Most of us find it difficult to accept the stressful events of life—the death of a loved one, serious injury, bankruptcy, divorce, and so forth. This is especially true when something "senseless" happens. How can family and friends come to terms with the death of a talented college student, not even twenty years old, from a terminal disease? Through its emphasis on God's grace, religion within the Christian faith allows us to "do something" about the calamities we face. In some other faiths, one can offer sacrifices or pray to a nonexistent deity in the belief that such acts will change one's earthly condition. An even more impersonal level of religion encourages us to view our personal misfortunes as relatively unimportant in the broader perspective of human history.

The church can be a very powerful agent of socialization.

This perspective may be much more comforting than the terrifying feeling that any of us can die senselessly at any moment.

ANTICIPATORY SOCIALIZATION AND RESOCIALIZATION

The development of a social self is literally a lifelong transformation that begins in the crib and continues as one prepares for death. Two types of socialization occur at many points throughout the life cycle: anticipatory socialization and resocialization.

Preparation for many aspects of adult life begins with anticipatory socialization during childhood and adolescence, and continues throughout our lives as we prepare for new responsibilities. *Anticipatory socialization* refers to the processes of socialization in which a person "rehearses" for future positions, occupations, and social relationships. A culture can function more efficiently and smoothly if members become acquainted with the norms, values, and behavior associated with a social position before actually assuming that status.

Anticipatory socialization is evident when high school students participate in college-prep classes or technologically focused classes that prepare them for their intended area of study at the post-high-school level.

At times when we assume new social and occupational positions, we find it necessary to unlearn our previous orientation. *Resocialization* refers to the process of discarding former behavior patterns and accepting new ones as part of transition in one's life. Often resocialization occurs when there is an explicit effort to transform an individual, such as in reform schools, therapy groups, prisons, religious conversion settings, and political indoctrination camps. Much more than socialization in general or even anticipatory socialization, the process of resocialization typically involves considerable stress for the individual.

overview

- Socialization is the process whereby people learn the attitudes, values, and actions appropriate to individuals as members of a particular culture. This chapter examines the role of socialization in human development, the way in which people develop perceptions, feelings, and beliefs about themselves, and the lifelong nature of the socialization process.

- God creates human beings as helpless infants who need human intervention in order to survive. It is through the process of social interaction that we become more fully human.

- Agents of socialization provide information, feedback, and social supports for role learning. The most important socializing agents in modern society are parents, peers, teachers, the mass media, and religion.

- The self is also a social product, shaped through the same socialization experiences by which the culture is internalized.

- Charles H. Cooley's "looking-glass self" captures the idea of seeing self through the reflected reactions of role partners.

- For George Herbert Mead, the social self is based on the unique human capacity for taking on the role of the other through play and games. This perspective is elaborated in Erving Goffman's work on self-presentation and impression management.

- Erik Erikson expanded the concept of identity development to encompass the entire life course, with emphasis on the set of self-perceptions called the ego. Major role transitions offer an opportunity to reorganize the self.

- Cognitive development refers to changes in the way people process information over time. Jean Piaget proposed a developmental theory of cognitive growth from his observations of children's changing cognitive styles. Lawrence Kohlberg extended Piaget's analysis to the study of moral development; that is, stages in the capacity for making judgments of right and wrong.

- Socialization is a lifelong process, as long as there are new roles to learn and old ones to relinquish. Some traits show relative stability across the life course, but most are flexible.

key concepts

Cooley, Charles H.
Social psychologist at University of Michigan; author of "looking-glass self" concept.

ego
The person we see ourselves as being; it attempts to reconcile the pressures between the raw drives of the id and the conforming demands of the superego.

Freud, Sigmund
Credited with the development of psychoanalysis.

generalized others
Third developmental stage proposed by Mead in which a child moves from taking the role of "significant others" to a view of society's role in general; internalizing broad social expectations.

"I"
George H. Mead's concept of an individual's view of her/himself as a total person; only one "I".

id
The total "raw" traits of a human; instinctual and compelling desires (Freud).

looking-glass self
Concept used by Charles Cooley to describe the process by which we estimate others' reactions to our behavior and feel corresponding feeling-states such as pride, embarrassment, or inadequacy in ourselves.

"me"
A person's idea of her/himself in a particular role; a "me" for each role he or she plays.

George Herbert Mead
Social psychologist at the University of Chicago who developed theories of mind, self, and society; stressed the impact of "generalized other" on the development of self.

other
Counterpart of "self" in a social situation; our view of the person in a dyadic relationship.

Piaget, Jean
Swiss biologist and psychologist who stated that humans pass through inevitable growth stages in reasoning and are active participants in their social development.

role
Expected behavior of persons in a particular position; may be ascribed or achieved.

self
The composite of one's perception, attitudes, and beliefs about himself or herself.

significant others
Persons who are most influential in helping to determine the behavior of the individual.

superego
Freud's concept that refers to that part of the self which has internalized social norms and attitudes; corresponds to Mead's concept of "me" and is popularly known as one's conscience.

endnotes

1. Both Anna and Isabelle were reported by Kingsley Davis in "Extreme Isolation of a Child," *The American Journal of Sociology* 45 (January 1940): 554-65; and in "Final Note on a Case of Extreme Isolation," *American Journal of Sociology* 52 (March 1947): 432-37.
2. Charles H. Cooley, *Human Nature and the Social Order* (New York: Charles Scribner's Sons, 1902).
3. George H. Mead, *Mind, Self and Society* (Chicago: University of Chicago Press, 1934).
4. Erving Goffman, *The Presentation of Self in Everyday Life* (Garden City, NY: Doubleday & Co., 1959).
5. See Sigmund Freud, *New Introductory Lectures on Psychoanalysis* (New York: W. W. Norton & Co., 1933).
6. See Erik Erikson, *Childhood and Society* (New York: W. W. Norton & Co., 1963; orig. 1950).
7. See Jean Piaget, *The Moral Judgment of the Child*, trans. Marjorie Gabain (New York: Harcourt, Brace & World, 1932) and *The Origins of Intelligence in Children*, trans. Margaret Cook (New York: W. W. Norton & Co., 1952).
8. Lawrence Kohlberg, *The Psychology of Moral Development: The Nature and Validity of Moral Stages* (New York: Harper & Row, Publishers, 1981).

CHAPTER SIX

Deviance, Crime, and Social Control

chapter outline

I. What is deviance?

II. Structural-functional perspective

III. Conflict perspective

IV. Theories of deviance
   A. Subcultural theories
   B. Strain theories
   C. Social control theories
   D. Labeling theory

V. Crime as a special case of deviance
   A. Statistics: the extent of crime
   B. Who commits crime?
   C. Who are the victims?
   D. Social control of crime

VI. Elite deviance

VII. Is all deviance bad?

VIII. How Christians can change the world

biblical reflection

"For rulers are not a terror to good conduct, but to bad. Do you wish to have no fear of the authority? Then do what is good, and you will receive its approval . . ."

—Romans 13:3

What is normative in one culture may be deviant in another culture. The Tanzanian warrior and American female impersonator: two men, two cultures.

WHAT IS DEVIANCE?

Strictly speaking, any failure to abide by norms is deviance. However, when sociologists discuss **deviant behavior**, they focus on behavior that violates a norm to such an extent that people will not tolerate it, usually because it threatens important values or has the potential for disrupting social order.

Practically everyone violates a norm now and then: driving over the speed limit, arriving a few minutes late to class or work, etc. Not all norms have the same degree of significance. Norms range from mundane expectations ("Wear socks with your shoes" or "Don't talk with food in your mouth") to more serious matters of role responsibilities (e.g., the husband and wife will carry out the traditional roles in the family), to such issues as respect for human life ("Thou shalt not kill"). Most of the time, we will not be too concerned with an occasional norm violation. It is when someone *habitually violates a norm or violates a norm we consider serious* (like murder) that we will determine that person to be *deviant*. A number of factors determine when a given behavior is viewed as deviance:

1. The nature of the norm that is violated.

2. The seriousness (or extent) of the violation.

3. Who does the defining.

STRUCTURAL-FUNCTIONAL PERSPECTIVE

Norms are important to the functioning of the social order. Because of norms, individuals understand the parameters under which they and the other members of the group operate. Consequently, they know what is expected of themselves as well as what can be expected of others. This makes communal life possible. Society considers certain norms (called *mores*) to be essential to its survival, and efforts will be made to bring the norm-violator's behavior back into conformity with the norm. This is what sociologists mean when they speak about social control.[1]

Every society seeks to ensure conformity to its norms, either formally or informally. The manner by which it does so is called **social control**. As mentioned earlier, those who do not conform are called deviants. One way society motivates people to conform is by the use of sanctions.

Every society has some means of encouraging conformity and discouraging deviance. These means are called **sanctions** and can be positive or negative. *Positive sanctions* are responses to behavior which increase (not ensure) the likelihood of that behavior occurring again. *Negative sanctions* reduce the likelihood of a reoccurrence of norm-violating behavior. It is clear from Scripture that negative sanctions, when used effectively, can deter deviance. After giving the Law and designating the types of sanctions that should be used for various infractions, God repeatedly notes that the purpose of the sanction is to "purge the evil from your midst" (Deut. 17:7b). As a result of faithfully administering the sanction, "the rest shall hear and be afraid, and a crime such as this shall never again be committed among you" (19:20).

Persons charged with the official responsibility of curbing deviance are *formal social control agents*, such as the police, the courts, and the prisons. Each of these is a component of the government, which God has established to sanction wrongdoers (Rom. 13:3-5). All others—family, peers, and acquaintances—are *informal social control agents*. Both formal and informal agents of social control have positive and negative sanctions at their disposal. Awards, applause, recognition of valued behavior, and promotions are positive sanctions. Ridicule, demotions, and imprisonment are negative sanctions.[2]

Undoubtedly, you have received many positive sanctions; you have even administered them. When you excelled in sports or

Sometimes deviance is functional, as in this Stamp Act Rebellion preceding the Revolutionary War.

Chapter Six: Deviance, Crime, and Social Control

academic studies, you received rewards such as National Honor Society certificates, pins, or varsity letters. Following an outstanding performance, you and other members of the audience applaud. From time to time, we hear reports of individuals who have "risen through the ranks" to become corporate executives. Such people have received promotions (positive sanctions) for their excellent job performance. Informal social control agents typically use applause and ridicule; formal agents tend to use awards, promotions, demotions, and imprisonment. In applying sanctions to encourage conformity, informal agents do so in more personal ways, whereas formal agents employ more standard methods.[3]

CONFLICT PERSPECTIVE

The conflict perspective is concerned with the power struggle to determine the norms of the society. Who defines what is deviant? Who determines which forms of deviance are serious enough to be called "crime"? It all depends on who has power and influence in the society.

Two important variables are linked to the issue of who is doing the defining: the *definer's view of reality* and the *amount of power the definer possesses*. People's views of reality impact their definitions of deviance. These views of reality can be positivist or subjectivist.

Positivists believe in objective reality and argue that certain behaviors are inherently bad or deviant. Such behaviors would be deviant for all time and all places. Christians, who believe in the objective truth of God's Word, argue that certain behaviors (e.g., stealing, murder, dishonesty) are inherently bad. Whether viewed from the perspective of the Ten Commandments (Ex. 20:13-17; Deut. 5:17-21), the things that God hates (Prov. 6:16; Mal. 2:16), or New Testament teachings (Eph. 4:17–5:7; Gal. 5:19-21), certain behaviors are inherently wrong.

Subjectivists counter that deviance is simply a subjective label that society has created for some behavior; thus, no behavior is bad in and of itself. This is why our society continues to define as deviant some of the behaviors that Scripture has defined as inherently bad (e.g., crime, violence, theft), but tolerates others (e.g., sexual immorality, homosexuality, gossip). Regardless of whether one is a positivist or a subjectivist, without power one's views are irrelevant to society.

Power, the ability to get others to do what you want them to do, is a crucial variable. People have power because of their political position or influence, social status or wealth. Those defining a behavior as deviant must be influential enough to get others to accept that definition. Davis and Stasz argue that the legal-

What prompts a person to commit a deviant act?

Sociology: A Christian Approach for Changing the World

ization of abortion was partly a function of a "shift in power groups"; a coalition of feminists, leftist activists, and members of the population growth movement were able to garner enough power to thwart the efforts of so-called "right-wing traditionalist segments."[4] Prior to these groups gaining that power, abortion was defined by our society as deviant.

Definitions of deviance may change from one group to another and from one point in time to another. As societal values change, normative expectations change. As normative expectations change, definitions of deviance change. Such changes are evident in our society. The United States' shift from its Judeo-Christian heritage has been accompanied by a corresponding shift in its definitions of deviance.[5] For example, we are seeing this shift reflected in how homosexuality is viewed by many in contemporary American society. It has undergone a number of social redefinitions: from sin to deviance to sickness to variant sexuality. Likewise, the traditional family (i.e., two-parent family with father as breadwinner and mother as homemaker) is often viewed as simply one among a number of alternative family forms (e.g., single parents by choice, divorced and blended families, and domestic partnerships) which in the past were considered deviant. Behavior that is deviant today may not be so defined in the future. However, regardless of modified definitions, God the Creator indicates no intention of changing His established standard of moral and ethical values.

THEORIES OF DEVIANCE

SUBCULTURAL THEORIES

Walter Miller and Edwin Sutherland's subcultural theories of deviance suggest that the values, norms, or conditions of given subcultures encourage deviant behavior. Miller presented deviance as a function of lower-class membership. He argued that lower-class families are different from middle-class families in many ways: they tend to have female-headed households and embrace lower-class **focal concerns**.[6] These lower-class focal concerns or values mitigate against conformity to middle-class norms. Miller believes that the focal concerns of the lower-class include:

1. *Trouble:* getting into trouble (e.g., fights or illicit drug use).

2. *Toughness:* an emphasis on not appearing soft but, instead, coming across as strong, unemotional, and tough.

3. *Fate:* the belief that luck controls both the good and bad aspects of one's life. A sense of control or mastery does not exist among the lower class.

4. *Autonomy:* the assertion of one's independence from the dictates of others; a rejection of authority.

5. *Smartness:* the ability to outsmart others.

6. *Excitement:* the value placed upon pleasure; the search for thrills in an attempt to escape the problems of lower-class life.

According to Miller, adherence to these values leads to deviance from society's norms.

Edwin Sutherland suggested that deviant behavior, like any other behavior, is learned. He added that deviant behavior is learned through interactions with primary groups. Deviant behavior results when an individual learns an excess of definitions favorable to norm violation. Definitions include values supportive of deviance and techniques and rationalizations for engaging in deviance. Whether one learns an excess of definitions favorable or unfavorable to norm violation depends upon the different primary groups with which one associates and the

> ### EXCERPT 6:1
>
> #### 1. TECHNIQUES OF NEUTRALIZATION & THE BELIEVER
>
> Sykes and Matza suggest that deviants have internalized the norms of society. Therefore, they must neutralize the constraining power of those norms in order to commit deviance. They suggest five techniques used to rationalize or justify deviant behavior. Let's apply these to the believer who chooses to engage in sin (and needs to rationalize it) or is unrepentant after sin (and must justify it).
>
> 1. **Billiard Ball** — attributes deviance to forces beyond one's control: e.g., "The devil made me do it" or "If you'd grown up in my home, you'd understand."
>
> 2. **Condemning the Condemners** — deflects attention away from one's deviance and onto social control agent; e.g., "Take the beam out of your eye before you try to take the speck out of mine" and "Judge not lest ye be judged."
>
> 3. **(S)he had it coming** — suggests that the deviance is in response to some wrong committed by the victim; e.g., "If she hadn't _____, then I would not have _____."
>
> 4. **Denial of the Victim** — excuses behavior because no one else was hurt; e.g., "I'm not hurting anyone but myself."
>
> 5. **Appeal to Higher Loyalty** — acknowledges behavior but resorts to a higher principle that supersedes the norm violated; e.g., "I have only God to answer to, not man."
>
> Since the Garden of Eden, people have rationalized their deviant behavior (Gen. 3:12,13). Instead of accepting personal responsibility for our sin (deviance from God's normative expectations), we often blame our circumstances or others. How do **you** respond when the Holy Spirit convicts you (John 16:8) or another person holds you accountable for your behavior (Matt. 18:15; Gal. 6:1)?

nature of those associations; hence, the concept of **differential association**.[7]

In *Techniques of Neutralization*, Matza and Sykes suggest that deviants neutralize the norms they have internalized to rationalize or justify deviant behavior.[8] (See Excerpt 6:1.)

Robert Burgess, Ronald Akers and Daniel Glaser attempted to strengthen Sutherland's theory by their concepts of differential reinforcement, differential anticipation, and differential identification. Burgess and Akers suggest that learning does not occur only in primary groups; it can be nonsocial as well (e.g., by modeling). Furthermore, reinforcement (rewards and the avoidance of aversive conditions) is a crucial factor: if learned behavior is reinforced, it will continue to occur. Thus, if deviance is rewarded or conformity punished, deviance is most likely to occur.[9]

Daniel Glaser viewed deviance as a function of both differential anticipation and differential identification.[10] A key question is, "With whom does a given individual identify?" If people identify with persons who view deviance as acceptable, then they will more than likely engage in deviance. Glaser also thinks that the identification can be with a real or imagined person. In addition to one's identification with others, the anticipated consequences of one's behavior will either reinforce or discourage deviance. It is not simply a matter of the ratio between definitions favorable to deviance and definitions unfavorable to deviance; instead, it is the ratio between favorable consequences and unfavorable consequences. If people *anticipate* fewer negative consequences than positive ones, then deviance will result.

STRAIN THEORIES

The basic assumption of **strain theories** is that certain people are frustrated in their efforts to achieve societal goals. The frustration may be due to the inaccessibility of normative means of achieving success, the inability to compete with others in society, or exploitation and discrimination. Robert Merton's anomie theory explains deviance as an adaptation to the absence of legitimate means to achieve success. He argued that both lower- and middle-class persons are exposed to the same success goals (wealth and the material symbols of success). However, lower-class individuals ultimately recognize that it is difficult, if not impossible, to achieve those goals legitimately. The typical lower-class persons will not be able to compete for the better jobs because of poor educational backgrounds. Even today, very few will achieve the middle-class lifestyle through professional sports. Merton argued that this created **anomie**, a gap between the goals of society and the legitimate means for achieving the goals. As a result, lower-class people must decide how to adapt.[11]

TABLE 6:1

MERTON'S TYPOLOGY OF DEVIANCE AND CONFORMITY

ADAPTATION	SOCIETY'S SUCCESS GOALS	SOCIETY'S NORMS
Conformist	Accepts	Accepts
Innovator	Accepts	Rejects
Ritualist	Rejects	Accepts
Retreatist	Rejects	Rejects
Rebel	Rejects/Establishes own	Rejects/Establishes own

Merton suggests five possible adaptations. Of these, the conformist adaptation is nondeviant. The deviant adaptations are innovation, ritualism, retreatism, and rebellion.[12]

1. *Conformists:* persons who choose to pursue society's norms to achieve success. Most people adapt in this way.

2. *Innovators:* strive to attain the success goals, but deliberately reject societal means of achieving those goals. Instead, they develop creative alternatives to achieving success (e.g., robbery, selling drugs, prostitution). Merton attributes this adaptation to inadequate socialization.

3. *Ritualists:* follow the norms of society meticulously but view the goals as unattainable. Some people become ritualistic in following a certain code of behavior, believing that their acceptance is accomplished solely by how they dress or according to some other particular practice.

4. *Retreatists:* have internalized both the success goals and norms regarding how to achieve the goals. However, the legitimate means are not available. Since they feel moral constraints against the use of illegitimate means, they "drop out" or retreat (e.g., drug addicts, alcoholics). They reject both the success goals and the socially acceptable means of achieving them. Some religious groups become retreatists because they are convinced they must separate from the modern world to assure their salvation.

5. *Rebels:* develop their own goals and a personally satisfying means of achieving them. Merton suggests that rebellion is a transitional response that seeks to *institutionalize* new ways of revising the cultural goals of a segment of society. Some Christians are looked upon as rebels whenever they seek to effect change by means of the Gospel.

Using the availability of legitimate means and American success goals as two variables, Merton developed a typology of deviance and conformity. (See Table 6:1.) While this typology was developed to explain lower-class deviance, examples of each form of deviance can be found within most social groups.

Merton later revised his structural theory and

categorized deviants as *nonconformists* and *aberrant*. These two differ in the openness with which they engage in deviance and the motivations for doing so. *Nonconformists* openly violate the norms and question their validity. Like the rebel, the nonconformist wants to bring about a change in norms. Unlike the nonconformists, *aberrants* do not question the legitimacy of the social norms. They acknowledge wrongdoing and therefore attempt to conceal deviant acts. Accordingly, aberrant individuals do not try to change the norms; their primary interest is avoiding detection. Are some Christians today in danger of becoming aberrants?

SOCIAL CONTROL THEORIES

Other theorists ask, "Why do people commit deviance?" Control theorists reply, "Why not?" Given the basic depravity of humanity, deviance should be expected. Hence, the question is not simply "Why?" but "Why not greater amounts of deviance?" Social control theorists like Travis Hirschi and Walter Reckless suggest that the nature of social control is the key to understanding deviance. If social controls are ineffective, deviance will be greater; if social controls are adequate, less deviance will occur.

SOCIAL BOND THEORY

Hirschi believes that the nature of one's social bonds determines the levels of deviance. According to Hirschi's *social bond theory*, four types of social bonds decrease the likelihood of deviance: *attachment, involvement, commitment, and belief*.[13] Developing these concepts in an effort to explain delinquency involvement, Hirschi argued that if a young person was sufficiently bonded to society, delinquency involvement was unlikely.

Violence is a particularly dysfunctional type of deviance.

1. *Attachment* is the development of relationships to others in society, especially parents, peers and teachers. Those who develop attachments with conventional persons and institutions of society are less likely to become deviant.

2. *Commitment* relates to the costs of deviance. If the consequences of deviance are too great, people will not violate the norms. Hirschi suggests that to the degree people are "committed to conventional lines of action," the consequences of deviant behavior would serve as a control against it.[14] That is, those involved in conventional lifestyles would not want to sacrifice their careers, reputations, positions of responsibility, or opportunities for achievement by committing a deviant act. Thus, their commitment to conventional activities serves as a deterrent to deviance.

3. *Involvement* in conventional activities also decreases the likelihood of deviance: a person who is busily engaged in school, family, and community activities has little time to think about deviance, much less engage in it.

4. *Belief* in the legitimacy of the law is the final bond. This is similar to internalization of conventional values of society: one's conformity to society's values is a result of the extent to which those values have been internalized. If those values are questioned or not internalized, deviance may result.

A strong bond to society, evidenced in attachment, commitment, involvement, and belief can deter persons from deviance. This would explain why many conservative Christians strongly conform to many of the norms of their society.

How would you label this man? What behavior would you expect?

THE CONTAINMENT THEORY

Walter Reckless proposes another control theory, the *containment theory*.[15] He envisions the individual as experiencing either *pushes* or *pressures and pulls* toward deviance. The pushes are internal factors; pressures and pulls are external. Pushes include extreme hostility, low self-esteem, and a need for immediate gratification. Adverse living conditions (e.g., poverty, minority group status) would be a pressure toward deviance; deviant peers and the mass media are examples of factors that might pull a person in the direction of deviance.

Reckless posits two types of control—inner and outer containment. *Inner containment* consists of those aspects of the self that serve to keep behavior within acceptable boundaries. Examples include a good self-concept, a high frustration tolerance level, and a goal orientation. *Outer containment* consists of those forces in one's immediate social environment that discourage deviance (e.g., supportive network, meaningful roles). If the inner and outer containments are adequate, they will work against deviance in most cases. Exceptions would be deviance that is a function of serious psychological problems (e.g., psychosis or phobias).

LABELING THEORY

Labeling theorists are more interested in the impact of being labeled a deviant than in discussing the etiology (cause) of deviance. According to Howard Becker, social groups create deviance.[16] They create deviance by:

1. Making rules whose infractions are defined as deviant.

2. Applying these rules to certain people who are labeled "outsiders" (norm-violators).

Thus, deviant behavior is deemed deviant because people with power and influence label it so. The point of the labeling theory is that two persons can commit the same act—one can be labeled a deviant while the other is not.

Primary and Secondary Deviance

Lemert distinguished between primary and secondary deviance.[17] *Primary deviance* is norm-violating behavior in which a person engages "without being noticed or sanctioned by the authorities."[18] Consequently, deviance does not become a part of the individual's self-concept. However, should a person be labeled a deviant, a process referred to as the dramatization of evil may occur. According to Tannenbaum, the community's reaction to the behavior may eventuate in a self-fulfilling prophecy.[19] Having "tagged" the individual as a deviant, that person may become the very thing that the society despises. This will occur if the individual develops a deviant self-image because he or she has accepted the community's definition.

At this point, *secondary deviance* occurs: the person begins to view him or herself as a deviant and, as a result, begins to orient his or her life around that deviant status. This is often referred to as a deviant career or a deviant lifestyle.

Labeling theorists emphasize the consequences of such labels. These include spoiled identity, restrictions, and additional deviance. *Spoiled identity* refers to the stigma that people experience as a result of being labeled a deviant. This often leads to guilt and shame, not only for the labelee but also for those with whom the labelee is associated (referred to as *courtesy stigma*). Employment restrictions, territorial restrictions, and social exclusion may also occur. Job opportunities are limited for individuals who have had a deviant status; in addition, persons with a deviant status are not wanted in certain places (e.g., a neighborhood resists the location of an ex-offenders' program in their community). *Social exclusion* refers to the tendency of conventional persons to dissociate themselves from the labelee. If such relationships exist, they are often strained. If a person is denied relationships with non-deviants, he or she will associate with other deviants who are also experiencing social exclusion. They may then develop values that promote further deviance.

CRIME AS A SPECIAL CASE OF DEVIANCE

As noted previously, *mores* are norms that have strong connotations of right and wrong attached to them. **Laws** are codified mores, established by a political body charged with the responsibility of creating laws. Violation of a law results in formal penalties by the government.

Criminal laws deal with behaviors that harm both society and its victims; thus, criminal law deals with public wrongs. Criminal law has three broad categories: physical violence, infringement on property rights, and crimes against health, morals, and public safety.[20] A **felony** is a crime that carries a penalty of more than a year. Many of these are index offenses, while many are not indexed (cf. discussion of *Uniform Crime Reports*); all other crimes are **misdemeanors**.

Civil laws involve behaviors that harm people but not society (*public wrongs*). Examples include libel, trespass, selling defective merchandise, and invasion of privacy.[21]

Since crime adversely affects society, not just individuals or groups, the state is the offended party when crimes are dealt with through the formal system. The law-violator (or defendant) has committed a crime against the state. In civil cases, an individual or group brings the judgment against the offending party. **Crime** is a violation of the law. When crime occurs, formal

FIGURE 6:1

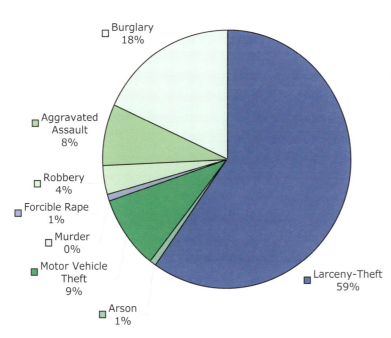

CRIME INDEX OFFENSES 1999

STATISTICS: THE EXTENT OF CRIME

social control agents are responsible for enforcing the law. These agents include the police, courts, and correctional institutions.

Crime is a serious social problem in our society. Questions such as the following are uppermost in many people's minds: How much crime is committed? Who are its victims? Who are its perpetrators? The best official sources of information for these questions are *The Uniform Crime Report* (UCR) and *The National Crime Victimization Survey*

TABLE 6:2

NUMBER OF REPORTED SERIOUS CRIMES IN 1992 AND 1999			
CRIME	1992	1999	PERCENT CHANGED
Violent Crime	1,923,270	1,430,695	-25.6
Murder/Non-negligent manslaughter	23,760	15,533	-34.6
Forcible Rape	109,060	89,107	-18.3
Robbery	672,480	409,670	-39.1
Aggravated Assault	1,126,970	916,383	-18.7
Property Crime	12,505,900	10,204,456	-18.4
Burglary	2,979,900	2,099,739	-29.5
Larceny-Theft	7,915,200	6,957,412	-12.1
Motor Vehicle Theft	1,610,800	1,147,305	-28.8

Adapted from *Crime in the United States: The Uniform Crime Report,* 1992, p. 58, and 1999, p. 65.

(NCVS). The Federal Bureau of Investigation (FBI) publishes the UCR annually. Based upon reports voluntarily submitted by local police agencies, the UCR provides information about crimes known to police and crimes cleared by arrest. *The National Crime Victimization Survey* estimates the extent of crime against persons and against households. It differs from the UCR in that it relies upon reports from those who have been victimized, some of whom have not reported their victimization to the police.

The UCR provides rates for two types of crime: Part I offenses are serious crimes, also referred to as index offenses; Part II offenses include crimes other than Part I offenses and traffic violations.

Part I offenses include violent crimes against persons (forcible rape, robbery, aggravated assault, homicide, and non-negligent manslaughter) and property crimes (burglary, larceny, arson, and automobile theft).

Alcohol, though legal, is commonly related to illegal activity.

Examples of Part II offenses include vandalism, prostitution, sex offenses, forgery, counterfeiting, trespassing, and embezzlement.

Table 6:2 provides information regarding the relative distribution of index crimes. Far more property crime is committed (87.7%) than violent crime (12.3%). Both violent crimes and property crimes are decreasing. From 1992 to 1999, violent crime decreased from 1,923,270 to 1,430,695; property crime from 12,505,900 to 10,204,456. This is a decrease of 25.6 and 18.4 percent respectively.

WHO COMMITS CRIME?

According to the UCR, a lower-class urban nonwhite male typically commits crime. Males comprise approximately 48.9 percent of the United States population; women make up 51.1 percent.[22] However, males accounted for 78.2% of the arrests in 1999; females, 21.8% of the arrests.[23] The U. S. Bureau of the Census estimates that Whites constitute about 82.4% of the total population; Blacks 12.8%; and Asian and Pacific Islanders, 4%.

However, 69.0% of those arrested in 1999 were Black; 28.6% were White; and 1.7% were Asian or Pacific Islanders.[24]

What accounts for the differences? A number of suggestions have been made: the nature of crimes reported in the Crime Index, prejudice and bias, and subcultural differences.

The types of crimes reported in the Crime Index are those most often committed by lower-class individuals (cf. discussion of *elite deviance*). In addition, because of the culture's emphasis on aggressiveness and toughness, males are most likely to commit serious crimes. Another explanation for the greater number of arrests for men is the differential treatment of men and women by the police—police are more lenient with women.

Subcultural explanations have also been offered for why certain groups commit crimes. The disintegration of the African American family and the resultant lack of an adequate male role model have been cited as contributing to the high African American male crime rate. Others, such as Walter Miller, argue that lower-class values encourage crime. On the other hand, both the success with which Asian Americans have assimilated into American society and their subcultural values have been used to explain their low rates of criminal involvement. The emphasis upon both community (as opposed to individualism) and avoidance of shame (to the community because of one's behavior) have held Asian American behavior in check. Others have suggested that prejudice and bias cannot be overlooked. Put simply, nonwhites and the poor are treated more harshly by the criminal justice system.

Young people commit a disproportionate amount of crime. Young people under eighteen years of age represented 28.3% of all arrests for index crimes: 16% of all violent crime arrests and 32.9% of all property offenses. While the arrest rates are decreasing, this age group still commits more crime than those eighteen years of age or older. From 1990 to 1999, arrests for index crimes decreased 20.5% compared to a 22.5% for those eighteen years of age or over.[25]

WHO ARE THE VICTIMS OF CRIME?

Those persons most likely to engage in serious crime are also most likely to be its victims—young, nonwhite, lower-class, urban males. Teenagers between the ages of sixteen and nineteen have the highest victimization rate (77.6 per 1,000), followed by twelve to fifteen year olds (74.5 per 1,000) and twenty to twenty-four year olds (68.7 per 1,000). At twenty-five years of age, the victimization rate drops about one-half (36.4 per 1,000) and continues to decline.[26] Blacks have the highest rates (19.5 per 1,000) for those over twelve years of age (in contrast to 10.2 for whites in the same age category).[27] In 1999, "males were victimized at rates 22% higher than females," with the exception of rape and sexual assault.[28]

Crime rates are higher in large urban areas as well. In 1999 metropolitan areas had crime index rates of 4,599.8; cities outside the metro-

EXAMPLE 6:2

EXAMPLES OF ELITE DEVIANCE

Ford Pinto
Some believe the company continued to produce the Pinto even though it was aware that a rear-end collision would cause the gas tank to explode.

The Dalkon Shield
Some contend that A. H. Robbins marketed its intrauterine device with the knowledge of its potential for infection. After it was banned in the United States, A. H. Robbins continued to sell it on the international market.

Beech-Nut Apple Juice
Some believe Beech-Nut sold caramel-colored water to mothers as "100 percent pure juice."

Love Canal
Hooker Chemicals and Plastic Corporation, after using this area of Niagara Falls for toxic waste disposal, sold it to the city for $1.00. Homes and a playground were built on the site. Families that resided there experienced many health-related problems: birth defects, cancer, and miscarriages, to name a few.

Savings and Loan Scandal
About 1.4 trillion dollars was lost as a result of bailing out failed savings and loans companies. Had they been allowed to fail, the cost would have been $3 billion.

Source: David R. Simon and D. Stanley Eitzen, *Elite Deviance*, 4th ed. (Boston: Allyn and Bacon, 1993), 52.

Some people call gambling a victimless crime. What do you think?

politan areas had a rate of 4,560.6, and rural counties had a rate of 1,900.6.[29] All areas of large cities are not equally plagued by crime: inner-city neighborhoods have higher rates of crime than do stable middle- and upper-class neighborhoods.

SOCIAL CONTROL OF CRIME

Societies promote stability by controlling deviance. Such controls include prisons, prison camps, and juvenile homes (training schools and camps). What purpose do these perform in the criminal justice system? Four suggestions have been offered: protection, retribution, deterrence, and rehabilitation.[30]

1. *Protection:* Those who commit serious offenses (e.g., homicide, rape) are often institutionalized. As long as they are kept in a state prison, federal prison, or juvenile facility, the public is protected.

2. *Retribution:* Retribution is punishment of the criminal; this view suggests that the criminal should pay for the crime. It is consistent with the view that people should accept the consequences of their behavior.

3. *Deterrence:* The deterrent function of institutions is related to the retribution function. Punishing people by restricting their freedom, it is believed, will serve to discourage crimes on the part of others.

4. *Rehabilitation:* Rehabilitation is the effort to reform the individual. While the individual is institutionalized, the institution attempts to help him or her through counseling and education. In some institutions, prisoners can earn college credit. Thus, the prison is not simply a holding tank or a means of punishment; instead, it is an opportunity for the prisoner to be rehabilitated and to start a new life.

How effective are our correctional institutions? Do they deter? Are prisoners rehabilitated? Some who oppose capital punishment challenge the notion of deterrence. They present research statistics that suggest that even capital punishment does not reduce murder rates.[31] (If capital punishment does not deter, can prisons deter?)

Recidivism rates (repetition of criminal or delinquent behavior) are so high that many question both the deterrent and rehabilitative functions of prisons.[32] Forty percent of defendants in the seventy-five largest U.S. counties in 1996 had prior felony convictions; twenty-two percent had two or more previous convictions.[33] Seventy-six percent of all state prisoners in 1997 were recidivists; 61% of those in federal prisoners had prior criminal offenses.[34] This suggests that the correctional system is ineffective.

ELITE DEVIANCE

Crime is not a lower-class nonwhite urban phenomenon. In 1949 Edwin Sutherland drew attention to crime on the part of middle- and upper-class individuals in his book, *White Collar Crime*.[35] He argued that crime was not necessarily a result of living in poverty. "Respectable" people in business and politics also commit crimes. Their crimes are either for personal advantage or of direct benefit to their employers. Examples of the former would be embezzlement, taking company equipment or supplies, padding expense accounts, and using company time or equipment for personal matters. Crimes committed for the benefit of the company include advertising fraud, antitrust violations, and willful sale of defective merchandise. Such crimes have far-reaching consequences and cause untold amounts of suffering and hardship. Sutherland noted that such crimes lead to large financial losses and create public distrust.

While some sociologists continue to use the term **white collar crime**, others prefer *corporate deviance* or *elite deviance*. Simon and Eitzen prefer elite deviance and define it as illegal or unethical behavior on the part of upper- and upper-middle-class individuals in government or corporations, which is committed for personal gain or to "enhance the power, profitability, or influence of the organizations involved."[36]

Studies indicate that elite deviance may be far more costly than conventional crime in terms of financial costs and the lives endangered or lost. In spite of this, those found guilty of elite deviance receive mild sanctions relative to those who engage in and are convicted of conventional crimes. Financial penalties are typically less than what the corporation gained by engaging in the behavior, and jail terms are relatively short.

IS ALL DEVIANCE "BAD"?

Deviance is a violation of a norm. One's tendency is to perceive the norm-breaker as bad, evil, or a misfit. But is all deviance bad? Consider the following deviant acts:

The colonists' refusal to continue to abide by England's taxation resulted in the Revolutionary War and the founding of the United States.

African American Rosa Parks' decision to keep her seat rather than relinquish it for a member of the white majority sparked the Civil Rights Movement.

Shannon Faulkner's application to the Citadel resulted in all evidence of her sex being removed from her transcripts. Her deviance highlighted the persistence of sex as a barrier to certain opportunities.

Each of these examples demonstrates two factors regarding deviance. First, whether it is viewed as good or bad depends upon one's perspective. Those who question the legitimacy of a norm will often applaud the deviant; those who support the norm will denigrate the deviant. Second, while deviance may cause some disruption of the social system, it may also be quite functional. Its existence reinforces the norms and values of society. Punishment of the deviant reasserts the social system's norms and values as well. Deviance can also lead to positive change in society by revealing problems in the social system. In each of the instances cited above, individuals had the courage to deviate from the system. Consequently, they helped to make the United States (and the world) a better place.

HOW CHRISTIANS CAN CHANGE THE WORLD

What happens when Christians must live in a society where certain norms violate their values? Some Christians tug back by quietly living a life that stands against the norms of society. Such deviance has social consequences: When you break a law, prepare to be fined or arrested. Think of the many days Paul spent in chains for preaching the gospel. At the very least, your quiet deviance may annoy others and lead to an isolated life.

Some deviance, however, is a product of sin. Such sin may be individual or social in nature.

In other words, deviance may stem from an individual deficiency or a social injustice. Thus, the believer must address deviance on both levels—individual and social.

On the individual level, deviance stemming from individual deficiency will be reduced considerably by individual repentance. Christians can help this process by sharing the gospel of Jesus Christ.

On the social level, one must examine how the social structure encourages deviant behavior in an attempt to address social sin. For example, the social values of materialism have significantly contributed to deviance in American society. Whether in the print media or on television, we are bombarded with images of the "good life," a life of comfort and affluence. According to Merton's social strain theory, when people internalize social values and give them a high priority, deviance may result.

Merton pointed to the role of education in deviance. When schools do not prepare people to achieve the American Dream, anomie can result. This may then lead to deviance. All children should receive a *quality* education that enables them to compete in the job market. Thus, educational institutions must address the problems (e.g., lack of resources, inequality) that make them less effective.

Our society has always assumed a relationship between education and employment. We have assumed that a good education leads to a good job and the ability to enjoy the American Dream. However, education and employment alone are insufficient. We need to de-emphasize materialism and cultivate a sense of community.

Sutherland underscores the importance of interpersonal relationships. Interactions in one's groups that assert the legitimacy of the law and promote conventional behavior can insulate one against deviance. When deviance has already occurred, resocialization can take place in the context of interpersonal relationships.

Therefore, Christians should try to develop interpersonal relationships with both deviants and at-risk populations. Options include Big Brother/Big Sister programs, prison ministries, mentoring, rehabilitation centers, and neighborhood outreach programs. This would afford believers the opportunity to point others to Jesus Christ, model biblical values, and possibly provide alternative activities.

In addition, we must establish a norm of responsibility. Since norms are a basis of order in society, each individual is responsible for contributing to that order. We cannot simply rely on formal sanctions to maintain that order. We must hold one another accountable for our behavior. Attempts to rationalize deviant behavior should not be tolerated. We must also recognize that ultimately each of us is accountable to God for our behavior and its influence upon others.

What would be a Christian perspective on the criminal justice system? Christians can influence the penal system to strive for justice. Minimally, this means two things. First, justice should be fair. All deviants—regardless of social class, race, or status—should be punished by the same standards (Lev. 19:15). Bribery is unacceptable (Ps. 26:9-10; Amos 5:12; Mic. 3:11; 7:3). Perjury must be punished (Deut. 19:16-19; Mal. 3:5). In addition, fairness suggests that intentionality must be considered when sanctions are administered (Lev. 4:2; Deut. 19:1-13; Josh. 20).

Second, justice should be restorative: the aim should be to correct the behavior, not denigrate the offender (Deut. 25:1-3). While specifically related to church discipline, the principle laid out by Paul in 2 Corinthians 2:5-8 is applicable: the goal is not only to maintain order in society but also to restore the citizen to the community once punishment has been meted out. God is just, but He is also merciful and compassionate. Believers, then, should balance justice with compassion.

Dealing with deviance requires addressing it on a number of levels. On the individual level, it is important to strengthen individuals' resolve to contribute to the stability of society. Empathy and a sense of responsibility are needed. On the interpersonal level, we need to be "iron sharpening iron"; that is, in our interpersonal relationships we should assert the importance of living responsibly. At the structural level, we need to take steps to strengthen those institutions that are linked to deviance and conformity—the family, education, and justice.

overview

- Deviance is a violation of a society or group's norms that threatens its values and social order. It results in social control efforts.

- Social control is the attempt to bring the deviant person back into line. Social control efforts can be formal or informal.

- Crime is a particular type of deviance. It is a violation of a law.

- People tend to see criminals as lower-class nonwhite individuals, but crime is pervasive among all classes and races. Persons in the upper classes of society usually commit white collar and corporate crime.

- Since adherence to society's law makes order possible, serious crime or delinquency will be dealt with by formal social control agents: the police, the courts, and correctional institutions.

- While public opinion changes regarding what should be done with criminals, there are three basic opinions: they should be punished, they should be put away for the protection of society, and/or they should be rehabilitated.

- Sociologists are interested in determining the causes of crime and deviance. Miller and Merton presented explanations for lower-class crime and deviance. Miller argued that it resulted from lower-class values that promote crime. Merton argued that the lower classes have the same values as the upper classes. However, he noted that the gap between the success goal and the legitimate means for achieving that goal caused some lower-class people to resort to crime to achieve the American Dream of success.

- Differential association and control theories explain crime and deviance regardless of social class. Sutherland argued that people, through their interaction with different primary groups, learn definitions that favor or reject crime and deviance. If a person learns more definitions that are favorable to deviance rather than unfavorable, deviance is likely to occur. Reckless and Hirschi argued that adequate social controls lessen the likelihood of deviance. Reckless posited two types of control: inner and outer containment. Before deviance can occur, both types of containment must be weakened. Hirschi, on the other hand, believed that strong social bonds decreased one's propen-

- sity for deviance: the stronger the bonds, the less likelihood of serious violations of societal norms.

- Unlike others, labeling theorists do not try to explain why deviance occurs, but rather what impact the deviant label has on a person and how the label affects internal and external control efforts. They suggest that being labeled a deviant may cause individuals to develop a deviant identity. Those who define themselves as deviant will act like deviants; Lemert referred to this as secondary deviance. Labeling theorists suggest that labeling persons as deviant may have a self-fulfilling effect.

- It is important to note that while people typically think of deviance as bad behavior, it is simply the violation of a norm. Depending on the nature of the norm, deviance may be good. When societal norms conflict with God's will as expressed in His Word, deviance is good.

- In addition, whether or not the deviance is defined as good or bad depends upon the definer. This chapter cited a few examples of deviance that had the potential for positive consequences.

- Christians may use their sociological understanding of deviance to address the problem. Each sociological explanation of crime and deviance has social policy implications. Both Sutherland and Miller's explanations suggest the need for alternative values. If the deviant has learned values that promote deviance, a different set of values can be learned to reject it. Thus, the deviant needs resocialization.

- Merton argued that educational barriers prevented the lower class from achieving the American Dream of success. As a consequence, some engage in crime. This would suggest removing the barrier or redefining the goal. While the barrier should be removed so that people can meet their needs adequately, that in itself is insufficient. The pursuit of the dream is inherently problematic; things do not satisfy.

key concepts

anomie
The gap between society's success goal and the legitimate means for achieving that goal.

crime
A violation of a law in a given society.

deviant behavior (social deviance)
Behavior that violates the norms of a society.

differential association
Developed by Edwin Sutherland, this theory states that people learn to be criminal when they have had an excess of experiences favoring law violation. They usually have these in primary groups.

felony
A crime that is usually punishable by at least one year or more in a state or federal prison.

focal concerns
Walter Miller states that lower-class youth have certain focal concerns—trouble, toughness, fate, autonomy, smartness, excitement—that lend themselves to criminal/delinquent behavior.

labeling theory
A theory associated with Howard Becker and Edward Lemert that contends deviance is not a quality of the act committed, but a consequence of others' defining the act as deviant; the person who moves from "primary" to "secondary" deviance accepts the label and embarks on a career as a delinquent or criminal.

law
A systematic rule enacted by political authority that involves formal penalties for violations.

misdemeanor
Offense punishable by not more than a year in a county jail.

recidivism
Repetition of criminal or delinquent behavior; usually referred to as recidivism rate.

sanction
A means of encouraging conformity and discouraging deviance; refers to either positive or negative sanctions or approving or disapproving behavior.

social control
Theories associated with Walter Reckless and Travis Hirschi that suggest weak social control mechanisms explain deviant behavior; either a formal or informal attempt to enforce conformity to society's norms.

strain theory
A theory (e.g., Merton's anomie theory) that suggests deviance may result when people are frustrated in their attempts to achieve a goal.

white collar crime (elite deviance)
Persons of high respectability and high social status who commit crime in the course of their occupation, amounting to billions more than "street" or "blue collar" crime.

endnotes

1. William Graham Sumner, *Folkways* (Boston: Ginn Publishing Co., 1906).
2. Ruth Shonle Cavan, "The Concepts of Tolerance and Contraculture as Applied to Delinquency," *Readings in Juvenile Delinquency,* 3rd ed. (Philadelphia: Lippincott Publishing Co., 1975), 5-20.
3. Marshall B. Clinard and Robert F. Meier, *Sociology of Deviant Behavior,* 6th ed. (New York: Holt, Rinehart & Winston, 1985), 14.
4. Nanette J. Davis and Clarice Stasz, *Social Control of Deviance: A Critical Perspective* (New York: McGraw-Hill Publishers, 1990), 48.
5. Marshall B. Clinard and Robert F. Meier, *Sociology of Deviant Behavior,* 8th ed. (Fort Worth, TX: Harcourt Brace Jovanovich, 1992), 7-8.
6. Jack E. Bynum and William E. Thompson, *Juvenile Delinquency: A Sociological Approach* (Boston: Allyn & Bacon, 1989), 175-77.
7. Edwin H. Sutherland, *Principles of Criminology,* 4th ed. (Philadelphia: Lippincott Publishing Co., 1947).
8. David Matza and Gresham Sykes, *Techniques of Neutralization: A Theory of Delinquency* (New York: Irvington Publishers, Inc., 1993).
9. R. L. Burgess and R. L. Akers, "Differential Association-Reinforcement Theory of Criminal Behavior," *Social Problems* 14 (1968): 128-47.
10. Walter C. Reckless, *The Crime Problem,* 4th ed. (New York: Meredith Publishing Co., 1967), 399.
11. Robert S. Merton, "Social Structure and Anomie," *Deviant Behavior: A Text-reader in the Sociology of Deviance,* 4th ed. (New York: St. Martin's Press, Inc., 1933), 119-29.
12. Ibid.
13. Travis Hirschi, *Causes of Delinquency* (Berkeley: University of California Press, 1969).
14. Ibid., 166.
15. Walter Reckless, "A New Theory of Delinquency and Crime," *Federal Probations* 25 (December 1961): 42-46.
16. Howard Becker, *Outsiders: Studies in the Sociology of Deviance* (New York: Free Press, 1963).
17. Edwin M. Lemert, *Deviance, Social Problems and Social Control* (Englewood Cliffs, NJ: Prentice-Hall, 1967).
18. Davis and Stasz, *Social Control of Deviance*, 46.
19. Frank Tannenbaum, *Crime and Community* (Boston: Ginn Publishing Co., 1938).
20. Gresham M. Sykes, *Criminology* (New York: Harcourt Brace Jovanovich, 1978), 46.
21. Ibid., 46.
22. *Statistical Abstracts of the United States—2000.* Table 11.
23. Federal Bureau of Investigation, *Uniform Crime Report—1999* (Washington, DC: U.S. Government Printing Office, 1999), 229. [Cited 11 March 2001]. Available from World Wide Web <http://www.fbi.gov/ucr/Cius.99/99crime/99 c4_06.pdf.>
24. Ibid., 230. [Cited 11 March 2001]. Available from World Wide Web <http://www.fbi.gov/ucr/Cius.99/99crime/99 c4_07.pdf.>
25. Ibid., 216. [Cited 11 March 2001]. Available from World Wide Web <http://www.fbi.gov/ucr/Cius.99/99crime/99 c4_03.pdf.>
26. United States Department of Justice, Bureau of Justice Statistics, "Violent Victimization by Age, 1973-1999." [Cited 11 March 2001]. Available from World Wide Web <http://www.ojp.usdoj/gov/bjs/welcome.html
27. United States Department of Justice, Bureau of Justice Statistics. "Violent Victimization by Race, 1973-1999." [Cited 11 March 2001]. Available from WorldWide Web <http://www.ojp.usdoj.gov/bjs/welcome.html

28. United States Department of Justice, Bureau of Justice Statistics, "Victim Characteristics." [Cited 11 March 2001]. <http://www.ojp.usdoj.gov/bjs/cvict_v.htm>
29. Federal Bureau of Investigation, *Uniform Crime Report—1999,* 65. [Cited 11 March 2001]. Available from World Wide Web <http://www.fbi.gov/ucr/Cius.99/99crime/99c2_13.pdf >
30. Charles Zastrow, *Social Problems: Issues and Solutions,* 3rd ed. (Chicago: Nelson-Hall, Inc., 1991).
31. *Sourcebook of Criminal Justice Statistics—1999* (Washington, DC: U.S. Government Printing Office, 1999), Table 5.55, 456. [Cited 11 March 2001]. Available from World Wide Web <http://www.albany.edu/sourcebook/1995/pdf/t555.pdf>
32. Davis and Stasz, *Social Control of Deviance*, 159.
33. *Sourcebook of Criminal Justice Statistics—1999*, Table 5.58, 458. [Cited 11 March 2001]. Available from World Wide Web <http://www.albany.edu/sourcebook/1995/pdf/t558.pdf>
34. Ibid., Table 6.39, 514. [Cited 11 March 2001]. Available from World Wide Web. <http://www.albany.edu/sourcebook/1995/pdf/t639.pdf.>
35. Edwin H. Sutherland, W*hite Collar Crime* (New York: Dryden Press, 1940).
36. David R. Simon and D. Stanley Eitzen, *Elite Deviance*, 4th ed. (Boston: Allyn & Bacon, 1993), 11-12.

CHAPTER SEVEN

Social Stratification

chapter outline

I. From social differentiation to social stratification

II. Why inequality?
- A. Structural-functional perspective
- B. Social conflict perspective
- C. Synthesis

III. Social class in America
- A. Occupation
- B. Income
- C. Education

IV. Subjective nature of social class

V. The impact of class
- A. Vertical vs horizontal mobility
- B. Global inequality

VI. Theories on poverty

VII. A Christian response

biblical reflection

"Do nothing from selfish ambition or conceit, but in humility regard others as better than yourselves. Let each of you look not to your own interests, but to the interests of others. Let the same mind be in you that was in Christ Jesus, who, though he was in the form of God, did not regard equality with God as something to be exploited, but emptied himself, taking the form of a slave, being born in human likeness. And being found in human form, he humbled himself and became obedient to the point of death, even death on a cross."

— Philippians 2:3-8

To Christians, God is a radical departure from the "gods" of ancient times. Ancient cultures viewed their deities as capricious, often angry beings that had to be appeased through sacrifice. But Christians know the True God as One who comes down to meet us on our level. Common people can be with and talk with the True God. And God talks to and works through common people. This must have been quite a shock to the Philippians who were part of a world where only those with very high status could come into the presence of God. The fact that God's Son came in the form of an ordinary human was inconceivable to many people of the time.

We still have a difficult time with the notion that people of high social status are no closer to God than those of low status. We like to believe that people in certain occupations with much education are somehow "better" than others. We like to believe that people of low socioeconomic status are there because of something they did or didn't do. We are uncomfortable with the notion that everyone is inherently equal. We, too, are confused by the fact that God's Son appeared not as someone of high social status, but as a lowly servant.

As Philippians 2:6 states, Jesus could have exploited His equality with God. Certainly many of us pretend to be as powerful as God. But grabbing high status and power can be disastrous. Jesus knew that. He had equality with God so He did not need to "grasp" it. Instead, He let go of His powerful position in the universe and identified with the lowly in society.

Unlike Jesus, humans have no right to "grasp" equality with God. Why then do we resist our rightful place as equals to the poor and powerless in society?

FROM SOCIAL DIFFERENTIATION TO SOCIAL STRATIFICATION

God creates each of us with unique characteristics. We tend to choose to interact with people who are similar to us. People of the same sex, age, and interests tend to *differentiate* themselves from other groups. Such **social differentiation** simply reflects our God-given differences and is generally not problematic in our daily interactions. However, **social stratification** occurs when some of these groups are perceived to be more important than others. From a Christian perspective, this is where we become estranged from God's original creative process. God did not create us with different characteristics in order for us to overpower others.

It is curious that some characteristics such as

hair or eye color are seemingly inconsequential in the structure of stratification in America. Yet equally curious is our preoccupation with the shade of one's skin or the presence or absence of certain sex organs. But we will talk about that more in coming chapters. This chapter will focus on inequality of rewards based on the type of work one does. For some reason we do not reward everyone equally for a day's work. Some people's work is much more highly valued than others. In fact, some kinds of work (e.g., housekeeping and child care) are often not rewarded economically at all. In this chapter we will explore the explanations and consequences behind such economic stratification.

Social stratification is structured inequality. While "equality" is one of our social ideals, in reality, we see a world around us in which some people are much more highly valued than others. But this is not an exclusively American dilemma. There are status differences in every society. As a result of social sin, all societies are *stratified*; i.e., divided into levels or *strata* that are ranked.

This is often disconcerting for Christians. The Bible acknowledges that God created each person with special gifts and talents (1 Cor. 12). Those talents and gifts are often differently rewarded by certain groups and organizations. However, it is clear that God's grace is available to all in equal measure: "There is no longer Jew or Greek, there is no longer slave or free, there is no longer male and female; for all of you are one in Christ Jesus" (Gal. 3:28).

WHY INEQUALITY?

If all societies (at least all beyond the most elementary) are stratified, is institutionalized inequality inevitable in human society? If so, why? There are two major schools of thought concerning the development of social stratification: **structural-functionalism** and **conflict theory**.

STRUCTURAL-FUNCTIONAL PERSPECTIVE

Functionalists such as Kingsley Davis and Wilbert Moore believe that stratification is both necessary and inevitable.[1] Some positions in society serve functions that are perceived as more important than others. They require special talent, skills, or training. Consequently, according to the functionalist, these positions should have special rewards. In this manner society assures itself that the most important positions are filled by the most qualified and competent people. If no differences were allowed and recognized in income, power, or prestige, there would be no incentive to encourage individuals to undergo the demanding preparation required by certain positions. The lengthy training of the medical doctor is often cited as a supporting example. Functionalism argues, then, that inequality exists because it enables society to function at the most efficient level.

Critics of structural-functional theory raise numerous questions concerning its testability. Who determines the functional importance of a given task? Or how do we define "reward"? If rewards refer to income differentials, positions are often rewarded out of proportion to their functional importance. A corporation executive may earn more than the President of the United States. Nor are highly rewarded positions necessarily important to the welfare of society (consider the movie star or professional athlete). In reality, high rewards seem to relate more to the profit-making capabilities of a given person than to his or her importance to society as a whole.[2]

Moreover, how do we know that the most qualified people fill the most important positions? The opportunity to compete for those positions is certainly unequal. A number of critics suggest that functional theory is supportive of the status quo, since it implies that the prevailing distribution of rewards is functionally necessary.[3] Theoretically, those at the top have the talent to be there and so their differential reward is both legitimate and essential. In this sense, structural-functionalism rationalizes inequality.

SOCIAL CONFLICT PERSPECTIVE

While *functionalists* see society as a stable system of interdependent parts cooperating on the basis of common values, *conflict theorists* conceive of society as a system of conflicting interest groups. According to their perspective, social order is based on group dominance and organized coercion, not on value consensus.

To conflict theorists, inequality is a matter of the wealthy exploiting the poor. Those who support this perspective do not agree that the survival of society is contingent on the unequal distribution of rewards. On the contrary, they believe that rewards should be more equally distributed among the members of society.[4] Conflict theorists also contend that stratification may result in lost talent because not all talented persons have the opportunity to develop their potential. Thus, instead of being useful (functional), stratification is often harmful (dysfunctional) to society—it fosters hostility rather than cooperation.

More specifically, conflict theory suggests that stratification is perpetuated not by the larger society for its own good, but by the holders of power in an effort to maintain their own positions. What appear to be *common* social values are really the values of the privileged groups in power.[5]

Criticisms of conflict theory are numerous.[6] It is difficult to test empirically in order to determine how dominance is established and perpetuated. It leads to the inference of conspiracy without factual base. It fails to explain the overwhelming and necessary persistence of social order. And it overplays the causal relationship between conflict and change.

SYNTHESIS

Obviously, structural-functionalists and conflict theorists view social inequality from very different perspectives. To the functionalists, the question is, "Who shall do the *important* work?" And their answer is, "The talented and the trained." Conflict theorists ask, "Who shall do the *dirty* work?" And their answer is, "The despised and the defeated."[7]

Neither theory is totally correct or incorrect. Both have strengths as well as weaknesses. The old Chinese saying, "Things that oppose each other also complement each other," suggests an appropriate synthesis of functionalism and conflict theory.[8]

Functionalism may explain how talented people are motivated to attain high positions. Consider again the example of the physician. Conflict theory explains how those in high positions are often able to maintain their superior reward level. In the case of the physician, the political power of the American Medical Association might be cited.

Too, every society has both order and conflict. Self-interest may be paramount in conflict situations; still, cooperation is essential to the survival of any society. The two schools suggest theoretical explanations for both conflict and cooperation. Functionalism and conflict theory thus provide complementary rather than contradictory perspectives on inequality. Certainly, both see societies as systems of interrelated parts and both emphasize the fact that inequality is the basis of social stratification.

SOCIAL CLASS IN AMERICA

In America, we tend to be very concerned with *occupation and education*. We are so fascinated by what people do for a living that we structure a very elaborate system of economic rewards and prestige based on a person's perceived value to society. We say we believe all people are created equal by God; in fact, not all people are treated equally in our society. **Social class** is a product of this social sin.

OCCUPATION

One of the first questions we ask (or would like to ask) when making a new acquaintance is "What do you do?" Knowing a person's occupation allows us to set him or her in social space. It determines whether deference is owed to or expected from that person.[9] Knowledge of what people do usually provides insights into their educational attainment, income level, recreational activities, and general lifestyle. In short, individuals are assigned a class status most often on the basis of their occupations.

Class and occupation are further related in that people usually find those occupations most open to them which are most appropriate to their present class status. Children born into upper-class families seldom become unskilled laborers. And those born into lower-class families seldom become physicians or top-level corporation executives.

Each of these people works hard. Yet some are paid much more for their labor. Why? The structural-functionalist says that some labor, requiring specialized training, is more highly valued by the society than other labor. Conflict theorists say that those who have more power exploit those who serve them by requiring them to work longer hours for low pay.

OCCUPATIONAL PRESTIGE

Occupations themselves are ranked on the basis of their social prestige. It is remarkable that, though we are all unique individuals, we tend to agree on what makes a person "important." We call this *occupational prestige*. Surveys of occupational prestige show little differences over the past twenty years.

Professional and managerial positions usually rank at the top, while unskilled laborers rank at the bottom. White-collar workers and skilled craftsmen fill the middle positions. See Table 7:1. The consistency of such rankings has been noted in numerous studies, both nationally and internationally.[10]

INCOME

While occupation is the basic key to understanding class structure, income must also be considered. The two are generally correlated so that the higher the income, the higher the prestige rating, but there are notable exceptions. The high school teacher, for example, has considerably more prestige than the auto mechanic but may make considerably less money. Some prostitutes may have higher incomes than bank executives, yet they rank considerably lower in the social status scale.

In recent years the unequal distribution of income has received increased attention, especially from the conflict theorists who note that individual wealth in the United States is heavily concentrated. Wealthy Americans now enjoy a greater share of the national wealth than ever before. In fact, the top 5 percent of the population controls more than half of all wealth in the United States. The poorest Americans (the bottom 20 percent) receive less than 5 percent of the total.[11]

The 1999 household income of families in the United States is shown in Table 7:2. As can be

TABLE 7:1

Social Prestige of Selected Occupations in the United States.

Occupation	Prestige Score	Occupation	Prestige Score
Physician	86	Librarian	54
Lawyer	75	Firefighter	53
University Professor	74	Social Worker	52
Architect	73	Funeral Director	49
Chemist	73	Bookkeeper	47
Aerospace Engineer	72	Mail Carrier	47
Dentist	72	Secretary	46
Member of Clergy	69	Bank Teller	43
Psychologist	69	Welder	42
Pharmacist	68	Farmer	40
Optometrist	67	Carpenter	39
Nurse	66	Child-care worker	36
Secondary-school Teacher	66	Hairdresser	36
Accountant	65	Auto Mechanic	31
Electrical Engineer	64	Salesperson	30
Elementary-school Teacher	64	Cashier	29
Veterinarian	62	Garbage Collector	28
Airplane pilot	61	Waiter/Waitress	28
Computer Programmer	61	Bartender	25
Sociologist	61	Janitor	22
Police Officer	60	Shoe Shiner	09
Actor	58		

General Social Surveys 1972-1996: *Cumulative Codebook* (Chicago: National Opinion Research Center, 1996), 1077-1085.

TABLE 7:2
Total Money Income of Families in the United States by Race/Ethnicity 1999.

TOTAL MONEY INCOME	PERCENT OF FAMILIES			
	TOTAL FAMILIES	WHITE FAMILIES	BLACK FAMILIES	HISPANIC FAMILIES
Under $5,000	2.9	2.3	6.3	3.9
$5,000 - 9,999	6.3	5.5	12.2	8.0
$10,000 - 14,999	7.3	7.0	10.1	9.7
$15,000 - 24,999	14.0	13.9	16.4	18.9
$25,000 - 34,999	12.7	12.6	13.7	15.8
$35,000 - 49,999	15.7	16.0	14.7	16.7
$50,000 - 74,999	18.5	19.1	14.0	15.2
$75,000 - 99,999	10.3	10.8	6.5	6.7
$100,000 & over	12.3	12.9	6.1	5.2
Total	100.0	100.0	100.0	100.0
Median Income	$40,816	$42,504	$27,910	$30,735

Source: U.S. Bureau of the Census, Current Population Reports, Series P60-209, *Money Income in the United States: 1999* (Washington, D.C.: U.S. Government Printing Office, 2000), Table 13, p. 60 and Table B-2, Appendix B, p. B-3.

seen, only 12.3 percent of American families reported $100,000 or more. In the same year, 30.5 percent of all Americans (more than 80 million people) had incomes below $25,000. The median family income in 1999 was $40,816. For Black and Hispanic families, it was considerably lower. In America today, more than 30 million people live below the poverty line (defined roughly as $16,000 for a family of four).[12]

EDUCATION

Both amount and kind of education affect the social class ranking that one is likely to attain. Higher education increases the likelihood of entrance into more prestigious occupations. Indeed, in many cases, it is a prerequisite (medicine and law, for example). Education often opens doors of opportunity that otherwise would remain closed. It also causes changes in a person's lifestyle, attitudes, goals, values, even speech patterns, which are important in terms of class recognition and acceptance. Education is often considered a requirement for "refinement." In fact, some sociologists believe that level of education (rather than occupation) provides the most important single clue to a person's social class.[13]

Education is closely tied to both occupation and income. All three provide fairly reliable

Long after the Civil Rights Movement of the 1960s, racial/ethnic minorities are still disproportionately poor.

clues to the total way of life that distinguishes social classes. However, the three are not always highly correlated. Some well-educated persons, for example, receive low incomes and work at various occupational prestige levels. The three criteria are widely used in social science research because they are readily available from census reports and are fairly easy to objectify. They also illustrate some of the confusion surrounding the delineation of an American class structure.

THE SUBJECTIVE NATURE OF SOCIAL CLASS

What is your social class? Most Americans categorize themselves as belonging to the *middle class*, despite how more objective criteria might classify them. Class in America is a state of mind more than a formal structure, and most Americans, regardless of income or education, have a middle-class mentality.

The "homogenizing" of lifestyles in America is one of the reasons class is not more formally structured. The externals of class have become and are becoming less and less distinctive. Dress and language differences are diminishing. A family-owned home, money in the bank, and a college education for the kids were once prerogatives of the rich; today, they are available to a larger segment of American society. The media have contributed to the "leveling out" of class differences. In many ways we have evolved from a *middle-class* to a *middle-mass* society.

THE IMPACT OF CLASS

Let's review for a moment. We have indicated that in God's Kingdom, social class is irrelevant. In fact, our occupations, education, or income have nothing to do with our salvation. We've also noted that social class seems to defy objective measures: social class is whatever we think it is. If social class does not exist for God, and there are few scientific measures of class, does it really exist? Certainly (in light of the fact that in America we can tell little about one's social class by observing a person's clothing, car, or other consumables), we would wonder if social class still exists. However, the consequences of social class are very real. One of the reasons sociologists study class is because of its impact on individual life chances. For example, one's physical and mental health, life expectancy, education, occupation, voting behavior, marriage choices, family size, divorce probability, religious affiliations, social life, etc., are all affected (in most cases strongly so) by class background.[14]

Statistics show that life expectancy is lowest and infant death rates are highest among the lower-class groups. Lower income persons are also more likely to die from violence, on death row, and in war.[15]

Mental health is also highly correlated with class background. The higher one's social class, the less the probability of mental illness, contrary to popular belief. Certainly, treatment for mental disorder is associated with class position—the best care being most available to the upper classes.[16]

Both education and occupation are strongly affected by class. The higher the class, the greater the educational opportunity. In terms of occupation, lower-class persons most often enter unskilled or semiskilled occupations. Middle- and upper-class persons most often move into professional or managerial positions. The poor work long hours at hard work for low pay, when jobs are even available. Worse, they are made to feel inferior and blamed for their own poverty. In actuality, most poor people are born into poverty, and social factors make it extremely difficult to rise to a higher level.[17]

Although recent research suggests considerable change, social class remains a major determinant of political attitudes and voting behavior. Members of the lower class typically have voted for the Democrats. They are economically liberal; they want what they *do not* have. Upper-class persons more often vote for Republicans. They are economically conservative; they want to keep what they *do* have. It is important to note, in this regard, that the lower-class people who have the greatest need for political power are those least likely to exercise their right to vote.

Even marriage stability is affected by class. The lower one's class, the greater the likelihood of divorce, separation, or desertion. Family life is more conflict-ridden for the poor. Lower-class persons marry younger and have more children than other class levels.

Social class even has a major impact on how we practice our religious faith. Upper-class persons tend to belong to religious groups that are more formal in their worship styles. Both upper- and middle-class people tend to respond to religion on an intellectual basis. Lower-class people respond more on an emotional level and are attracted more to fundamentalist sect groups.

Community involvement is also strongly affected by class position. The higher one's class, the more likely one is to be involved in community affairs. It is middle-class and upper-class people who are most actively involved in civic groups, club programs, political parties, school boards, and the great variety of other programs through which modern communities operate.

VERTICAL VS. HORIZONTAL MOBILITY

By definition, class implies the *opportunity* for mobility, although *unequal* opportunity is evident in any complex society. *Social mobility* is movement from one social class to another. **Horizontal mobility** involves movement within

Social class has a great impact on one's life chances. What are the life chances of these children compared to your children?

a particular level with no appreciable change in class ranking. A computer specialist for a large oil company who resigns for personal reasons and is hired by a large bank (at the same salary level) is demonstrating horizontal mobility. On the other hand, **vertical mobility** is defined as movement up or down the class scale. It *does* involve a social class change. Vertical mobility is popularly known as "climbing the ladder to success." In this type of movement, the climber achieves a higher status than his ascribed birth status.

GLOBAL INEQUALITY

We have seen that stratification (and inequality) is an important part of American society. But this is only one part of a much larger context of global poverty. In our world there is a vast difference between the lives of the majority, who are poor, and the minority, who are rich. There is a large (and growing) gap between the "haves" and the "have nots"—where the richest 20% of the earth's population controls 85% of the world's wealth, and the poorest 20% controls less than 2%. This is a reality that must be faced in any review of the status of the world's population. This difference in wealth is even more disturbing when other statistics are revealed. Out of approximately six billion people, more than two billion have no access to adequate health care—resulting in eleven million children under age five dying every year from preventable diseases. About two and a half billion people lack access to basic sanitation, and one billion are not able to obtain clean water. Two billion individuals live without adequate electricity, and over one billion survive on less than one dollar per day.[18] The comparative wealth of the West, especially in America, is a huge contrast to the harsh circumstances in which many people live.

Why has there been so much more economic growth in Western nations? Why have they gotten wealthy while many other nations have stayed poor? Several historical reasons have been given for the advance of European societies, beginning with basic environmental factors: the availability of land in relation to the population size, as well as the abundance of natural resources and the ability to produce enough food.[19] In addition, there are social factors: the rise of literacy and the availability of books, combined with openness to change and innovation. Technological factors are also thought to be significant: the use of science to create new tools and (eventually) machines, in addition to better navigation and transportation methods.[20]

All these reasons lay a foundation for the wide range of economic factors that contributed to the dominance of the West: the growth of private property, more markets with the rise of cities, and greater incentives through economic freedoms. These circum-

Despite their living conditions, these children are loved and valued by God.

FIGURE 7:1

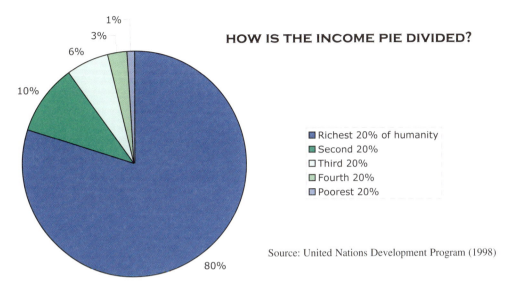

This figure demonstrates the dramatic inequality of income in the world.

stances worked together with the environmental, social, and technological elements to create a much higher level of living.

As history has demonstrated, the rise of industrialization and colonial expansion in the eighteenth and nineteenth centuries expanded the economic reach and dominance of the West. This situation continues to this day, with a resulting stratification of poor countries and rich countries. The core of the capitalistic worldview is based on strong individualism, with each person free to work for his or her own advantage. Along with historical advantages, this has led to large differences among the peoples of the world, with resulting inequalities.

THEORIES ON POVERTY

But we may still ask: why are so many people in the world today so poor? Several answers have been given, many that build on the structural-functional and conflict theories we have already reviewed. Here we will focus on just two of the most influential theories. The first is **modernization theory**, which takes its name from the assumption that history is a movement from a "traditional" to a "modern" way of life. It is based on the social thinking of sociologists such as Emile Durkheim, who were concerned with the differentiation of labor and the resulting weakening of social groups.[21] It is also influenced by the work of Talcott Parsons, who emphasized the interdependency of all aspects of society and the differentiation of functional roles in "modern" industrial social systems.[22] Americans have come to believe that their economic experience was the model for *all* other "developing" nations to follow; in other words, all nations should copy the path taken by the United States. Parsons and others believed that modernization takes place when the economy is separated from other sections of a society (such as the religious institutions), and therefore becomes more "rational" and advanced.[23]

Another sociologist who contributed to the

idea of modernization was Max Weber, who looked at this issue from a religious perspective. His main interest was how Protestant (especially Calvinist) theology contained features that led to rational, individualistic economic activity for profit.[24] Weber believed that Protestantism led to the attitudes and values necessary for the growth of capitalism, and thus to "modern" society. He stressed that this "Protestant work ethic" led to individual achievement and the material progress of the whole society.[25] Another writer who built on Weber's ideas was David McClelland, who proposed that certain societies (especially American society) have an *achievement motivation*—an individual's desire for personal achievement.[26] McClelland believed that when this motivation is highly valued and common in a society, everyone benefits from increased economic production.

In all these theories, sociologists (like everyone else) were greatly influenced by their own cultural assumptions. For example, some social observers examined such variables as a society's time focus (future as opposed to past), concepts of authority (individual freedom as opposed to rigid hierarchy), and attitudes toward work (rewards for innovation as opposed to insistence on conformity).[27] In each of these areas, the Western way was perceived to be better.

Modernization theory was especially important in the 1950s and 1960s, as many new nations were established in former colonies around the world. The United States was very interested in promoting development through capitalism, and assumed that assistance was needed from the West to help these new countries modernize.[28] Underlying this assumption was the conviction that the United States was the best example of success, and that the Western model was the one other nations should follow.

But these ideas have been criticized by many social scientists, who questioned whether modernization should be equated with the American way of life.[29] The concept of *social development* began to replace economic growth as a measure of progress. In particular, critics of modernization theory were opposed to its acceptance of Western superiority and the idea that all nations had to follow the same (Western) path to development. Some researchers criticized the notion that transformation of developing countries would automatically take place through the *diffusion* of Western economic and technological methods.[30]

Therefore, new ideas began to emerge about the reasons for poverty around the world. Gradually more attention was paid to the unbalanced relationships between rich and poor countries and how this caused more poverty. This view eventually came to be called **dependency theory**. In some ways it is similar to conflict theory. Its central point is that certain (rich) nations are in the center of the world's economic and sociopolitical systems, while other (poor) nations are on the outside and are dependent for their survival on what the powerful countries want. The rich nations will exploit the poor ones for their economic and political advantage.[31]

Based in part on a Marxist analysis, dependency theory sees poverty as being caused by external factors. Rich nations take raw materials and exploit cheap labor, setting up unequal bal-

This Mexican child has become dependent on the handouts of others. Dependency theory is critical of rich nations handing economic relief to poor nations because it does little to truly develop the people.

As a Christian, what is your obligation to these people? Is sharing the gospel enough?

themselves or demonstrate independent or self-sustained economic growth.[34] It places them in a situation from which they will never be able to rise above their poverty. It also fails to produce a new definition of "progress"—is the Western one the only valid idea? It seems that dependency theory, like modernization theory, subtly accepts the conviction that to advance, other countries must follow the American model.

To greatly oversimplify these two theories, it can be said that dependency theory blames the world's rich for the problem of poverty, while modernization theory blames the poor. Clearly, each position leads to very different approaches to development and to different solutions to solve world poverty.

A CHRISTIAN RESPONSE

ances of trade. They send profits out of the poor countries, and keep these nations subordinate.[32] They also ruin the natural environments of poor countries for their own advantage.[33] Dependency theory sees poverty as a *created* condition, not as the fault of the poor. Nations are seen as occupying a class-like position in the world economy, with unequal access to resources and power. Here we see social stratification on a global scale.

Critics of dependency theory say that it seems to question the ability of poor nations to help

Some authors, particularly Christian ones, have focused on the human systems that keep people poor.[35] In this they are influenced by structural-functional theory. They believe that God's concern for the poor (expressed throughout the Bible) should be a model for all Christians. Injustice of any kind should be resisted. For example, it's clearly wrong when poor countries have to sell their resources at low prices, while having to buy expensive finished products from richer countries. Most of all, Christians should value people over property, and try to bring about more equality in how nations are treated in the global economy. Unfortunately, many Western Christians strive to become part of a higher class, and this may cause them to be less concerned with the needs of the world's poor.[36] What should the Christian response be?

As we said at the beginning of this chapter, God sees everyone the same. People are not better because they have more wealth, or have higher status, or live in a certain country. Those who live in poor nations are not "lower" than Americans. They are not inferior or less important. Rather, they are often poor because of historical or current events beyond their control. They are still loved by God, and He has as much concern for them as for each of us. This is the starting point for any worldview that is based on biblical foundations.

Christians then need to be focused on this world and have a realistic view of the problem of global inequality. They should "wake up to the Biblical alternative to the Western dream," as Tom Sine stated.[37] This alternative in many ways is the reverse of the American idea of success, for it depends on God, not human technology. While a Christian view recognizes the benefits of market-oriented economics, it doesn't see personal consumption as a way to find meaning or happiness. And while it sees the importance of each individual, it focuses more on the concept of community. This makes the Christian view one that values people for more than their economic worth.

Many Western Christians confuse the secular idea of "progress" with the advance of God's Kingdom. But this fails to realize that the Christian's main goal is not to sustain Western culture, but rather it is to build a Christian culture that has biblical values. Instead of seeking worldly status, Christians should seek God's way. And instead of seeking worldly goods, Christians should consider what has *eternal* value.

overview

- Inequality leads to status differences in every society. When those differences are institutionalized (stabilized) into hierarchical arrangements, we speak of social stratification.

- Two contrasting schools of thought explain the development of such institutionalized inequality: structural-functionalism and conflict theory. Functionalists believe that stratification is essential for the well-being of society. Some positions are more important than others. They require special skills or background preparation and, therefore, deserve special rewards.

- On the other hand, conflict theorists describe society as a system of conflicting interest groups. Inequality is seen as a matter of the powerful exploiting the powerless.

- In the United States, occupation, income, and education are major determinants of class placement. Occupation is usually cited as the single most important index of class.

- Vertical mobility is the hallmark of an open-class society. Certainly, much of it occurs in this country. However, most mobility is between adjacent class levels. The "rags to riches" success idealized by the American Dream is a rare exception, not a frequent occurrence. Still, our belief in equality remains strong.

- Two views of global poverty have been promoted. Modernization theory sees the problem as a lack of economic and technological "progress"; dependency theory sees the source of poverty as poorer nations being overly dependent and controlled by stronger nations.

key concepts

conflict theory
Stratification theory that conceives of society as a system of conflicting interest groups; suggests that social order is based on organized coercion.

dependency theory
An explanation of global poverty that says nations become poor when they are denied access to self-development strategies because of colonialism and economic dominance by well-developed nations.

horizontal mobility
Movement within a particular social stratum.

modernization theory
An explanation of global poverty that says nations are poor because they have not "modernized" by adopting Western economic systems and technology.

social class
An economic interest group that has both social recognition and a sense of in-group awareness.

social differentiation
The separation of social categories such as race, gender, or age.

social stratification
The institutionalization or stabilization of status differences into hierarchical arrangements.

structural-functionalism
Stratification theory that justifies inequality as necessary to the efficient functioning of society. Through unequal rewards society assures itself that the most important positions are filled by the most competent people.

vertical mobility
Movement up or down the class scale.

endnotes

1. Kingsley Davis and Wilbert E. Moore, "Some Principles of Stratification," *American Sociological Review* 10 (April 1945): 242-49.
2. Burke D. Grandjean and Frank D. Bean, "The Davis-Moore Theory and Perceptions of Stratification: Some Relevant Evidence," *Social Forces* 54 (September 1975): 166-80.
3. Beth Ensminger Vanfossen, *The Structure of Social Inequality* (Boston: Little, Brown & Co., 1979), 30.
4. Bruce J. Cohen, *Introduction to Sociology* (New York: Schaum's Outline Series, McGraw-Hill Book Co., 1979), 114.
5. Vanfossen, *Social Inequality*, 33.
6. Ibid., 46-50.
7. Kaare Svalastoga, "Social Differentiation," in *Handbook of Modern Sociology*, ed. R.E.L. Faris (Chicago: Rand McNally Publishing, 1964), 533.
8. *Selected Works of Mao Tse-Tung*, vol. 1 (Peking: Foreign Language Press, 1967), 343.
9. R.W. Dellinger, "Keeping Tabs on the Joneses," *Human Behavior* 6 (November 1977): 24.
10. Vanfossen, *Social Inequality*, chapters 3 and 7.
11. U.S. Bureau of the Census, Current Population Reports, Series P60-209, *Money Income in the United States: 1999* (Washington, DC: U.S. Government Printing Office, 2000), Table 10, 40-45.
12. Ibid.
13. Andrew Hacker, "The Boy Who Doesn't Go to College," *New York Times Magazine* 24 (June 1962): 11ff.
14. Cohen, *Sociology,* 113-14.
15. Vanfossen, *Social Inequality*, 354.
16. H.B. Hollingshead, R. Ellis, and C. Kirby, "Social Mobility and Mental Illness," *American Sociological Review* 19 (October 1954): 577-84.
17. Michael Harrington, *The New American Poverty* (New York: Viking/Penguin, 1985), 13.
18. United Nations Development Program, *Human Development Report 2001* (Cary, NC: Oxford University Press, 2001).
19. Carlo M. Cipolla, *Before the Industrial Revolution: European Society and Economy, 1000–1700*, 3rd ed. (New York: W. W. Norton & Co., 1993).
20. Julian Simon, *The Great Breakthrough and Its Cause* (Ann Arbor, MI: University of Michigan Press, 2001).
21. Emile Durkheim, *The Rules of Sociological Method* (New York: Free Press, 1982).
22. Talcott Parsons, *Essays in Sociological Theory*, rev. ed. (New York: Free Press, 1954).
23. Eva Etzioni-Halevey, *Social Change: The Advent and Maturation of Modern Society* (London: Routledge & Kegan Paul, 1981).
24. Sidney Burell, "Calvinism, Capitalism, and the Middle Classes: Some Afterthoughts on an Old Problem," in *The Protestant Ethic and Modernization: A Comparative View*, ed. Shmuel Eisenstadt (New York: Basic Books, Inc., 1968).
25. Leslie Sklair, *The Sociology of Progress* (London: Routledge & Kegan Paul, 1970).
26. David McClelland, *The Achieving Society* (Princeton, NJ: Van Nostrand Publishing, 1976).
27. Lawrence Harrison, "Underdevelopment is a State of Mind," in *Development and Underdevelopment: The Political Economy of Inequality*, ed. Mitchell Seligson and John Passe-Smith (Boulder, CO: Lynne Rienner, Publishers, 1993).
28. Andrew Webster, *Introduction to the Sociology of Development* (London: Macmillan Publishers Ltd., 1984).
29. Jessie Lutz and Salah El-Shaklis, eds., *Tradition and Modernity: The Role of Traditionalism in the Modernization Process* (Washington DC: University Press of America, Inc., 1982).
30. Ankie Hoogvelt, *The Sociology of Developing Societies,* 2nd ed. (London: Macmillan Education Ltd., 1978).
31. Raymond Boudon, *The Analysis of Ideology* (Chicago: University of Chicago Press, 1986).
32. Paul Baran and Paul Sweezy, *Monopoly Capital: An Essay on the American Economic and Social Order* (New York:

Monthly Review Press, 1966).

33. Lester Brown, ed., *State of the World 2001* (New York: W. W. Norton & Company, 2001).
34. John Browett, "The Newly Industrialized Countries and Radical Theories of Development," *World Development* 13 (1985): 7.
35. Ronald Sider, *Rich Christians in an Age of Hunger* (Dallas: Word Publishing, 1997).
36. Linford Stutzman, *With Jesus in the World: Mission in Modern Affluent Societies* (Scottsdale, PA: Herald Press, 1992).
37. Tom Sine, *Wild Hope: Crises Facing the Human Community on the Threshold of the 21st Century* (Dallas: Word Publishing, 1991).

additional resources

Peter M. Blau and Otis Dudley Duncan, *The American Occupational Structure* (New York: John Wiley & Sons, 1967).

Richard Centers, "The American Class Structure," in *Readings in Social Psychology*, ed. Theodore M. Newcomb and Eugene L. Hartley (New York: Henry Holt & Co., Inc., 1947), 481-93.

Joan Ferrante, *Sociology: A Global Perspective* (Belmont, CA: Wadsworth Publishing Co., 1992). See especially Chapter 2 ("Theoretical Perspectives") and 9 ("Social Stratification and the Effects of Race, Class, and Gender").

J. O. Hertzler, "Some Tendencies toward a Closed Class System in the United States," *Social Forces* 30 (March 1952): 313-23.

Diana Kendall, *Sociology in Our Times*, 3rd ed. (Belmont, CA: Wadsworth/Thompson, 2001).

Gerhard E. Lenski, *Power and Privilege: A Theory of Social Stratification* (New York: McGraw Hill Book Co., 1966).

Gustavo Logos, *International Stratification and Underdeveloped Countries* (Chapel Hill: University of North Carolina Press, 1963).

John Macionis, *Sociology*, 7th ed. (Upper Saddle River, NJ: Prentice-Hall, 1999).

John E. Schwarz and Thomas J. Volgy, *The Forgotten Americans* (New York: W. W. Norton & Company, 1992).

Larry J. Siegel and Joseph J. Senna, *Juvenile Delinquency: Theory, Practice, and Law* (Belmont, CA: Wadsworth/Thompson, 2000).

Jennifer Cook Sterling, "The American Dream, Then and Now," *Newsweek Education Program*, 12 (New York: Newsweek, Inc., 1993).

W. Lloyd Warner and Paul S. Hunt, *The Social Life of a Modern Community* (New Haven: Yale University Press, 1941).

CHAPTER EIGHT

Race and Ethnic Stratification

chapter outline

I. Definitions
   A. Race
   B. Ethnicity
   C. What is a social minority?

II. Why racial/ethnic stratification?
   A. Structural-functional perspective
   B. Conflict perspective
   C. Why prejudice?

III. Social dynamics of race and ethnic relations
   A. Assimilation
   B. Pluralism
   C. Segregation
   D. Extermination or genocide

IV. How Christians can change the world

biblical reflection

"There is no longer Jew or Greek, there is no longer slave or free, there is no longer male and female; for all of you are one in Christ Jesus."

—Galatians 3:28

Racial and ethnic stratification is a particularly insidious form of social sin. It is clear that we were all created with equal potential to be children of God. Yet we purposely impose social barriers that prevent certain categories of people from fulfilling their potential. In their attempt to reconstruct the social reality to give themselves more power, some groups go to great lengths to pretend that they are somehow "better" than "those" people. It's a silly game we play and it betrays our insecurity with our own salvation. In the last chapter we challenged the taken-for-granted notion that some people "deserve" more status than others. Humans sin when we forget that we are all God's children. In this chapter we will look at two of the many forms this insidious game takes: racism and ethnicism.

DEFINITIONS

RACE

Race is an ascribed status. It consists of biologically inherited characteristics such as skin pigmentation, hair texture, eye shape and color. Like flowers, human beings come in many colors, shapes, and sizes. Scientists have attempted to classify people into races or discrete biological categories with similar physical characteris-

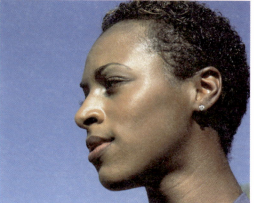

Does race really exist, or is it simply a socially constructed reality? What is the race of each of these women? How do you know?

tics. To date, however, there is great variation in thought and little agreement among biologists, geneticists, physical anthropologists, and physiologists about the empirical or factual basis of race. Race as a scientific biological concept is very inaccurate.[1] Ashley Montague, a physical anthropologist, noted that while some scientists find only two races, others have found as many as two thousand. In his opinion, there are at least forty races based on scientific facts.[2]

Yet people are not blind to or unconcerned about physical differences. They notice skin colors, body types, hair textures, and facial features. At times, in various places and for various reasons, legislative bodies have instituted legal or administrative racial categories. For example, in the late apartheid system of South Africa, people were legally classified as White, Coloured, Asian, or Black, and this affected people's lives profoundly. The Sandra Laing story in Excerpt 8:1 is a dramatic example of apartheid.[3]

EXCERPT 8:1
Forbidden Love Outlives Apartheid

A black woman is reunited with her white mother after apartheid kept them apart for 30 years.

It took 30 years, the death of her father and the end of apartheid for Sandra Laing – a black child born to white parents – to be reunited with her mother. The two were torn apart by a genetic quirk, in an enduring tragedy of South Africa's racist system.

Last week Sandra's mother, Sannie, wept as she finally kissed the daughter she had turned her back on.

"At last. My daughter, Sandra," she said as they were reunited at a Pretoria retirement home. "Can it be true. Is it really my daughter?" All Sandra Laing could muster through her tears was: "Mammie, mammie."

The two women did not even know if the other was alive until a few days ago, when years of heartache came to an end.

Sandra Laing was born in 1955 in Piet Retief, a small town as conservative as any in apartheid South Africa. Her Afrikaans-speaking parents were white, as were her two brothers. But Sandra's skin was notably darker, and became more so as the years passed. Her tightly curled black hair helped seal her fate.

"In 1966, when I was 10, the police came to take me away from my school. Mr. Van Tonder, the principal, said I was not white and could not stay. Two policemen drove me to my father's shop in Panbult," she said.

"They said I was being expelled because I looked different. My father cried," she told the Johannesburg *Sunday Times* recently.

Why Sandra was born black has never been explained, but probably has roots in the considerable "inter-breeding" that took place after the Dutch settled in South Africa at the beginning of the 18th century.

Nine other white schools refused to accept Sandra. The state tried to reclassify her as "coloured," or mixed-race. Sandra's father fought the decision until the laws were changed to say that the child of two white parents must be classified as white.

Sandra's parents had blood tests to prove she was their daughter. The education department then ruled that she could be readmitted to her old school but recommended that she did not become a border.

Yet being classified as white did not prevent restaurants and bus drivers from turning Sandra away. Neighbours shunned her. She was not even welcome at the local church.

"I felt a lot of pain and thought it would be best if I left and stayed with people I felt happier with," she said.

(continued on page 124)

Chapter Eight: Race and Ethnic Stratification

> At 16 Sandra left home to live with Petrus Zwane, a black Zulu-speaker. In 1973 she went home with her newborn son, but Mrs. Laing gave her daughter a box of baby clothes and told her not to return.
>
> "My father was furious because I married a black man. He threatened to shoot first me and then himself if I ever put foot over his threshold again," she said.
>
> Apartheid officials told Sandra she was entitled to a white identity card but that they would take away her two children by Mr. Zwane because different races could not live in the same house.
>
> Sandra spent the next nine years getting herself reclassified as "coloured" so she could legally live with her son and daughter.
>
> After Sandra's father died in 1988, she wrote to her mother. Mrs. Laing wrote back to say she was moving [to a new] house and would not reveal her new address. Even her brothers, Adriaan and Leon, refused to speak to her.
>
> Sandra had given up hope of finding her mother until their story was featured in the Johannesburg *Sunday Times* as a personal tragedy of apartheid. The newspaper helped Sandra, who now runs a creche in Tasaki township on the East Rand, to search for her mother.
>
> Eventually, police records led to the Pretoria retirement home where Mrs. Laing has lived for years.
>
> — *The Guardian,* January 24, 2000

Today we are still required to indicate our race categories on numerous forms, a practice that is quite inaccurate and arbitrary. Many people do not fit neatly into the categories. For example, how would you classify a person with Irish American and Japanese American parents? What about German American and Filipino American parents, or German American and African American parents?

ETHNICITY

Ethnic groups are categories of people with a distinctive cultural heritage that is usually reflected in national origin, names, language, religion, dress, food habits, mannerisms, and lifestyle. Ethnicity is usually quite noticeable in the first generation, but as acculturation sets in, the distinctiveness declines in succeeding generations. For example, while a foreign language may be the first generation's mother tongue, succeeding generations usually switch to English.

Ethnic groups have enriched American society enormously. This is evident around the nation in city names, street names, house styles, foods, and music. Parrillo writes, "Multiculturalism is neither new nor a threat to the stabilization and integration of American society. It is an old, continuing presence that strengthens not weakens, enriches not diminishes, nourishes not drains, a civilization whose character and temperament have long reflected the diversity of its people."[4]

In America a marked tendency has been to lump people (native and immigrant) into larger categories. Saxons, Scots, Swedes, Norwegians, Finns, Germans, Dutch, and other northern and western Europeans became WASPs (White Anglo-Saxon Protestants).[5] People of Italian, southern German, Polish and other eastern and southern European origins that are predominantly Roman Catholics became White Ethnics. The Navajos, the Cherokees, the Choctaws, the Seminoles and other indigenous people were called Indians and then Native Americans. The Japanese, the Chinese, East Indian, Pakistani, Filipino, Vietnamese and other peoples from eastern and southern Asia are designated Asians. People from various southern African countries, Jamaica, Haiti, the West Indies, and Latin

America are called Blacks or African Americans. People from countries around the Mediterranean Sea are called Middle Eastern Americans. Finally, Mexicans, Central and South Americans are called Hispanics or Latina/Latino Americans.

Because of this tendency in America to group people, individuals have to deal with the reality of ethnicity, even though they may not identify strongly with—or have the same interests, priorities, or goals of—the broader categories of people. For example, Cuban, Puerto Rican, and Mexican Americans are considered Hispanics or Latinas/Latinos, but they have distinctive identities, cultural traits, and interests. They were not equally concerned about such issues as Proposition 187 in California (designed to deny public education and certain social services to illegal aliens), or refugees from Cuba who were taken to the U. S. Canal Zone in Panama until a decision could be made about their immigration status. Similar examples abound for Haitians, Jamaicans, and Ethiopians, or for the Japanese, the Chinese, and Filipinos, or for the Navajos, the Hopis, and the Choctaws—or for any number of other groups.

The connection between race and ethnicity needs careful consideration. In some cases, ethnic groups include several races. For example, Cuban Americans or Puerto Ricans may be of European, Middle Eastern, Asian, African or Native American backgrounds or various combinations of these. In other cases, some races include several ethnic groups.

WHAT IS A SOCIAL MINORITY?

The status of racial or ethnic **minority** has little to do with numbers. For example, Blacks in South Africa are a numerical majority, yet remain a social minority because they have been systematically denied access to positions of power in the society. Minority groups have several characteristics:

1. They are distinct from the **dominant group** in some way.

2. They compete with the dominant group for scarce resources, such as land, employment, and housing.

3. They are less powerful than the dominant group.

4. They suffer prejudice and discrimination from the dominant group.

5. They are more self-conscious than the dominant group. They have a greater "we-feeling."

Minority status may be based on appearance, behavior, and/or beliefs.[6] The stigma of some minority groups is attached to such physical or biological differences as skin color. Women, older people, and physically and mentally challenged people are now called the "new minorities." Additionally, certain forms of behavior may be a stigma, restricting life chances and influencing social interactions. For example, homosexuals, drug addicts, mentally ill, and welfare recipients often suffer prejudice and discrimination because many (in both the dominant and minority groups) find their behavior offensive and/or socially unacceptable. Finally, some minorities are unacceptable to the dominant groups (and to many minority group members) because of their beliefs (e.g., political or religious beliefs).

The establishment and maintenance of racial and ethnic social stratification systems require certain necessary conditions. First, there must be *readily discernible physical and/or cultural differences* between racial and/or ethnic groups. Groups have used any number of traits to distinguish themselves from others: for example, physical features, religion, language, and food habits. In America, whiteness became the deciding factor years ago. As early as 1751,

Benjamin Franklin was writing that Spaniards, Italians, Russians, Germans, and Swedes were all "of what we call a swarthy complexion," while the Saxons and the English were "the principal body of white people on the face of the earth."[7] A German traveler in 1809, noticing the similarity between the notions of whiteness in America and nobility in Europe, wrote: "In a country dominated by whites those families of whom it is assumed that they are least intermingled with Negro or mulatto blood are the ones most highly honored; just as it is considered a kind of nobility in Spain to be descended neither from Jews nor Moors."[8] In America, whiteness still has its privileges and the symbolism is most powerful. Many Whites seem surprisingly unaware of this.

Competition over scarce and valued resources is a second necessary condition for the establishment and maintenance of a racial and ethnic stratification system. There has been and continues to be much competition between the dominant group and minority groups over land, education, employment, political power, housing, medical services, recreational services, and other valued resources. In addition, minority groups often compete or contend with one another over scarce resources; for example, the tense relationships between African Americans and Korean American grocers.[9]

A third necessary condition for the establishment and maintenance of a racial and ethnic social stratification system is *unequal power between at least two groups*. In America, White Anglo-Saxon Protestants became the dominant or majority group and were able to deal with other racial and ethnic groups as they pleased. This was not the case in early American history when European settlers received help and traded with many native peoples. Even after the Thirteen Colonies declared their independence from England in 1776 and established the United States, they continued to treat Native Americans as nations and signed treaties with them. As the colonies/states grew in power over the years, however, they began dealing with Native Americans as they wished—practically ignoring the Native Americans' opinions on matters.

While not necessary, a final condition that certainly reinforces a racial and ethnic stratification system is an *ideology* that one group is superior to other groups. Ideologies usually contain several elements. First, ideologies identify a society's problems. Second, they identify the causes of the problem. Third, they identify the solution and, finally, they call for a commitment to the struggle to save the society. For example, Nazism faced war-devastated Germany, inflation, unemployment, and numerous problems after World War I. It identified Jews and other allegedly inferior peoples as the cause of the problems. It then offered the "Final Solution" as the cure, requiring the German people to commit to the struggle to save Germany.

Stereotypes play a significant role in ideologies. Unable to distinguish among individuals, "in-group" members see "out-group" members as silhouettes in white, black, yellow, brown, etc. Stereotypes may be positive or negative and they often fuel the negative conceptions in prejudices. Robert K. Merton noted years ago that the same characteristics admired in members of the dominant group may be despised in members of minority groups.

WHY RACIAL AND ETHNIC STRATIFICATION?

THE STRUCTURAL-FUNCTIONAL PERSPECTIVE

Racial and ethnic stratification functions to protect the privilege of the dominant group. As a society becomes more complex, diversity is sometimes seen as a threat to stability. That is why stratification becomes more intense as a community grows into a large city. In a small town, members of racial and ethnic groups will probably live near members of the dominant group; all social classes tend to live together. As the population grows, however, there is a tendency for differing groups to segregate into separate neighborhoods on the basis of race, ethnicity, and social class.

Segregation of races results in neighborhoods with sharply different lifestyles. Majorities often perceive that minorities have inferior values that lead to lower motivation and achievement. Discrimination appears functional. Some may cite evidence indicating that since some racial and ethnic groups have lower educational attainment, it appears reasonable that they will earn less. A higher crime rate among some racial/ethnic groups may be a function of such lower educational attainment.

From a functional perspective, then, racial/ethnic discrimination is functional because minorities have values that are sometimes dysfunctional to the society. This is the same argument cited in the previous chapter about the "culture of poverty"; i.e., racial/ethnic minorities are more likely to be raised in an "inferior culture" which transmits values and norms leading to lower achievement.

CONFLICT THEORY PERSPECTIVE

Recall the previous chapter's critique of the functional perspective of stratification. Once again, the conflict theorist would say that the functionalist is "blaming the victim"; i.e., blaming minorities themselves for the prejudice and discrimination against them. The conflict theorist would say we are being very ethnocentric by claiming that racial/ethnic neighborhoods have an inferior culture.

Instead, the conflict theorist looks to the social structure as the source of discrimination. The structure of segregation results in fewer opportunities for minorities. They are often made to feel uncomfortable in institutions that are predominantly White. These subtle forms of discrimination are called *institutional racism*. For example, Black students are often reluctant to attend a predominantly White university because they may wonder, "What are my opportunities for dating people of the opposite sex?" or "How can I develop good relationships with these people who speak and act so differently from me?"

Prejudice is a social disease that is passed from one generation to the next.

A functionalist may blame minorities themselves for making such decisions that exclude them from opportunities for achievement. However, the conflict theorist would look at ways in which the predominantly White university is an unfriendly environment for diversity.

The situation is similar to the German fable of a lion, a donkey, and a fox that go on a hunt. At the end of the hunt, the lion orders the donkey to share. The donkey says: "One for you, one for you, and one for me," giving an equal share to each hunter. Angrily and in an awesome display of power, the lion roars, kills the donkey, and orders the fox to share. Trembling in fear, the fox takes a small item and gives everything else to the lion. Beaming with contentment, the lion roars again and says: "You really know how to share! Who taught you how to share?" The fox responds, "The dead donkey!" In conflict perspective, racial and ethnic stratification is a "win-lose" situation. The powerful dominant group takes what it wants and leaves the leftovers for the minority. The happiness of the dominant group results in the suffering of racial and/or ethnic minority groups.

WHY PREJUDICE?

Much research has been conducted in an effort to discover why people are prejudiced. Some writers have suggested that prejudice is caused by personality factors such as frustration over life's challenges and difficulties, and a need for aggression against others who are in a weaker position. These *authoritarian personalities* tend to have rigid views of the world and are intolerant of people different from them. Adorno and others have found that people with little education and those raised by very strict parents tend to develop authoritarian personalities. Many of these people also hold strict, conservative religious views.[10] This finding—that religious people tend to be more prejudiced than less religious people—is troubling to many of us with a strong religious commitment. It seems so contrary to the example of Jesus Christ, who related so easily and genuinely to everyone He dealt with, treating each person as a unique human being.

Another suggested cause of prejudice is *lack of contact*, which leads to ignorance of other groups. It does appear that if interaction increases between people prejudiced against one another, the prejudice decreases—but only when the interaction is among people of fairly equal economic status. If the statuses are unequal, prejudices are actually reinforced. Prejudices are most likely to decrease when out-group members: 1) have traits that challenge negative stereotypes, and 2) are encouraged to interact in productive meetings in which members of different groups work toward common goals.[11]

While **prejudice** is an attitude, **discrimination** is differential or special treatment of a particular group or group members on the basis of perceived physical, behavioral, and/or belief differences. Discrimination may be positive and beneficial, as when we design buildings to provide maximum accessibility to physically challenged people like the blind, deaf, short, or those confined to a wheelchair. This enables them to realize their full human potential and make valuable contributions to society.

Discrimination is negative and detrimental when people are refused admittance to our churches because of physical, behavioral, and/or cognitive differences. Discrimination is legal and most appropriate when we require proof of qualifications before allowing people to perform certain important tasks; for example, performing surgery or flying a passenger airplane. It is illegal when we refuse to hire or rent to people only because of their physical, behavioral, and/or cognitive differences. It is reasonable and in the best interests of a community to discriminate and imprison someone who is dangerous, but it is often most unreasonable to exclude individuals simply because of irrelevant physical, behavioral, and/or belief differences. Finally, discrimination may be individual and/or structural—built into the social structures of society. In this latter situation, individuals may discriminate routinely, without even being aware of it.

THE SOCIAL DYNAMICS OF RACIAL AND ETHNIC STRATIFICATION

The presence of a minority group creates tensions within a society. In order to preserve social stability, the society must develop a pattern of relationships by which to accommodate diversity. Historically, several patterns have been tried—with varying degrees of success. The patterns of relationships in which the dominant group has dealt with minority groups in

America include assimilation, pluralism, segregation, and extermination or genocide.

ASSIMILATION

The pattern of relationships in which the minority group adopts the dress, language, and behavior of the majority group is called **assimilation**. It is probably the most common pattern of behavior among minorities. Milton M. Gordon suggested at least seven levels of assimilation, of which the following five are most prevalent:[12]

1. *Acculturation* - when minority group members are socialized into WASP culture, at times by force, but usually on a voluntary basis.

2. *Secondary Structural Assimilation* - when minority members have relationships with the dominant groups in such places as grocery stores, company work, and recreational facilities.

3. *Primary Structural Assimilation* - when minority groups relate intimately with the dominant group in such places as family groups, work groups, play groups, and private clubs.

4. *Marital Assimilation* - when minority group members intermarry with members of the dominant group.

5. *Civil Assimilation* - when minority group members identify with the dominant group and feel no distinct cultural identity.

Why is assimilation so common? It appears to meet the needs of the dominant group. For instance, as the United States was emerging as a nation, there was a need to establish a common culture and language. Thus, White Anglos had a goal of a "**Melting-Pot**," in which all cultural differences were blended, resulting in a new American culture. Some Native American children were taken from their parents and raised in boarding schools, forced to speak English, and punished if they were caught speaking their mother tongue. This was in part the result of much dominant group ethnocentrism. More often, however, minority group members were desirous of becoming like the dominant group. In the United States this process was helped by public schools, which taught a common language (English), patriotism, and a common history (U.S. history).

PLURALISM

It has become increasingly obvious in recent years that some groups have not and will not lose their racial and/or ethnic identities. In fact, since the 1960s, we seem to be experiencing a kind of ethnic revival in America—a strengthening of ethnic ties and a celebration of cultural differences. American-style **cultural pluralism** is a minority-group adaptation to the dominant society that stops short of either full assimilation or the eradication of cultural differences. Cultural pluralism is the retention of cultural differences without prejudice. As an example, some American Jews and Amish people have succeeded in retaining much of their unique culture, such as dietary habits, language, family customs, and religious practices.

Some Mexican Americans advocate bicultural and bilingual pluralism, a milder form of cultural pluralism. This is especially true in the southwest, where their roots and their presence predate their Anglo conquerors. Another example of cultural pluralism can be found in Hawaii, where about 20 percent of the people are Native Hawaiians. In 1993, Governor Waihee, the first governor of Native Hawaiian ancestry, sought federal recognition of a "Hawaiian nation" that would coexist with the state and have its own representatives.

A more egalitarian form of pluralism includes *bilingualism* and *biculturalism*. Here differences between the dominant and minority groups are mutually accepted and respected. There is equal protection under the law, a modest level of secondary structural assimilation, a low level of primary structural assimilation, and no significant marital assimilation. Perhaps the best examples of this are found in Switzerland and Quebec or French Canada.[13]

Ideally, cultural pluralism appears to be a workable solution to America's dominant and minority group conflicts, especially for those minorities who have not, cannot, or do not want to be assimilated. In reality, however, it is difficult to achieve. First, the dominant group, like all groups, is ethnocentric. Second, the dominant group is more powerful than the other groups and continually exerts pressure on them to Americanize (especially on young people through schools and the mass media). Third, "success" in America seems to require a good deal of Americanization for any individual or group to make it up the ladder. As a result of these factors, cultural pluralism may be restricted to selectively celebrating certain traditional holidays and talking about "ethnic consciousness." Novak calls this superficial display of ethnicity "Saturday ethnics."[14] Machado refers to it as "cultural schizophrenia."[15]

SEGREGATION

Native Americans offer perhaps the best example of legal and forced segregation. At times the reservations were established to protect Native Americans from settlers. More often, however, Native Americans were transferred by force from land the government and/or settlers

Cultural pluralism can reduce prejudice when people learn to accept one another's differences and interact in a natural way.

had deemed valuable and desirable.

In the 1940s, wartime hysteria joined with national and economic interests to produce prejudices against Japanese Americans. About 110,000 Japanese Americans—around two-thirds of them American-born—were transferred legally and by force to Hawaii and the West Coast to inland Relocation Camps. A few years ago the Federal Government apologized to survivors of the Relocation Camps and gave each person a token monetary compensation of $20,000 for their loss of homes, farms, businesses, and other belongings.

Despite the efforts of the Civil Rights Movement and its hard-won legislation, most data show that American cities are currently quite segregated by race and ethnicity. While some segregation is voluntary, most of it is the overt or covert design of the dominant or majority group. Massey and Denton argue that Whites have used many strategies to keep about a third of the Black population in sixteen segregated urban areas. In addition, they argue that this is a major reason for the existence of a Black underclass trapped in poverty.[16] Years ago Kyle Haseldon wrote that racial segregation is immoral because "it denies and violates on the grounds of race that human oneness which is obvious in nature, which is proclaimed by the highest order of government, and which is a central doctrine of the Christian religion."[17]

EXTERMINATION OR GENOCIDE

The American dominant group has on occasion engaged in extermination or genocide of Native Americans. After the American Revolution, the new government attempted to negotiate treaties of land cession with Native Americans. When the new government failed to reach agreements with them, it confronted them with military force. Many treaties were signed; few were kept. Generally speaking, Native

As a result of nineteenth-century political policies, Native Americans are now America's most impoverished minority.

Americans were defeated and their lands expropriated. Private property is considered a cornerstone of American society, but the American government considered Native Americans to have little or no property rights. Of the many extermination or genocide attempts, the following are illustrative:

- At Sand Creek, Colorado, in 1864, militiamen descended upon an encampment of Cheyenne who had been guaranteed safe conduct and, instead, slaughtered most of them.

- In the frigid Plains winter of 1890, United States forces armed with Hotchkiss machine guns mowed down nearly three hundred Sioux at Wounded Knee, South Dakota.

- On October 12, 1885 (on Columbus Day, ironically), *The New York Times* reported that in Arizona and New Mexico:

... the ranchers and cowboys in Cochise, Pima and Yavapai counties are organizing in bodies for the purpose of going on a real old-fashioned Indian hunt, and they propose to bring back the scalps and obtain the reward. Word now comes from Tombstone ... that the reward in that county has been increased to $500 for a buck Indian's scalp ... Pima and Yavapai have taken steps to increase the reward to $500 ... Yuma, Apache, and Maricopa counties will follow suit.

This reward system, while it may seem savage and brutal to the Northern and Eastern sentimentalists, is looked upon in this section as the only means possible of ridding Arizona of the murderous Apaches ...

From time immemorial all border counties have offered rewards for bear and wolf scalps and other animals that destroyed the pioneer's stock or molested his family. Why, therefore, ask the Arizona settlers, should not the authorities place a reward upon the head of the terrible Apache, who murders the white man's family and steals his stock like the wolves? 'Extermination' is the battle cry now, and the coming winter will witness bloody work in this section.

In 1972, Carlson and Colburn stated:

"Today, the Indians are America's most impoverished minority. The reason for their tragic circumstances is directly traceable to the policies of the Federal Government beginning in the early nine-

By opposing racism in our own neighborhoods and churches, Christians can change the world.

teenth century. The brutal elimination of the Indian came to an end with the close of the century and a more patronizing attitude to him was adopted . . . When Indian reservations were discovered to rest on valuable lands, Congress still did not hesitate to appropriate them . . . In spite of the well-meaning reforms of the period between 1890 and 1930, the Indians lost almost two-thirds of their land."[18]

HOW CHRISTIANS CAN CHANGE THE WORLD

It's obvious that racial prejudice/discrimination is a great sin shared not only by individuals but also by societies as a whole. We have discussed ways to eliminate the individual sin of prejudice, such as contact and integration. Likewise, the elimination of institutional racism through social integration has alleviated the social sin of prejudice. There is evidence of much progress. Civil Rights legislation eliminated segregation in the United States many years ago. The "Colored" and "White" drinking fountains and restrooms, as well as chairs in bus stations labeled "Colored" and "White" are almost forgotten today. Many may not know that some Southern courtrooms had separate "White" and "Colored" Bibles for swearing in witnesses. No longer do we see signs on some businesses that read "No Niggers or Mexicans served here." Older African Americans still remember when they could only get take-out food from the back door of a White restaurant, even though they paid the same price as Whites who were served in the front. Older Jewish Americans still remember when they could not stay in certain hotels, enroll in some schools, or belong to some social clubs. Some Mexican Americans still remember being punished because they spoke Spanish in school. Some Native Americans still remember boarding schools where they were taught that their tribal way of life was barbaric.

We must not be lulled into the complacency of thinking that things are "all right." Things are only better! We have reduced the most blatant forms of racism to infrequent or atypical incidents. However, those aspects of racism that remain are difficult to attack; they are subtle, often hidden, and frequently confused with economic and political issues. Preferential treatment programs—combined with general economic problems—have been blown out of proportion and have created a backlash of conservatism and racism. Organizations such as the Ku Klux Klan and the American Nazi groups are once again openly and proudly espousing their racist beliefs. Even a casual reading of the daily paper will indicate evidence of continued racism, inequality, and sporadic incidents of racial violence. In this climate, it is not surprising that certain issues have become hot topics again: for example, multiculturalism, bilingualism, immigration, profiling, and affirmative action.

We find ourselves working side by side in a pluralistic society Monday through Friday, but forming clusters of Black/White/Hispanic/Asian congregations on Sunday. However, Christians need to examine themselves continually for evidence of segregation and should strive for racial reconciliation. DeSanto and Paloma note that this becomes a matter of concern to the effectiveness of our missionary efforts:

"While we willingly send our missionaries to minister to and to convert 'the heathen,' rejoicing at reports that they are turning to Christ in record numbers, when they come to our shores we have difficulty accepting them as equals – brothers and sisters in Christ. Why? Do we suffer from a bad case of ethnocentrism and an even worse case of pride and superiority?"[19]

As a further concern for Christians, several studies suggest that religious people—those of us who believe in "love thy neighbor"—tend to be more prejudiced than nonreligious people.[20] This must be reversed! We need only cite the parable of the Good Samaritan (Luke 10:30-37) to support the notion that God intends for us to care for ***all*** our neighbors, regardless of race or ethnic background. Some see racial prejudice/discrimination as stemming from the social sin of giving greater sovereignty to our Christian culture (complete with its music, dress, and language) than to our God. Such "culture worship" results in ethnocentric attitudes, excluding those who come from diverse cultures.

Christians ought to be leaders of social change in the area of racial/ethnic stratification. Examine the racial composition of your own church. Suggest some intercultural dialogue and joint worship with other churches. If your church will not budge on cultural diversity, join a multiracial church. In other words, do not tolerate racial/ethnic segregation on Sunday morning!

Racial prejudice and discrimination are perennial, worldwide problems. We have only reduced or disguised these problems. Minority and dominant group relationships remain perhaps our greatest barrier to achieving the ideals of the Christian ethic and our democratic creed. In the past, leadership in the cause of racial and ethnic equality came from unexpected sources—for example, the Supreme Court, an institution far removed from the people and their daily lives. Those institutions that should, predictably, have been on the "front lines," leading the cause of equality with moral and religious fervor, have often been silent. Martin Luther King, Jr. and countless other Christians and churches have fought for equal rights and continue to do so, but for the most part churches have not been at the forefront combating racism and inequality.

We do not all have equal opportunity, because the past has rendered us unequal, and present reality works to maintain that inequality.[21] We cannot rewrite the history of minority and dominant group relationships in America. Guilt at this time is nonproductive and pointless. However, we are morally obligated to "right" injustices rather than to continue them, and to remember our soiled past—lest we forget and perpetuate or repeat it.

overview

- Races are biological categories of peoples.

- As a scientific concept, race is practically meaningless. As a legal term and a popular idea, however, race has been used frequently to influence social organization and social interactions.

- Ethnicity refers to a distinctive cultural heritage shared by a people and is reflected in language, religion, dress, lifestyle, and mannerism.

- Most multiracial and/or multiethnic societies are stratified, and racial and/or ethnic groups share unequally in the benefits and disadvantages offered.

- Minority groups are racial and/or ethnic groups who share identifiable differences (in appearance, culture, and/or behavior) from a dominant group, and for whom these differences mean unequal treatment, restricted life choices, and limited rewards and/or achievements.

- Prejudice is "thinking ill of others without sufficient warrant," and involves negative

- feelings, negative beliefs, and negative tendencies to act toward racial and/or ethnic groups.

- The dominant group may pursue different policies toward racial and/or ethnic minority groups. The dominant group may attempt to assimilate minority groups.

- Pluralism means that racial and/or ethnic minority groups adopt enough of the dominant group's culture to function in society, but also retain traits of their racial and/or ethnic heritage.

- The dominant group may also pursue policies of segregation and extermination or genocide when the dominant group believes that the minority group cannot be assimilated or controlled.

- Prejudice and discrimination against racial and ethnic groups continues to be a problem in the United States, despite gains made in the 1960s and 1970s. Christians need to be more involved to change the attitudes of the public.

key concepts

assimilation
The fusion of formerly distinctive groups, resulting in the disappearance of any differences that serve as the basis for prejudice and discrimination.

cultural pluralism
A minority group's retention or preservation of cultural differences without prejudice or discrimination; difference with respect and equality.

discrimination
Behavior in relation to a particular group or group member which is determined or influenced by perceived racial or cultural differences in that group; it may be positive or negative.

dominant group
The group in power and the one that other groups are expected to imitate in order to gain acceptance; the dominant group in America is White, Anglo-Saxon, and Protestant.

ethnic groups
Groups that share certain cultural differences which set them apart from the dominant group. National origin, language, religion, or general lifestyle offer the most common evidence of a group's ethnicity.

melting pot
An idealistic version of how diverse races and ethnic groups fused into one, creating the amalgam that is America.

minority group
A group sharing certain identifiable differences in appearance, culture, or behavior, and for whom these differences mean unequal treatment, restricted life choices, and limited rewards and/or achievements.

prejudice
Negative feelings, beliefs, and tendencies to act against certain people because of their race, ethnic background, or behavior.

race
A population sharing genetically or biologically inherited characteristics.

endnotes

1. Martin Marger, *Race and Ethnic Relations, American and Global Perspectives*, 2nd ed. (Belmont, CA: Wadsworth Publishing Co., 1991).
2. James M. Henslin, *Essentials of Sociology*, 2nd ed. (Boston: Allyn & Bacon, 1998).
3. Chris McGreal, "Forbidden Love Outlives Apartheid," *Daily Mail and Guardian* (Johannesburg, South Africa, January 24). http://www.mg.co.za/mg/news/2000jan2/24jan-sandra.html/
4. Vincent N. Parillo, "Diversity in America: A Sociohistorical Analysis," in *Sociological Forum* 9, no. 4 (1994): 523-45.
5. Charles H. Anderson, *White Protestant Americans: From National Origins to Religious Groups* (Englewood Cliffs, NJ: Prentice-Hall, 1970).
6. William M. Newman, *American Pluralism: A Study of Minority Groups and Social Theory* (New York: Harper & Row, 1973).
7. Stephan Thernstrom, ed., *Harvard Encyclopedia of American Ethnic Groups* (Cambridge, MA: Harvard University Press, 1971).
8. Werner Sollors, "How Americans Became White: Three Examples," in *MultiAmerica: Essays on Cultural Wars and Cultural Peace*, ed. by Ismael Reed (New York: Penguin Books, 1997), 3-5.
9. Moon Jo, "Korean merchants in the black community: prejudice among the victims of prejudice," in *Ethnic and Racial Studies* 15, no. 3: 343-47.
10. T. W. Adorno et al., *The Authoritarian Personality* (New York: Harper and Row, 1950).
11. Douglas T. Kenrick, Steven L. Neuberg, and Robert B. Cialdini, *Social Psychology: Unraveling the Mystery* (Boston: Allyn & Bacon, 1999).
12. Milton M. Gordon, *Assimilation in American Life* (New York: Oxford University Press, 1964).
13. S. Dale McLemore, *Racial and Ethnic Relations in America* (Boston: Allyn & Bacon, 1980).
14. Michael Novak, *The Rise of the Unmeltable Ethnics* (New York: Macmillan Publishing Co., 1971).
15. Manual A. Machado, *Listen Chicano!* (Chicago: Nelson-Hall Publishers, 1978).
16. Douglas S. Massey and Nance A. Denton, *American Apartheid: Segregation and the Making of the Underclass* (Cambridge, MA: Harvard University Press, 1993).
17. Kyle Haseldon, *The Racial Problem in Christian Perspective* (New York: Harper & Row Publishers, 1964).
18. Lewis H. Carlson and George A. Colburn, eds., *In Their Place: White America Defines Her Minorities*, 1850-1950 (New York: John Wiley & Sons, 1972).
19. C. P. DeSanto and M. M. Paloma, *Social Problems: Christian Perspectives* (Winston-Salem, NC: Hunter Textbooks, 1985), 267.
20. Gordon Allport, *The Nature of Prejudice* (Cambridge, MA: Addison-Wesley, 1954).
21. Joseph Barndt, *Dismantling Racism: The Continuing Challenge to White America* (Minneapolis: Augsburg Fortress, 1991).

additional resources

Joan Ferrante, *Sociology: A Global Perspective*, 3rd ed. (Belmont, CA: Wadsworth Publishing Co., 1998).

George Eaton Simpson and J. Milton Yinger, *Racial and Cultural Minorities: An Analysis of Prejudice and Discrimination*, 5th ed. (New York: Plenum Press, 1985).

Rodney Stark, *Sociology*, 4th ed. (Belmont, CA: Wadsworth Publishing Co., 1992).

Ronald G. Stover, Melodie L. Lichty, and Penny W. Stover, *Industrial Society: An Evolutionary Perspective* (Upper Saddle River, N.J.: Prentice Hall, 1999).

George Brown Tindall and David E. Shi, *America, A Narrative History* (New York: W.W. Norton & Co., 1996).

Benn J. Wattenberg, *The First Universal Nation: Leading Indicators and Ideas about the Surge of America in the 1990s* (New York: Free Press, 1991).

James W. VanderZanden, *American Minority Relations*, 3rd ed. (New York: Ronald Press Co., 1972).

———, *The Social Experience: An Introduction to Sociology*, 2nd ed. (New York: McGraw-Hill, 1990).

CHAPTER NINE

Gender and Society

chapter outline

I. Definitions
   A. Sex
   B. Gender

II. Why gender stratification?
   A. Structural-functional perspective
   B. Conflict perspective

III. The gender socialization process – interactionist perspective
   A. Family
   B. School
   C. Peers
   D. Media
   E. Religion
   F. Masculine and feminine roles today

IV. How Christians can change the world

biblical reflection

"So if anyone is in Christ, there is a new creation: everything old has passed away; see, everything has become new!"

—2 Corinthians 5:17

In the last two chapters we have investigated social stratification—one of the most insidious forms of social sin. In this chapter we will continue the discussion of structured social inequality by examining ways in which societies are structured to promote gender inequality. Such social sin is not exclusive to non-Christian groups. In fact, some religious organizations have been adamant in their promotion of a culture that excludes women from leadership positions.

The Bible verse cited at the beginning of this chapter reminds us that Christians should stand against those aspects of the culture that constrain us from asserting our "newness" in Christ. Being a new creation in Christ means that we need to be open to God's call that may take us beyond traditional gender roles.

DEFINITIONS

SEX

Sex is an ascribed status. God created us with specific chromosomes making us biologically male or female. Our sex constrains our behavior to some extent. Women's small hands enable them to excel at small detailed manual work (such as sewing or typing). Men's bigger frames lend themselves to heavy manual labor. However, these physical aspects do not restrict men and women to narrowly defined roles. Sewing is not limited to women and moving heavy objects is not limited to men.

GENDER

Gender is an achieved status. We are born male/female but we become **masculine/feminine**. Through socialization, boys and girls grow up learning different forms of communicating, different ways of thinking, and different patterns of interacting. While our sex differences are created by God, gender differences are created by our society.[1] This is evident in the social variations we see throughout the world. For example, there are societies in which men do the cooking and women work in the fields. There are no biological constraints that prevent

We can't tell the sex of the baby on the left. Yet, as we see by the little girl on the right, it is not long before gender becomes unmistakable.

Sociology: A Christian Approach for Changing the World

women from taking a traditionally masculine role (e.g., the woman who chooses to play basketball) or men from taking a traditionally feminine role (e.g., child rearing). In fact, in contemporary American society, it would seem that most young people are **androgynous**—they share both masculine and feminine characteristics in their roles.

WHY GENDER STRATIFICATION?

God created us with biological differences. It is clear that there are important social functions to such differences—how else would we reproduce? Yet gender stratification occurs when one gender is considered inferior to the other and thus experiences discrimination. Jesus challenged such behavior. See, for example, His treatment of the woman who anointed Him (Mark 14:3-9), as well as Mary Magdalene and the other Mary, who were the first to see Him after His Resurrection (Matt. 28:1-10). Nevertheless, throughout history societies have attached social value to one's biological sex, so that opportunities are limited for one sex.

"In every society, in every century, people have assumed that males and females are different not only in basic anatomy but in elusive qualities of spirit, soul, and ability . . . Every society has distinguished men's work from women's work and created barriers between the sexes."[2]

The tie between gender and society is strong. Once we are labeled male and female, our lives will never be the same because society demands certain behaviors subsumed in the term "gender." Gender roles permeate all areas of life, including appropriate dress, body posture, emotional reactions, and even occupational choices. No matter what else we accomplish in life, we are always that *plus* our male or female designation (e.g., rich man or a woman doctor).

STRUCTURAL-FUNCTIONAL PERSPECTIVE

Structural-functional theory sees society as a system of integrated structures (institutions like family, religion, education, economics, and government) that remain balanced overall and that adjust if strains occur. Gendered behavior clearly can be functional in a society, especially as a means of dividing labor. As seen in "hunter-gathering" societies, one way of dividing labor was for the men to hunt and the women to gather. Nursing females were not free to travel on hunts. Somehow such societies came to *value* one function over the other—the male task was so chosen. (In this case, the meat was defined as more valuable since it was less available.)

Why such gender inequality? A structural-functionalist would cite ways in which individuals perpetuate attitudes and behaviors that discriminate against women. The source may be men who make sexist jokes or refuse to hire or promote women. Or the source may be women themselves when they choose life paths that lead to low wages and limited opportunities.

Are gender differences functional today? How many of the differences between masculine and feminine roles are rooted in the way God created us, and how many are just a product of society? If masculine and feminine roles are "locked in"—ordained by God—then efforts to change gender roles would be futile. However, if gender roles are merely a human social creation, then change is not only possible, it is preferable. If in the creation of gender roles society limits God's plan for the fulfillment of human potential, then Christians need to work toward change.

Robert Merton points out that for many women the gender roles of the 1950s became dysfunctional, oppressive, self-defeating, and alienating.[3] Gender issues strained society and collectively women moved to change such roles. When change in gender started within families, it spread throughout the society (social system) to the institutional patterns of religion,

If gender roles were mandated by God, a man might not be allowed to cook nor a woman to play sports.

the media, the economy, the workplace, and other areas. Today we are still experiencing the effects of these changes in such issues as the increasing number of women pastors, the debate over homosexuality, and the determination of rights in reproduction issues.

Scholars have long debated the functions of gender stratification. Many have argued that our biology determines our destiny and that men and women are biologically limited in what they can do. Today we generally accept that some combination of biology and social learning must be the answer in explaining human behavior. This debate is important to Christians in planning for social change. We cannot change the way God created us. But we must change aspects of society that limit our fulfillment of God's plan for our lives.

THE CONFLICT PERSPECTIVE

The social conflict perspective looks at the ways in which the social structure limits opportunities for men or women. While a functionalist would point to individuals as the source of gender stratification, the conflict theorist would point to a social system as perpetuating inequality. Such **institutional sexism** may take the form of rigid job expectations that make it difficult for women with young children to excel. Or it may take the form of loneliness at the top of the corporate ladder where women have few colleagues with whom to interact.

The conflict theorist would say that rather than *choosing* to take life paths that lead to low wages, women are victims of a *system* that creates barriers for them. Examples of these barriers can be seen in the socialization process to which we now turn.

THE GENDER SOCIALIZATION PROCESS: INTERACTIONIST PERSPECTIVE

Through our interactions with agents of socialization, we learn a gender identity. This gender identity influences our attitudes and behavior. The system of socialization makes us believe certain behaviors are just "natural" and that any violations of traditional gender roles are "unnatural." As we have seen in earlier chapters, the five basic socializing agents are family, school, peers, media, and religion. We will focus on the gender expectations influenced by these groups.

THE FAMILY

When born into your family, you were a captive learner, completely ignorant of sex differences and gender roles. Before too long, you probably detected some differences in "mothering" and "fathering," even before you observed differences in males and females. This is because most parents see children through gender-colored glasses that exaggerate the differences between males and females. Therefore, many families consciously and unconsciously treat their sons and daughters differently, even while loving them equally.[4] Within three to five years, the "self" becomes a very definite boy-self or girl-self. This is what we earlier referred to as "sexual identity," and it develops before either racial or social class identity.

Within twenty-four hours—day one—studies show that parents treat their girl and boy babies in line with traditional gender roles.[5] Except for genitalia, children at this age appear no different; yet, when parents were asked to describe their babies, they saw major differences. Parents described infant daughters as tiny, soft, weak, inattentive, and delicate, while infant sons were described as strong, coordinated, and alert. Fathers offered more stereotypical descriptions than did mothers, confirming that men sanction gender expectations more severely.[6]

Parents first hold an image difference, but then the process continues with specific interactions along gender-traditional lines. Parents obviously possess great vested interest in having their children identified properly in their assigned sex. Shakin and Sternglanz examined a major basis of gender attribution—clothing. Ninety percent of the infants studied in a shopping mall wore traditional gender-typed clothing. Parents donned girls in pink or yellow, while boys were clad in blue or red.[7] Style varied as well, with girls wearing laced, ruffled dresses for special occasions and pastel, flower- or heart-decorated casual clothes. Boys wore suits for special occasions and overalls or pants in basic or military color for casual wear.[8]

Even before children learn to talk, parents play with them differently and according to the child's sex. Girls are cuddled, held tenderly, and handled as if fragile, while boys are more likely to be tossed in the air, played with roughly, and talked to less. Girl babies are picked up more quickly when they cry, even though boy babies cry more and sleep less than girl babies do. In talking to sons, mothers and fathers speak "more explicitly, teach and question them more, and use more numbers and action verbs."[9]

During early childhood development, verbal communication assumes great importance. Learning to talk requires more than understanding a certain vocabulary—it involves using words appropriately and learning that they are *just* symbols. A feminist might say man-made symbols show a negative bias against the female gender. Why do we refer to a boat as "she" or "her," an unknown dog as "he," and a strange cat as "she"? Parents teach children not to call a male "pretty" or a female "husky" or "rugged." Acquired language shapes the viewing screen for seeing the world; thus, children's glasses begin to take on a gender-colored tint!

As children get older, gender-role socialization continues in the choices of different toys, games, books, and bedroom decorations—all of which occur along traditional gender lines. Parents continue to encourage proper behavior according to cultural standards; i.e., girls are to be more gentle and verbal, while boys are to be more active. Into the 1990s, parents still reported feeling that only sons should mow the lawn,

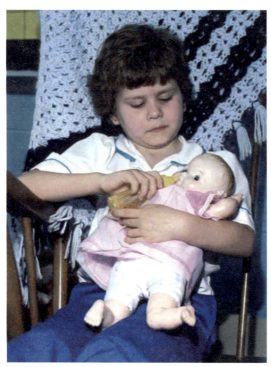

Children learn gender by imitating their parents.

carry out the garbage, and help with repairs. Many parents give little thought to the "why" behind childrearing practices and may, therefore, merely accept traditional gender roles. How do these practices affect children?

We must remember that the predictions your family made about you becoming a doctor, an athlete, or a musician—a particular kind of male or female—contribute to the process Merton called the **self-fulfilling prophecy**.[10] In effect, he said that if you are told frequently that you have long, agile "surgeon's" fingers, a sharp, "scientific" way of looking at situations, and a keen concern for people, you might get the message that being a doctor is all that you are meant to be. Possibly some of these same traits also could make you an effective music therapist in a mental hospital, or a very good high school band director! However, the point is that families frequently recommend the role that fits your gender.

We have already suggested that mothers, fathers, brothers, and sisters form our first significant others and our most available, impressive gender role models. People in many American homes feel that traditional gender roles are the "right" models for a strong, "normal" family.[11] Thus, while the family is the undisputed regulator of the child's environment, other influences outside the home require that we understand what happens there as well.

THE SCHOOL

The sheer number of hours children spend at school means something surely must rub off. From nursery school or kindergarten through the elementary school grades, the curricula are ostensibly identical for girls and boys. However, the past predominant use of male examples to illustrate key historical figures or contemporary roles of leadership has come under fire in recent years. Those seeking to eliminate sexism in the school are concerned about including female figures who have played significant roles in history. Often extracurricular activities in grade school are sex-segregated, as well. By high school, elective subjects are often sex-selective. How many boys in your grade dared take home economics? If so, did your school change the name to "family living"? How many girls took mechanical drawing or shop? If they had wanted to take these courses, would the school administration have permitted it?

A close look at the educational system convinces many social scientists that sexism in education begins as early as formal training does. **Sexism** is the belief that one sex group, in this case male, is innately superior to the other (female) and thus has the right to dominate. Decide for yourself if sexism existed in your past school experiences. In grades one through seven, how many male teachers did you have? However, what sex was your principal? In high school, who taught science, was head coach,

Girls tend to learn best in a cooperative setting.

directed the band, or sat in the principal's chair? Generally, early public education is female-predominant and male-dominant. By high school, the curricula subjects are often sex-related among the faculty; for example, men teach science and math and women teach English. Just as a child's bedroom decorations affect gender, so does the general school environment.

According to Renzetti and Curan, teachers sexually separate students, which has at least three interrelated consequences:

First, sex separation in and of itself prevents boys and girls from working together cooperatively, thus denying children of both sexes valuable opportunities to learn about and sample one another's interests and activities. Second, it makes working in same-sex groups more comfortable than working in mixed-sex groups—a feeling that children may carry with them into adulthood and which may become problematic when they enter the labor force. Third, sex separation reinforces gender stereotypes, especially if it involves differential work assignments.[12]

Many studies document the loss of academic potential and self-esteem by girls during the educational process. Girls are high achievers in the lower grades, but until recently fewer have gone to college. Now more than 55 percent of undergraduate college students are women. In college, there are fewer role models for female scholars, since there is only one woman for every four men on the faculty—even fewer are among the full-time, tenured faculty. In spite of pressures for equal opportunity in hiring and pay, women remain a small minority of administration.[13] As students, therefore, children and young adults see gender stereotypes among superiors.

PEERS

As adolescents and young adults, we tire of hearing about peer influence. However, we should never underestimate the importance of peers, especially in play groups that shape values and teach appropriate gender roles. Mead considered play an essential element in the development of self and sexual identity.[14] When you were very young, your solitary play was imitative—you took the roles of nurse, mother, cowboy, truck driver, and you firmed up your image of what those roles required, whether you would ever assume them or not.[15]

Even when you began to play with others in organized games, you acted out the reciprocal nature of doctor-patient, storekeeper-customer, cowboys-Indians, mother-child. Perhaps you grew up in a neighborhood in which you played with both boys and girls. Did you ever swap out in appropriate gender role-games (e.g., the girls would agree to play cops and robbers, if the boys would agree to play "house")? In these kinds of anticipatory role-games, frequently the complementary roles were/are gender-typed. For example, in playing house, the girl will be the wife-mother and the boy will be the father-breadwinner. While the boys play football, the girls practice twirling and cheerleading in the face of rejection as a team member.[16]

Toy manufacturers cooperate by catering to sex-typical games and toys that reinforce traditional gender. Toy catalogs generally have clear-cut divisions for boys and girls, with a neutral, in-between section for games, creative playthings, and puzzles. Boys are pictured with trucks, astronaut outfits, footballs, and builder sets. Girls have cooking sets, nurse's outfits, manicure sets, toy vacuums, and dolls of all sorts. Even male dolls are not meant for boys to play with—the nearest thing to a doll for a very young boy is a teddy bear, some other stuffed animal, or an army figure.[17]

Usually in our society, same-sex groups characterize most childhood play, especially after preschool.[18] No doubt children respond to societal pressure by avoiding cross-sex play that might cause teasing, such as, "You love a gir-l, You love a gir-l," a chant detested by a young boy. Such sanctioning socializes children into same-sex groupings. Yet, whenever children are least pressured (i.e., fewer adults are around), the tendency to sex-segregate grows even stronger. Perhaps at some basic level we tend to be more comfortable with those most like us—especially at play. If this is true, then the fact that similarity of interests does not seem to matter in these groups shows how much significance sexual and gender identity assume for children.

Finally, Maccoby describes how these same-sex groups reinforce traditional gender.[19] Girls cooperate, allow open communication, and persuade each other with talk. Boys act competitively, interrupt each other, and push and shove for attention. If girls do play with boys, girls are apt to be even more passive. After grade school, some change occurs as males and females begin dating; however, they still retain the strong bond of same-sex peers who keep them on gender track.

On the traditional college campus, the peer culture of beauty and romance tends to overshadow academic achievement for young women. As a result, some women who come to college often become ambivalent about academic and career decisions and instead preoccupy themselves with social activities.[20] Such an approach to college work may help to explain why women who are college graduates tend to earn less in their lifetimes than male college graduates.

THE MEDIA

Television programs and preschool books have rid themselves more effectively of racial stereotypes than sex stereotypes. Children's shows and cartoon programs are not as blatant in sex typing as even a decade ago, but women and girls still predominate in roles that portray domestic, clerical, or nursing activities, while men or boys play aggressive, creative, adventurous roles.

Media executives make decisions concerning script content and character development that often have subtle implications for gender value

Boys tend to be competitive with one another, while girls are cooperative in their play.

transmission. Furthermore, a study of the portrayal of women over three decades of prime-time television found that women are now more likely to be depicted as having careers, yet the focus of most programs is on women's romantic or family lives.[21] Renzetti and Curran (1995) point out that media, including magazines, television, and advertisements, portray men and women in very stereotypic roles.[22] Women are depicted as homemakers and sex objects, serving men and children. Women with high career success are often portrayed as incompetent in romantic and family relationships. Men are portrayed as aggressive and selfish, very concerned with physical and sexual appeal. Men as seen in the media are most likely to have occupations associated with power and material success: doctors, lawyers, detectives.

RELIGION

Most world religions are very far from treating women as equals in society. In fact J. S. Hawley, in a book about the fundamentalist resurgence in world religions, claims that conservative religions are the last bastion of sexism in contemporary society.[23] Despite the fact that some religions, particularly some Protestant denominations, encourage the ordination of women, children around the world see few women who are imams, priests, rabbis, or senior pastors—while seeing increasing numbers of women who are practicing medicine, law and other professions.

Language usage, when referring to God, may also be confusing. When one hears an omnipotent God being referred to as "He," one may begin to question the importance of women. It may seem inconsistent that modern books most often use gender-neutral language, while many of the religious texts most often refer to humans as "men." This may create a barrier for evangelism, as some may think the religious texts "outdated" or "irrelevant."[24]

MASCULINE AND FEMININE ROLES TODAY

The gender role socialization process described above results in women and men who still lean toward traditional gender expectations. Feminists and others concerned with the overall well-being of humankind might ask: Are these roles maximizing human potential? Let's look at some of the disadvantages of traditional masculine and feminine roles, as these often form the basic premise for social change.

FEMALE EFFECTS

Beginning with women, we must say they still hold an inferior position in society and any pursuit for equality is often questioned. The language of our society continues to imply role insignificance:

> When a woman marries, the couple is pronounced "man" (the human being) and "wife" (the possession of the man) . . . When a woman goes to work she is part of "manpower." If she is injured on the job she is entitled to "workman's compensation." If she is physically abused she is "manhandled" . . . Daily, women open letters addressed to "Dear Sir." They are called "gals" or "girls" by their employers until they are in their eighties . . .[26]

However, over time it seems plausible, given the tremendous significance of symbolic language, that these usages reinforce inferior female status. As expressed by Henley et al:

> In addition to derogating women, linguistic sexism involves defining women's place in society unequally and also ignoring women altogether . . . We may consider the commonly used titles of respect for men and women in our society. Men are addressed as Mr., which reveals nothing about their relationship to women. But how are women typically addressed? The titles Miss and Mrs. define women in terms of their relationship to men. Even when a woman has earned a higher status title, such as Dr., she is still likely to be addressed as Miss or Mrs.[27]

The most blatant way that our language ignores or excludes women is through the use of the supposedly generic "he" and "man." As we saw earlier with the use of these words in the Bible, some women may wonder if certain biblical passages apply just to men or to women as well. Recent research raises serious doubts as to whether this he/man approach is really neutral or generic.[28]

If one could convincingly argue that women are not really in inferior positions, but are high-

Young girls tend to be happy and self-confident. When they become teenagers, girls are less confident and have a lower self-esteem.

ly respected as wives and mothers, we would still have to address the fact that women feel inferior. At all ages, girls and women carry the excess weight of low self-esteem.[29] As children, they respect their fathers as being smarter than their mothers.[30] Another study showed that seventy-one percent of high school boys think it is "great" to be male, but only fifty-four percent of the girls felt it "great" to be female. Adolescent girls also worry more about appearance and generally have a low view of themselves.[31] Women continue to struggle with these feelings in adulthood. Ironically, women will give an essay they think has been written by a male a better evaluation than the same essay written by a female. Inferior status seemingly translates into inferior self-feelings, underlining how societal ascriptions affect a sense of who we are.

MALE EFFECTS

Men also have problems associated with traditional gender. As two authorities in family and gender study express it:

> There has been a growing awareness that the traditional pattern of sex-role differentiation has costs for men as well as women . . . It is a strain to have to act tougher, stronger, more dominant, and more competent than one really is inside. It is also a strain to have one's masculine status constantly dependent on success at work and providing well for a family of dependents.[32]

Men often outdistance even themselves by pushing their superiority beyond their own capabilities. The pressure to succeed may take a toll on their mental and physical health, evidenced in consistently lower life expectancies. Furthermore, while assigned the goal of being superior, men must "arrive" at this without showing the emotions that accompany inevitable failures along the way. Havemann and Lehtinen call this "The Burden of Being 'Superior.'"[33] These kinds of problems, for both men and women, led to the call for social change; i.e., a change in the structuring of gender roles.

HOW CHRISTIANS CAN CHANGE THE WORLD

While the Civil Rights Movement for racial equality began in the Christian churches in the South, the Feminist Movement has developed largely outside the church. In fact, many Christians have vehemently opposed it. **Feminism**, in and of itself, is the belief that women are equal in worth to men and entitled to the same opportunities, rights, and privileges. Ideologically, there is little here for Christians to disapprove. However, some positions being promoted by the Feminist Movement—such as gay/lesbian and abortion rights—have caused many Christians to avoid association with it. As a result, the Women's Movement has occurred largely without the help and support of Christians.

Social change takes time. The Feminist Movement began about 150 years ago. No doubt it was encouraged in the early 1800s by the first efforts to achieve education for women, particularly higher education. The second major impetus for women's rights was the suffrage movement, an effort to gain civil rights for "Negroes" and for women, particularly in the form of the voting franchise. That twenty-year effort succeeded in getting the voting privilege for all races, but not for the female sex. It took a half-century after ratification of the fifteenth amendment to the Constitution (1870) to gain the same right for women in the "Susan B. Anthony" or nineteenth amendment (1920). After a pall of forty years, the contemporary spirit of feminism revived with the publication of Betty Friedan's book, *The Feminine Mystique* (1963). Within five years of its publication,

Women can now be found in many types of careers, though in most jobs they still earn less than men.

more than a dozen organizations were following the lead of the National Organization of Women, and within ten years roughly 100,000 women had joined.[34]

Contemporary feminism has become a relatively quiet movement. In fact, many modern women shun being called a "feminist" since they feel the word has many negative connotations. Today's women are no longer beating on corporate doors in an effort to gain access to jobs and civil rights. The earlier successes of the movement have given women access to corporate America. The contemporary movement is about changing the systems to remove barriers to success in corporate America.[35]

There is more work to do. Christians interested in social justice should note that there is still an income gap between men and women. The 1999 median income for men was $30,121. For women it was $18,777.[36] The gap remains, in part, because women enter lower-paying occupations, usually along traditional gender lines. Persons seeking equality for women often demand *comparable worth*; i.e., work of equal value requiring the same skill level should receive equal pay. In the United States, for example, women salespersons make less money selling clothes than males doing the exact same work. According to Doyle and Paludi:

> Even when we compare working women with working men who have comparable educational status and occupational credentials, and who have pursued their

> careers full time throughout most of their working years, we still find great disparity between the women's and men's incomes . . . Part of this salary disparity is due to the cultural belief that men should earn more than women because men supposedly are the primary "breadwinners" of the family . . .[37]

Women continue to enter the job market in traditional gender occupations (e.g., secretaries, clerks). Furthermore, when women enter an occupation category, its status lessens. Glen and Feldberg showed that when men filled clerk positions, esteem and salary were higher than for the women who increasingly took over those positions.[38] On the other hand, observe the opposite changes that occurred when men entered the traditionally female fields of stewardess and nurse—esteem and salary have gone up and males have advanced to top levels faster. As is typical, the name stewardess had to become flight attendant to keep males from doing anything remotely female in orientation.[39]

On the home front, not much has changed. Sociological studies have shown that the essential division of labor in the majority of families has remained intact. Housework continues to be the domain of women, whether they are homemakers or part-time or full-time employees.[40] Hochschild actually calls the wife's work at home "the second shift," the time when women do two-thirds of household chores, especially the daily ones.[41] Berk argues this is not likely to change because housework continues to be a primary way to retain segregation and superiority for males.[42]

God calls each of us to a unique place in the Kingdom. Traditional gender roles should not present a barrier to our full participation in God's work. If you understand how gender structures and forms our culture, you are equipped to experience your place in society and the church in a new way. Moreover, you should have encountered here the encouragement to see if further changes are needed in our society. Persons who care enough to act ultimately affect social changes.

Sociology teaches us to understand the roles of others—to take their perspective for additional understanding and even truth. It teaches that there is always more than one way to look at a subject: society is bad; society is good. Many Christians are very troubled by Scriptures that seem to constrain women to certain roles. But take a second look. Perhaps the reason Paul said, "Wives, be subject to your husbands" and "Husbands, love your wives" is because he was diverting our attention to the area of living that is most difficult for each of us. Men do have more trouble loving and women often have trouble submitting. In the first part of this scriptural passage, Paul says, "Be subject to one another out of reverence for Christ" (Eph. 5:21). He knew that this best forms a family. Perhaps

Though women have gained access in many professions, there is still a glass ceiling preventing many women from high-level management. Women can see the top but they cannot reach it.

Chapter Nine: Gender and Society

this is the change we should work for.

What should a Christian do to stand up against gender stratification? First, examine your own heart for evidence of sexist attitudes and behaviors, then change your ways. Second, do not tolerate sexist attitudes and behaviors in your friends, family, church, workplace, or school. Speak the truth in love: "Let the word of Christ dwell in you richly; teach and admonish one another in all wisdom" (Col. 3:16). Many Christians, unaware of ways in which their behavior hurts women, would appreciate a loving nudge in the direction of social justice. Finally, do not tolerate institutions that create barriers for women's achievement. Advocate an understanding of ways in which your church, school, or workplace practices institutionalized sexism. If necessary, refuse to participate in organizations that will not remove barriers based on sex.

No doubt there has been some change, but clearly ceilings still persist, barriers abound, and we have not yet as a society fully heeded the often forgotten words of Paul:

"There is no longer Jew or Greek, there is no longer slave or free, there is no longer male and female; for all of you are one in Christ Jesus."

Galatians 3:28

overview

- Sex is an ascribed status. It is determined at conception by differing chromosomes. Gender is an achieved status. We learn to be "masculine" and "feminine" through socialization with family, school, media, peers, and church. Gender stratification occurs when opportunities are limited based on one's sex.

- A structural-functionalist explanation of gender stratification notes the functions gender plays in reproduction and the social structure of a nonindustrial society. Men's large frames were well suited for hunting, while women were better suited to stay home nursing their babies and keeping the home fires burning. In explaining gender inequality, the functionalist would point out ways in which individual men and women promote sexism.

- Conflict theorists would look at ways in which the social system promotes gender stratification. They would note examples in which institutional sexism creates barriers for achievement.

- Once in place, gender structure is continued via the socialization process, in which children, adolescents, and adults learn gender roles and attitudes.

- The chapter concludes with a look at gender today and the changes or lack thereof that have taken place. The effect of gender structuring on males and females shows a need for maximizing unrealized human potential—something we have not yet accomplished.

- Feminism is the leading movement calling for changes to rectify the inequality surrounding gender. The changes that have occurred, however, have hardly been revolutionary.

key concepts

androgyny
Having the characteristics of both male and female; being neither distinctively masculine nor feminine.

feminism
A reaction to sexist attitudes in society; the belief that women have been subordinated and must be given equal opportunities and status in all areas and institutions of society.

gender
The characteristics a society considers appropriate for males and females.

institutional sexism
Practices within a social organization that systematically discriminate against men or women, making it more difficult for them to achieve.

masculinity/femininity
The social image of being male and female as determined and taught by society.

self-fulfilling prophecy
Robert K. Merton's theory of the process of becoming what you are predicted to be; the prediction becomes a causal factor in the learning process.

sex
The biological characteristics of being male or female; manifested in several ways: the chromosomes, the internal reproductive system, the gonads, the hormones, and the external genitals.

sexism
The belief that one sex is superior to the other and thereby entitled to exploit the other sex through stereotyping, work discrimination, laws, family, and other systems.

endnotes

1. For a thorough discussion of the essential need to clarify the biological versus the sociological definitions of sex versus gender, see: J. A. Doyle and M. A. Paludi, *Sex and Gender: The Human Experience* (Dubuque, IA: William C. Brown, 1991).
2. C. Travis and C. Offir, *The Longest War* (New York: Harcourt Brace and Jovanovich, 1977).
3. R. K. Merton, *Social Theory and Social Structure*, rev. ed. (Glencoe, IL: Free Press, 1957).
4. For research confirming this statement, see: L. C. Coombs, "Preferences for sex of children among U.S. couples," *Family Planning Perspective* 9 (1977): 259-65; N. E. Williamson, *Sons or Daughters?* (Beverly Hills, CA: Sage Publications, Inc., 1976).
5. For research support, see: A. Lake, "Are We Born into Our Sex-Roles or Programmed into Them?" *Woman's Day* (January 1975): 24-25; J. Z. Rubin, F. J. Provenzano, and Z. Luria, "The eye of the beholder: Parents' views on sex of newborns," *American Journal of Orthopsychiatry* 44 (1974): 512-19.
6. Rubin contends that this result—males as *doing* and females as *being*—accounts for many of the negative consequences seen in women's self-concepts and esteem. We are a "doing" society: men are what they do occupationally, while women are still being good, sweet, kind wives and mothers. Beyond that "being," even if they work outside the home, women still have trouble saying "who they are."
7. M. D. Shakin and S. H. Sternglanz, "Infant Clothing: Sex Labeling for Strangers," *Sex Roles* 12 (1985): 955-64.
8. C. Renzetti and D. J. Curran, *Women, Men, and Society* (Boston: Allyn & Bacon, 1995).

9. N. B. Weitzman, B. Binis, and R. Friend, "Traditional mothers' communication with their daughters and sons," *Child Development* 56 (1985): 895-96.
10. Merton, *Social Theory and Social Structure*.
11. S. F. Anders, "Gender and Society," in *Sociology: A Pragmatic Approach*, 3rd ed., ed. J. C. Bridges (Winston-Salem, NC: Hunter Text Books, 1986).
12. Renzetti and Curran, *Women, Men and Society*, 118.
13. Ibid.
14. M. Mead, *Sex and Temperament in Three Primitive Tribes* (New York: Mentor Books, 1935).
15. Anders, "Gender and Society" in *Sociology: A Pragmatic Approach*.
16. Ibid.
17. Ibid.
18. E. Maccoby, "Gender as a social category," *Developmental Psychology* 24 (1988): 755-65.
19. Ibid.
20. D. C. Holland and M. A. Eisenhart, *Educated in Romance: Women, Achievement, and College Culture* (Chicago: University of Chicago Press, 1991).
21. A. L. Press, *Women Watching Television: Gender, Class, and Generation in the American Television Experience* (Philadelphia: University of Pennsylvania Press, 1991).
22. Renzetti and Curran, *Women, Men and Society*.
23. J. S. Hawley et al., *Fundamentalism and Gender* (New York: Oxford University Press, 1994).
24. Charles W. Peck, George D. Love, and L. Susan Williams, "Gender and God's Word: Another Look at Religion, Fundamentalism, and Sexism," *Social Focus* 69 (June 1991): 1205-1221.
25. Hawley et al., *Fundamentalism and Gender*.
26. G. Allen, "How Your Daughter Grows Up to Be a Man," *Humanist* 40 (1990): 34.
27. N. Henley, M. Hamilton, and B. Thorne, "Womanspeak and Manspeak: Sex Differences and Sexism in Communication," in *Beyond Sex Roles*, ed. A. G. Sargent (New York: West Publishing Co., 1985).
28. Renzetti and Curran, *Women, Men, and Society*.
29. This author contends that the lower self-esteem of females results from traditional gender socialization as Rubin explains it. Unless we change childhood socialization, we will continue to set girls up to need validation from others so much, that they inevitably become more dependent and less coequal.
30. L. Ollison, "Socialization: Women, Worth and Work." Unpublished paper, San Diego State University. Cited in: E. Havemann and M. Lehtinen, *Marriages and Families: New Problems and New Opportunities* (Englewood Cliffs, NJ: Prentice-Hall, 1975).
31. P. Orenstein, *School Girls: Young Women, Self-Esteem, and the Confidence Gap* (New York: Doubleday & Co., 1994).
32. A. Skolnick and J. H. Skolnick, *Intimacy, Family, and Society* (Boston: Little, Brown & Co., 1974). Cited in E. Havemann and M. Lehtinen, *Marriages and Families: New Problems and New Opportunities,* 2nd ed. (Englewood Cliffs, NJ: Prentice-Hall, 1990).
33. Havemann and Lehtinen, *Marriages and Families*.
34. Anders, "Gender and Society" in *Sociology: A Pragmatic Approach*.
35. N. Wolf, *Fire with Fire* (New York: Random House, 1993).
36. A median is the value that is exactly in the middle of a variable, such as income. Therefore, one-half of men have an income higher than the median value and one-half have an income lower than the median value.
37. Doyle and Paludi, *Sex and Gender*, 258.
38. E. Glen and R. Feldberg, "Degraded and Deskilled: The Proletarianization of Clerical Work," *Social Problems* 25 (1977): 52-64.

39. This type of change clearly demonstrates the inferiority of women's positions. Why couldn't men be called stewardesses or stewards? It is difficult to think of an occupation where the name has been changed to accommodate females. Names have been modified (e.g., policeman to police officers; firemen to firefighters).
40. P. Blumstein and P. Schwartz, *American Couples* (New York: Morrow & Co., 1983).
41. A. Hochschild, *The Second Shift* (New York: State University Press, 1989).
42. S. F. Berk, *The Gender Factory: The Apportionment of Work in American Households* (New York: Plenum Press, 1985).

additional resources

J. M. Bardwick, *Psychology of Women* (New York: Harper and Row, Publishers, 1973).

L. Gould, "X: A Fabulous Child's Story," *Ms* 1 (December 1992).

S. J. Kessler and W. McKenna, *Gender: An Ethnomethodological Approach* (New York: John Wiley and Sons, 1978).

E. Maccoby and C. Jacklin, *The Psychology of Sex Differences* (Stanford: Stanford University Press, 1974).

W. Martyna, "Beyond the 'He/Man' Approach: The Case for Nonsexist Language," *Signs* 5 (1980): 482-93.

J. Money and A. A. Ehrhardt, *Man and Woman, Boy and Girl* (Baltimore: Johns Hopkins Press, 1972).

J. Money and D. Mathews, "Prenatal Exposure to Virilizing Progestins: An Adult Follow-Up Study of Twelve Women," *Archives of Sexual Behavior* 11 (1982): 73-83.

J. M. Nielsen, *Sex and Gender in Society: Perspectives on Stratification*, 2nd ed. (Prospect Heights, IL: Waveland Press, 1990).

J. H. Pleck, *Working Wives and Working Husbands* (Beverly Hills: Sage Publications, Inc., 1985).

M. Sadker and D. Sadker, "Striving for Equity in Classroom Teaching," in *Beyond Sex Roles*, ed. A. G. Sargent (New York: West Publishing, Co., 1985).

R. G. Simons and F. Rosenberg, "Sex, Sex Roles, and Self-Image," *Journal of Youth and Adolescence* 4 (1975): 229-58.

L. Thompson and A. J. Walker, "Women and Men in Marriage, Work, and Parenthood," *Journal of Marriage and Family* 51 (1989): 845-72.

U. S. Bureau of Census (Washington, DC: U. S. Department of Commerce), 1999.

I. Weis, *Class, Race and Gender in American Education* (New York: State University Press, 1987).

CHAPTER TEN

Aging

chapter outline

I. **Age Structure**
   A. Age norms
   B. Age stratification

II. **Changing age structures: Demographic processes**
   A. An aging world
   B. An aging America

III. **Normal aging**
   A. Sociological theories of aging
   B. What does aging cause?

IV. **Adaptation to life events**

V. **Illness and long-term care**
   A. Chronic illness
   B. Institutionalization and long-term care

VI. **Death and dying**

VII. **How Christians can change the world**

biblical reflection

"For everything there is a season, and a time for every matter under heaven."

—Ecclesiastes 3:1

In a culture that is fixated on youth, aging is sometimes seen as an ugly, debilitating process. However, when seen as one of God's seasons of life, aging can be beautiful.

Victor Hugo, the nineteenth-century poet and novelist, once remarked, "Forty is the old age of youth; fifty is the youth of old age." He was probably referring to the important changes that occur at mid-life, but Hugo also may have been pointing out that age is a basic characteristic of human societies that helps to organize daily life. Age structures social life in a multitude of subtle but important ways. Many a young person has heard the parental refrain, "It's about time for you to get a job." This is one illustration that our lives are lived on a time line and that society expects certain actions of people at given ages. In this chapter we examine age as a basic feature of social organization and how social life influences the **aging** process. We begin by examining age structure. We then turn to a consideration of what aging means in the social context and how social life influences the process of growing older. Sociologists who study aging are sometimes referred to as engaged in social **gerontology**—the study of the relationship between age and social life.

AGE STRUCTURE

AGE NORMS

Human behavior is shaped by many factors ranging from genetic and biological properties to social and cultural forces. Thinking as sociologists, we are interested in identifying the social forces that influence beliefs, values, and behavior. Chief among the social forces is the normative order of society. Norms are shared expectations of appropriate behavior. Yet, what people often fail to notice about norms is how many of them are linked to age.

The mass media is often drawn to spectacular human-interest stories such as the senior citizen who, when attacked by a mugger, called out for help while she hit the man repeatedly with her umbrella. We marvel at her courage and strong will precisely because we generally do not *expect* people to fight off muggers. Thus, when an *older person—especially* a *woman*—does so, we think that is pretty special.

Or consider the man who wanted to bungee-jump on his eightieth birthday. We may think: "He shouldn't do that *at his age*." The point is not whether bungee-jumping and fighting off a mugger are the best or most rational actions to undertake; rather, the key thought here is that our expectations of what people should and can do are strongly colored by their age. Therefore, we can say that **age norms** are *shared expectations of appropriate behavior for people at a given life stage*. Some age norms are linked to particular ages such as sixteen, twenty-one, or sixty-five, but most often they are tied to stages or periods of the life course. Age norms may be codified in law or they may be quite informal, as in the case of appropriate dress. Most age norms are passed on through tradition, but social movements and legal action are challenging many today.

Consider the example of commercial airline pilots. The Federal Aviation Agency's regulations of 1959 established a mandatory retirement age of 60 for commercial pilots. Citing airline safety, the agency (renamed the Federal Aviation Administration in 1967) viewed older pilots as probably lacking adequate reaction time and/or visual acuity to fly. Some people would argue that today's sixty year olds are in much better health than those of that age forty years ago, and that they have experience to compensate for some deficits in functional ability. This debate ensues, as do similar ones for firefighters and police.

Some age norms are obviously good for society. Can you imagine a ten-year-old pilot or a twelve-year-old police officer? But the fact that some age norms have changed over time suggests that some expectations were unfair to people of certain ages—young or old. When considering society as a whole, we can envision a conglomeration of age norms functioning with other norms, exerting pushes and pulls on what people think they should do. Sometimes these pushes and pulls are quite subtle; at other times they are quite explicit. From a sociological perspective, age norms help structure society, but they may also be a source of conflict and injustice.

When she was in her late twenties, Pat Moore sought help from a professional make-up artist to disguise herself as an "older person." Her book *Disguised* convincingly details her three-year adventure and offers a fascinating account of the influence of age norms.[1] For instance, she describes how she received very different *treatment* by a male office supply clerk on two occasions when she went to purchase the same item—one time as the young woman, without her costume, and one time disguised as the older woman. The young adult clerk almost gushed over the young Pat Moore, but neglected and showed little cordiality to the older Pat Moore. **Ageism** refers to negative attitudes and behaviors toward older people based on their chronological age. Pat Moore felt targeted by numerous ageist actions during her research, but also reported numerous occasions of beneficence and good will to the older Pat Moore. For this chapter, the critical point is that we see how the social system uses age as a basic organizing criterion to create a system of age stratification.

AGE STRATIFICATION

Social stratification refers to the unequal distribution of social resources in a social system. As is the case for other social categories such as sex and race, there is stratification between different age groups in all societies.[2] We can refer to this concept as **age stratification**: *an unequal distribution of social resources based on chronological age*. Age is, therefore, one of several overlapping systems of stratification; it represents one way of stratifying or layering society where age groups comprise the strata of society.[3]

Viewing society as an age-stratified system highlights several important social processes. Perhaps the best way to illustrate them is by an analogy. Consider the escalator. Stepping onto the escalator signifies birth, and aging is signified by progress to higher floors. Imagine reaching the first floor as becoming ten years old, the second floor as reaching twenty, and so on. As you are aware, you were not the only one born on your birthday or during that given year. Sociologists refer to people born during a similar period of time—usually a ten-year period—as a **cohort** or birth cohort. (One can define a cohort for any time period, but the most common demarcations are one-year and ten-year periods.) So each of us started riding the escalator with other people; we are aging together as members of a specific cohort. The unfortunate part is that some members of each cohort will not even make it to the first floor, fewer still to the second floor. By the time one reaches the seventh, eighth, or ninth floors, the cohort has shrunk appreciably.

When viewing society as involving a system of age stratification, one can also see the links between individual aging and social history. **Matilda Riley**, the chief architect of the age stratification perspective, identified these links by stating that the perspective has three foci: *individual aging, cohort flow*, and *changing age structures*.

Of course, we all know what individual aging is, but perhaps not in the sociological sense. *Individual aging* is seen as "a life-course process of growing up and growing *older* from birth to death, not simply growing *old* beyond some arbitrary point in the life course."[4] Because age norms operate in every society, growing up and growing older imply adopting certain roles and giving up others. Certain roles are expected of children, youth, young adults, and older adults throughout the life course. To continue in certain roles after the norms specify exiting the role is a case of *asynchronization*. It is acceptable for a five year old to wear a holster with a "six-shooter" cap pistol, but a twenty year old doing the same is absurd; he is "off time" or out of sync with his cohort. The seventy-two-year-old father of a newborn is another illustration of asynchronization. Fathering a child in one's seventies is not a typical expectation.

The age stratification perspective also emphasizes the role of *cohort flow*. While the individual ages, the cohort of which he or she is a part flows through history. Using the escalator analogy, a cohort ages together or rides to subsequent floors together. Each cohort changes as it moves through historical time. Some cohorts in America have experienced a World War, while some have only been alive through Desert Storm. Thus, specific world, national, or regional events will affect or "imprint" each cohort differently. For a simple illustration from public health, think about the difference in dental health due to the discovery and application of fluoride. While previous cohorts struggled to maintain their oral health, recent cohorts have a tremendous advantage because of fluoridation of public water systems and dental applications of fluoride for children.

The third focus of the age stratification perspective is the role of *changing age structures*. Because cohorts flow and experience different events, there is always the possibility for changing age structures. Wars, epidemics, natural disasters, or advances in public health are just some of the many factors that can affect the age structure of a population. It can also be affected by social and cultural practices that influence fertility, mortality, or migration. Studying the relationship between population and social processes is referred to as *demography*. American demographers have been acutely aware of how our age structures are changing in dramatic fashion. American society has gotten older (i.e., a larger percentage of its population is older), and this trend will continue. Indeed, the world in general is experiencing population aging.

FIGURE 10:1
Life Expectancy at Birth in Selected Nations: 2000

World	**66**
More Developed	75
Less Developed	64
North America	**77**
United States	77
Canada	79
Northern Europe	**77**
Sweden	79
Norway	78
United Kingdom	77
Western Europe	**78**
France	79
Austria	78
Germany	77
Belgium	78
Southern Europe	**77**
Greece	78
Italy	78
Eastern Europe	**69**
Bulgaria	71
Poland	73
Hungary	71
Romania	69
Russia	67
Other More Developed	
Japan	81
Australia	79
New Zealand	77
Israel	78
Other Less Developed	
Mexico	72
China	71
Brazil	68
Kenya	49
Egypt	65
India	61
Uganda	42
Nigeria	52
Bangladesh	59

Source: 2000 World Population Data Sheet. Washington, DC: Population Reference Bureau.

CHANGING AGE STRUCTURES: DEMOGRAPHIC PROCESSES

AN AGING WORLD

American society is similar to most modern societies in this aging of the population. The process of modernization typically is accompanied by changes in mortality and fertility rates—what is referred to as the "demographic transition." Public health interventions, better nutrition, and improved sanitation often lead the way to lower death rates, including lower infant mortality. As a result, a larger proportion of the society lives into adulthood and later life. And, as longevity increases, the society ages. Most modern or more developed societies have rates for **life expectancy** in the middle seventies. As shown in Figure 10:1, Japan has the highest life expectancy at 81. Life expectancy in the United States is about 77, quite similar to most of northern and western Europe.

Even beyond the modernized societies, many developing nations are also experiencing changing age structures. India had a life expectancy of fifty-seven in 1991, but that figure rose to sixty-one in the past decade. If one considers the period between 1985 and 2025, the most rapid *growth* in the older adult population will occur in developing countries such as Guatemala (357%), Singapore (348%), and Mexico (324%). Thus, while most modern nations have already experienced a dramatic change in their age structure, numerous highly populated, developing nations will also experience a similar shift in the next few decades. Granted, most of the less developed nations now have a small percentage of older adults, so that the change rate is high. Nonetheless, it is clear that the world's population is rapidly aging. Changes in life expectancy, along with other demographic factors—especially lower fertility and the prevalence of abortion—will combine to make the world much older.

The way the age structure changes will also affect social relations. Consider the example of China's implementation of strict population controls in 1980. Recent decades have seen a drop in the fertility rate, as couples have not been permitted to have more than one child. Thus, for several years, China's most recent cohorts have been the "4-2-1 babies" (i.e., an only child born to two parents and four grandparents). Family sociologists have long known that only-child families are quite different from families in which a child has siblings with which to play, fight, and learn. Popular Chinese culture has dubbed this recent cohort of youngsters, especially the boys, as "little emperors." China can anticipate further change in coming decades due to relaxing the "one child" population control policy in urban areas. To be clear, change in age structures can affect significant change in social structures and vice versa.

AN AGING AMERICA

America is part of a trend toward an aging society common to much of the world, but the changes in its age structure are also unique. One of the major reasons is that fertility and, hence, cohort flow have been fairly uneven in the past sixty or seventy years. Whenever the fertility rate fluctuates substantially, *disordered cohort flow* occurs. By analogy, the number of people boarding the escalator varies widely from cohort to cohort. Consider the changes in fertility in the United States since 1920. Fertility dropped in the 1930s, probably in part due to the economic depression. The national birth rate for the period 1929-1935 was only 17.69.[5] Fertility increased substantially in the 1940s, especially so in the latter part of that decade, and the national birth rate climbed to over 24 by 1950. There is debate about just how much the end of World War II caused this rise in fertility, but it is clear that a "baby boom" occurred between 1947 and 1960. Many of the large numbers of babies born during that period were birthed in crowded hospital nurseries, went to crowded public schools, faced stiff competition for college admission, and even stiffer competition for their first jobs. In short, social and economic institutions were not ready for the large cohort. To make matters worse, the fertility rate declined in the 1960s and 1970s; thus, many of the institutional accommodations for the baby boom were not needed two decades later (e.g., public school closures and mergers in the 1980s).

The baby boomers are now in middle age and will start turning sixty-five years of age in the period from about 2012 to 2025. While the United States now has about 12.7 percent of its population at sixty-five years of age or older, that figure will jump to over 17 percent by 2020. To clarify these changes, Figure 10:2 displays the percentage of the population sixty-five years and older from 1950 to 2050. Notice the sharp increase in the percent of the population sixty-five years or older during the period 2020 to 2030. Some sociologists and gerontologists claim that we now need **"2020 vision"** to prepare for the tremendous age shift the United States will experience in less than thirty years.[6] One way of thinking of the change is that the proportion of the U.S. population over sixty-five during the year 2020 will be similar to the current proportion of people sixty-five years or older in Florida.

Further evidence that our society is aging comes from the fact that the oldest segments of the older population are growing the fastest. Observe also in Figure 10:2 that the proportion of the older adult population that is eighty-five years of age or older is also growing rapidly (85+/65+). Indeed, if one considers the proportion of the older adult population that is eighty-five years of age or older in 1950 and 2050, a quadrupling of that population may be observed. Thus, while we will see a sharp shift

FIGURE 10:2
Aging of the United States Population: 1950 to 2050

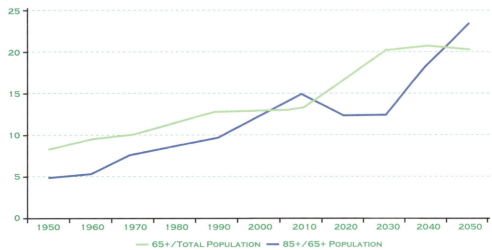

Source: National Center for Health Statistics, *Health, United States, 1999 with Health and Aging Chartbook* (PHS), 99-132 (Hyattsville, MD: National Center for Health Statistics, 1999).

in the proportion of people over sixty-five years of age, we have already witnessed dramatic growth in the proportion of people eighty-five years of age or older. The number of centenarians (persons 100 years or older) has also reached an all-time high. In short, the American population is aging, and the senior citizen population itself is also aging. It is also important to note that America's growing ethnic diversity will increasingly manifest itself among the older population. The populations of African, Hispanic, and Asian Americans have, on average, been younger populations. But we are witnessing increasing life expectancy among these groups, which translates to a more ethnically diverse older population in the future.

Some people interpret the aging of America in an alarmist or "social problem" framework, but this is an inaccurate interpretation. The aging of our population represents an incredible success due to changes in public health and lifestyle behaviors. And as stressed throughout this chapter, *older people are survivors*. They have managed to avoid accidents and have lived in such a way as to make it into their later years. As a result, the older population is somewhat of an elite group, and one with many positive qualities—higher political, voluntary, and religious participation and lower rates of criminal activity, just to name a few.[7] Assuredly, we must prepare for the dramatic change in the age structure of our population, but we can also view older people as a valuable resource to meet the challenges ahead.

It is intriguing to ponder how our society has been and will be shaped by its changing age structures. However, given what sociologists and gerontologists have learned about the aging process, many popular ideas about what "normal aging" entails will probably need to be revised. Indeed, it may be that those who are not aware of some of the most basic features of normal aging are most likely to be anxious about the aging of our world. For the remainder of the chapter, we turn our attention to popular myths and realities of normal aging, especially in modern societies. We begin with a brief overview of sociological theories of aging and show that their development has greatly shaped what we now know to be normal aging.

NORMAL AGING

SOCIOLOGICAL THEORIES OF AGING

The first "implicit" sociological theory of aging developed in the 1950s and became known as the **activity theory**; it grew out of the more general, symbolic, interactionist theoretical perspective. "In its simplest form, this theory posits that the more active older adults are also more satisfied with life."[8] Whereas growing older often entails the loss of social roles (e.g., retirement and widowhood), activity theorists hypothesized that people who substitute new roles or compensate for the loss adjust better and manifest higher life satisfaction.

Disengagement theory emerged in the 1960s with disdain for the "implicit" activity theory. Cumming and Henry argued instead that social disengagement is a natural part of the aging process; indeed, they argued that it is functional for both society and the older person. Disengagement theory stressed that the decrease in social participation attendant with growing older was both a natural and inevitable response.[9] This also could be seen as "functional" for society, as older workers and leaders would then make room for younger ones. For this, they drew sharp criticism, but the idea that the social life of elders shows an overall trend toward decreasing social participation is still quite popular.

The decade of the 1970s witnessed the resurgence and further development of activity theory, as well as the emergence of the age stratification perspective noted earlier. It may not be an oversimplification to say that these theories were developed in reaction to disengagement theory. Sociological research on aging mushroomed as scholars sought to see if disengagement was a valid theory. The vast body of studies showed that disengagement is neither a natural nor inevitable response to growing older.

Findings on activity theory tended to support the major hypotheses but showed that the link between activity and well-being is not as simple as originally thought.[10] For instance, some people prefer limited social activity but also have fairly high life satisfaction. Other theoretical perspectives—such as viewing aging as exchange, and the political economy of aging—were developed in the 1970s and 1980s in an attempt to debunk the disengagement theory. But a second aim of the theories was to articulate what normal aging is. Therein lies one of sociology's most substantial contributions to the study of human aging.

WHAT DOES AGING CAUSE?

In the attempt to describe what is normal or usual aging, sociologists observed that age is correlated with many sociological variables. However, they also pointed out that a correlation between two variables does not necessarily imply a causal link. Because advanced age is correlated with higher prevalence of chronic disease and institutionalization, there is a tendency to think of advanced age as the cause of these and many other phenomena. Yet, among sociologists and gerontologists there is widespread dissatisfaction with the use of age as a causal variable.[11] Age and cohort are very important markers of life events, historical experiences, and resources, but age, in and of itself, is typically regarded as an impotent causal variable. Psychologist Jack Botwinick stated this most eloquently:

> Age, as a concept, is synonymous with time, and time in itself cannot affect living function, behavior, or otherwise. Time does not 'cause' anything . . . Time is a crude index of many events and experiences and it is these indexed events which are 'causal.'[12]

Another way of stating this point is that aging all too often gets a bad name for things it did not cause. Myriad biological, neurological, psychological, and social forces influence human thought and action across the life course. A substantial body of research now indicates that the typical changes often observed in later life can be substantially modified or slowed by interventions of various types. Social gerontologists often refer to **normal aging** as the naturally developmental processes of growing older, as distinct from pathological processes that are more likely attributable to disease.[13]

An older population is a very diverse population, and this diversity is one piece of evidence that normal or usual aging does not inevitably cause disease or decline in function.[14] To posit that aging causes certain declines foolishly ignores the many individual differences in the rate of changes in social and physical functioning. There are eighty-year-old men and women who can swim two miles, and able-bodied forty year olds who cannot swim one mile (even though they know how to swim).

Our society usually exaggerates the contribution of "aging" to changes associated with age. All too often we neglect the true causal variables, such as unhealthy lifestyles, environmental toxins, mental illness, or limited social support. These and other factors create major differences in what the typical aging experience entails; thus, sociologists stress the importance of a **life-course perspective** when studying aging.

Most older people stay active well after retirement.

Chapter Ten: Aging

The life course perspective is a view of aging that emphasizes the relatedness of an individual's thought and behavior at given life stages to previous life stages. If we want to understand behavior in later life, our best predictors are usually that person's behavior in earlier life. People who are very social rarely develop into recluses in later life. And rarely do cynical and bitter middle-aged persons become elders full of encouragement and praise. Although adult learners are a diverse group, most have displayed an aptitude for learning earlier in life, and some life events may accentuate this aptitude. Assuredly, people change. The *way we change*, however, is inextricably related to our previous behavior. Therefore, adjustment problems at one point in the life course often lead to similar problems in later life. Some people develop a tremendous sense of coherence in managing life's problems and seem to face subsequent problems with resiliency.[15] Others who struggle with life events in earlier life often struggle in later life when confronting events commonly experienced by older people.

ADAPTATION TO LIFE EVENTS

Life events have played a key role in helping scholars understand the aging process. As noted earlier, sociologists are skeptical that aging can cause much of anything. Along with social class and environmental conditions, sociologists often look at life events as key causal variables for at least two reasons. First, later life typically entails several undesirable life events as one's cohort shrinks and chronic illness affects human functioning. Second, adaptation to undesirable events experienced earlier in life may not have been adequately resolved—the problems experienced earlier have shaped personality in ways that make successful adaptation more difficult in later life.

So how do people face the key events of retirement, widowhood, and the probability of developing a chronic illness? Obviously these events spark major immediate change in the individual's life. But what about the long-term effects? Does retirement bring about health declines? Do widows become recluses? Let's consider retirement first.

Though some people may characterize it as a crisis, Atchley and others assert that a "crisis" orientation to retirement is an oversimplification and perhaps a distortion of the reality in America.[16] To begin, if adequate pensions are available, a significant proportion of workers in modern societies opt for "early retirement," at which time they can engage in other activities. While many people may consider retirement hazardous to health, the evidence has become quite compelling that this is not true. When people die shortly after retirement, it is almost always their failing health *before* retirement that both prompted the retirement and led to death. There is even evidence that retirement may *improve* health in some cases.[17]

There is no sound empirical evidence that retirement leads to social isolation and depression, either. While this may occur for some people, the majority of retirees find new avenues for social life and seem to adjust fairly well.[18] Retirement is a realignment of role relationships rather than sheer loss, although the outcomes of the adjustment are contingent on several characteristics, most notably social class standing.[19]

Widowhood is another common role transition for older adults, especially older women. In terms of the degree of life change expected, this event has been characterized as one of the most stressful. Certainly, by comparison to retirement, widowhood is a more existentially challenging event, in part because of the lack of control over its happening. There is, in fact, considerable evidence to show that widowhood spurs decrements in physical and mental health, at least for the time immediately following the event. Yet, the bulk of the research shows that most widows emotionally recover from the event after about one year of grieving.[20] Even more revealing is that social participation does not generally decline. Instead, it appears from **longitudinal research** that widows, even in advanced old age, are fairly active in social life relative to their level of activity before the event. Indeed, when adjustment patterns such as mortality and morbidity are considered, the harshest effects of widowhood appear to be on younger widows. Older couples generally have enjoyed years together, and although they may despise the thought of losing a spouse, they are more likely to have given serious thought to it (i.e., widowhood is a normative event for older women). A younger person often feels "blindsided" at the death of a spouse (i.e., a nonnormative event). Like retirement, widowhood spurs a realignment in social life, often fostering high levels of social activity with friends who have also experienced the event. In both cases, disengagement in social relationships is not the inevitable result. The emotional catastrophe of widowhood is severe in many cases, but older adults—especially older women—show considerable resiliency in adjusting to such a major form of loss.

Several explanations emerge when trying to understand why so many (but not all) older people can be so resilient and positive in the face of adversity. Two explanations appear salient. First, *older adults are survivors*. They *have coped*. They have avoided accidents, in part, because many of them avoided high-risk behaviors. They have faced numerous problems over the life course and have probably learned strategies that help them deal with adversity. Second, numerous studies show that *older adults generally have higher levels of participation in religious activities* than is the case for younger adults.[21] Higher religious participation may help in two specific ways. First, religion has long been found to be an important coping mechanism. Religion frequently helps provide meaning to life, especially in the face of adversity; that is, it often helps the person *think through*

Older women who are widows often develop strong support systems with other widows.

the adversity—why it occurs and what it might mean. Second, religion often provides beneficial social relationships. Many occur informally, but there is also an increase in the integration of religious and secular helping organizations designed to benefit older adults. Oftentimes, such programs are designed to enhance service provision to elderly persons, as churches and temples facilitate their efforts with the educational and technical assistance of mental health professionals.[22]

ILLNESS AND LONG-TERM CARE

CHRONIC ILLNESS

Some life events can be devastating in their effects; others appear fairly benign. One of older people's greatest concerns is confronting a chronic illness. Illness, especially chronic illness, may have the power to alter dramatically the person's lifestyle. Again, aging does not cause the illness, but it does increase the likelihood of illness. Some of the themes touched on earlier, however, become very clear when data on health and illness are examined. To illustrate,

Table 10:3 provides some basic information on health and illness among three groups of older people.

First, consider assessed health—asking people to rate their own health. Notice that for good health ratings, there is only a slight difference in the percentages as we compare the three age groups. The percentage of the oldest subjects reporting excellent or very good health is less than those 65-74 years of age, but slightly more than those 75-84 years of age. Looking at it another way, it is intriguing that in the eighty-five-years-of-age or older group, the highest proportion is not in the middle category of good health. As noted earlier, *heterogeneity is often positively associated with age in a population.* People eighty-five years or older are just such an example. Indeed, the excellent or very good health ratings among people eighty-five years or older is even more interesting when one considers the health problems they face. A substantially higher proportion of them have at least one difficulty performing the tasks defined for Activities of Daily Living (ADL). Despite the

TABLE 10:3

Health Status and Problems Among Three Categories of Older Adults

	65-74	75-84	85+
ASSESSED HEALTH			
% Excellent or Very Good	38.3	33.6	35.1
% Good	33.4	32.1	30.4
% Fair or poor	28.3	34.4	34.5
ADL DIFFICULTY			
% None	77.4	68.2	55.5
% One	8.1	10.2	11.8
% Two	4.6	6.0	8.3
% Three	9.9	15.7	24.3
ARTHRITIS			
Rate per 1,000	453.1	460.6	279.4
DEATH BY CAUSE			
Heart Disease	139.4	227.5	240.0
Cancer	156.7	156.3	69.9
Cerebrovascular Disease	24.9	54.1	61.3
Diabetes	16.3	19.6	11.4

Sources: J.F. Van Nostrand, S.E. Furner, and R. Suzman, editors, *Health Data on Older Americans: United States, 1992 (Vital and Health Statistics, Series 3: No 27)* (Hyattsville, MD: National Center for Health Statistics, 1993). U.S. Bureau of the Census, Statistical Abstract of the United States, 2000 (Washington, DC: U.S. Government Printing Office, 2000).

problems they face, however, they are not health pessimists—their health ratings are higher than what we might expect.[23]

Although it is rarely implicated as a primary cause of death, the prevalence of arthritis among the older population is also extensive. Nearly half of the persons age 65-84 are afflicted by arthritic problems, but the bulk of them manage to function with the assistance of others and/or technical devices. Finally, notice mortality or deaths by cause over the three age groups at the bottom of Table 10:3. The prevalence of these conditions is not simply related to age. The prevalence of some conditions such as diabetes increases from ages 65-74 to ages 75-84 and then decreases by ages eighty-five and older. What we are witnessing here is population change due to mortality. The cohorts are shrinking, so that those who *survive* to eighty-five years of age are probably the most fit. Women are much more likely to survive into this period, despite the fact that they suffer from more musculoskeletal problems—men are more likely to have died earlier due to life-threatening conditions such as heart disease.

Given the changing age structures of the coming decades, it is clear that we need to prepare for the prevalence of functional disabilities associated with chronic disease. Engineers, designers, and health care professionals are all beginning to respond by developing products and services to enable persons with chronic disease to be functional in society. It is clear that people, especially women, will live many years with chronic disease. It is incumbent upon us to create a society where people can remain independent as long as possible.

As people age, their priorities change.

INSTITUTIONALIZATION AND LONG-TERM CARE

No one issue does more to spark interest in maintaining functional independence than institutionalization or what is popularly called placement in a nursing home. To many people, being institutionalized is *the* event that epitomizes growing older. As long as they are independent and living in their homes, many people do not even identify themselves as older people. Clearly, when illness so wrecks the body that the individual can no longer function independently, the person's sense of self is challenged in new ways.

But just how many people will actually succumb to such a lot in life? In other words, will most people who reach sixty-five or seventy-five years of age be institutionalized? Is this a normal part of growing older? Both responses are no. If we were to calculate all the people in nursing homes today and divide that by the total proportion of older adults, we would arrive at a figure of about 5 percent. It would appear that nursing home admissions are fairly rare—a source of good news.

However, the 5 percent figure could be called misleading or a fallacy.[24] We would arrive at that figure by conducting a **cross-sectional analysis**. We know the proportion at that one point in time. Yet, nursing home populations turn over—some people die there, others go home, still others go back to the hospital or to live with family members. Therefore, sociologists find it more meaningful to estimate the **total chance of institutionalization**; that is, the likelihood that a person age sixty-five or older will ever be placed in an institutional setting such as a nursing home. This rate is much higher, generally identified to be about 25 percent.[25] In addition, three risk factors greatly affect the total chance of institutionalization: (1) advanced age; (2) diagnostic condition—higher rates for chronic heart failure, broken hip, Alzheimer's disease, and stroke; and (3) living alone.

Certainly the total chance of institutionalization at one in four—higher if one has one or more of the three high-risk factors—sounds more formidable than the 5 percent number. Yet, even the total chance figure is not as bleak as it may seem. The inverse is that the majority of the older adult population (about 75 percent) will *not* be admitted to a nursing home during their lifetime. These are the people that some writers have called the "invisible elderly." They do not get all the news coverage as those with Alzheimer's disease who are abandoned by their children or are the victims of nursing home abuse. Rather, they are the relatively healthy, relatively independent older adults who are living in their homes, shopping at local markets, being visited by children and grandchildren, and engaging in leisure pursuits. They need help with certain tasks from time to time, but by and large they are fairly independent.

Social gerontologists and health care providers have learned that a system of long-term care better meets the needs of elders who experience health problems. It can help a larger proportion maintain their independence. **Long-term care** is the sustained provision of one or more services to enable people with chronically impaired functional capacities to maintain their maximum levels of psychological, physical, and social well-being.[26] Long-term care is actually a hybrid of medical care and social care.

There are two basic types of long-term care, the most obvious of which is *institutionalization*. The other, *community-based care,* is provided to the person outside of institutional settings and includes: (1) adult day care; (2) home health care; (3) foster care; (4) hospice; (5) protective services; and (6) respite care. Many of these forms of community-based care can delay the onset of preventable disease, lengthen functional independence of people with chronic disease, and improve the quality of the person's life. Federal policies during the 1980s (Omnibus Budget Reconciliation Act of 1980 and the Prospective Payment System implemented in

Many elderly people benefit from the stimulation of interpersonal relationships that nursing homes provide.

1983) liberalized Medicare benefits to several of these community-based care services. These programs are usually less costly and they substantially affect quality of life. It appears both likely and desirable that future policy will again enhance the development of these forms of long-term care to prevent institutionalization whenever feasible. Most of the "invisible elderly" are residing in their homes, and community-based long-term care seems best for reducing and/or delaying the risk of institutionalization.

DEATH AND DYING

To many people, growing older is frequently associated with dying. There is good reason why many people think in these terms. Just going back to nineteenth-century America, death was much more likely to occur at earlier stages of the life course. Death in the first year of life was common, and about one third of the population died before age twenty.[27] The successful public health improvements over the past century have raised average life expectancy to the point that older people are now the age group with the highest proportion of deaths. The other major change since the nineteenth century is the location of most deaths. A century ago, most people died at home, but now the majority of people die in hospitals. Thus, the experience of death is in many ways "hidden" from the public, not only because of the location of most deaths, but because of the specialized occupations surrounding the death industry (e.g., morticians).

Despite the changes in where and when death occurs, there is no evidence to suggest that older people are more anxious about or afraid of death. Most of the research indicates that older people are more aware of their finitude, but they are not necessarily afraid of death. The deaths of close family members and friends spur more contemplation about death *throughout the life course*. Thus, it should come as no surprise that older people think about and discuss death more often because they have lost more friends and family members to death.

What concerns most older people is not so much the occurrence of death as *how* they might die. High technology medicine now means that life can be extended beyond the level of what most of us consider functional independence. In American society, functional dependency is widely accepted in infancy and childhood but not in adulthood. Older people, therefore, face the specter of growing dependency and institutionalization due to chronic conditions such as stroke and Alzheimer's disease. Again, anxiety grows not so much about the termination of life, but how the person's life is ended.[28] Finally, there are important differences in how people think about and prepare for death. Previous research indicates that death anxiety is also much lower among persons who are strongly religious and, to a lesser extent, among affirmed atheists. People who are uncertain about their religion or only sporadically participate in it have the highest levels of **death anxiety**.[29]

HOW CHRISTIANS CAN CHANGE THE WORLD

Christians need to recognize the importance of working against the ageism present in most modern societies, especially if present in the church. Negative images and attitudes about aging permeate our society, but Christians need to be transformed by thinking about aging in a new light. To begin with, more pastors and church leaders can teach and preach about honoring the older members of the church and society as a whole. In addition, it is important for world-changers to seize opportunities to reward and honor long-term, faithful service to society or the church. These are important steps to generating beneficence toward older people in our midst. We also need to walk a fine sociological line regarding age integration while ministering to older people. Although many older people want activities and services for similarly aged persons, some do not prefer age-segregated activities. Remember also that many older people do not identify themselves as "older people." Christians need to be sensitive to the preferences of older people to learn how to best minister to them.

Some of the most exciting ways to deliver services to people across the life course is through intergenerational programs—intentionally linking people of different ages. Young people benefit from spending time with older people and vice versa. We should cultivate relationships that can be mutually beneficial, and allow the older person to contribute to it—not trap the older person into the "receiver" corner. Jesus taught that it is more blessed to give than to receive, and we need to find opportunities for older people to *contribute* to social relationships, even when they have reduced functional capacities. Social contributions may be impossible for some, but in such cases we must advocate for the dignity of human life regardless of functional capacity.

overview

- Our consideration of the sociology of aging has led to several conclusions, perhaps the first of which is that age is a basic criterion by which society is organized. Age is the basis for one of several overlapping systems of stratification, and age norms operate to guide human thought and action. Therefore, in tandem with race, gender, and other stratifying criteria, age influences the socialization and allocation processes whereby people adopt certain positions and enact roles attendant with those positions. As Christians, we need to evaluate these norms to see if they hold solid moral and social fiber or are simply traditions in need of revision.

- Aging also provides the link between personal biography and historical change. Not only does a person age, but also as a member of a cohort, he or she experiences many events at the same age as others in the cohort. Thus, individual aging and cohort flow help to index social and historical change and provide the framework to see society as a system of stratification.

- We also noted that the world's population is rapidly aging. While developed nations have "aged" during recent decades, we will also experience substantial growth in the proportion of the population over sixty-five years of age in developing countries. The changing age structures in America are the subject of much interest, as the baby boom becomes a senior boom in about the year 2020. There are many ways that Christians can respond. Churches are beginning to recognize this shift and are organizing ministries to meet the needs of older adults. At the same time, we need to be vigilant not to create age-segregated churches. Young people need to interact with older people and vice versa; unfortunately, some churches are so oriented to one period of the life course that people at other stages often feel they do not belong.

- As sociologists have sought to understand the aging experience, it appears that certain ideas once widely held have now been widely rejected. We now know that aging is not a very potent causal variable and that aging does not entail a natural and inevitable disengagement from social participation. Even in coping with major events such as retirement and widowhood, older people show considerable resilience in adapting to major changes. Older people also face a number of challenges to physical functioning and health maintenance. Despite the prevalence of health problems they encounter, most older people rate their health fairly well and report some of the highest levels of life satisfaction in the population. The majority of older people will never be placed in a nursing home, but the majority will need help coping with life's exigencies and chronic illness. Many churches have played—and will continue to play—valuable roles during such times. Community-based long-term care and intergenerational assistance also appear to pay strong dividends in aiding the older person to maintain his or her independence. Maintaining independence is very important to how older people think about their later years.

- Sociologists choose to view aging from a life-course perspective, noting that behavior and behavioral change in later life are usually related to behaviors exhibited earlier in the life course. There is much we need to learn to prepare for the accelerated aging of our society and the world. Not only are sociologists giving more attention to studying human behavior using the life-course perspective, but also other disciplines—including law, medicine, engineering, and industrial design—will give increased attention to the role of aging in society.

- Christians can work against ageism in society and the church by helping others see the negative images about aging that permeate society. They can urge pastors to preach informatively on the subject of aging and work to avoid age segregation in congregations. They can also organize intergenerational programs to link people of different ages.

key concepts

activity theory
Organized set of hypotheses viewing social activity as beneficial to the well-being of older adults.

age norms
Shared expectations of appropriate behavior for people at a given life stage.

age stratification
An unequal distribution of social resources based on chronological age. Age is one of several overlapping systems of stratification.

ageism
Negative attitudes and behaviors toward older people based on their chronological age.

aging
A life-course process of growing older from birth to death and passing through a set of social positions and roles.

cohort
A set of people born (or experiencing an event) during a given period of time, typically one or ten years.

cross-sectional analysis
Research that collects data at one point in time.

death anxiety
Diffuse form of fear related to the termination of one's life.

disengagement theory
Perspective that presumes that age is accompanied by an inevitable and mutual withdrawal in social life.

gerontology
Scientific study of aging.

life-course perspective
View of aging that emphasizes the relatedness of an individual's thought and behavior at given life stages to previous life stages.

life expectancy
Number of years remaining in life, often calculated at birth or at key ages.

longitudinal research
Research collecting data at two or more points in time.

long-term care
Sustained provision of one or more services to enable people with chronically impaired functioning to maintain their maximum levels of performance.

normal aging
Naturally developmental processes of growing older as distinct from pathological processes which are more likely attributable to disease.

Riley, Matilda White
Sociologist and major architect of age stratification theory.

total chance of institutionalization
Lifetime risk of nursing home placement.

"2020 vision"
Recognition of the major demographic and social changes occurring about the year 2020.

endnotes

1. Pat Moore, *Disguised: A True Story* (Waco, TX: Word Publishing, 1985).
2. Matilda White Riley, Anne Foner, and Joan Waring, "Sociology of Age," *Handbook of Sociology*, ed. N. J. Smelser (Newbury Park, CA: Sage Publications, Inc., 1988), 243-90; Matilda White Riley, "On the Significance of Age in Sociology," *American Sociological Review* 52 (1987): 1-14.
3. Talcott Parsons, "Age and Sex in the Social Structure of the United States," *American Sociological Review* 7 (1942): 604-616.
4. Matilda White Riley, "Age Strata in Social Systems," *Handbook of Aging and the Social Sciences*, ed. R. H. Binstock and E. Shanas (New York: Van Nostrand Reinhold, 1985), 374 (emphasis in original).
5. U.S. Bureau of the Census, *Statistical Abstract of the United States, 1987* (Washington, DC: U.S. Government Printing Office, 1986).
6. Kenneth F. Ferraro and Harvey L. Sterns, "'2020 Vision' and Beyond," *Gerontology: Perspectives and Issues*, K. F. Ferraro, ed. (New York: Springer Publishing, 1990), 357-60.
7. Erdman Palmore, "The Advantages of Aging," *The Gerontologist* 19 (1979): 220-23.
8. Kenneth F. Ferraro, "Sociology of Aging: The Micro-Macro Link," *Gerontology: Perspectives and Issues*, K. F. Ferraro, ed. (New York: Springer Publishing, 1990), 113.
9. Elaine Cumming and William E. Henry, *Growing Old: The Process of Disengagement* (New York: Basic Books, 1961).
10. Bruce W. Lemon, Vern L. Bengtson, and James A. Peterson, "An Exploration of the Activity Theory of Aging: Activity Types and Life Satisfaction among Inmovers to a Retirement Community," *Journal of Gerontology* 27 (1972): 511-23.
11. George L. Maddox, "Aging Differently," *The Gerontologist* 27 (1987): 557-564.
12. Jack Botwinick, *Aging and Behavior* (New York: Springer Publishing 1978), 307.
13. Ewald W. Busse and George L. Maddox, eds., *The Duke Longitudinal Studies of Normal Aging, 1955-1980* (New York: Springer Publishing, 1985).
14. John W. Rowe and Robert L. Kahn, "Human Aging: Usual and Successful," *Science* 237 (1987): 143-149.
15. Aaron Antonovsky, *Unraveling the Mystery of Health: How People Manage Stress and Stay Well* (San Francisco: Jossey-Bass Publishing, 1988).
16. Robert C. Atchley, "Retirement and Leisure Participation: Continuity or Crises?" *The Gerontologist* 11 (1971): 13-17; Robert C. Atchley, *Social Forces and Aging* (Belmont, CA: Wadsworth Publishing Company, 1991).
17. David J. Ekerdt, "Why the Notion Persists that Retirement Harms Health," *The Gerontologist* 27 (1987): 454-57; David J. Ekerdt, Raymond Bosse, and Joseph S. LoCastro, "Claims that Retirement Improves Health," *Journal of Gerontology* 38 (1983): 231-236; and Gordon F. Streib and C. J. Schneider, *Retirement in American Society* (Ithaca, NY: Cornell University Press, 1971).

18. Raymond Bosse, Carolyn M. Aldwin, Michael R. Levenson, Avron Spiro III, and Daniel K. Mroczek, "Change in Social Support after Retirement: Longitudinal Findings from the Normative Aging Study," *Journal of Gerontology: Psychological Sciences* 48 (1993): 210-17.
19. Kenneth F. Ferraro, "Aging and Role Transitions," *Handbook of Aging and the Social Sciences,* 5th ed., ed. R. H. Binstock and L. K. George (San Diego: Academic Press, 2001), 313-30.
20. Helena Z. Lopata, *Widowhood in an American City* (Cambridge, MA: Schenkman Books, Inc., 1973); Kenneth F. Ferraro, "Widowhood and Health," *Aging, Stress, and Health*, ed. K. S. Markides and C. L. Cooper (Chichester: John Wiley & Sons Ltd, 1989), 69-83; and Kenneth F. Ferraro, Elizabeth Mutran, and Charles M. Barresi, "Widowhood, Health, and Friendship Support in Later Life," *Journal of Health and Social Behavior* 25 (1984): 245-54.
21. David O. Moberg, "Religion and Aging," *Gerontology: Perspectives and Issues*, K. F. Ferraro, ed. (New York: Springer Publishing, 1990), 179-205.
22. Rachel Filinson, "A Model for Church-based Services for Frail Elderly Persons and Their Families," *The Gerontologist* 28 (1988): 483-85.
23. Kenneth F. Ferraro, "Self-Ratings of Health among the Old and the Old-Old," *Journal of Health and Social Behavior* 21 (1980): 377-83.
24. Robert J. Kastenbaum and Sandra E. Candy, "The 4 Percent Fallacy: A Methodological and Empirical Critique of Extended Care Facility Population Statistics," *International Journal of Aging and Human Development* 4 (1973): 15-21.
25. Jersey Liang, and Edward Jow-Ching Tu, "Estimating Lifetime Risk of Nursing Home Residency: A Further Note," *The Gerontologist* 26 (1986): 560-63.
26. Stanley J. Brody, "Goals of Geriatric Care," *Hospitals and the Aged: The New Old Market*, ed. S. J. Brody and N. Persily (Rockville, MD: Aspen Publishers, 1984), 51-62.
27. Peter I. Uhlenberg, "Study of Cohort Life Cycles: Cohorts of Native Born Massachusetts Women, 1830-1920," *Population Studies* 23 (1969): 407-20.
28. Victor W. Marshall, "Socialization for Impending Death in a Retirement Village," *American Journal of Sociology* 80 (1975): 1124-44.
29. Richard A. Kalish, *Death, Grief, and Caring Relationships,* 2nd ed. (Monterey, CA: Brooks/Cole Publishing Co., 1985).

CHAPTER ELEVEN

Marriage and Family

chapter outline

I. What is the family?
   A. Basic concepts

II. Theoretical analysis of the family
   A. Structural-functionalist perspective
   B. Conflict perspective
   C. Symbolic interactionist perspective

III. A Christian perspective

IV. Families in multicultural perspective
   A. Ethnicity and race
      1. African Americans
      2. Latinos
      3. Asian Americans
   B. Gay and lesbian families

V. How the American family has changed
   A. Trends in marriage
   B. Trends in cohabitation
   C. Trends in divorce
   D. Trends in family structure

VI. Is the American family declining?

VII. Social change and the future of the family

VIII. How Christians can change their world

biblical reflection

"Therefore a man shall leave his father and his mother and shall cleave to his wife, and the two shall become one flesh."

—Genesis 2:24

Consider Pauline, a young woman reaching adulthood in 1962. Following high school graduation, Pauline worked as a secretary at an automobile dealership until she married. She moved out of her parents' home and formed a new household with her husband. In her early twenties, Pauline began a family soon after marriage. She then quit her job and stayed home to care for their four children. Pauline was expected to have the primary responsibility of caring for the home and children, since her husband had a steady job that paid enough to support their family comfortably.

Fast forward to the early twenty-first century. Novella is a young woman reaching adulthood in 2001. She is not likely to marry before her twenty-fifth birthday. Before marriage, she will work and attend college. She is likely to move in and out of her parents' household several times, perhaps living by herself, with a boyfriend, or with roommates. Novella marries shortly after the birth of her first child. Unlike Pauline, she does not drop out of the labor market, but continues her career in public relations. Novella questions the traditional gender-based organization of home life, but readily accepts divorce, cohabitation, single parenthood, and sex outside marriage.[1]

Whether watching the news, reading the newspaper, seeing almost any television program, attending a political event, or listening to conversations at a social gathering, you hear about the family. Over the last forty years, the American family has undergone dramatic change in structure and values, and often elicits passionate debate over its current status.

WHAT IS THE FAMILY?

Since we are all born into some type of family, we all know what a family is, right? Wrong. Familiar and commonplace as the *notion* of family may be, a universally agreed upon *definition* of the family remains elusive. A definition of the family should encompass a range of family structures, dynamics, and functions. Hence, the **family** is two or more people who are committed to each other over time, sharing intimacy, resources, values, and decision-making responsibilities, as well as assuming responsibility for the care of children.[2] (Conflicting definitions of the family are presented in Excerpt 11:1.)

EXCERPT 11:1
Conflicting Definitions of the Family

- A family is any two or more persons related by birth, marriage, or adoption and residing together (U.S. Bureau of the Census, 1997).

- Family is a group of people who love and care for each other (Associated Press, Random Sample of 1,200 People).

- A family is defined as two or more persons who share resources, share responsibility and decisions, share values and goals, and have a commitment to one another over time (American Association of Family and Consumer Sciences).

- A family is a group of individuals related to one another by marriage, blood, or adoption (Focus on the Family).

- The family is a social institution found in all societies that unites people in cooperative groups to oversee the bearing and raising of children.

Source: John Macionis, *Sociology*, 8th ed. (Upper Saddle River, NJ: Prentice-Hall, 2001), 462.

BASIC CONCEPTS

Family structures and patterns vary tremendously across cultures. For example, in the developing world, large families are necessary for subsistence agriculture and the production of goods necessary for the family's survival. Typical to these regions are **extended families**—consisting of parents, dependent children, and other relatives. With increasing urbanization, industrialization, and social mobility, large families are economically disadvantageous, while nuclear families prosper. **Nuclear families** consist of one or two parents and their children. Pauline and Novella both live in nuclear families. The family Pauline was born into is known as her *family of orientation*, and the family she entered into as an adult was her *family of procreation*.

In most industrialized nations, monogamy is the dominant cultural norm. **Monogamy** is marriage to one spouse at a time. In many developing nations, however, especially in Africa and southern Asia, polygamy is permitted. **Polygamy** is marriage to more than one spouse at a time. Polygamy takes two forms. The most common is **polygyny**—a family in which a man can marry more than one woman at a time. In Islamic nations in Africa, for example, a man is permitted to marry up to four wives. Although illegal in the United States, polygyny still exists in parts of Utah and Idaho. In less than 1 percent of the world's families, polyandry is permitted. **Polyandry** is a family in which a woman can marry more than one husband at a time. (Polyandry will be discussed in greater detail later in the chapter.) Despite the permissibility of polygamy, most actual marriages are monogamous. **Kinship** refers to family ties established through marriage or lines of descent. **Marriage** is the socially acknowledged and approved union between a man and a woman for the purpose of founding and maintaining a family.

THEORETICAL ANALYSIS OF THE FAMILY

A theory is a logically related set of explanations used to describe, understand, and predict some aspect of human social behavior. Several theoretical approaches—mainly functionalism, symbolic interaction, and conflict theory—explain family behavior and guide our research.

Nuclear family is the norm for White American culture. Extended families are celebrated at family reunions, but are rarely used for subsistence.

THE STRUCTURAL-FUNCTIONALIST PERSPECTIVE

Functionalists are interested in how society is structured in order to maintain its stability. Functionalists begin by looking at the four primary tasks the family performs in every society.

1. ***Socialization***. The family is the primary setting for socialization—the place where we learn about society, language, sexual rules, gender roles, and behavioral norms that help us become well-integrated, contributing members of society. Families also provide members with a sense of self and identity.

2. ***Regulation of Sexual Behavior and Reproduction.*** Families are expected to regulate the sexual activity of their members, and thus control reproduction as it occurs within specific boundaries. All cultures regulate sexual activity and restrict sexual relations and reproduction among family members. One universal cultural norm is the *incest taboo*, a cultural norm forbidding sexual relations or marriage between certain family members. Families also ensure that they replace dying members of society with new generations in an orderly fashion.

3. ***Social Placement.*** Families confer social status, and place children in various social hierarchies. It is in the family that children consciously and unconsciously learn the value and meaning of ethnicity, religion, and social class. Patterns of inheritance and descent also are tied to social placement. For example, many societies use *patrilineal descen*t, where the family name is traced through the father's lineage, and sons and male relatives inherit family property. This line of descent is most common throughout Asia, Africa, and the Middle East. If the family name or inheritance is traced through the mother's lineage, it is known as *matrilineal descent*. Common in most Western societies is *bilineal descent,* where the family name and inheritance can be traced to both parents.

4. ***Protection, Affection, and Companionship.*** The family provides the necessary economic and emotional support to its members. For many, the family is a "haven in a heartless world"—providing physical protection, emotional support, and financial assistance.

A functional analysis is beneficial when looking at "the big picture" and understanding the family's contribution to society. Does Pauline have a more stable family than Novella? Why? Functionalists, for example, would be concerned that Novella may surrender some part of family socialization to other institutions. Pauline, for example, probably controlled more of the practical and moral training of her children until they reached adulthood. Novella, however, may have given up some of this responsibility to religious and educational institutions. Novella's children may now learn many of the necessary skills and values for responsible membership in society from school rather than from home. Functionalists would be interested in the long-term consequences of this transition on the stability of society.[3]

THE CONFLICT PERSPECTIVE

The conflict perspective examines society not in terms of its stability and harmony, but in terms of power, conflict, inequality, and struggle. Conflict sociologists examine how the social structure promotes divisions and inequality based on dominance and coercion. Conflict sociologists see families as small versions of society, where some members benefit from the social arrangement more than others. A conflict sociologist might be interested in how racial discrimination affects family life, or how economic trends like corporate downsizing and globalization affect the power structure within families. A conflict sociologist would argue, for example, that Novella has more power in the family than Pauline because of her position in the economic system. Her income provides her new choices and more influence in family decisions. However, despite economic gains, Novella would still bear most of the responsibility for child rearing and domestic chores.[4]

THE SYMBOLIC INTERACTIONIST PERSPECTIVE

The symbolic interactionist perspective attempts to understand society through the personal day-to-day interactions of people. Symbolic interactionists focus on symbols, shared meanings, and interactions based on verbal and nonverbal communication. During interaction with others, attempts are made to interpret what is meant and what others' motives might be. Another important idea in symbolic interaction is the *definition of the situation*—when a situation is defined as real, it has real consequences. For example, if Pauline's husband is very jealous because he believes she is flirting with other men and may be potentially unfaithful, there will be real, perhaps damaging consequences. Or perhaps one of Novella's children interprets family life to be peaceful and supportive, while another child perceives family life as burdensome and conflictual. Each child will act, behave, and respond to the family depending upon his/her definition of the situation. Symbolic interactionists may also be interested in how gender or media images influence perceptions of family experiences.[5]

A CHRISTIAN PERSPECTIVE

What is God's intention for family life? Tough question! The Christian family is based on nine general premises:

1. The family is created in the image of God, and is designed to honor the Creator.

2. The family proclaims the dignity and value of each individual in partnership with the larger community. The family unites the individual to larger social structures and institutions. The family is the God-given institution in which children learn the virtues required to become good citizens, parents, and workers.

3. Children are a blessing from God. Parents are mandated to bring their children to faith in Jesus Christ. The psychological well-being of children depends on positive parent-child interactions fostered by discipline, love, dignity, and praise.

4. The family sets the boundaries for moral behavior, and is the cornerstone of moral order in society.

5. The church must resemble the family by extending grace, empowering others, and fostering intimacy. The church is called to provide a coherent structure of beliefs, values, and activities that enhance family life.

6. Family life cannot escape the presence and power of sin. Excessive demands of

the economic marketplace, flawed governmental policies, and a poisonous popular culture weaken the family, and diminish its connection, influence, and ability to function.

7. The family is called to promote human welfare in both material and spiritual ways. Great extremes of wealth and poverty weaken the family. Consumerism and careerism are tempered by a focus on relationships, mutual empowering, servanthood, and the sharing of resources. Families and churches are encouraged to seek economic and social justice.

8. Biblical family relationships are based on:

- *Commitment*—trust, honesty, dependability, faithfulness, and Christ-centeredness.

- *Grace*—forgiveness, avoiding blame, compromise, hope, appreciation and affection, the ability to cope with stress, openness to change, and resilience.

- *Empowering*—mutual submission, serving and being served, avoiding blame, respecting individuality, recognizing strengths, giving compliments, and avoiding control.

- *Intimacy*—common faith, sharing

Healthy families develop connection and love rituals.

Sociology: A Christian Approach for Changing the World

beliefs, positive, open, and honest communication.

9. The family must be intentional—maturating a plan to build and maintain family ties is essential for Christian families. Healthy families develop:

- *Connection rituals*—everyday opportunities for family bonding.

- *Love rituals*—developing individual intimacy by making individual and family members feel special and important.

- *Community rituals*—major family events that link families to their communities.[6]

FAMILIES IN MULTICULTURAL PERSPECTIVE

We began this chapter by talking about the family lives of Pauline and Novella. Their experiences, however, are characteristic of primarily White, middle-class American women. Consider Nimbatu, a woman of the Toda tribe in the Nilgiri Hills of India. The Toda culture practices *polyandry*, a tradition where a wife has multiple husbands. Nimbatu's marriage was initially arranged, and when Nimbatu married, she not only married one man, but also all of his brothers. All of the brothers have full sexual rights, and marital privileges are rotated equitably among the brothers. When Nimbatu becomes pregnant, there is no call to determine biological parenthood, so a community celebration is convened. If none of the brothers volunteers to assume paternity, the oldest brother will select the father. After two or three children are born, another brother will be selected for subsequent

In urban areas such as Chicago, nonwhite families now outnumber white families.

children. Toda men can also seek mates from women who are already married.[7] Clearly, the family experiences of Nimbatu are dramatically different from Pauline or Novella.

Hannah is a thirty-five-year-old woman who grew up in a kibbutz—a Jewish agricultural settlement in Israel. Her kibbutz features collective ownership of all property and communal living. In the kibbutz, the community raised Hannah, and her parents played almost no role in her socialization or discipline. Hannah saw her parents no more than one hour per day when she was young, and progressively less as she entered adolescence. Nurses and teachers raised Hannah, not her parents. She ate and slept in special quarters throughout high school, sharing the same room and using the same showers and toilets as her age cohorts. Following high school and required military service, Hannah returned to the kibbutz. After a brief period of cohabitation, she married shortly after the birth of her first child in a ceremony designed to satisfy Israeli law by conferring legal rights to the child. Once kibbutz members are married, all domestic work is shared equally, and the equality of the sexes is scrupulously observed. Although nuclear families are more central in contemporary kibbutzim, commitment to the communal way of life is still central to Hannah and her family.[8]

> **EXCERPT 11:2**
> Stereotypes and Strengths of African American Families
>
> **STEREOTYPES**
> - Lower class/Welfare dependent
> - Criminals
> - Drug abusers
> - Promiscuous
> - Less intelligent
> - Absent fathers
>
> **STRENGTHS**
> - Strong kinship bonds – extended family is important
> - Hard working – dual-job households are common
> - Flexibility in family roles – sharing by husband and wife
> - Strong religious orientation
> - Strong bonds between parents and children
>
> Source: David H. Olson and John DeFrain, *Marriage and the Family: Diversity and Strengths*, 3rd ed. (Mountain View, CA: Mayfield Publishing, 2000).

> **EXCERPT 11:3**
> Stereotypes and Strengths of Latino Families
>
> **STEREOTYPES**
> - Poorly educated
> - Large families
> - Migrants or illegal immigrants
> - Male dominated and emotionally cold
> - Alcohol abusers
>
> **STRENGTHS**
> - High family cohesion
> - Commitment to extended family
> - Supportive kin network
> - Strong ethnic identity
> - Hard working
> - Family flexibility
>
> Source: David H. Olson and John DeFrain, *Marriage and the Family: Diversity and Strengths*, 3rd ed. (Mountain View, CA: Mayfield Publishing, 2000).

ETHNICITY AND RACE

The proportion of ethnic and minority families in the United States has experienced phenomenal growth. According to Census Bureau projections, by 2025, 62 percent of the U.S. population will be White, down from 86 percent in 1950. This trend illustrates the growing presence and power of minority families.

AFRICAN AMERICANS

While African Americans made significant economic progress during the last half of the twentieth century, they still face economic disadvantages. The typical African American family earned $30,439 in 2000, roughly 66 percent of the median income for Whites. Moreover, African American families are characterized by fewer marriages and higher divorce rates. African American women experience parenthood at earlier ages, become single heads of households, and are less likely to remarry. Despite these economic hardships, 90 percent of African Americans feel close to their families and highly value family responsibility and loyalty.[9] (See Excerpt 11:2.)

LATINOS

One of the fastest growing segments of the American population is the Latino segment. It is estimated that by 2030, Latinos will be the largest ethnic group—approximately 20 percent of the U.S. population. The Latino population is very diverse; immigrants come mainly from Mexico, followed by the Caribbean, and Central

> **EXCERPT 11:4**
>
> Stereotypes and Strengths of Asian American Families
>
> **STEREOTYPES**
> - Rigid gender roles
> - Highly intelligent
> - Obedient children
> - Hard working
> - Emotional distance
> - Competitive
>
> **STRENGTHS**
> - Strong family orientation
> - Filial piety
> - High value on education
> - Support of extended family
> - Family loyalty
>
> Source: David H. Olson and John DeFrain, *Marriage and the Family: Diversity and Strengths*, 3rd ed. (Mountain View, CA: Mayfield Publishing, 2000).

and South America.

Latino families tend to be relatively large and stable, with lower divorce rates compared to other ethnic groups. Traditionally, many Latino families have very supportive nuclear and extended families. Because the family is highly valued, there is also a strong emotional commitment to the family. Latino parents often exercise more control over children's courtship, and adhere more rigidly to conventional gender roles.

Latino families encourage machismo—strength, daring, and sexual prowess for men. On the other hand, women are expected to follow the values of marianismo—the glorification of motherhood, sacrifice, submission, and acceptance of a difficult marriage. While some Hispanics have prospered, particularly Cubans, the typical Latino family in 2000 had an annual income of $33,447, only 79 percent of the national standard. Many Latino families continue to wrestle with the stresses of unemployment and other poverty-related problems.[10] (See Excerpt 11:3.)

ASIAN AMERICANS

Asian American families are also one of the fastest growing ethnic minorities in America. Although Asian American families are very diverse, most share several patterns. Among these are strong collectivist kinship traditions and marriages that are often arranged by kin. Compared to other ethnic groups, Asian Americans have one of the highest marriage rates and lowest divorce rates. Extended families are normative, and children are expected to be obedient and loyal to parents and kin. As well, women are expected to be subordinate to males in the family structure. Hard work, achievement, self-control, dependability, good manners, thrift, and diligence are highly valued. While traditional expectations for marriage are dissipating, new family norms emphasizing romantic love and choice are creating new sources of intergenerational conflict.[11] (See Excerpt 11:4.)

GAY AND LESBIAN FAMILIES

In 1989, Denmark was the first country to recognize same-sex marriages. Since then, Norway and Sweden have lifted their ban on gay marriages. In the United States, homosexual marriages are illegal in all fifty states, although Hawaii, Vermont, and the cities of San Francisco and New York have allowed limited marital benefits to gay and lesbian couples. It is estimated that one million gay couples are raising children. Undoubtedly, research on gay and lesbian families is emotionally charged and politically motivated. Critics of gay and lesbian families argue that the children in these families face disproportionate risks: confusion over sex-

Increasingly, same sex partners are raising children.

ual identity, greater risk of relational instability, higher likelihood of suffering from depression and other emotional difficulties, and greater risk of losing a parent to AIDS, substance abuse, or suicide.[12]

In one recent nonconclusive study, Stacey and Biblarz report "no differences between heterosexual parents and homosexual partners regarding parenting styles, emotional adjustment, and the sexual orientation of the children."[13] That is one issue that will come under increasing study in the future. Despite the psychological, political, legal, and moral consequences of homosexual partnerships, gay men and lesbian women will contine to challenge traditional marriage and family values and practices. Christians have an obligation to prevent this social change through prayer and the teaching of a biblical worldview.

> ### EXCERPT 11:5
> Facts About Marriage
>
> - African Americans have been most affected by the decline in marriage.
>
> - An increased number of people who get divorced choose not to remarry.
>
> - In about half of all marriages, one or both people have been married before.
>
> - Engagements last an average of 9 months.
>
> - The average U.S. wedding costs about $15,000.
>
> - The average age of divorce is 36 for males, and 33 for females.
>
> - The average length of marriage is 7 years.
>
> Source: U.S. Bureau of the Census, 1997

HOW THE AMERICAN FAMILY HAS CHANGED

TRENDS IN MARRIAGE

While marriage is still the most popular and predominant institution, it plays a less dominant role than in previous generations. The *marriage rate*, the proportion of unmarried women age fifteen and over who get married in a year, continues to fluctuate. The rate of marriage has declined from a high of 68 percent of the population in 1970, to 59 percent in 1996.[14] While more than 85 percent of Americans eventually marry, the number of households with just one person doubled from 13 percent in 1960 to 26 percent in 2000.[15] Moreover, people are delaying marriage. The median age for first marriage is now 26.8 years for men and 25.0 years for women. Women and men are now marrying at an older age than at any time in American history. In 1960, for example, men married at 22.8 years of age, and women at 20.3 years.[16]

Despite the overall decline in marriage, Linda Waite and Maggie Gallagher discovered a number of positive effects of marriage on individuals. They argue that married people experience greater physical, material, and spiritual health. Generally, married people live longer, have better health, earn more money and accumulate more wealth, feel more emotionally fulfilled, enjoy more satisfying sexual relationships, and have happier and more successful children than those who remain single, cohabit, or get divorced.[17]

TRENDS IN COHABITATION

Cohabiting has gained such widespread acceptance that most unmarried couples today are cohabiting.[18] Rates of cohabiting have increased dramatically due to an increased uncertainty of the stability of marriage, an erosion of social norms against cohabitation, increased individualism and secularism, and the wider availability of birth control. Currently, four million couples are cohabiting, an eightfold increase since the 1960s. Approximately 40 percent of unmarried couples marry within five to seven years. Overall, cohabiting couples are more egalitarian, less bound to traditional sex roles, and more likely to be multiethnic.[19] Almost half of cohabitants are couples with children.

Despite the growing popularity of cohabiting, it is not a good predictor of a successful marriage. People who cohabit usually have divorce rates that are equal to or higher than non-cohabitants and, subsequently, have lower rates of marital satisfaction, adjustment, and commitment to marriage.[20] Moreover, gender differ-

---

EXCERPT 11:6

Facts About Divorce

- In 1996, there were 2.3 million marriages and 1.2 million divorces.

- Approximately one million children each year are affected by divorce. About 65 percent of divorces involve children.

- Most divorced people remarry within five years.

- Lower income, less education, insecure employment, and a very brief courtship place families at greater risk for divorce.

- When couples are demographically dissimilar – not comparable in age, race, religion, attitudes and values – the risks of divorce increase.

Source: U.S. Bureau of the Census, 1998.

---

ences shape how the relationship is perceived. Women view the cohabiting relationship as a trial marriage, whereas men view the relationship as an alternative to marriage and a means of sexual gratification.[21]

TRENDS IN DIVORCE

We are number one! The United States has the highest divorce rate in the world; twice as high as Canada, four times higher than Japan, and ten times higher than Italy.[22] The U.S. divorce rate rose sharply between 1960 and 1980, and now more than four in ten marriages end in divorce.

The high U.S. divorce rate can be attributed to many factors:[23]

1. **Rise of individualism.** Today's families spend less time together, and have a greater interest in personal fulfillment and individual happiness. Since marriage is now perceived as an exchange of emotional gratification, couples are less inclined to stay together if their marriages do not provide emotional satisfaction and happiness.

2. **Women's increasing participation in the paid labor force.** Increasing participation in the labor force has reduced wives' economic dependency on husbands.

3. **Contemporary marriages are more stressful.** Public policy and private decision-making have tilted heavily against the sacrificial, nonmarket activities of families. Families have found their roles increasingly difficult as managerial greed, tax and housing policies, pop psychology, and a poisonous entertainment industry have declared a silent war against families.

4. **Divorce is socially acceptable.** Because of the decreasing influence of religion in people's lives, divorce no longer carries the powerful social stigma it did a century ago.

5. **Divorces are easier to obtain.** Changes in divorce laws have made it easier for people in unsatisfying marriages to obtain a divorce. Prior to *no-fault* divorce laws, courts were required to show fault (i.e., adultery, abuse) for a failed marriage. Today, all states allow divorce if a couple agrees that their marriage has failed.

Divorce has profound effects for the divorcing couple, but may be hardest on children. Divorce can alter a child's home environment and social surroundings, entangle them in bitter feuding, and distance them from a parent they love. In many cases, children blame themselves for their parents' breakup. Most studies concur that children of divorced parents have much higher rates of emotional, relational, and behavioral problems. Moreover, children of divorced parents experience more problems in dating, have higher rates of cohabitation, generally have less happy marriages, and experience greater stress from parenting. Many experts counter, however, that divorce is better for children than staying in families marked by tension and violence.[24]

One positive trend is that fathers are spending more time with their children.

Sociology: A Christian Approach for Changing the World

TRENDS IN FAMILY STRUCTURE

The number of single-parent families with children under eighteen is increasing dramatically. In 1970, only 12 percent of children lived in single-parent families; by 1998, almost 30 percent of children lived in single-parent families. Caucasians and Hispanics have the highest rates of two-parent homes (79 percent and 69 percent respectively), and about half of African American children (53 percent) live in two parent households.[25]

Rising divorce and remarriage rates have also increased the number of *stepfamilies*—families where one or both partners have children from a previous marriage. The United States has the world's highest remarriage rate—almost 70 percent of divorced people eventually remarry.[26] In 2000, about 25 percent of all U.S. families were stepfamilies.[27]

One of the positive new trends, however, is the increased role of fathers. Fathers are expected to be involved in care-giving, and are spending more time with their children than fathers from previous generations. In 1998, married fathers reported spending four hours per day with their children, up from 2.7 hours in 1965.[28] In addition, between 1950 and 2000, the number of father-only families increased from 220,000 to 1.8 million.

IS THE AMERICAN FAMILY DECLINING?

Going to a family reunion can be an enjoyable and informative experience for sociologists. Often they are asked by family members to give an opinion on a variety of issues, particularly on the condition of the American family. Some will argue that the family is deteriorating, disintegrating, and bereft of hope and value. Other family members will note the new freedoms and opportunities available to all family members. Much to their dismay, all of their opinions are mostly right!

Nijole Benokraitis has developed a model of understanding family change based on four general perspectives.

- *Conservatives* are convinced that the family is declining and deteriorating due to moral decay, indicated by high rates of divorce, out-of-wedlock births, and single-parent families. Conservatives develop family policies that restore religious faith, stigmatize divorce and out-of-wedlock births, and reduce government involvement in the family.

- *Centrists* feel that the family is declining because of increased selfishness, individualism, excessive parental permissiveness, and the negative influence of the media. Centrists pursue family policies that emphasize communal and parental responsibility, provide economic incentives for intact families, and develop programs to combat selfishness and rampant individualism.

- *Liberals* argue that the family is changing, but not deteriorating. The family is changing because the economic structure and demographic patterns have altered family functions and gender roles. Liberals advocate policies that minimize the negative impact of changes in the economic structure. They advocate programs to help women and children become economically secure by expanding training and job opportunities for low-income workers, and implementing universal health care.

- Finally, *feminists* assert that the family is not deteriorating, but improving because women and men have more options and opportunities. Feminists develop policies that provide more institutional support for dual-earner and single-parent families, create more family-friendly workplaces, and provide universal child care and health insurance.[29]

SOCIAL CHANGE AND THE FUTURE OF THE FAMILY

We know some of the issues that Pauline faced as she formed a new family during the turbulent sixties and seventies. But what about Novella? What kinds of questions, resources, and dangers will she face as she navigates a family through the twenty-first century? Sociologists cannot predict the future, but here are seven likely trends:

- Sexuality will continue to be a matter of personal choice, not bound to marriage or childbearing. As sex pervades the American cultural landscape, more women will have unplanned pregnancies, increased adolescent pregnancies, and a greater risk of extramarital affairs. Despite advances in medical technology, people also will be increasingly at risk for the contraction of STDs (sexually transmitted diseases).[30] AIDS will continue to be a global health crisis.

- There will be an erosion of stigmas. Childlessness, out-of-wedlock births, single parenthood, divorce, cohabitation, and homosexuality will be more common, acceptable, and based on individual choices. Marriage will play a less dominant role.[31]

- Lower birthrates and lower death rates will result in a growing population of those over seventy-five years of age. People will spend a smaller portion of their lives parenting young children, yet grandparenthood will become increasingly more integral in the family life cycle. Financial, emotional, and social support for elderly family members will still largely be the responsibility of younger generations.[32]

- The blending of gender and family roles. (Gender roles: the traits and behaviors assigned to females and males in a culture.) In new roles of authority, women are being encouraged to be more assertive and to command respect. Similarly, men are encouraged to be less aggressive and more honest and open about feelings. Moreover, as women continue to enter the labor force in record numbers (79% in 1998), domestic responsibilities will become more equitable, although not totally. Traditional notions and responsibilities of husbands and wives will abate, as men take more active roles in fathering and domestic chores. Families will also need to find new ways to blend work and family responsibilities.[33]

- Disappearance of childhood. The private and public lives of families will continue to be distorted, and childhood will no longer be an extended period of sheltered time, free from adult anxieties. Children will face much greater exposure to violence, drugs, and alcohol.[34] In addition, families will be increasing their use of child care outside of the family. In many cases, children will be in multiple child-care arrangements, combining care by relatives (particularly grandparents), non-relatives, and organized facilities. The long-term effects of these child-care arrangements on children's social and emotional health are unknown.

Furthermore, it is estimated that seven million five- to fourteen-year-old children are regularly left unsupervised, another trend that is likely to continue.[35]

- Proliferation of legal and ethical issues. Recent medical advances in reproductive technology are raising fascinating and troubling questions: sex selection for nonmedical purposes, commercial preconception arrangements, ectogenesis (creation of artificial womb), cloning, formation of animal/human hybrids by combining animal and human genetics, fetal tissue research, partial birth abortions, and the increasing number of multiple births. In addition, legal issues, particularly surrounding the role of government, will generate new ethical questions. Among them are: the place of biology in reproduction and custody; family subsidies for child care, elder care, health care, and greater choice in children's education; relationship between the workplace and family life; rights of adoptive and genetic parents; euthanasia and physician-assisted suicide.[36]

- Disintegration of community and the integration of the commodity. The American family's rootedness in local communities will continue to erode, fragmenting and isolating families. Families will become increasingly confronted with and dependent on bureaucracy and mass society.[37] Moreover, families will be faced with a growth in advertising and marketing to children and youth, and a growing preoccupation with individualism, pop psychology, and progressive insignificance.[38]

HOW CHRISTIANS CAN CHANGE THEIR WORLD

Challenging some of these trends in family relations can be difficult. Christians should look first to their own family relations to examine areas of personal failure. Often it is easier to be a good Christian role model in our school or workplace than in our own family. Consistently living up to Christian standards in front of our spouse, children, and parents can be challenging.

Within our families, we can study the precepts and models presented in God's Word (Josh. 1:8, "Meditate on it day and night"), always showing compassion (John 15:12-13) and generosity (Luke 6:38). We can teach our child(ren) the necessity of being encouragers (Prov. 15:23) and servants (Matt. 23:11-12). Parents should strive to effect Christian character and growth in their children's lives.

We must work to alleviate the social sins of violence and abuse within families. Christ calls us to be peacemakers (Matt. 5:9; John 14:27), beginning in our own families and extending as beacons to families in trouble. Work with your church to promote Christian counseling to families in need. Work to meet the needs of single-parent families by offering quality child-care services, shelter, and food. For example, Willow Creek Community Church in Illinois has a Cars Ministry that repairs donated cars and gives them to single mothers in need.

The changes cited in this chapter are trends but are not inevitable. Christians, working together, can be a powerful force to change these trends. We often say that what happens in someone else's family is "none of my business." However, Christian social responsibility (Matt. 25:21) demands that we change this attitude. By seeing marriage and family as a community responsibility rather than a private affair, Christians can begin to truly minister to those in need.

overview

- A family is two or more people who are committed to each other over time, sharing intimacy, resources, values, and decision-making responsibilities, as well as assuming responsibility for the care of children.

- The nuclear family, including one or two parents and their children, is the prevailing family form in developed nations. The prevailing form in developing nations is the extended family, consisting of parents, dependent children, and other relatives.

- Monogamy is the law in the United States. However, the most common form of marriage in developing nations is polygamy, which is marriage to more than one spouse at a time.

- The functionalist perspective sees the family as fulfilling some important social functions to promote stability in a society.

- The conflict perspective looks at power struggles within families.

- The symbolic interactionist perspective looks at the way families create social definitions of everyday situations. Our families define our reality.

- The Christian perspective sees family as honored by God, setting boundaries for moral behavior, and promoting human welfare.

- Families vary by ethnicity and race. Each has its own strengths and stereotypes.

- The American family has undergone many changes in the past fifty years. Cohabitation, divorce, individualism, and dual-career marriages are now prevalent.

- The future will continue to see tremendous social change within families. Christians need to act to challenge some of these changes and reach out to families in need.

key concepts

extended family
Parents, dependent children, and other relatives.

family
Two or more people who are committed to each other over time, sharing intimacy, resources, values, and decision-making responsibilities, as well as assuming responsibility for the care of children.

kinship
Family ties established through marriage or lines of descent.

marriage
The socially acknowledged and approved union of a man and a woman for the purpose of founding and maintaining a family.

monogamy
Marriage to one spouse at a time.

nuclear family
One or two parents and their children.

polyandry
Marriage to more than one husband.

polygamy
Marriage to more than one spouse at a time.

polygyny
Marriage to more than one wife.

endnotes

1. For an excellent summary of some of the recent changes in the American family, see Suzanne M. Bianchi and Lynne M. Casper, "American Families," *Population Bulletin* 55, no. 4 (December 2000); Stephanie Coontz, *The Way We Really Are: Coming to Terms with America's Changing Families* (New York: Basic Books, 1997); "Decade in Review: Understanding Families in the New Millennium" Special Issue, *Journal of Marriage and Family* (November 2000).
2. David Olson and John DeFrain, *Marriage and Family: Diversity and Strengths*, 3rd ed. (Mountain View, CA: Mayfield Publishing, 2000), 10-11.
3. Talcott Parsons and Robert Bales, *Family, Socialization, and Interaction Process* (New York: Free Press, 1955); Joan Aldous, "Symposium Review: Families by the Book," *Contemporary Sociology* 20 (1991): 660-62.
4. B. Thorne and M. Yalom, *Rethinking the Family: Some Feminist Questions* (New York: Longman Publishers, 1982); Friedrich Engels, *The Origin of the Family* (Chicago, IL: Charles H. Kerr and Company, 1902, orig. 1884).
5. Robert H. Lauer and Jeanette C. Lauer, *Marriage and Family: The Quest for Intimacy*, 4th ed. (Boston, MA: McGraw-Hill, Inc., 2000); David Newman, *Sociology of Families* (Thousand Oaks, CA: Pine Forge Press, 1999), 136-42.
6. Jack O. Balswick and Judith K. Balswick, *The Family: A Christian Perspective on the Contemporary Home*, 2nd ed. (Grand Rapids, MI: Baker Books, 1999); William J. Doherty, *The Intentional Family* (Reading, MA: Addison Wesley, 1997); W. Bradford Wilcox, "Conservative Protestant Childrearing: Authoritarian or Authoritative?" *American Sociological Review* 63, no. 6 (December 1998): 796-809.
7. Stuart A. Queen, Robert W. Habenstein, and Jill S. Quadagno, *The Family in Various Cultures*, 5th ed. (Cambridge, MA: Harper and Row, Publishers, 1985), 17-35.
8. Queen, Haberstein, and Quadagno, *The Family in Various Cultures*, 90-103.
9. Harriet McAdoo, "African-American Families," in *Ethnic Families in America: Patterns and Variations*, ed. C. Mindel, R. Habenstein, R. Wrights, Jr. (Upper Saddle River, NJ: Prentice-Hall, 1998), 361-81; Harriet McAdoo, *Black Families*, 3rd ed. (Thousand Oaks, CA: Sage Publications, 1997); S. Hatchett; J. Veroff, and E. Douvan, "Marital Instability among Black and White Couples in Early Marriage," in *The Decline in Marriage Among African-Americans*, ed. M. Tucker and C. Mitchell-Kernen (New York: Russell Sage Foundation Publications, 1995).
10. U.S. Census Bureau, *Household and Family Characteristics: March 1998*, Update (Washington D.C.: The Bureau, 1999); R. Horowitz, "The Expanded Family and Family Honor," in *The Family Experience: A Reader in Cultural Diversity*, ed. M. Hutter (Boston, MA: Allyn & Bacon, 1997); Ross Parke and Raymond Buriel, "Socialization Concerns in African American, American Indian, Asian-American, and Latino Families," in *Contemporary Ethnic Families in the United States: Characters, Variations, and Dynamics*, ed. Nijole Benokraitis (Upper Saddle River, NJ: Prentice-Hall, 2002); David Newman, *Sociology of Families*, 90-92.
11. Linda Lindsey and Stephen Beach, *Sociology*, 2nd ed. (Upper Saddle River, NJ: Prentice-Hall, 2002); Harry Kitano and Roger Daniels, *Asian Americans: Emerging Minorities* (Englewood Cliffs, NJ: Prentice-Hall, 1995); S. Blair and Z. Qian,

"Family and Asian Students' Educational Performance: A Consideration of Diversity," *Journal of Family Issues* 19, no. 4 (1998): 355-74; Ronald Takaki, *A Different Mirror: A History of Multicultural America* (Boston, MA: Little, Brown & Co., 1993).

12. Lynn Wardle, "The Potential Impact of Homosexual Parenting on Children," *University of Illinois Law Review* (1997): 833-919; Paul Cameron and Kirk Cameron, "Homosexual Parents," *Adolescence* 31 (1996): 757-76; David Blankenhorn, *Fatherless America: Confronting Our Most Urgent Social Problem* (New York: Basic Books, 1995).

13. Judith Stacey and Timothy Biblarz, "(How) Does the Sexual Orientation of Parents Matter?" *American Sociological Review* 66, no. 2 (2001): 159-83. See also Mike Allen and Nancy Burrell, "Comparing the Impact of Homosexual and Heterosexual Parents on Children: Meta-Analysis of Existing Research," *Journal of Homosexuality* 32 (1996):19-35.

14. U.S. Bureau of the Census, *Statistical Abstract of the United States* (Washington, DC: Government Printing Office, 1997), 55-56.

15. U.S. Census Bureau, March supplements of the Current Population Surveys, 1960 to 2000.

16. Bianchi and Casper, *American Families,* 8; Olsen and DeFrain, *Marriage and Family*, 11; Tom W. Smith, "The Emerging 21st Century American Family," National Opinion Research Center, University of Chicago, *GSS Social Change Report No. 42* (November 24, 1999), 1.

17. Linda Waite and Maggie Gallagher, *The Case for Marriage: Why Married People Are Happier, Healthier, and Better Off Financially* (New York: Doubleday & Co., 2000).

18. U.S. Bureau of the Census, Current Population Report, Series P20-514: *Marital Status and Living Arrangements,* March 1998; Larry Bumpass and Hsien-Hen Lu, "Trends in Cohabitation and Implications for Children's Family Contexts in the United States," *Population Studies* 54, no. 1 (March 2000): 29-41; Smith, "The Emerging 21st Century Family," 2.

19. Bianchi and Casper, "American Families," 21.

20. Elizabeth Thomspon and Ugom Golella, "Cohabitation and Marital Stability: Quality or Commitment," *Journal of Marriage and the Family* 54 (1992): 259-67; Susan Brown and Alan Booth, "Cohabitation versus Marriage: A Comparison of Relationship Quality," *Journal of Marriage and the Family* 58, no. 3 (1997): 668-78.

21. Eleanor Macklin, "Cohabitation in the United States," in *Current Issues in Marriage and the Family*, ed. J. Gipson (New York: Macmillan Publishing Co., 1998), 215-45.

22. U.S. Bureau of the Census, "Marital Status and Living Arrangements," (March 1998), Update.

23. For an extensive discussion of divorce, see Arland Thornton, "Changing Attitudes Toward Separation and Divorce: Causes and Consequences," *American Journal of Sociology* 90, no. 4 (January 1985): 856-72; Linda Waite, Gus Haggstrom, and David Kanouse, "The Consequences of Parenthood for the Marital Stability of Young Adults," *American Sociological Review* 50, no. 6 (December 1985): 850-57; Lenore Weitzman, *The Divorce Revolution: The Unexpected Social and Economic Consequences for Women and Children in America* (New York: Free Press, 1985); Naomi Gerstel, "Divorce and Stigma," *Social Problems* 43, no. 2 (April 1987): 172-86; Frank Furstenberg and Andrew Cherlin, *Divided Families: What Happens to Children When Parents Part* (Cambridge, MA: Harvard University Press, 1991); Sylvia Ann Hewlett and Cornel West, *The War Against Parents* (Boston, MA: Houghton Mifflin, 1998); John Macionis, *Sociology*, 8th ed. (Upper Saddle River, NJ: Prentice-Hall, 2001), 476-77.

24. Paul Amato and Alan Booth, *A Generation at Risk: Growing Up in an Era of Family Upheaval* (Cambridge, MA: Harvard University Press, 1997); Christy Buchanan, Eleanor Maccoby, and Sanford Dornbusch, *Adolescents after Divorce* (Cambridge, MA: Harvard University Press, 1996); Judith Wallerstein and Sandra Blakesless, *Second Chances: Men, Women, and Children a Decade after Divorce* (New York: Ticknor & Fields, 1996).

25. National Center for Health Statistics, *National Vital Statistics Reports* 48, no. 3 (March 2000).

26. U.S. Bureau of the Census (1997), 107.

27. Olson and DeFrain, *Marriage and the Family*, 15.

28. Elizabeth Pleck and Joseph Pleck, "Fatherhood Ideals in the United States: Historical Dimensions," in *The Role of the Father in Child Development*, 3rd ed., ed. Michael E. Lamb (New York: Wiley and Sons, 1997), 33-48; Bianchi and Casper, *American Families*, 23.
29. Nijole Benokraitis, "How Family Wars Affect Us: Four Models of Family Change and Their Consequences," in *Feuds About Families: Conservative, Centrist, Liberal, and Feminist Perspectives*, ed. Nijole Benokraitis (Upper Saddle River, NJ: Prentice-Hall, 2000), 14-24.
30. David M. Newman, *Sociology of Families*, 473-87.
31. David Olson and M. Kilmar Hanson, eds., *2001: Preparing Families for the Future: NCFR Presidential Report* (St. Paul, MN: National Council on Family Relations, 1990).
32. Bianchi and Casper, *American Families*, 4-8.
33. Bianchi and Casper, *American Families*, 32-36; Melissa Milkie and Pia Peltola, "Playing All the Roles: Gender and the Work-Family Balancing Act," *Journal of Marriage and the Family* 61, no. 2 (May 1999): 476-90; Scott Coltrane, *Gender and Families* (Thousand Oaks, CA: Pine Forge Press, 1996).
34. Hewlett and West, *The War Against Parents*, 43-52; Newman, *Sociology of Families*, 480-81.
35. U.S. Bureau of the Census, *America's Children at Risk,* Census Brief, 97-2, (Sept. 1997).
36. Laurence Houlgate, *Morals, Marriage, and Parenthood: An Introduction to Family Ethics* (Belmont, CA: Wadsworth Publishing Company, 1999).
37. Robert D. Putnam, *Bowling Alone: The Collapse and Revival of American Community* (New York: Simon and Schuster, Inc., 2000); Smith, *The Emerging 21st Century American Family,* 9-12; Jack O. Balswick and Judith K. Balswick, *The Family: A Christian Perspective on the Contemporary Home* (Grand Rapids, MI: Baker Books, 1991).
38. Michael Jessup, "Truth: The First Casualty of Postmodern Consumerism," *Christian Scholar's Review* XXX: 3 (Spring 2001): 289-304.

CHAPTER TWELVE

Religion

chapter outline

I. Defining religion
   A. Structural-functionalist definition
   B. Substantive definition
      1. The sacred
      2. A set of beliefs
      3. Ritual behavior
      4. Community of worshipers
II. Functions and dysfunctions of religion
   A. Functions of religion
      1. Support, consolation, and reconciliation
      2. Means to identity
      3. Norms and values
      4. Prophetic activity
      5. Growth and maturation
   B. Dysfunctions of religion
      1. Religion and change
      2. Religion as conflict
III. Religious commitment
IV. Sect and church
V. The growth of churches
VI. The future of religion

biblical reflection

"By rejecting conscience, certain persons have suffered shipwreck in the faith."

—1 Timothy 1:19

The sociological study of religion poses some peculiar problems. Religion deals with **sacred** concerns, with the areas of life set aside for special consideration. Because these concerns are to be approached with such reverence, it is difficult to subject them to the same scrutiny that one might use in studying deviant behavior, voter preference, or bureaucratic rules.

Ironically, the problem manifests itself whether or not one is religious. Those who are deeply committed to religion in the traditional sense may find it difficult to look at their beliefs objectively, much less in a neutral manner. They may think of themselves as disloyal to their faith if they seriously consider research findings that are contrary to their beliefs. Similarly, those who are disenchanted with traditional religion may be resistant to the sociological study of religion because they are unable to accept research findings that support religious claims. Both kinds of findings are frequent in sociology.

Yet, the problem of studying religion sociologically goes much deeper than this. From the believer's point of view, what is most important about religion is its meaning to those who have faith. The beauty and majesty of religion are found only as one makes a commitment to it. For example, while God is available to all people, Christians believe that one cannot really know God without faith in Christ. To set this faith aside as a means of comprehending religion is self-defeating, for one is setting aside the very ingredient that is necessary for religion to be meaningful. Religion is irreducibly religious; it must be understood as religion, not as some psychological projection or economic compensator.[1]

Nonetheless, if religion is to be studied from a sociological perspective, it must be examined empirically. Sociologists study those aspects of religion that can be seen and understood by all persons who are properly trained. Thus, sociology eliminates much of what believers consider most important about religion. Does this mean that sociology is an exercise in futility?

Consider J. Milton Yinger's analogy from *The Scientific Study of Religion*.[2] Yinger points out that the beauty and majesty of a stained glass window are visible only from inside the sanctuary of a church. As the sunlight passes through the multicolored collage, the vision from inside can be magnificent. Nevertheless, some observations about a stained glass window cannot be made from the inside. For instance, the window is part of a larger plan and fits into the external design as well as the internal décor. We can also note that the window has historical significance; it was designed and constructed by an artist to symbolize some event. Furthermore, the window is both similar to and different from other windows. The point is that not everything necessary to understanding a stained glass window can be seen from the inside.

Likewise, not everything important about religion is visible to those on the inside. Sociology cannot answer all questions having to do with religion, but it can offer some important insights into the role and practice of religion by seeing it from the outside.

DEFINING RELIGION

To investigate religion sociologically requires defining the term **religion**. An inquiry conducted in an unbiased manner must not favor one religion over another. The task is formidable. If the definition is to be value-free, it must be inclusive of not only Christianity and Judaism—which would pose little problem for most Americans—but also Islam, Hinduism, Jainism, Buddhism, Taoism, Shintoism, and maybe Confucianism. Special problems are posed by Jainism, Theraveda Buddhism, and Confucianism because they are nontheistic religions. An inclusive definition becomes more troublesome when the diversity of "new" religious movements is considered. Particularly challenging to our value-free position is Satanism, a religion that seems to invert many of the theological and ethical tenets to which most Americans subscribe.

In sociology, the attempt to solve the problem of defining religion has typically taken one of two directions.[3]

STRUCTURAL-FUNCTIONALIST DEFINITION

The first approach to definition is called a *functional definition*. In this approach, religion is defined in terms of what it does or accomplishes in society. Yinger, following Paul Tillich, uses this definition in asserting that religion is "that which concerns man ultimately."[4] In proposing this definition, Yinger emphasizes that the nature of "ultimate concern" may vary widely across different cultures and subcultures. People may be anxious and seek to find "salvation" through escape from suffering, ugliness, boredom, or sin. Yinger also observes that religion may share with medical institutions an interest in health, but he believes the importance of this function decreases as technology develops to offer more immediate answers to medical problems.[5]

It should be apparent that the functional approach to defining religion is particularly useful in comparative studies. It allows one to see some unusual ways of fulfilling religious impulses. For example, in 1919 Morris Cohen wrote an intriguing essay titled "Baseball as a National Religion."[6] In a similar vein, a young man once explained a Bible story by relating it to the time sequence of a football game. The first incident in the biblical character's life was described as similar to the first quarter; the second series of actions represented the second quarter and took him to halftime, and so forth. What is important to note is that the football game was used to interpret the Bible story, rather than vice versa. The events in the game of football had become the basis for understanding life, thus taking on a religious function.

Similarly, sociologist Michael Jindra has described the movement that developed around the *Star Trek* television series as a religious phenomenon. In addition to an origin myth, he found that "**Trekkies**" are guided by beliefs in progress, discovery, science, and egalitarianism—beliefs that they then try to transmit to others.[7] This missionary outlook is clearly seen in the following quote:

> In this light *Star Trek* becomes almost a sort of scripture, doesn't it? What the Bible does in 66 books, *Star Trek* does in 79 episodes . . . I can't think of a series that really spoke to the future of humankind with as much clarity and vision as *Star Trek*.[8]

Using a functional definition, one can appreciate the way in which political ideologies like Communism or Nazism seek to fulfill purposes in some societies in much the same way traditional religions like Islam or Catholicism do in others. Thus, the functional approach tends to open our minds to the myriad ways in which the religious impulse may be expressed in different settings.

SUBSTANTIVE DEFINITION

The *substantive definition* defines religion in terms of what it is or what it contains.[9] The substantive method asserts that categories of behavior, attitudes, and ideas are found in all religions regardless of their situational or cultural settings. In using this method, any phenomenon that lacks these characteristics is excluded, irrespective of its consequences or functions. The challenge, of course, is to identify the unique content or substance of religion.

Perhaps the most widely accepted definitions of religion among sociologists are based on the work of Emile Durkheim.[10] Using anthropological materials taken from the Australian Arunta, Durkheim attempted to delineate the elementary forms of religious life. He concluded that a "religion is a unified system of beliefs and practices relative to sacred things . . . which unite into one single moral community called a Church, all those who adhere to them."[11]

This definition sets four elements presumed to be present in all religions. According to Durkheim, a religion is characterized by sacred items, a set of beliefs, rituals for relating to the sacred, and a community of worshipers.[12]

THE SACRED

The **sacred** refers to things set apart for special consideration; i.e., things not treated according to the standards of everyday life. For example, Christians generally set the Bible apart from other books. From their perspective, it is divinely inspired like no other book; therefore, its teachings must be given more respect. It is sacred.

The sacred stands in opposition to the **profane**, which refers to the areas of life that receive no special treatment. If the Bible is held to be sacred, then other books are profane. Sacred/profane distinctions are relative to the society in which they are found. In Saudi Arabia, for example, it is the Koran which is held to be sacred, while among most of the population of India, the Vedas and Upanishads are the sacred writings.

There is an important distinction between religious and sociological perspectives: from the believer's point of view, the Scriptures *are* sacred; from the sociological viewpoint, the Scriptures are *believed to be* sacred. There is no way for sociologists to determine whether or not the claims of a particular religion are true. Within sociology, *sacredness is an attitude toward something*, not a characteristic of those things. Sacredness depends upon the group's definitions. Some Christian groups, for example, believe that bread and wine are transformed into sacramental elements during the communion worship service. Others reject that viewpoint. Sociologists concern themselves with the attitudes of believers towards the sacramental elements, not with the inherent sacredness of the elements themselves.

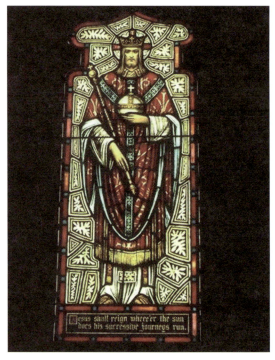

Every religion has symbols of the sacred.

A SET OF BELIEFS

All religions develop and disseminate a set of beliefs regarding the sacred. We have just discussed two such beliefs, that of belief about Scriptures and belief about the sacraments. Typically, religious beliefs will be elaborated into theologies, recorded in sacred writings, and eventually summarized by creeds.

RITUAL BEHAVIOR

The third element in Durkheim's definition is ritual. **Ritual** prescribes the proper way of relating to the sacred. It identifies the behavior that allows one to know when and how to approach the sacred. Prayer, singing, dancing, burning incense, and giving to religious causes are ritual practices found in most religions.

Rituals are often used to maintain boundaries between the sacred and the profane. In modern churches, prayer is frequently used to mark a boundary between worship (being in the presence of the sacred) and everyday life (profane activity). Put differently, worship services are begun with prayer to announce to participants that they are now involved with sacred things, and then these services are concluded with prayer to announce that the involvement has ended.

A COMMUNITY OF WORSHIPERS

For religion to exist, a group must perpetuate it. In other words, religion is of interest to sociologists only if it embraces social experience. However, sociologists should exercise caution

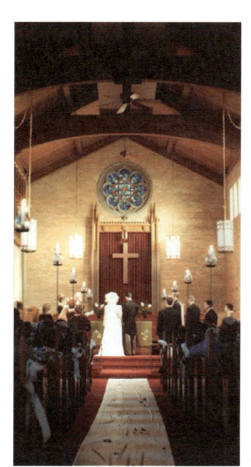

Every religion has rituals to mark the important events of life: birth, marriage, death.

before imposing any rigid notions of the frequency of meetings or the types of contact among adherents. The Australian aborigines meet for their religious gatherings during the dry season; they may stay from several days to several weeks, after which they will not reconvene for several months. In contrast, modern Christian churches offer worship services one or more times weekly. Yet both groups meet Durkheim's criterion of a community of worshipers because they have regular meetings in which they share beliefs and rituals regarding their group's notion of the sacred.

THE FUNCTIONS AND DYSFUNCTIONS OF RELIGION

A central issue that sociologists who study religion discuss on a continuing basis is whether or not religious commitments are essentially beneficial (**functional**) or harmful (**dysfunctional**) to society. As discussed in Chapter Two, the functional model assumes that a structure that survives over time does so because it is meeting needs important to the survival of society. But such a structure usually has multiple consequences, and at least some of these tend to be harmful or negative for some groups or individuals. The functional model cautions against assuming that the conditions one personally believes to be good and proper are necessarily the same conditions needed to maintain society in a stable system of relations.

Not surprisingly, there is no consensus within the discipline of sociology about the effects of religion. Nevertheless, O'Dea and Aviad identify five consequences that have general acceptance among sociologists.[13] In considering these, one might ask if these same functions can be met by structures that are nonreligious. The question is, does religion make a *unique* contribution to society, or not?

Religion serves some basic psycho-social functions.

THE FUNCTIONS OF RELIGION

SUPPORT, CONSOLATION, AND RECONCILIATION

We each face three problems that appear to be endemic to the human condition: pain, injustice, and uncertainty or confusion.[14] Any member of society may suffer emotional and/or physical injury. Ironically, such pain often seems to fall upon those who least deserve it, and these persons become distressed and confused as they try to cope with the situation. Some individuals begin to ask, why keep trying?

Consider the situation of a single mother,

whose only child had graduated recently from high school and was preparing to enter a career in modeling. This daughter accepted a ride home from a party with a young man who had been drinking. Driving down the highway at high speed, the young man rammed a parked car, throwing his passenger into the windshield and then out of the car to slide some two hundred feet on the concrete. The eighteen-year-old girl remained in a coma for about two months, then died. Ironically, the driver, who had a previous conviction for drunk driving, received only a bruised elbow. His punishment was a small fine and a suspended license.

This incident contains all three problems identified above: *pain*, both physical (for the daughter) and emotional (for the parent); *injustice*—the driver suffered only a minor disruption of his lifestyle, while the passenger's life was ended; and the mother's genuine state of *confusion* over how such a situation could occur. Where was the fairness? Where was God?

Most of us could cite similar events. We recognize the difficulties posed for the persons involved, but many overlook what is at stake for society. Because these persons are demoralized and perplexed, society cannot count on their continued participation. Unless they can be consoled and reconciled, these persons may decide to withdraw or even rebel. Enter the religious community to provide sympathetic support. Through interaction with others, participation in ritual, and understanding of belief, those who are adversely affected by such events may find meaning in the unfortunate situation. They accept their loss and experience revitalization. In the case described above, the mother was able to accept her daughter's death by believing that "God takes the loveliest roses for His own garden," thus being assured that she would see her daughter in heaven. While others might rationalize the tragedy differently, the point is that religion provided a satisfactory explanation of the events and brought comfort to a distraught parent.

A MEANS TO IDENTITY

O'Dea and Aviad propose a second function, the contribution that religion makes to identity. Religion helps to establish identity by answering questions of who or what we are. To know that one is a Presbyterian or Methodist allows others to know something about oneself and to predict what kinds of behavior might be appropriate. Beyond the external dimensions of identity, religion strengthens the sense of self and provides security. At the core of this function is the **nonempirical referent** of religious identity. A person may be a husband and a college professor, two facets of selfhood that are very important. However, both of these status-positions can be undermined by changes in the empirical world—one may be divorced or fired or both—which leaves the individual feeling vulnerable. But a religious identity, a sense of being a child of God does not depend upon empirical events. One's relationship to God is secure, regardless of changes in the empirical world. The biblical story of Job illustrates this function well.

NORMS AND VALUES

A third function of religion is to *sacralize* norms and values. Because there are some practices in society that are vital to its identity (and perhaps its survival), it is important that society set them apart as *the* legitimate way things are done. Such practices are attached to the sacred, thereby turning what is customary and useful into what is supernaturally demanded. Thus, Christians assert that marriage is not just a civil requirement, but a union of a man and a woman by God. Likewise, testimony given in court is "the truth, the whole truth, and nothing but the truth, so help me God." If I then perjure myself, I have not just violated the legal statute, but I have also disobeyed God. The norms of marriage and of the courtroom have been given sacred reinforcement. In sacralizing norms and values, religion is contributing to social control.

PROPHETIC ACTIVITY

A fourth function of religion provides believers with a set of values and expectations by which they can evaluate social practices and advocate social change. Put differently, religion can lead to **prophetic activity**. An illuminating example can be found in the widespread participation of ministers in the civil rights movement. These ministers proclaimed that God demands social justice for minorities, using their belief not only to motivate protestors against discrimination, but also to disturb the consciences of those who were involved in discriminatory practices.

GROWTH AND MATURATION

Finally, religion promotes growth and maturation in individuals. In some respects, religion motivates persons to move through various stages of life. For example, religion typically calls upon its adherents to become contributing members of society; i.e., to get an education and obtain a job, to find a spouse and have children, and to accept responsibility for one's aging parents. In its institutional form as the church, religion frequently gives ceremonial recognition to important life events such as marriage and the birth of children. Religious groups also promote growth by teaching moral and spiritual truths to their members.

THE DYSFUNCTIONS OF RELIGION

Sociologists have also identified some typical dysfunctions of religion. Perhaps the most pervasive critique came from Karl Marx.

RELIGION AND CHANGE

Marx was a materialist who believed that human life is dominated by economic struggles between those who have significant amounts of resources (the haves) and those who lack such resources (the have nots). While the content of the resources that provide one group power over another changes over time, he believed the basic form of the struggle dominates history until a worldwide revolution eliminates economic inequality.

The role played by religion in this struggle is to serve as an "opiate for the masses." By masses, Marx refers to those in the lower class (the have nots). For these persons, religion has a narcotic effect. First, religion lulls the lower class into accepting discomfort and turning attention away from social injustices. Second, it promises these persons a future relieved of present burdens if they will behave—meaning not upset the system that benefits the upper class (the haves). In essence, the primary function of religion is to enhance control by the upper class. Thus, according to Marx, religion is dysfunctional in two ways: for those in the lower class, it prevents recognition of problems and thwarts attempts at solution; and for the total society, it restricts efforts to promote change.

Ignoring the question of whether or not change is inherently beneficial, Marx's argument can be evaluated more objectively if we consider Max Weber's classic study, *The Protestant Ethic and the Spirit of Capitalism*. In this book, Weber asserts that sometimes religion facilitates change.[15]

Weber notes that the capitalist economic system developed most easily in those countries in Europe that were predominantly Protestant, because Protestantism promoted ways of thinking that enhanced the appeal of capitalism. In the first place, Protestant theology was Calvinist, attributing absolute sovereignty to God. On the important question of salvation, **Calvinists** asserted the doctrine of predestination, which meant that there was nothing humans could do about their eternal destiny. In fact, because God was absolutely in control, the Calvinist position was that individuals would not be certain until death whether or not they were among the "**elect**."

There was a twist to this, however. Although one could not be certain, one could "probably" know because God's grace in the life of a believer would have positive consequences. Thus, if a person was successful in life, it was taken as a sign that he or she was probably among the elect. Such a belief supplied a powerful motive to seek success, not only for economic benefits but also for religious reasons.

This motivation was channeled into business activity by another Protestant belief that Weber called "inner-worldly **asceticism**." Catholics had long utilized ascetic (self-denying) practices to show devotion to God. For example, one might leave the world and its pleasures—taking vows of silence, of celibacy, or of poverty—to concentrate on otherworldly (spiritual) goals. The Protestant innovation was to promote "being in the world but not of the world." Their devotion to God was demonstrated by being holy in the midst of worldly pursuits. In practice, this was interpreted to mean living in a frugal, sober manner.

Weber argued that this kind of lifestyle was ideally suited to the development of capitalism. That is, individuals who were motivated to success as a means of relieving their religious anxiety—encouraged to demonstrate their affection for God by achievement in worldly activity, but discouraged from consuming their earnings by their beliefs—were likely to accumulate the surplus capital necessary for investment. At the same time, they would be willing to risk their earnings in business ventures in the hope of proving their status in the elect.

Therefore, Weber concluded that religion may facilitate change, at least in some situations. The issue of whether or not capitalism was functional for the lower class is not addressed in Weber's treatise. However, Rostow and others claim that capitalistic economy produces and distributes wealth more broadly than others. Capitalism thus provides a higher standard of living than socialist systems.[16] Nevertheless, many sociologists would be reluctant to argue that capitalism is an unmixed blessing to the poor, given the wide gaps that continue to exist between the haves and the have nots.

It is certainly true that religion sometimes facilitates change. During the decades just prior to the Civil War, many Christian ministers were strong advocates of the abolition of slavery. For another example, the Shiite revolution in Iran during the late 1970s ushered in a return to conservative Islamic practices in that nation.

RELIGION AS CONFLICT

Another dysfunctional consequence of religion is its propensity to generate and/or to sustain conflict among adherents of different religious viewpoints. A brief survey of recent world history would uncover numerous examples of such conflict. Despite repeated attempts to reduce tensions, Jews and Palestinians continue to fight over territorial claims to the West Bank. This is merely one aspect of the larger antagonism between Israel and the Arab states, fostered in large measure by religious differences. In India, there is serious conflict between Hindus and Sikhs. Also in India, Hindu extremists have hindered efforts by Christian organizations to provide relief to earthquake victims. Although recent efforts to establish peace have been initiated, Catholic/Protestant tensions in Ireland continue to smolder just below the surface. Religiously based protests and even abortion clinic bombings have occurred in the United States. Attempts to strengthen or bridge church-state separation—such as removing prayer from the public schools or offering federal support for faith-based initiatives—often lead to conflict.

One reason that religious conflict is so intense and enduring is that, by definition, religious issues deal with the sacred—those areas of special concern. Coser points out that conflict involving deeply held beliefs is seen to transcend personal interests, so that one believes he or she is fighting for truth and righteousness, not for personal gain. [17]

RELIGIOUS COMMITMENT

Religiosity is the term sociologists use to refer to all the ways in which religion is expressed. A large body of literature attempts to explain the different dimensions of religiosity or religious commitment. While there is no consensus on these dimensions, the scheme proposed by Charles Glock has received widespread acceptance.[18]

Glock identifies five areas of commitment that are anticipated in all religions: experiential, ideological, ritualistic, intellectual, and consequential.

- The *experiential* area of commitment deals with feelings. All religions expect their followers to experience some feeling or emotion. Research by Stark suggests that this feature of religion may become more pronounced as people grow older.[19]

- The *ideological* dimension refers to the beliefs of the group. Every religion expects its followers to believe in its central doctrines. To be sure, every group does not promote the same beliefs, but each of them does demand acceptance of its beliefs.

- The *ritualistic* dimension requires commitment expressed in some type of participation. Adherents should attend meetings, offer prayers, sing hymns, read sacred writings, burn incense, or make financial contributions.

- The *intellectual* dimension insists that believers must become informed about their particular group and its beliefs. Committed followers are expected to learn the history and rationale behind the group's practices. Baptists, for example, are expected not only to undergo immersion but also to learn why their church reserves baptism for believers only.

- The *consequential* dimension requires adherents to manifest their commitment by integrating their religion into their lifestyle; that is, as a result of the other four areas of commitment—emotion, belief, ritual, and knowledge—religious groups anticipate that their religion will be expressed in daily life. Put in religious terms, religious followers are not to be hypocrites (insincere in their commitments). Religion must affect behavior.

Findley Edge has suggested an intriguing test of one's religion in American society. After identifying "love your neighbor as yourself" as a norm promoted in almost all churches, Edge asks how we should love our neighbors as ourselves when buying a new car. This is a very common experience and one in which our love for others should be apparent. If we genuinely love those we do business with, we should seek a profitable transaction for the dealer as well as ourselves.

In his book, *The Greening of the Church*, Edge writes that the next time he wanted to buy a car, he planned to drive into the dealer's lot and say something like, "I want a new car of the same model as my present automobile. There are several things wrong with my present car." He then intended to enumerate them.[20] Having done this, he would ask the dealer for a price that he initially planned to pay without question.

But upon reflection, Edge realized that the dealer's love for his customer might lead him to cut his profit margin too thin, so he proposed to add fifty dollars to the dealer's price and write a check for that amount.

Edge concludes his discussion with two questions. The first is: Does that seem stupid to you? In an informal survey over the years, no one has ever said, "No, it does not seem stupid." But the second question always makes people uncomfortable: How, then, does a Christian show love for a neighbor when buying a new car?[21]

Using historical materials, Rosabeth Kanter offers a different way of talking about commitment. Rather than asking how it is expressed, she asks how commitment is built. By studying nineteenth-century communes, she was able to specify six commitment-building processes.[22]

1. *Sacrifice.* Persons are required to give up something in order to become members. They "sacrifice" something of value for the sake of their religion. Alcohol or tobacco would be typical examples.

2. *Investment.* Investment is the second element in developing commitment. Instead of asking followers to give something up, they are required to give something to the group, usually time or money. As persons place things of value (energy, money) into the group, the group becomes more valuable to the persons.

3. *Renunciation.* Potential members are expected to relinquish outside activities and relationships. This separates them from outside influences such as newspapers and letters, and they are sometimes asked to wear distinctive costumes that establish boundaries from other groups. In extreme cases, contacts with family members are restricted. The effect of such renunciation is to increase the importance of the group because it has become the sole source of self-definition.

4. *Communion.* This involves spending time with group members in worship, recreation, and leisure activities. It corresponds to the notion of fellowship in some churches.

5. *Mortification.* Through participation in public confession of shortcomings and failures, the person is led to a sense of worthlessness and humility. The self of the individual is assaulted to expose any evidence of selfishness, conceit, or egotism, quickly followed by ritual acceptance to teach how much one is loved. Mortification thus offers a dual benefit to the group: confession of unworthiness leads the person to devalue his or her own opinions as residual egotism, which can be replaced by the pronouncements of leaders. The alternation of guilt and restoration engenders a strong sense of union.

6. *Sense of Transcendence.* Because religious groups are bearers of ultimate truth and meaning, they are able to vest everyday activity with special significance (everyday life is sacralized). Thus, such mundane activities as cooking a meal or cleaning the meeting hall gain significance when one views them as preparations for God's special prophet.

SECT AND CHURCH

Writing out of the backdrop of European history, Ernest Troeltsch characterized religious organization in terms of two sets of traits.[23] His position was that a religious group would appear as either *church* or *sect*, a view reflecting the historical situation in Europe around 1500.

The **church** type is a religious body oriented toward merger with the secular world. It is conservative with respect to its doctrines and ethical standards, and it claims universal authority within the society to effect those standards. Membership is inclusive in that the individual is born into the church; therefore, all are expected to give loyalty to it.

The **sect** stands apart from both other religious groups and the secular world. Membership is exclusive in that it is voluntary—one must decide to join—and requires a conversion experience or conscious affirmation. The sect emphasizes a literal interpretation of Scripture and a purity of lifestyle leading to otherworldly rewards.

Later scholars, surveying the religious scene in the United States, have added two more categories. H. Richard Niebuhr introduced the notion of *denomination* as a hybrid of the other two (church and sect).[24] Similar to the church, denominations accommodate themselves to prevailing cultural standards, but do not attempt to merge with the secular order. Like sects, denominations have voluntary membership and try to influence society primarily through the participation of their members in other spheres of life. The theological and ethical positions of denominations tend to arise from more liberal interpretations of Scripture than either church or sect.

Another scholar, Howard Becker, developed a fourth category—the **cult**. This term refers to groups that are small and loosely organized, with membership defined mostly by participation. Doctrines and practices are drawn from a variety of sources and are often vague and inconsistent. The sustaining force in these groups is usually a powerful leader. [Unfortunately, the term "cult" has been co-opted in recent years to identify those groups perceived as unrespectable or deviant, depriving the concept of analytical usefulness.] [25]

Sociologists have subjected this classification to scrutiny, and have generally agreed that it has two main limitations: first, the church-sect typology is difficult to use in societies where Christianity is not the dominant religion; and second, the boundaries of the types are not clearly evident even in Western societies. Nevertheless, the categories continue to be discussed and used in research.[26]

One area of interest has been in the development of sects. Literally thousands of such groups come into existence, but most of them go unnoticed by outsiders. What happens to them? There appear to be three possibilities:

1. **The sect may die**. Two interrelated problems face a group if it is to survive over time. In the first place, it must successfully socialize a second generation who may not have the kind of background experiences that made the group attractive to the parents. Equally important is the problem of leadership succession; even among the original adherents to the sect, there may be disagreement about who should replace the leader.[27]

2. **The sect may stabilize and become an established sect.** Examples of this kind of adaptation are the Amish, the Quakers, and the Primitive Baptists. Retaining the sect-like features of a group in the midst of a modern society is a precarious undertaking. It seems to require that members limit their participation in outside activities, as the Amish have done.[28]

3. **The sect may grow and become a denomination**. Methodists, Baptists, Assemblies of God, and others originated as sects but have become institutionalized as denominations. As part of this development, the initial goal of purifying society has been diluted.[29]

The Amish Community is an example of an enduring religious sect.

THE GROWTH OF CHURCHES

Many studies have attempted to determine the factors associated with church growth.[30] The findings in these studies sometimes question the established beliefs about church growth. For example, the United States has long been characterized as the most religiously active society in the industrial world (see Table 12:1). However, recently a team of researchers has produced evidence to challenge the figures that show the United States to have higher rates of participation than other countries. They suggest a moratorium on claims about the uniqueness of church participation in the United States.[31]

In any event, religious groups neither participate at the same levels (e.g., Catholics attend more frequently than Protestants) nor experience similar rates of growth (e.g., religiously conservative groups grow more rapidly than religiously liberal groups).[32] Dean M. Kelley argued that conservative churches grow (see Table 12:2) because they are better able to provide answers for life's troubling questions. Furthermore, he asserted that success in religion depends in part on making strict demands for sacrifice and discipline, traits that he believed had largely disappeared from the liberal churches.[33]

Among those studying church growth, a key element of Kelley's thesis is the primacy of institutional factors (those which the church can control) over contextual factors (those which are mostly outside the control of the church). For example, churches can require certain types of behavior from their members, but they cannot exert much control over demographic and economic changes in the surrounding neighborhood.

TABLE 12:1

Comparison of Religious Activities and Beliefs in 10 Industrial Countries: National Adult Samples, by Percent, 1981-1983

	ACTIVITY			BELIEFS	
	ATTEND CHURCH WEEKLY	ATTEND CHURCH MONTHLY	PRAY	GOD	LIFE AFTER DEATH
U.S.A.	42.5	59.4	85.3	95.6	70.5
Australia	17.2	23.3	33.9	80.1	49.1
Belgium	30.2	38.0	54.4	76.0	36.9
Britain	13.8	22.9	49.0	72.8	46.5
Canada	30.8	45.1	73.1	90.6	61.2
Finland	3.3	10.7	14.2	—.—	—.—
France	10.7	16.5	40.7	59.0	35.0
Germany	18.5	33.9	54.7	68.2	36.0
Italy	32.3	48.1	70.0	82.2	46.4
Sweden	5.5	13.9	33.2	51.9	27.6

Source: adapted from Robert A. Campbell and James E. Curtis, "Religious Involvement Across Societies: Analyses for Alternative Measures in National Surveys," *Journal for the Scientific Study of Religion* 33 (September 1994): 221.

Dean R. Hoge, a prominent sociologist of religion, directly tested hypotheses derived from Kelley's work and concluded that contextual factors are more important than institutional factors.[34] In other words, it appears that location in the suburbs of a city or the average age of church members is typically more important in church growth than the theological or ethical demands made on members. Later work has largely substantiated but also clarified these findings, especially in demonstrating that *less important is not equivalent to inconsequential*.[35]

Reference has already been made to differences between the United States and other societies. Table 12:3 contrasts the distribution of religious adherents in this country with the worldwide pattern, underscoring the uniqueness of the American scene.

THE FUTURE OF RELIGION

In 1968, two prominent researchers in the sociology of religion announced that people appeared to be abandoning traditional religion in the United States.[36] They were not alone, for many believed that **secularization** was the irreversible trend of the nation. More recent events seem to point in the opposite direction: religious

TABLE 12:2

Comparison of Growth Rates for Selected U.S. Denominations, 1970-1988, by Theological Orientation

THEOLOGICAL ORIENTATION	% CHANGE
LIBERAL	
Lutheran Church	-6
Methodist Church	-13
Episcopal Church	-25
Presbyterian Church	-27
CONSERVATIVE	
Southern Baptist	+27
Nazarene	+42
Seventh Day Adventist	+61
Assembly of God	+246

Source: Yearbook of American and Canadian Churches

activity and interest appear to be on the upswing, even in areas—such as university campuses—where its influence has often been highly circumscribed. Moreover, it is not clear just what secularization means.[37] We can, however, identify the following trends as suggestive of possible future directions:

TABLE 12:3

Estimates of Religious Adherents* as a Percentage of World and U.S.A. Populations, circa 2000

RELIGIOUS TRADITION	% OF WORLD POPULATION	% OF U.S. POPULATION
Christian	33.0	86.2
Muslim	18.0	1.5
Hindu	16.0	0.3
Jew	0.3	2.0
Buddhist	6.0	0.7
Nonreligious	16.0	8.5

* Adherent is a broader category than member or preference. Thus, the percentages for all groups except nonreligious are probably at the high end of reasonable estimates.

Source: www.adherents.com (1/25/01)

The major dividing line in religion today is increasingly the conservative versus **liberal** boundary, as identified by Robert Wuthnow.[38] Hunter's important book, *Culture Wars*, describes some of the ways this may be manifest even in nonreligious arenas.[39]

Within the major faith traditions of Protestant, Catholic, and Jew, Gallup Poll data indicate that between 1947 and 2000 Catholics gained about seven percentage points as religion of preference, while Protestants and Jews lost approximately eleven and three percentage points respectively. Those with no religious preference grew from 6 percent to a high of 11 percent in the early 1990s, before leveling off at 8 or 9 percent.

Immigration and dissemination of nontraditional religions are becoming established in the Gallup Poll data, indicating the combined number of Muslims, Buddhists, and Hindus is almost seven million. Mormons (Latter Day Saints) exceed five million. Denominations are showing a preference for developing ethnic-based churches rather than trying to integrate heterogeneous populations, a practice likely to reinforce differences and increase diversity.

overview

- It is difficult to study religion sociologically. Both those who are strong supporters of religion and those who oppose religion are often resistant to findings that threaten their positions. Many do not believe religion can be studied effectively by outsiders.

- Sociologists do not agree completely on the definition of religion. Some favor functional definitions, defining religion in terms of its consequences, while others favor substantive definitions, defining the subject in terms of its content. According to Durkheim, religion contains four elements: the sacred, beliefs, rituals, and a community of worshipers.

- O'Dea and Aviad suggest six main functions of religion: 1) support, consolation, and reconciliation; 2) establishing identity; 3) strengthening identity and providing security; 4) sacralizing norms and values; 5) evaluating social practices and advocating change; and 6) promoting growth and maturation among society's members.

- Marx proposed that religion has an overall dysfunctional consequence for society because it distracts the lower classes from their true problems, thus retarding the process of change in society.

- Weber attempted to refute Marx by claiming that at least sometimes religion facilitates social change. Sociologists generally agree that religion often generates or sustains conflict between groups.

- Religiosity refers to all the ways in which religion is expressed, or to how commitment is shown. Glock discussed five dimensions of religious commitment: experiential, ideological, ritualistic, intellectual, and consequential. Alternatively, Kanter examined the six processes by which a group gains commitment: sacrifice, investment, renunciation, communion, mortification, and transcendence.

- A major theoretical tool in the sociology of religion has been the sect-church typology suggested by Troelstch. Niebuhr added the category of the denomination to the original two categories, and then Becker provided the notion of cult.

- The future of a sect may include dissolution, becoming an established sect, or growing into a denomination. O'Dea discussed five dilemmas faced by religious groups in the process of their institutionalization.

- Sociologists have studied the factors that influence church growth. An important study by Kelley proposed that conservative churches experience growth more than liberal churches. A direct test of this hypothesis supported Kelley's basic findings, but found that the factors most responsible for growth were things over which the church had little control.

- An area of controversy in church growth studies is the finding that churches with a homogeneous membership experience growth while heterogeneous church memberships decline or remain stable.

- Three trends are at work affecting religion in the United States: conservative versus liberal developments; growth and declines in membership among Protestants, Catholics, and Jews; and the establishment of imported nontraditional religions.

key concepts

asceticism
Self-denial in the interest of showing religious devotion.

Calvinists
Believe human beings can do nothing about their eternal destiny (predestination).

church
Religious group that seeks merger with the secular world, expects loyalty from all persons in a given area (inclusive membership), and generally takes a conservative position regarding doctrine and ethics.

cult
Small, loosely organized religious group that takes an eclectic approach to doctrine, tends to have poorly defined membership standards, and is held together by the force of the leader's personality.

the "elect"
Those destined for salvation.

liberal
Religious orientation that emphasizes the symbolic nature of religious truth, accepts a variety of interpretations of Scripture, and believes in a continuing unfolding of revelation from a variety of sources. True liberals disdain fundamentalism.

nonempirical referent
Experience not directly verifiable through the physical senses.

profane
Common, everyday attitude toward behavior or objects; things that demand no special treatment.

prophetic activity
A set of values and exceptions which can be used to evaluate social practices and advocate social changes.

religion
A group of people who meet together on some regular basis, who share similar beliefs, and who practice similar rituals regarding their notion of the sacred.

religiosity
Ways of expressing religious commitment.

religious dysfunction
Harmful effects of religion upon society.

religious function
Beneficial effects of religion upon society.

ritual
Ways of relating to sacred things; stereotyped ways of acting toward the sacred.

sacred
Things set apart for special consideration; that which is holy.

sect
Religious group that stands apart from the secular world, requires conversion to become a member, tends toward literal interpretation of Scripture, and emphasizes otherworldly rewards.

secularization
The decline of religious influence or participation or both.

Trekkies
Star Trek fans guided by beliefs in progress, discovery, science, and egalitarianism.

endnotes

1. Mircea Eliade, *Myth and Reality* (New York: Harper & Row, 1968); Robert A. Segal, *Religion and the Social Sciences* (Atlanta: Scholars Press, 1989).
2. J. Milton Yinger, *The Scientific Study of Religion* (New York: Macmillan Co., 1970), 2.
3. Meredith B. McGuire, *Religion: The Social Context*, 3rd ed. (Belmont, CA: Wadsworth Publishing Co., 1992), 10.
4. J. Milton Yinger, *Sociology Looks at Religion* (Toronto: Macmillan Co., 1969), 19.
5. Ibid., 20.
6. Morris R. Cohen, "Baseball as a National Religion," in *Religion, Culture, and Society,* ed. Louis Schneider (New York: John Wiley and Sons, 1964), 36-38.
7. Michael Jindra, "Star Trek Fandom as a Religious Phenomenon," *Sociology of Religion* 55 (1994): 27-51.
8. Jeffrey Mills, as quoted in Jindra, "Star Trek Fandom," 34.
9. McGuire, *Religion: The Social Context*, 11.
10. Emile Durkheim, *The Elementary Forms of Religious Life* (New York: Free Press, 1915).
11. Ibid., 62.
12. Ibid., 51ff.
13. Thomas F. O'Dea and Janet O'Dea Aviad, *The Sociology of Religion*, 2nd ed. (Englewood Cliffs, NJ: Prentice-Hall, 1983), 14-15.
14. Keith A. Roberts, *Religion in Sociological Perspective* (Homewood, IL: Dorsey Press, 1984), 30ff.
15. Max Weber, *The Protestant Ethic and the Spirit of Capitalism* (New York: Charles Scribner's Sons, 1958).
16. Walt W. Rostow, *The Stages of Economic Growth: A Non-Communist Manifesto* (New York: Cambridge University Press, 1960).
17. Lewis A. Coser, *The Functions of Social Conflict* (New York: Free Press, 1956), 121ff.
18. Charles Y. Glock, "On the Study of Religious Commitment" (Research Supplement), *Religious Education* 57, no. 4 (1962).
19. Rodney Stark, "Age and Faith: A Changing Outlook or an Old Process?" in *Religion in Sociological Perspective*, Charles Y. Glock, ed. (Belmont, CA: Wadsworth Publishing Co., 1973), 48-62. (Originally published in *Sociological Analysis*, 1968.)
20. Findley B. Edge, *The Greening of the Church* (Waco, TX: Word Books, Publisher, 1971).
21. Ibid., 145ff.
22. Rosabeth M. Kanter, *Commitment and Community* (Cambridge, MA: Harvard University Press, 1972).
23. Ernest Troeltsch, *The Social Teachings of the Christian Churches* (New York: Harper & Row, 1931).
24. H. Richard Niebuhr, *The Social Sources of Denominationalism* (New York: Meridian Books, 1929).
25. Howard Becker, *Systemic Sociology* (New York: John Wiley and Sons, 1932). On the pejorative use of the term "cult," see James A. Beckford, "Politics and the Anti-Cult Movement," *Annual Review of the Social Sciences of Religion* 3 (1979): 169-90.
26. For example, see Roland Robertson, *The Sociological Interpretation of Religion* (New York: Schoecken Books, 1970); Peter L. Berger, *The Sacred Canopy: Elements of a Sociological Theory of Religion* (Garden City, NY: Doubleday & Co., 1967); Benton Johnson, "On Church and Sect," *American Sociological Review* 28 (1963): 539-49; Roger O'Toole, "Understanding Traditions in the Study of Sectarianism: Non-Religious Uses of the Concept 'Sect,'" *Journal for the Scientific Study of Religion* 15 (1976): 145-56; William H. Swatos, Jr., "Monopolism, Pluralism, Acceptance, and Rejection: An Integrated Model for Church-Sect Theory," *Review of Religious Research* 16 (1975): 174-85. See also John Wilson, *Religion in American Society: The Effective Presence* (Englewood Cliffs, NJ: Prentice-Hall, 1978).
27. John Wilson, *Religion in American Society*, 139ff.
28. Bryan R. Wilson, *Sects and Society: The Sociology of Three Religious Groups in Britain* (London: Heinemann Publishing,

1961), 10.
29. Dean M. Kelley, *Why Conservative Churches Are Growing* (New York: Harper & Row, 1977).
30. For example, see Dean R. Hoge and David A. Roozen, eds., *Understanding Church Growth and Decline, 1950-1978* (New York: Pilgrim Press, 1979); David A. Roozen and C. Kirk Hadaway, eds., *Church and Denominational Growth* (Nashville, TN: Abingdon Press, 1993).
31. C. Kirk Hadaway, Penny L. Marler, and Mark Chaves, "What the Polls Don't Show: A Closer Look at U.S. Church Attendance," *American Sociological Review* 58 (1993): 741-52; Dean R. Hoge and David A. Roozen, eds., *Understanding Church Growth and Decline*, 17.
32. Dean Kelley, *Why Conservative Churches Are Growing*.
33. Dean R. Hoge, "A Test of Theories of Denominational Growth and Decline," in *Understanding Church Growth and Decline, 1950-1978*, Hoge and Roozen, 178-97.
34. Ibid.
35. Roozen and Hadaway, *Church and Denominational Growth*.
36. Rodney Stark and Charles Y. Glock, *American Piety* (Berkeley: University of California Press, 1968), 240ff.
37. Larry Shiner, "The Concept of Secularization in Empirical Research," *Journal for the Scientific Study of Religion* 6 (Fall 1967): 207-20.
38. Robert Wuthnow, *The Restructuring of American Religion* (Princeton, NJ: Princeton University Press, 1988).
39. James D. Hunter, *Culture Wars: The Struggle to Define America* (New York: Basic Books, 1991).

CHAPTER THIRTEEN

Education

chapter outline

I. Why education?

II. A comparison of educational systems
   A. Brazil
   B. China
   C. Germany
   D. India
   E. Japan
   F. United Kingdom
   G. United States

III. Structure and culture in education

IV. Theoretical perspectives
   A. Structural-functionalism
   B. Conflict theories
   C. Symbolic Interactionist theory

V. How Christians can change the world

biblical reflection

"You shall put these words of mine in your heart and soul, and you shall bind them as a sign on your hand, and fix them as an emblem on your forehead. Teach them to your children, talking about them when you are at home and when you are away, when you lie down and when you rise."

—Deuteronomy 11:18-19

WHY EDUCATION?

How did education get transferred from the family to a very complex, impersonal system? It appears the nature of society has changed. In earlier forms of societies, enabling children to fulfill their potential was a much easier task than it is in modern societies. This is because of changes in the *amount* and *complexity* of what people need to know and because in modern societies what they will need to know will probably *change during their lifetimes*. In earlier forms of human societies, the skills and knowledge people needed to learn were often passed on from parents to children. Hunting and gathering societies lived a nomadic life, foraging for food as they traveled. Early agricultural societies primarily worked in agriculture, using animals and simple farming technology like plows pulled by animals. In **industrialized societies** (where things are produced through manufacturing) and **postindustrial societies** (like the United States, where the number of manufacturing jobs has declined and more people work with information than things), the amount of material to be learned has become too large, too complicated, and too quickly outdated for the old forms of education to succeed. In a complex society, parents put their trust in a complex system of schools to prepare their children for many possible directions in life. Even in adulthood, knowledge about certain techniques or topics becomes obsolete within a few decades or years. Workers find themselves having to "retool"—having to learn new skills and abilities as they shift occupations or other life circumstances.

And so, in today's modern societies hundreds of millions of people need to be exposed to vast amounts of information—information that changes at an amazing rate. The delivery of this information through education is accomplished in large systems of interconnected jobs and organizations. In the United States a combined effort of the federal government's Department of Education, state departments of education, and local school boards maintains and orients this huge system. Local elementary schools, middle or junior high schools, and senior high schools manage hundreds or thousands of staff members, work with huge curricula on many topics, and try to effectively determine if anyone is learning anything! And then we have an enormous collection of public and private colleges continuing the process. You are probably reading these words as part of your own involvement in that large system. You may also have noticed that our modern world offers an overwhelming abundance of educational resources that are constantly being revised, updated, improved, or negated as technological advances dictate. This indicates a strong probability that you will revisit some facet of the educational system throughout your lifetime as you try to gain the right education to succeed wherever you are in the competitive society of today's United States.

A COMPARISON OF EDUCATIONAL SYSTEMS

The world is full of different kinds of educational systems at different stages of development. As noted earlier, the educational systems to which we are accustomed developed as part of the industrialization process. We are now postindustrial, which means that most of the jobs in our country deal with information instead of agriculture or manufacturing.

Countries with growing populations and burgeoning industry need more literate work forces that are trained to the time schedules of manufacturing companies. This normally means some form of primary (elementary) schooling and, as industry becomes more predominant, more secondary (junior high and senior high) schooling. After countries become postindustrial, there is a greater call for a third level of schooling: college.

In this section you'll look at the educational systems of several different countries. These are just some illustrative cases, but they will allow you to compare some of the differences that exist in educational systems. Describing the basic shape of some of the world's educational systems is not a simple matter. Data for some countries is difficult to obtain. Any description fails to disclose many other factors as well, such as the varying regions and social classes within a country. All of these "snapshots" are of the countries' education systems in the late 1980s or early 1990s.

Table 13:1 provides some useful information for the countries discussed. In particular, note the differences in the first column. This number shows the number of students in secondary school for every hundred students in primary school, having adjusted for the number of grades involved. That probably sounds complicated but the number is actually easy to interpret. If the number is close to 100, it means most of the students in the country *do* continue on through secondary school. Four countries in the table have that pattern: Germany, Japan, the United Kingdom, and the United States. But three countries in the table have a number well below 100: Brazil, China, and India. This means that a large portion of the students in primary school do *not* go on to complete secondary school. The reasons for these differences are discussed for each individual country in the descriptions below. As you read these descriptions, try to imagine how your involvement with the education system would change if the United States adopted any of the educational systems described below.

BRAZIL

Brazil is still in the process of industrializing. Over a fourth of the population works in agriculture (27%) and just over a fifth works in manufacturing (21%). The country's education system in the mid-1990s required eight grades of primary schooling, followed by three grades of secondary schooling. The secondary schooling is offered in four different forms: a regular academic track, a teacher training track, a business-oriented track, and an agricultural track.

Since Brazil still has a large proportion of people working in agriculture and a growing proportion of people in manufacturing, most of the students in Brazil only complete the primary schooling. As can be seen in Table 13:1, there

TABLE 13:1
International Comparison of Education

COUNTRY	% OF SECONDARY STUDENTS PER 100 PRIMARY STUDENTS	% OF WORK FORCE IN AGRICULTURE	% OF WORK FORCE IN INDUSTRY	PERCENT WHO MAKE IT TO FIFTH GRADE	PERCENT OF PEOPLE OVER 15 WHO CAN READ AND WRITE
Brazil	35.7	27	21	70	83
China	50.8	56	17	88	82
Germany	72.5	3	36	95	—
India	44.6	—	—	62	52
Japan	95.0	6	33	100	—
United Kingdom	96.5	2	30	—	—
United States	89.3	3	23	94	—

*Cells for countries where data were not available are indicated with a dash.
Source: *United Nations Statistical Yearbook*, 43rd edition, 1996, viii.

Brazil is still in the process of industrializing, so its educational system is not highly developed.

Since half the country's population works in agriculture and less than a fifth works in industry, there is little motivation for most Chinese to be highly educated.

are only 35.7 secondary students in each grade of secondary school for each 100 students in each grade of primary school. International data also informs us that only a third or so of the small number of people who finish secondary schooling go on to college. The primary reason for such limited educational attainment in Brazil is the lack of utility for it. Most people's lives will not be greatly influenced by how much education they have.[1]

CHINA

China is a huge country with about a sixth of the world's population. Roughly half of the country's population works in agriculture (56%) and less than a fifth work in industry (17%). It is a country struggling to modernize across large land areas and a large population. Primary schooling in China lasts five or six years; secondary schooling has a three-year junior stage and a two- or three-year senior stage. About six in ten students leave schooling after their primary years (43% continue). This is quite a change from earlier Chinese society. In 1952 only 49 percent of students even made it *into* primary school. Access to schooling, particularly college training, is carefully controlled in China.

Access to the education system in any particular country is usually controlled in one of three ways: merit tests and academic accomplishment, economic realities of cost, or government control of access. In China, most people will have little reason to attain high levels of education since the largest area of employment is in agriculture. Those who do wish to go on must confront governmental control of access to advanced education.[2]

GERMANY

Germany was split into two countries at the close of World War II. The western section of the country became an influential member of the community of countries from western and northern Europe. The eastern section of the country became an influential part of the community of countries in the state-socialist (what was commonly referred to as communist) system headed by the former Soviet Union. In 1990 the two Germanys reunited into a single country. The education system in contemporary Germany takes most of its form from the former Federal Republic of Germany, which was more commonly called West Germany. Before the unification, West Germany was a very industrialized country and had shifted to some extent to a postindustrial economy. East Germany was also an industrialized country, but less so, and had not shifted toward a postindustrial economy. Neither country depended on labor-intensive agricultural techniques. In contemporary Germany, only 3 percent of the population works in agriculture since technology is used extensively in the agricultural process. A large proportion of the contemporary German population still does work in industry. In fact, more than a third of the working population works in manufacturing (36%). This creates a need for more educated workers.

A large proportion of children attends kindergarten (80% of five years olds, for example), though this is not mandatory. Mandatory schooling begins with four years of primary school and continues through one of four kinds of secondary schooling: a basic secondary schooling with limited academic demand (hauptschule); a secondary schooling that offers a somewhat more extensive academic training, as well as some vocational training (realschule); a strong academic schooling that prepares a student for college (gymnasium); or a hybrid secondary school that tries to integrate the strengths of the other three types of secondary schools (gesamtschule).

These integrated schools (the gesamtschule) have not been particularly popular. Interest in the basic secondary schooling (the hauptschule) has declined considerably since World War II as the need for postindustrial and high technology workers has increased. Instead, the gymnasium secondary schools have become more and more popular in the past fifty years. While only 11 percent of primary school graduates went on to gymnasium secondary schools in 1952, 30 percent of the primary school graduates went to gymnasium schools in 1992.

A very important aspect of the German education system is that access to higher levels of education is controlled through academic achievement. Students at the gymnasium schools identify specific areas of study for their last two years of secondary schooling. At the end of those two years they are scored on their grades in those areas and their performance on the certification test for those areas. In 1991, 23.6 percent of the graduates passed this testing process and were qualified for entrance to the German universities. Although these universities are free to those who qualify, some students must still wait to be admitted since the colleges can only accommodate so many in certain fields of study.[3]

INDIA

India is a poor country with a very large population that mostly works in agriculture. In the last decade or so, an industrial base has been developing, but it accounts for very little of the employment in the country. During the 150 years of British colonial rule, the educational system was constructed to cater to the needs of the society's elite segment. Since then (independence came in 1947), massive efforts have focused on constructing a more comprehensive educational system. Only half of the country's population is able to read and write, but increased access to education for children suggests that literacy rates are surely better for younger generations than older ones.

Primary education is required and runs

through five grades. Middle education lasts through three grades and the remaining secondary education consists of four more grades. Dropout rates from the primary schools were high and ran above 60 percent through at least the 1980s. While more recent data are not available, it seems probable that the dropout rates are still high, although probably not as high as they once were. Because cultural expectations are low for women and certain caste positions, these children drop out at higher rates than others do. Since education has limited utility in a primarily agricultural society, overall educational attainment is low.[4]

JAPAN

Japan's manufacturing economy has created large shifts in postindustrial occupations. Only 6 percent of the work force work in agriculture or food production, while a third work in manufacturing. Thus, more education is needed for success in the economy. Most Japanese children go to preschools (in 1994, 64 percent of first-grade children had attended some preschool earlier). Primary schooling is mandatory and lasts six years. It is followed by an additional three years of required junior high school. The next three years of high school are not mandatory. In fact, successful performance on entrance examinations is necessary for a student to get into a high school. About 91 percent of the students who completed junior high school in 1994 were able to get into a high school. In 1994 about a fourth (26%) of high school students attended a high school with a vocational specialization, while the rest attended academic high schools.

Access to colleges is very competitive in Japan and is determined by performance on entrance examinations. For men eligible to enter college in 1993, only about 18 percent qualified and made it in. Several screening processes led to this low number. First, only about half of the men felt qualified enough to apply. Of those that tried, only a third were accepted (36.6%). Figure 13:1 presents this process as a graph.

For women completing high school in 1993, only 4.5 percent enrolled in college. Just over a fifth (23.5%) applied for entrance and of those that applied only 19 percent were accepted. It has become a common practice for high school graduates to put their lives on hold and spend a year or two after high school studying and taking the college exams each year, hoping to get into college. For men, this waiting process is viewed as acceptable for a couple of years. For women, it is assumed that the process will usually last a year at most.

Since access to education is so very competitive in Japan, it has become more common for students to attend private schools beyond their regular schooling. These schools (called juku) are expensive and students spend a lot of additional time each week in these "second schools." All of this points out the limited access to education in Japan. It is in great part a system based on academic achievement. No

FIGURE 13:1
Access to College in Japan for Men

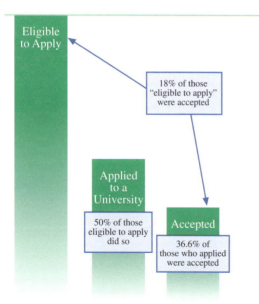

Sociology: A Christian Approach for Changing the World

matter how much money you have, you cannot assume you will get into a college of your choice—or perhaps into any college at all. But wealth is still critically important. Students from wealthy families can afford to go to juku and have much better access to educational aids at home.[5]

THE UNITED KINGDOM

The United Kingdom only has about 2 percent of its labor force in agriculture and just under a third in manufacturing (30%). Children enter mandatory schooling when they are five and move through the system more by age grouping than by grade level. Required education runs through age sixteen. Students age five through age eleven attend primary school ("infant" schooling is from five to seven years of age and "junior" schooling runs through eleven years of age). Secondary schooling starts with middle schools, where students are educated until they reach fourteen years of age, and continues with comprehensive schools that teach them until they are sixteen (or eighteen if they are successful enough to be allowed into the advanced level courses).

When students are fourteen and finishing middle school, they begin the selection process that will determine how much more education they will receive. From age fourteen through age sixteen, they focus on the courses necessary to achieve a General Certificate of Secondary Education (GCSE). Successful performance on the examinations associated with the GCSE allows a student to stay in school for the advanced levels, which are the primary means to get into college. The testing is rigorous and roughly a third of the students actually perform well enough to enter the advanced levels. Of those who pass the tests, some do not continue on. Only one in four students actually enters the advanced schooling for ages seventeen and eighteen.

In contrast to less developed nations, U.S. schools are well equipped, contributing to a knowledge gap between rich and poor nations.

The General Certificate of Education (GCE) examinations assess performance in the advanced levels and determine access to college. In the advanced level schooling, students usually focus on three A-level courses (which is to say, they specialize in three specific fields of study). To gain entry to a college, the students take a series of exams (most of which are essay and oral and last several hours) in each specialized area they have chosen. In 1992 only 21 percent of the students passed the GCE. Since not all of those students went on, only 12 percent of the students actually entered college. Clearly, the primary limitation on access to greater amounts of schooling in 1992 was merit. Even so, financial background also influences ability to continue education. The universities, for example, are free to those who are accepted. Students also receive a housing grant for living expenses, although it usually is not enough for low-income students.[6]

THE UNITED STATES

The United States has a small proportion of its workers in agriculture (only about 2 or 3%) and just over a fifth (23%) working in manufacturing. Most of the employed work force is involved in postindustrial employment. This type of employment structure is particularly dependent on an educated population. In the U.S., education is generally mandatory from ages six or seven through sixteen. Students usually attend one of two forms of school systems. The first common form consists of primary schooling for grades one through five, middle schooling for grades six through eight or nine, and secondary schooling through grade twelve. The second common form substitutes a junior high for the middle school, placing grades seven through nine in the junior high school.

Most students (87%) continue past primary schooling into secondary schooling. In 1998, 83 percent of adults (people eighteen or older) had graduated from high school. If we look at only people who are younger (but beyond traditional college age), the rate is much higher—91 percent of people age twenty-five through thirty-four have at least graduated from high school. Access to education in the United States is partly based on achievement, but far less so than in some of the countries already discussed. In most states in the United States, colleges accept students if they have completed high school (which usually has not required a test performance similar to the United Kingdom or Japan) and can pay the costs. More elite colleges demand higher achievement on entrance tests. These are provided by nonprofit organizations that are not part of the government-controlled education system. But, even then, these schools also cost substantially more than state-provided colleges and the financial expectations serve at least as great a control on access as achievement.[7]

STRUCTURE AND CULTURE IN EDUCATION

All countries have a social structural system that determines who can and cannot access education. These social structures also determine the form of the educational system. But countries also have a set of cultural views about education's role and importance. Both of these factors (structure and culture) affect each other. The structural system reflects the cultural assumptions about education. Each generation's cultural assumptions are formed in part by the system they have experienced. In the preceding summary descriptions, you have had a brief look at the structures of the educational systems in several countries. But it is important to note that each country has cultural views about education that are equally important.[8]

For example, the Japanese culture has a great concern for and value of education.[9] Student clubs build and reaffirm a pro-education focus and family life is built around a high value on educational success. This, together with the structural limitations on access to higher education explains why so many families spend so much on supplementary schooling like juku.

In the United Kingdom, the political process has tended to be guided in recent decades by the Labour and Conservative parties. Each party represents particular packages of beliefs and assumptions from the larger culture. They have expended notable amounts of effort to create the current educational system so that it is in keeping with those cultural perspectives. An illustration of this process is the movement in past decades from more elitist "grammar" schools for secondary education to "comprehensive" secondary schools that lessen the early tracking

Standardized education functions to insure that each member of the society has a certain knowledge base.

in the school system. This is a change the Labour party has promoted in particular.[10]

In the United States you may be familiar with the cultural underpinning of free education. Early in this country's development there was (and to a great extent there still is) a cultural belief that democracy depends on a literate and intelligent population.[11]

Whenever you consider the nature of an educational system in society, it is always wise to look for both the cultural and structural factors that have shaped it.

THEORETICAL PERSPECTIVES: EXPLAINING THE DIFFERENCES IN EDUCATIONAL SYSTEMS

Each of the three broad theoretical approaches (Structural-Functionalism, Conflict Theory, and Symbolic Interactionism) provides a special insight about educational systems.

STRUCTURAL-FUNCTIONALISM

Since functionalism looks at large systems in societies and what purposes they serve to keep the society operating, it is a great perspective to use when looking at large social institutions like education systems.

Education serves several important purposes for most countries. The obvious purpose is to "educate" the young. This refers to both training them to work in the society's economy (as we saw in the preceding comparison of educational systems) and socializing them to fit into the society's culture. Education systems also serve two other purposes that are not quite as obvious: sorting students into different ability classifications and creating new knowledge for the society. These four purposes are the main **manifest** (intended) functions of education systems.

There are also some **latent** (unintended) purposes for education systems. Along with the manifest functions, this chapter will include discussion of one of the latent functions: custodial care of children.

Manifest Function: Transmission of Knowledge

For any society to work, we must learn how to perform the skills and use the knowledge that our social systems depend on. Modern societies do this by gathering in school buildings (or gain education through some alternative means) where we are taught the basic information and abilities we need in order to be contributing members of society (**transmission of knowledge**). Imagine a society where people did not know how to write or speak, where they did not know how to take an appropriate role in their political system, or where they did not know their own country's history (as well as other countries' histories) well enough to understand what was happening around them. Such a society could not continue very long before it fell apart.

Manifest Function: Socialization

All of us have learned—from someone, somewhere—how to act and think correctly to fit into a particular situation. Whether we are starting a new job or moving to a new neighborhood, we soon learn the way "things are done" there. We are being socialized—taught to fit into the existing set of social systems. Schools are places that do a lot of **socialization**. We teach children (and adults) how to behave through the ways we organize them. Have you ever wondered why we all sit in rows the way we do, or why we raise our hands to get permission to speak? Do these practices teach us something about how to behave in certain social settings? And just what do we learn from our peers at school? In all of these ways and many more we are (or were) all socialized in the education system. A much-debated, contemporary example that focuses on the socializing function of schools is William Bennett's *The Devaluing of America: The Fight for Our Culture and Our Children*.[12]

Manifest Function: Sorting Students by Ability

If you started your own company and wanted to hire some people, how would you evaluate their competence to do the job? Most of us would consider many factors, including their performance in school. Having earned a high school diploma or a college diploma often indicates that a person has learned certain skills and abilities (knowledge and skills were transmitted to them). But we would probably look at their grades as well. When we learn that some students have a lot of "A's" and some others have a lot of "D's," we usually conclude something about how much knowledge they learned and also how competent or capable they are. We use schools to identify the students who have higher abilities.

Manifest Function: Creating Knowledge

In many colleges, the professional faculty members not only transmit knowledge, foster the socialization of their students, and aid in the sorting process, but they also create new knowledge. It is in the higher education organizations that people try out new ideas, attempt to find new answers to existing questions, or even develop new avenues of wording questions that help us understand things in a new way. Still, in comparison to commercial or other nonacademic endeavors, the creation of new knowledge on campus is a fairly inefficient, trial-and-error process. We all joke about academics who seem to have their heads in the clouds or have great "book smarts" but no "street smarts." But it is in these hit-and-miss efforts that new political ideas like democracy can be born. They can also result in new economic theories that may later guide the development of societal economies. And they can give us new ways to understand the workings of the physical world. We usually are willing to accept the loss of time and effort in failed theories because in this process we discover those insights that prove to be great advances for humankind.

Latent Function: Custodial Care of the Young

While "babysitting" is not one of the reasons we build schools, the schools serve that purpose nonetheless. When societies are primarily agricultural and children provide useful labor on the farm, parents often question the rationale of sending their kids to school. But in industrial and postindustrial countries, when adults contribute wages to the family through jobs outside the home, provisions have to be made for the **custodial care of the young**. For the same reason that day care centers have developed in these countries, education has come to be useful for a custodial-care purpose. Once all the kids are in school, both parents can have jobs and still avoid the child-care costs associated with day care.

CONFLICT THEORIES

While conflict theorists look at the larger aspects of societies (much as functionalists do), they study those aspects of the system characterized by domination and exploitation. Most of us figure out relatively early in life that the social systems around us are not always fair. We notice that some people seem to have easier access to the positions that matter. We may even notice that some *kinds* of people (as compared to just individual people) have better chances to get where they want to be. These inequities are clearly present in education systems as much as anywhere else. Conflict theorists point out that the education system often serves the interests of certain classifications of people more than others. In particular, conflict theorists often refer to the education system's role in the creation and maintenance of social inequality.[13]

One way education systems create and maintain social inequality is by serving the interests of those who have higher-class positions. Unequal funding drives a lot of these processes.[14] Consider, for example, the role property taxes play in funding school systems. Most U. S. schools rely on local property taxes for most of their funding. But property tax revenues vary greatly, depending on the wealth of the local area. Where there are large company plants (assuming they have not had their taxes set aside to attract them to the area) or where more expensive housing exists, there will be higher property tax revenues. Where housing is primarily for the poor and there are no large company sites, property tax revenues will be much lower. From this we have school systems in the country whose funding varies greatly—money that is used to buy better equipment, add buildings, and hire better teachers. The current

TABLE 13:2
Percentage of people 15 years old and older who cannot read and write

COUNTRY	EVERYONE	MEN	WOMEN
Brazil	16.7	16.7	16.8
China	17.8	10.1	25.5
India	48.0	34.5	62.3

system works very much to the advantage of those who have more money. Additionally, those who are very wealthy also have the option of sending their children to the best private schools. This is particularly important since research indicates that students in private schools usually do better academically than those in public schools. This research holds true even after factoring out the indirect effects of wealth (e.g., children in wealthy homes have better resources like books and personal computers, as well as families that tend to support and encourage their efforts to do better in school).[15]

Beyond class, other categories of people experience disparity in the education system. Women, for example, have greater difficulty in most societies getting an education equal to the one men receive. The differences can vary widely from one country to another, however. Table 13:2 demonstrates this with a comparison of the percentage of men and women who cannot read and write in three less developed countries.[16] In Brazil literacy is common. Only about 17 percent of men or women can *not* read and write. In China 90 percent of the men can read and write (10.1% are illiterate) but only three-fourths of women can read and write (25.5% are illiterate). In India there is even greater discrepancy. Two thirds of men can read and write (34.5% are illiterate), but only one third of women can read and write (62.3% are illiterate).

Many different kinds of people do poorly in the education system, some more dramatically than others. In a classic book on this topic, Randall Collins has even argued that the education system in the United States is intended to provide credentials (degrees and certificates) in a way that gives unfair advantages to some types of people and limits the opportunities of others.[17]

SYMBOLIC INTERACTIONIST THEORY

Since symbolic interactionists are more interested in the issues associated with interpersonal social reality (as compared to large social systems), they tend to look at the education system through the experiences of people in the system. In other words, symbolic interactionists still look at the functions of education and how education creates inequality. But they analyze the experiences of individuals and small groups in the system more than they consider large systems or classifications of people.

The work of Robert Rosenthal and Lenore Jacobson, for example, deals with both socialization and the creation of inequality.[18] After administering tests to students in elementary school, they then indicated to the teachers which students would show noticeable improve-

Education can change the world.

ment in that coming school year. But the tests were not actually intended to measure potential for future change in ability. The researchers were just trying to see what would happen if teachers had a different symbolic understanding of these students' potential. At the end of the school year they found that their predictions were mostly correct. Since the students they predicted would do well were randomly chosen, however, the change was due to the way they were perceived (and then treated) by the teachers. Symbolic interactionists identify this use of symbolic labeling as a critical process in the development of who we are. Notice that the way people label us in the education system affects our socialization into certain identities and abilities. It also points out how important the expectations of the key people in the education system can be in determining outcomes—the unequal outcomes—of education.

Rosenthal and Jacobson's research has created a great deal of discussion about how education is done. However, it is a very contested issue. Efforts to replicate their research (create the same results) have found little support for claims that expectations guide student outcomes —at least in the way Rosenthal and Jacobson said it did.[19]

HOW CHRISTIANS CAN CHANGE THE WORLD

In this chapter we have reviewed some of the issues that challenge educational systems worldwide. The overarching issue has been that of equal access to fulfilling each person's God-given potential. Each system we have reviewed has come short of guaranteeing each citizen equal educational opportunity.

God has given all of us work to do. The educational system can help us prepare for that work . . . or it can squelch the potential within us. Christians need to work toward creating educational systems that will enable all of us to do God's work.

Christians have responded to the inadequacies in education in a number of ways. Many have sought to return to the Old Testament command for parents to teach their children what they need to know. This has resulted in a number of Christian families choosing to homeschool their children. While there are some indications that homeschooled children can be very high achievers, they may not be exposed to social diversity or to the high-tech laboratory equipment necessary to prepare them for a complex society. Christians who choose to homeschool can make an impact by conscientiously integrating their children into the general society. Examples include taking them to the public library or performing public service at the local school.

Many Christians have established separate Christian schools. Most of these schools produce graduates who are, on average, higher achievers than their public school counterparts. Some of these schools have the funding to provide high-tech equipment but may still lack social diversity. Yet, because of the costs of private tuition, not everyone has equal access to this form of education. Many private Christian schools become havens from the increasing numbers of public school children who are members of minority groups or who live in poverty. Thus, they can unknowingly perpetuate prejudice and discrimination. Christians should work to establish schools that provide not only excellence in academics, but promote principles of social justice. Examples might be scholarship programs and other special efforts to reach underserved populations.

Finally, Christians need to stay involved in the public school system to ensure that it provides equal opportunity for each person to fulfill his or her God-given potential. You can do this by volunteering at your local school, becoming part of the local school board, or helping to establish new programs for the underserved. These are just a few examples of the many ways Christians can change the world by impacting the educational institutions. A good educational system can promote social justice by removing the barriers to achievement for the poor and minorities. Educators can become mountain-movers:

> *"If you have faith the size of a mustard seed, you will say to this mountain, 'Move from here to there,' and it will move; and nothing will be impossible for you."*
>
> –Matthew 17:20

overview

- A comparison of education systems indicates that societies with growing populations and burgeoning industry need work forces that are more literate and are trained to the time schedules of manufacturing companies. This normally means some form of primary schooling. As industry becomes more predominant, more secondary schooling is needed. After countries become postindustrial, there is a greater need for college.

- A structural-functionalist explanation of education looks at manifest functions of schooling: transmission of knowledge, socialization, sorting students by ability, and creating knowledge. Latent functions include custodial care of the young.

- Conflict theories look at ways educational systems promote inequality in societies. This is usually done by limiting access to quality education. Worldwide studies indicate that women, minorities, and the poor generally receive a less quality education, which results in lower achievement.

- Symbolic interactionists have looked at ways in which schools shape self-concept. Studies indicate that when some students are labeled "slow" while others are labeled "smart," there are dramatic effects on academic achievement.

- Christians need to work to ensure that all people have equal opportunity through quality school systems to achieve their God-given potential.

key concepts

custodial care of the young
A latent function of education in which schools keep children out of harm's way until they are contributing members of the society.

industrialized society
Society that emphasizes manufacturing jobs.

latent function
An unintended function of education; custodial child care is a latent function.

manifest function
An intended function of education; sorting students by ability and creating knowledge are two manifest functions.

postindustrial society
Society in which most of the jobs deal with information instead of agriculture or manufacturing.

socialization
A manifest function of education in which the school teaches members of a society how to fit in.

transmission of knowledge
A manifest function of education wherein schools teach students what they need to know to be successful members of the society.

endnotes

1. Information about the education system in Brazil is drawn from E. Bauzer Medeiros's entry on Brazil in *The Encyclopedia of Comparative Education and National Systems of Education,* T. Neville Postlethwaite, ed. (New York: Pergamon Press, 1988); U.S. Department of Health, Education, and Welfare, *The Brazilian Education System: A Summary* (Washington, DC: United States Office of Education, 1970); and Fay Haussman and Jerry Haar, *Education in Brazil* (Hamden, CT: Archon Books, 1978).
2. Information about the education system in China is drawn from Dong Chun-Cai's entry on China in *The Encyclopedia of Comparative Education and National Systems of Education*; and *Chinese Education: Problems, Policies and Prospects*, Irving Epstein, ed. (New York: Garland Publishing, 1991).
3. Information about the education system in Germany is drawn from J. Naumann and H. Kohler's entry on the Federal Republic of Germany in *The Encyclopedia of Comparative Education and National Systems of Education*; *International Comparisons of Entrance and Exit Examinations* (Washington, DC: U.S. Department of Education, 1997); and *The Education System in Germany: Case Study Findings* (Washington, DC: U.S. Department of Education, 1999)); and Val Rust and Diane Rust, *The Unification of German Education* (New York: Garland Publishing, 1995).
4. Information about the education system in India is drawn from A. Bordia's entry on India in *The Encyclopedia of Comparative Education and National Systems of Education*.
5. Information about the education system in Japan is drawn from T. Kanaya's entry on Japan in *The Encyclopedia of Comparative Education and National Systems of Education*; *International Comparisons of Entrance and Exit Examinations*; and Angela Wu, *The Japanese Education System: A Case Summary and Analysis* (Washington, DC: U.S. Department of Education, 1999).
6. Information about the education system in the United Kingdom is drawn from C. Booth's entry on The United Kingdom in *The Encyclopedia of Comparative Education and National Systems of Education*; *International Comparisons of Entrance and Exit Examinations*; and Robin Alexander, *Policy and Practice in Primary Education* (New York: Routledge, 1992).
7. Information about the education system in the United States is drawn from M. A. Eckstein's entry on The United States in *The Encyclopedia of Comparative Education and National Systems of Education*.
8. Statistics for many countries of the world can be found in sources like *Statistical Yearbook* from the United Nations. Information came from the forty-third issue of this publication (1996) to construct Table 13:1. All columns except column one are directly from the U.N. statistical yearbook. The ratio of average students per grade in secondary schooling to average students per grade in primary schooling was calculated using this formula: [(number of students in secondary school / number of years of secondary school for that country) / (number of students in primary schooling / number of years of primary schooling provided in that country)].
9. See Angela Wu, *The Japanese Education System*, for a look at the roles motivation groups play in the promotion of education as a cultural value.
10. Robin Alexander, *Policy and Practice in Primary Education*.
11. Steven Brint in *Schools and Societies* (Thousand Oaks, CA: Pine Forge Press, 1998) provides a good summary discussion of this process.
12. W. J. Bennett, *The Devaluing of America: The Fight for Our Culture and Our Children* (New York: Summit Books, 1992). Another example is E. D. Hirsch Jr., *Cultural Literacy* (New York: Viking Press, 1987).
13. A classic book on this subject is Christopher Jencks et. al., *Who Gets Ahead: The Determinants of Economic Success in America* (New York: Basic Books, 1979).
14. Jonathon Kozol, *Savage Inequalities: Children in America's Schools* (New York: Crown Publishers, 1991).

15. In 1981 James S. Coleman, Thomas Hoffer, and Sally Kilgore wrote one of the classic analyses on this issue, *Public and Private Schools: An Analysis of Public Schools and Beyond* (Washington, DC: National Center for Education Statistics, 1981).
16. United Nations, *Statistical Yearbook* (Paris: UNESCO Publishing, 1998).
17. Randall Collins, *The Credential Society: An Historical Sociology of Education and Stratification* (New York: Academic Press, 1979).
18. Robert Rosenthal and Lenore Jacobson, *Pygmalion in the Classroom* (New York: Holt, Rinehart & Winston, 1968).
19. J. Finn, "Expectations and the Educational Environment," *Review of Educational Research* 42 (1972): 387-410.

CHAPTER FOURTEEN

Health and Society

chapter outline

I. Health care as a social institution

II. Basic definitions
    A. Concepts that relate to individuals
    B. Concepts that relate to cultures or societies
    C. Quality of life indicators

III. Theoretical perspectives on health and medicine
    A. Structural-functionalist perspective
    B. Social conflict theory
    C. Symbolic interactionist theory

IV. Epidemiology
    A. Leading causes of death
    B. Life expectancy and mortality
    C. Social class
    D. Race
    E. Gender
    F. Infant mortality and the quality of life
    G. Morbidity and gender

V. AIDS

VI. Religion and health

VII. How Christians can change the world

biblical reflection

"The blind men came to him; and Jesus said to them, 'Do you believe that I am able to do this?' They said to him, 'Yes, Lord.' Then he touched their eyes and said, 'According to your faith let it be done to you.'"

—Matthew 9:28-30

Jesus was the Great Physician. People came to Him for physical healing as well as for spiritual enlightenment. Health issues have always been among the primary concerns of societies around the world. This chapter will discuss ways in which societies institutionalize health care. After introducing a few key terms, we will explore health and medicine from a variety of theoretical perspectives.

Following this theoretical foundation, we will examine how diseases are distributed according to gender, race, and social class. This section also includes a discussion of the growing presence of the AIDS virus, both in the United States and worldwide. The chapter concludes with a discussion of a research note of special concern to social researchers who are also interested in religion. To what extent and in what ways do religious beliefs and practices contribute to or detract from good health? Read to the end and find out!

HEALTH CARE AS A SOCIAL INSTITUTION

Health care, defined by the work of hospitals, health maintenance organizations, insurance companies, and your local family physician, is as fundamental to our society as the government, the economy, the family, education, and religion. In recent years, sociologists have come to understand and describe health and medicine in the same way they study these other social institutions. What's more, organizational components of other social building blocks relate to the health care system in ways that are often surprising. For example, a growing body of research suggests that affiliating with a church might help you stay healthy. The closing section of this chapter addresses that particular issue in more detail.

Many of these components of society overlap and need to be understood together. One could not fully understand the decisions doctors make when caring for their patients without accounting for the ways these decisions are influenced by the insurance industry. Is the patient employed? Does he or she have the resources to pay for expensive exploratory testing? What if the doctor can expect only partial reimbursement from state-funded public assistance programs such as Medicaid? These questions point toward ways in which the government protects the free enterprise of business, and also the manner in which states limit health-care options for the impoverished.

It wasn't always so complicated. Prior to World War II, doctors saw patients most often during routine house calls.[1] Now the presence of a physician in a private home generally means there is a party going on. And the doctor will likely leave early (after having been beeped) to go to his or her office or the hospital to care for a patient who has left home seeking professional care. Examining how these changes happen and also the consequences of these changes is another way sociologists study health and medicine.

BASIC DEFINITIONS

Understanding the following sets of concepts is especially helpful when studying the complex social relationships that occur as people seek to stay well or recover from sickness.

CONCEPTS THAT RELATE TO INDIVIDUALS

A **disease** is a biologically defined disorder of an organism that impairs its ability to function. Doctors define "disease" for us; they have studied biological pathways for the actions of bacteria, viruses, and fungi. We accept or reject these assessments based on how we feel or what we come to believe. At this stage we acknowledge that we have an **illness**, an individual's awareness of the presence of disease in his or her body. When others become aware of the presence of a disease in someone else, an awareness that causes them to change their behavior toward that person, we refer to the term **sickness**. Other people react to what doctors say about the "sick" person and what that person comes to accept; "sickness" changes our social relationships.

On the other hand, "health" is a bit more complex. **Health** is a state of complete physical, mental, and social well-being, not merely the absence of disease. Not only does health refer to what we don't have—germs or broken bones—health means all is well. Our relationships are fine; we're emotionally stable and happy; our bodies are functioning normally. People declare themselves to be healthy as they assess their own situations and as they gather information from doctors and others.

CONCEPTS THAT RELATE TO CULTURES OR SOCIETIES

Epidemiology is a systematic study of how diseases are distributed within a culture or society. Epidemiologists measure both the incidence and prevalence of diseases such as tuberculosis, malaria, and AIDS. By **incidence** we mean the number of new cases of a disease that occur in a population over a specific period of time (usually a particular year.) **Prevalence** represents the total number of cases present in a population at any given time. This includes new cases as well as all previously existing cases. These measures tell us how much impairment there is, how fast the problem is growing, or how well a treatment is working.

QUALITY OF LIFE INDICATORS

The **mortality rate** is the incidence of death in a population. The **morbidity** rate is the incidence of disease in a population. Morbidity and mortality rates are usually measured in terms of the number of people per 100,000 in a population that become sick, are sick, or who die over a specified period of time. The **infant mortality rate** measures the number of infants who, after having been born alive, die before their first birthday. Infant mortality rates are reported as the number of deaths in the first year of life per 1,000 live births. **Life expectancy**—the average number of years a person can expect to live—is calculated on the basis of one's birth year. For example, someone born in the United States in 1997 can expect to live 76.5 years.[2] These statistical measures are used to provide some indication of what it is like to live in a particular place at a particular time.

While there is some use for overall rates in a given population, these measures are more helpful when comparing subgroups within populations. For example, while average life expectancy in the United States is currently just over 76 years, life expectancy for males born in 1997 is 73.6 years; for females born in 1997 it is 79.4 years. Quite a difference!

The overall infant mortality rate in the United States was 7.2/1000 live births in 1997. Again, however, this measure doesn't begin to tell the whole story. The infant mortality rate for African American babies is currently twice the rate for Anglo-American babies—14.1 in 1997. These concepts will be discussed in more detail below as epidemiological data are compared according to gender, race, and social class.

THEORETICAL PERSPECTIVES ON HEALTH AND MEDICINE

Why do people behave as they do? What are the social rules for acceptable behavior? Why do some people follow these rules more than others? Who are these people most likely to be? Sociologists have developed theories to answer these types of questions. Outlined below are three specific theoretical perspectives that address questions regarding human behavior within the context of institutional medicine.

A STRUCTURAL-FUNCTIONALIST PERSPECTIVE

As the name implies, structural-functionalist sociology seeks to explain how and why social processes work. What social factors produce a stable, ordered, and efficient society? A functionalist perspective helps us find out. Talcott Parsons, a Harvard sociologist who wrote extensively in the 1940s and 1950s, described society as a system within which individuals are socialized to obey rules of behavior. His book *The Social System* is a complex analysis of society that details how and why people function as they do within the cultural context in which they live.[3]

Functionalist theory defines health and medicine in terms of social expectations. Sickness, in and of itself, is dysfunctional to social order. Sick people cannot do what is expected of them. They cannot build automobiles, cook french fries, change diapers, or shovel snow. Functionalists then ask, in effect, how can social order and efficiency be maintained when some of us are sick? The answer is deceptively simple. Social order is maintained if sick people follow some simple rules for behaving like sick people should.

What are these rules? Parsons answers that question with his concept of "the sick role." This concept defines what a functional society can reasonably expect from people who are sick. The sick role can best be understood in terms of the following four assumptions:

1. Illness is a condition that exempts individuals from normal social responsibilities. The sicker you are, the greater the exemption. You can "call in sick" and be excused from doing your job. You can, that is, if you're really sick. Part of this assumption depends on someone other than you validating your condition. Employers routinely require corroborating evidence from your doctor. Teachers require that sick students at least present a note from their moms. This requirement, in exchange for exemption, prevents malingering.

2. The sick person is not responsible for his or her illness. As Parsons defines this concept, he argues that becoming sick is not the fault of the individual; hence, he or she is entitled to exemption from responsibilities.

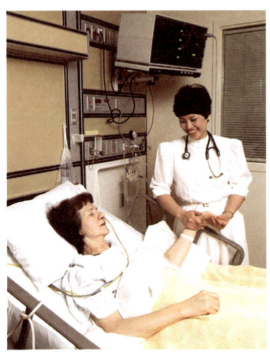

Social order is maintained if sick people adequately play the sick role.

3. The sick person must want to recover. The first two assumptions rest upon this one. Even though sick people are exempt from their jobs, they must demonstrate a desire to return to their normal mode of behavior. People suspected of "faking it" or not trying to get well no longer get the exemption.

4. Sick people must seek competent help and do what they are told. "Go to the doctor and take your medicine." That's how one demonstrates the willingness to recover. Again, failure to do this forfeits the benefits of the sick role.

Clearly, these assumptions define several sets of social relationships. Synthesizing these rules, rights, and obligations creates a society within which sickness can be efficiently redressed and order restored. Society *functions*.

SOCIAL CONFLICT THEORY

There is more than one way to look at society. Competing theories seek to explain how and why social institutions function as they do. Social conflict theory addresses a totally different set of questions than does functionalism. Rather than explaining how to keep order and stability within a social system, *conflict theory* addresses questions of social inequality. Which groups of people are more likely than others to benefit from the way society is arranged? How do these groups seek to maintain access to those benefits? Who suffers in that process?

With respect to health care, *conflict theory* is most useful in explaining how institutional medicine gives some groups of people more social benefits than others. Conflict theory points first to the objective reality that health care in the United States is a commodity to be purchased, not a basic right of citizenship. Those with the most purchasing power get better service.

Conflict theorists argue that this simply preserves the power of those who already have it.[4]

In 1998, more than 44 million people in the United States had no health insurance, a figure equal to over 16 percent of the entire population. What's more, 7.5 million of those uninsured persons *had* full-time, year-round jobs! Finally, these U.S. citizens who are uninsured are much more likely to be members of minority groups, single parents, and children.[5]

Conflict theorists argue that institutional medicine has become an agent of social control as much as it is a source of healing. For example, take the power that physicians have to diagnose illness and distinguish between the "sick" and the "well." Is this not also the power to discredit people?[6] Consider especially issues of mental health or addiction. The power to label individuals in those ways places "the sick" in a socially and morally subservient position to those who are "well."

Feminist Catherine Kohler Riessman argues that "medicalization" concentrates power in the hands of physicians who "monopolize the provi-

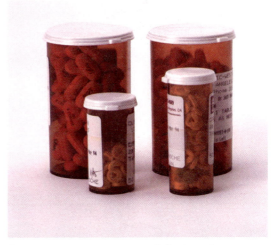

Doctors assert power over socially dependent populations by using jargon and prescribing treatment that is often not understood outside the medical field. We just trust that "doctor knows best."

sion of treatment" to the detriment of "structurally dependent populations . . . like children . . . and women."[7] From this perspective, women yield status and power to physicians. They do this when giving birth, seeking to prevent or terminate a pregnancy, or redefining their bodies through cosmetic surgery and crash diets. Females are motivated to do these things by largely unreasonable expectations about what it means to be a woman in American society.

To summarize, localizing social power in the hands of powerful individuals or members of powerful groups tends to create a society in which problems and solutions are defined and implemented by a few on behalf of many, not all of whom are going to be treated fairly.

SYMBOLIC INTERACTIONIST THEORY

Sociologist Herbert Blumer claimed that during an encounter between two or more individuals, "human beings interpret or 'define' each other's actions instead of merely reacting to each other's actions."[8] Symbolic interactionist theory focuses on these definitions and interpretations; these assessments determine attitudes and behavior. W. I. Thomas put it this way: "If (people) define their situations as real, they are real in their consequences."[9] *Symbolic interactionism* helps us understand how and why doctors and patients behave as they do when encountering one another.

Imagine you've been invited to a campus gathering at which several business executives will be on hand to interview prospective employees. The meeting begins with an informal reception where you, the executives, and other job seekers mingle. You notice a well-dressed older man standing alone near the punch bowl and you strike up a conversation. For the next ten minutes, you assume that your natural wit and engaging personality will make a good impression on this person you are sure will ultimately decide to hire you. Imagine your surprise when you later discover that the man by the punch bowl is actually another job seeker. The real boss is on the other side of the room, a woman you thought was a secretary. Who these people actually were had no bearing on how you behaved. You defined the encounter at the punch bowl as a job interview; it became a job interview from your point of view and you goofed!

Imagine now how encounters between patients and health-care professionals can become complicated and emotionally charged. A doctor sends you to the radiology department for an X ray because he or she thinks there was something "suspicious" about the headaches you described. On the way down the hall, you decide you've got a brain tumor. The technician smiles and you feel some relief. Then you hear someone in the next room say, "Oh no," as they develop your X ray. You're dying again! These assumptions emerge from our perceptions, stories we've heard from others, and our prior experiences. "Reality" becomes what we define it to be.

Imagine how complicated interactions can be when the individuals involved come from vastly different cultural backgrounds, carrying with them conflicting assumptions about what the encounter means. William Madsen describes just such a situation in his book, *The Mexican-Americans of South Texas*:[10]

> *We saw the doctor in his office after a long wait while many Anglos went in first. The doctor asked my wife, "What is wrong?" I told him. I said my wife had no energy and often no appetite. I told him how she had bad dreams and cried in her sleep. I explained she . . . had not responded to the treatment of a curandero (a Mexican folk healer). I said I had come to him because my brother thought he could probably cure this disease. The doctor sat there smiling as I talked. When*

I finished, he laughed at me. Then he sat up straight and said sternly, "Forget all that nonsense. You have come to me and I will treat your wife. It is my job to decide what is wrong with her. And forget about those stupid superstitions. I don't know how a grown man like you can believe such nonsense!" He treated me like a fool.

Madsen then reports the doctor asked the man to leave the room and told his wife to disrobe for an examination. The man refused. He took his wife away and they never returned.

By now you can perhaps understand how complex the study of health and medicine from these various sociological perspectives can be. At this point, we move from a discussion of theory to reports of how social circumstances produce different health outcomes for different groups of people. As you read and think about these data pertaining to health and illness in society, think about how a functionalist, conflict, or interactionist perspective helps you imagine strategies for changing these outcomes.

EPIDEMIOLOGY: THE DISTRIBUTION OF DISEASE AND DEATH

As we saw earlier, epidemiologists analyze data on death (mortality) and disease (morbidity) within societies. These investigators—often described as detectives—search for linkages and patterns among groups of people who are classified according to characteristics such as age, race, gender, education, income, and social class. What are these differences and how do they change over time?

LEADING CAUSES OF DEATH

Table 14:1 below lists the ten major causes of death in 1900 and 1997. What advances in medical knowledge do you think have produced these differences? What social conditions that shape modern society were unheard of at the turn of the century? How do these changes contribute to the differences noted in the table?

TABLE 14:1
Leading Causes of Death in 1900 and 1997

1900	1997
1. Influenza and pneumonia	1. Heart disease
2. Tuberculosis	2. Cancer
3. Gastritis	3. Cerebrovascular disease
4. Diseases of the heart	4. Chronic pulmonary disease
5. Cerebrovascular disease	5. Accidents
6. Chronic kidney disease	6. Pneumonia and influenza
7. Accidents	7. Diabetes
8. Cancer	8. Suicide
9. Diseases of early infancy	9. Kidney disease
10. Diptheria	10. Liver disease

Source: Rose Weitz, *The Sociology of Health, Illness, and Health Care: A Critical Approach* (Belmont, CA: Wadsworth, 2001), 31.

LIFE EXPECTANCY AND MORTALITY

We have defined life expectancy earlier in this chapter. But how has the average number of years one can expect to live changed over time? Since 1900, life expectancy has increased by thirty years (from 47 to 77). However, the life span has remained about the same. People only live so long, and some people in every period of time have lived to a ripe old age. In the early 1900s, infant mortality was high and it was fairly common for women to die during childbirth. These factors, of course, reduced the average life span. But those who managed to survive infancy and childbearing could expect to live as long as we do today. At this point, let's consider some more interesting variations in life expectancy and mortality by looking at differences in social class, race, and gender.[11]

SOCIAL CLASS

People with low incomes live seven years less than the more affluent. Levels of education and occupational status are the two most important components of this concept with respect to health and life. Higher levels of education and occupational status are associated with lower levels of stress, healthier and safer working environments, and a more nutritious diet. People with higher education and occupational status also use more preventive health services and are less likely to delay seeking care. Why do you suppose that is? Who, more than others, do you imagine has more direct access to good health care and educational opportunities? What might a conflict theorist have to say about these differences?

RACE

The average life expectancy for an Anglo-American born in the United States in 1997 is just over 77 years. But an African American born in 1997 can expect to live about 72.5 years. What accounts for these differences? A major factor is income. Blacks are three times more likely than Whites to live below the poverty level. Another reason has to do with Blacks having more high risk factors such as smoking, high blood pressure, and high cholesterol levels. Finally, and most important, diminished access to health care and medical services also produces the variation we observe in health status between African Americans and Anglo-Americans. Does this create a functional society? What might a conflict theorist have to say about these data? Why do you suppose it is that African Americans are more likely than Anglo-Americans to live in impoverished conditions?

Poor people do not have equal access to quality health care.

GENDER

An Anglo-American male born in 1997 can expect to live 74 years; an Anglo-American female born in 1997 can expect to live nearly 80 years. An African American female born in 1997 can expect to live a bit longer than an Anglo-American male (76 years), but life expectancy for an African American male is only 69 years—eleven years less than Anglo females. What accounts for these dramatic differences? Epidemiologists argue that the difference is due to different rates at which men and women die from heart disease, cancer, or are accident and homicide victims (especially for African American males). Men are more likely to be smokers; they also seem to have a greater propensity to abuse alcohol and other drugs. Men are also exposed to a wider array of hazards in the workplace. These include exposure to carcinogenic materials and accidents. Men also drive more miles, drive faster, and violate more traffic regulations than women.

INFANT MORTALITY AND THE QUALITY OF LIFE

Among the more common indicators of cultural quality is the infant mortality rate—the number of infants/1000 population who, after having been born alive, die before their first birthday. Table 14:2 compares the year 2000 infant mortality rates for selected countries around the world.

As is apparent, the United States ranks better overall than most other countries listed, but not compared to Western Europe, Canada, and Japan, where access to health care is universal. Moreover, the average again does not tell the whole story. For children born to African American mothers in the United States, the infant mortality rate is about double the national average (14.1 in 1998). Why these dramatic differences?

TABLE 14:2
Infant Mortality Rates by Selected Country

NORTH AMERICA		
	United States	6.8
	Canada	5.1
EUROPE		
	France	4.5
	Germany	4.8
	United Kingdom	5.6
LATIN AMERICA		
	Chile	9.6
	Cuba	7.5
	Mexico	26.2
AFRICA		
	Egypt	62.3
	Ethiopia	101.3
	South Africa	58.9
ASIA		
	India	64.9
	Japan	3.9
	Saudi Arabia	52.9

Source: U.S. Bureau of the Census, 2000.

Infant mortality is linked to low birth weight, which is most often the result of poor or absent prenatal care. High rates also result from poor maternal health, poor nutritional habits during pregnancy, insufficient access to health care, inadequate care once they obtain health care, and medical treatment that does not adequately address the needs of African American women living in poverty. Does this create a functional society? What might a conflict theorist say about this?

MORBIDITY AND GENDER

We've defined morbidity as the amount of disease, impairment, and accident in a population; we've distinguished between incidence (number of new cases) and prevalence (total

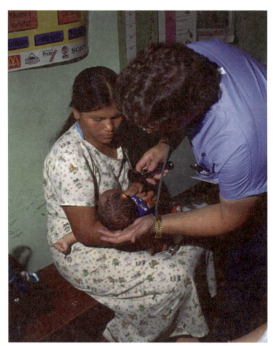

This baby in Latin America is less likely to survive to age one than a baby in the United States.

number of cases) in a population. How do these issues vary according to gender?[12]

Women's lives are filled with more health problems, but these problems tend to be less serious. Women have higher incidences of acute conditions (such as flu and cold, infectious and/or parasitic diseases) and a higher prevalence of most nonfatal chronic conditions (such as sinusitis, hay fever, migraines, arthritis, diabetes, high blood pressure, and asthma).

Compared to men, women's symptoms are more likely to be bothersome but not life threatening, and their limitations are mild or moderate rather than severe, at least until they advance in years. Having more nonfatal problems and fewer fatal ones means women live longer but experience more years of sickness and dysfunction. By contrast, men have fewer illnesses, but when ill health does strike, it is more likely to be fatal. Women's lives are compromised in quality; men's lives are compromised in length.

Why does this occur? We have already listed many of the reasons in the discussion on mortality rates. Some evidence suggests women are biologically protected from some diseases; other differences are clearly associated with acquired risks, such as illness and injury on the job or while engaging in dangerous recreational activities.

However, some of the statistical data might be open to question. Evidence exists which suggests women are more likely to seek medical help for conditions that are not life threatening. Thus, their cases are more likely to be noted by researchers who count up illness reports and doctor visits. Finally, women's tendencies to seek care earlier may lead to earlier diagnoses and more persistent management of these problems.

AIDS

The Human Immunodeficiency Virus (HIV) disables the immune system and enables normally benign infections to take over the body and kill the infected person. The first cases of AIDS were officially recognized by the U.S. Centers for Disease Control in 1981. The disease is now considered to be a worldwide plague.

As is now widely known, common targets for the HIV virus are IV drug users and gay and bisexual men. Educational efforts promoting "safe sex" appear to be associated with a decline in new cases among the gay community. Less than half of new HIV cases in America (and less than 10 percent worldwide) are linked to homosexual activity. However, an increasing proportion of new cases is being documented among heterosexuals, particularly African American and Hispanic women.

Research suggests that new AIDS cases are associated with the exchange of sex for drugs such as crack. Adolescent women are increasingly engaging in very large numbers of sexual contacts to support their addiction. AIDS is more and more becoming defined as a drug-related disease. This raises a very controversial issue that is worth some reflective thought.[13]

AIDS is transmitted through the drug-using sub-culture by the sharing of contaminated needles, or by engaging in sexual contact with someone who has been infected by a dirty needle. Based on the shifting nature of new AIDS cases, some have suggested a very controversial approach. What if IV drug users had available to them a place where they could obtain clean, sterile needles for individual use, rather than depending on the common practice among users to share contaminated needles with one another? Would this lead to an increase in drug use? Research suggests otherwise. A study published in 1997 by the National Institutes of Health reports that needle exchange programs "show a reduction in risk behaviors as high as 80 percent in injecting drug users, with estimates of a 30 percent or greater reduction of HIV."[14] Moreover, that report also cited several other studies indicating that drug-using behavior does not increase simply because addicts have clean needles available to them.

No one wants to appear to be promoting drug use. Many people believe offering the opportunity to exchange needles would do just that. There is a ban on federal funding to any drug treatment program that utilizes needle exchange. On the other hand, a 30 percent reduction in HIV would save many thousands of lives and hundreds of thousands of dollars in health care costs. Which do you think is the more ethical approach?

RELIGION AND HEALTH

Are religious people healthier than people who do not believe in God or practice their faith? Can praying real hard make you get well faster?

Previous research does not give clear answers to these questions. But sociologists of religion and medicine have noted some interesting things.[15] One early study suggested regular church attendance lowered blood pressure. Others also reported that religiosity (belief and practice) improved physical health and lowered mortality.

But other researchers are quick to point toward other social factors—such as age and gender—as more important indicators of health status than the role of religion in individuals' lives. And another study of Mexican American Catholics suggested the positive relationship between religious attendance and health status relies on something else entirely. People who attend religious events are healthier than those who do not, in part because being able to get out of the house requires a basic level of good health to begin with.

Others have suggested that positive associations between religion and health are related to health-protective behavior. This is the result of affiliation with religious groups that prohibit or restrict smoking, drug use, and alcohol use.

Ferraro and Koch's recent study seeks to clarify and specify the manner in which one's religion and health might be positively related. These researchers wondered: Is the *relationship* between religion and health stronger or weaker for Anglo-Americans than it is for African Americans? The logic for this research question emerges from what we have already noted from census data. That is, there are significant differences in morbidity and mortality rates between Blacks and Whites. African Americans are much more likely to get sick more often, be sick longer, and die earlier than Anglo-Americans. Ferraro and Koch reported these two rather interesting results from their research:

1. Religious practice (prayer, Bible reading, watching religious television or listening to religious radio programs, and attending worship) does seem to be linked to better health for Blacks, but not for Whites.

2. African Americans are much more likely to turn to the church when in a health crisis.

What do these findings mean? We know that African Americans are more likely to *be* in a health crisis than are Anglo-Americans. Research indicates that Blacks turn to the church more than Whites when this occurs. Could it be that African Americans do this because they believe they are more likely to get fair treatment and help from the church than from other social institutions? Could this be the "smoking gun" of a kind of discrimination that still exists within institutional medicine? This is a rather controversial conclusion.

Finally, the researchers wondered whether the differences in health between Anglo-Americans and African Americans would be even worse were it not for the African American Church.

What do you think?

HOW CHRISTIANS CAN CHANGE THE WORLD

This chapter has summarized ways in which access to quality health care is unequally distributed. Not everyone has an equal opportunity to enjoy life with the fullest health. Christians need to be aware of such social injustice and investigate ways to celebrate the human dignity of ALL persons. In Jesus' day the Great Physician did not discriminate by race, gender, social class, or "worthiness." In fact, He was known to touch lepers and a hemorrhaging woman—people who were considered very "unclean" in His culture. Yet all He asked was that they believe they could be healed.

Christians can help promote equal opportunity to health care by serving or supporting those who serve in health missions to poverty areas. Christian ministries for pregnant women or new mothers can insure their babies get a healthy start. Ministries to the elderly and homebound can insure that they get at least one healthy meal a day. Many health education ministries in schools and churches promote knowledge about healthy lifestyles and preventive medicine. Like Jesus we ought not to be afraid to go into the "unclean" areas: Churches need to have ministries to substance abusers and teen mothers.

overview

- This chapter outlines several complex and interesting issues related to health and medicine in our society. You have read a variety of perspectives from which to examine the social dynamics within the health care industry, and among health care workers and their patients.

- A structural-functionalist perspective seeks to find social stability.

- A conflict orientation examines the causes and consequences of social inequality.

- An interactionist perspective looks more closely at how individuals who are sick and the people who care for them get along with each other.

- Social epidemiology is the study of how illness and death occur within different social groups. Data demonstrate that there are significant differences in the rates of morbidity and mortality for men and women, Blacks and Whites, and rich and poor. A conflict perspective helps us examine and understand why these differences occur.

- Finally, researchers report there might be some interesting work yet to do when examining the relationship between religion and health.

key concepts

disease
A biologically defined disorder of an organism that impairs its ability to function.

epidemiology
A systematic study of how diseases are distributed within a culture or society.

health
A state of complete physical, mental, and social well-being, not merely the absence of disease.

illness
An individual's awareness of the presence of disease in the body.

incidence
The number of new cases of a disease which occur in a population over a specific period of time (usually a particular year).

infant mortality rate
The number of infants who, after having been born alive, die before their first birthday.

life expectancy
The average number of years a person can expect to live with respect to the year of his/her birth.

morbidity rate
The incidence of disease in a population.

mortality rate
The incidence of death in a population.

prevalence
The total number of cases present in a population at any given time; includes new cases as well as all previously existing cases.

sickness
One's awareness of the presence of a disease in someone else which then causes that person to change his or her behavior toward the sick individual.

endnotes

1. C. D. Gibson and B. M. Kramer, "Site of Care in Medical Practice," *Medical Care* 3 (1965): 14-17.
2. This particular statistic, as well as the subsequent indicators of morbidity and mortality are taken from the following source: *U.S. Bureau of the Census, Statistical Abstract of the United States: 2000,* 120th ed. (Washington, DC: U.S. Government Printing Office).
3. Talcott Parsons, *The Social System* (Glencoe, IL: Free Press, 1951), 436-39.
4. For an excellent collection of readings that address health care issues from a conflict perspective, see Peter Conrad and Rochelle Kern's edited volume entitled *The Sociology of Health and Illness: Critical Perspectives,* 4th ed. (New York: St. Martin's Press, 1994).
5. Two sources are used for this information, both of which provide an even more comprehensive analysis of inequities in the delivery of health care in America. They are:
   Jennifer A. Campbell, "Health Insurance Coverage, 1998," *Current Population Reports* Series (1999): 60-208.
   Rose Weitz, *The Sociology of Health, Illness, and Health Care: A Critical Approach* (Belmont, CA: Wadsworth Publishing Co., 2001), 223-47.
6. Irving Kenneth Zola, "Structural Constraints in the Doctor-Patient Relationship: The Case of Noncompliance," reprinted as Reading 6 in Howard D. Schwartz, *Dominant Issues in Medical Sociology*, 3rd ed. (New York: McGraw-Hill, 1994), 76-113.
7. See Reading 13 in Schwartz, above, 193.
8. Herbert Blumer, *Symbolic Interactionism: Perspective and Method* (Englewood Cliffs, NJ: Prentice-Hall, 1969), 79.
9. See Morris Janowitz, ed., *W. I. Thomas on Social Organization and Social Personality* (Chicago: University of Chicago Press, 1966), 301, original quote, 1931.
10. William Madsen, *The Mexican-Americans of South Texas,* 2nd ed. (New York: Holt, Rinehart & Winston, 1973), 95.
11. See Weitz, cited above, pp. 18-111, for full documentation of these statistics.
12. These insights are aptly summarized in Gregory L. Weiss and Lynne E. Lonnquist, *The Sociology of Health, Healing, and Illness* (Englewood Cliffs, NJ: Prentice-Hall, 1994), 49-59.
13. For a more complete discussion of this issue, see James D. Wright and Joel A. Devine, *Drugs as a Social Problem* (New York: Harper Collins, 1994), 74-75.
14. "Consensus Development Statement on Interventions to Prevent HIV Risk Behaviors." Report published by the National Institutes of Health, March 1997.
15. A comprehensive literature review of the issues mentioned in the chapter can be found in Kenneth F. Ferraro and Jerome R. Koch, "Religion and Health Among Black and White Adults: Examining Social Support and Consolation," *Journal for the Scientific Study of Religion* 3, no. 4 (1994): 362-75.

CHAPTER FIFTEEN

Economic Life

chapter outline

I. Christian economic challenges

II. Barter vs. money economies

III. Three economic sectors

IV. Premodern economies
  A. Hunting and gathering societies
  B. Pastoral societies
  C. Horticultural societies
  D. Agricultural societies

V. Modern economies
  A. Industrial societies
  B. Postindustrial societies

VI. Features of modern economies
  A. Separation of home and workplace
  B. Separation of ownership and control
  C. Women's entry into the labor force
  D. Globalization

VII. Capitalism vs. socialism
  A. Classic free market capitalism
  B. Socialism and the Marxian critique of capitalism
  C. Democratic socialism and the welfare state
  D. Underdevelopment, overdevelopment, and misdevelopment

VIII. How Christians can change the world

biblical reflection

"Sell your possessions and give alms . . . For where your treasure is, there your heart will be also."

—Luke 12:33-34

CHRISTIAN ECONOMIC CHALLENGES

The economy is that institution or sector of society in which people produce, distribute, and consume goods and services. If you are tempted to minimize the importance of the economic sector, consider how you personally would respond to the following:

If grocery stores, cafeterias, and restaurants suddenly closed and our food distribution network shut down, how would you get food? Could you grow your own? Even if you could, how much effort would it take and would you have time left to do anything else?

If banks closed and money became worthless, how would you obtain and pay for the things you need and want? What could you offer of value to trade for them?

Even if you are not currently a wealthy producer or distributor of a good or service, the choices we all make as consumers give us a good deal of power, especially if we work together as African Americans did during the 1955 bus **boycott** in Montgomery, Alabama.

If you are tempted to think that economic matters are of no concern to Christians, consider these additional questions:

1. Is Christianity compatible only with **capitalist** economic systems? Or does it allow some to wallow in undeserved wealth and condemn others to a life of abject poverty? Does **Christian socialism** as practiced by the **Hutterites** free people from jealousy and envy more so than capitalism would? Is it perhaps more compatible with the spirit of Acts, chapter two? But if so, can **socialism** work in national economic systems, or only for small religiously committed groups like the Hutterites or Israeli **kibbutzim**? Do you know any persons who live or have lived in Christian communes that practice economic sharing?

2. Can individual Christians—even relatively poor college students—influence the production and distribution of goods and services by boycotting the products of firms that produce morally offensive things? If so, which boycotts would you be prepared to join? Similarly, should Christians with money to invest practice **social responsibility investing** by investing only in companies that produce products compatible with a Christian lifestyle?

3. Do you agree with Christians and other religious leaders who call for a modern **Jubilee**, asking wealthy nations and financial institutions to cancel or reduce the debts of poor debtor nations to help them escape poverty? Can such efforts allow us to be Christian world changers?

BARTER VS. MONEY ECONOMIES

In many premodern societies, people simply exchanged goods and services in personal transactions. I might trade you four coconuts for two fish. You might offer to cut my hair if I pulled your aching tooth. No money would change hands, perhaps because money would not yet exist. This is called a **barter economy**.

Gradually, however, people began to use what was valuable to them in their transactions, whether cowry shells, cocoa beans, or precious stones or metals. Governments such as that of the Romans minted and stamped coins—often with the emperor's image—to facilitate economic transactions. These coins had value beyond their intrinsic value because people learned they could use them as a medium of exchange to obtain things they lacked, such as food. Modern societies now print lightweight paper money and even exchange funds electronically. Whether dollars or *euros* are used, all monetary systems rely on peoples' faith and trust that the coins, bills, or electronic money they exchange for goods and services are all "good as gold." Should we ever lose faith in the value of our money, we might be forced to return to a barter economy. When German money lost its strength before Hitler rose to power, the German people resorted to trading sacks of potatoes.

THE THREE ECONOMIC SECTORS

All modern economies have three sectors: the **primary** or extractive sector, the **secondary** or manufacturing sector, and the **tertiary** or services sector. These have varying levels of importance and employ varying numbers of workers. While this depends mostly on the level of technological development of the society in question, it also is influenced to some degree by the presence of natural resources, skilled labor, climate, and international cooperation.

The primary sector includes all economic activity devoted to extracting or producing goods from nature. Agriculture is central here, since all people must eat. Also included are hunting and fishing, forestry, and mining. In each case, something is being taken from nature or produced with the aid of natural resources such as land, water, and sunshine. Farmers or gardeners who grow corn, tomatoes, or potatoes—whether for sale or home consumption—are working in the primary sector. So are fishermen, loggers, and miners. This sector and these workers predominate in societies that are not highly developed technologically. Most human beings for most of human history worked in this sector, because producing food was so arduous in **preindustrial** times. As agriculture, logging, mining, and fishing become mechanized, employment in these sectors declines markedly, as it has in the United States, Western Europe, Japan, and Australia.

The secondary or manufacturing sector involves transforming products extracted or produced from nature into something that does not exist in nature. Cornflakes, tomato paste, and potato chips do not exist in nature. The persons who produce them work in the secondary sector (e.g., **blue-collar workers** in factories). Likewise, persons who produce automobiles (whether for Toyota, Daimler-Chrysler, or General Motors), computers, nylon stockings, toothpaste, and even those who print this sociology textbook are all working in the secondary sector. This sector of the economy becomes the leading sector of growth during rapid industrialization, as happened in the United States in the late nineteenth and early twentieth centuries. Indeed, this sector is often called the "industrial" sector. However, since there are also primary and tertiary sector industries, it is best to avoid confusion and refer to this sector as the manufacturing sector.

The tertiary sector employs all persons who provide services to others. Such workers do not extract anything from nature nor do they manufacture tangible goods. However, they provide valuable services to individuals and businesses. How would you like to take a sociology class without a teacher, or have your hair styled by a robot? A few other obvious examples of service workers are nurses and doctors, cooks and waitresses, lawyers, accountants, cashiers and clerks, police and probation officers, pollsters and punsters, truck drivers and airline pilots, garbage collectors, rocket scientists, and computer programmers. Salaries and benefits enjoyed by service workers vary greatly, as does their prestige. Those who work in traditionally male-dominated managerial and professional services with generally high salaries and benefits are called **white-collar workers**. Women who work in predominantly female occupations (e.g., dental hygienists, bank tellers, and secretaries, usually with lower pay and benefits than white-collar workers) are sometimes called **pink-collar workers**. Whatever their gender, race, pay, or prestige, service workers have become the majority of the **labor force** in modern societies. Most of my students expect to work by providing services to others. In what sector of the economy do you expect to be employed following graduation? If you work now, in what sector do you work?

PREMODERN ECONOMIES

Most of human history has been experienced prior to the modern age. The chief imperative people faced was that of obtaining food. Anthropologists and sociologists find that societies can be meaningfully categorized by the way they obtain food and do other work. Furthermore, the way societies meet the need for subsistence has implications for society far beyond simple survival. It has strong implications for family life, education, religion, and government; in fact, it impacts virtually all other sectors of society beyond the economy.

HUNTING AND GATHERING SOCIETIES

Before modern technology came into being, humans spent most of their time gathering food from nature. People have hunted for birds and animals, fished, gathered nuts and wild fruits and roots far longer than they have farmed or eaten in restaurants or food courts. A few of us still hunt and fish or gather wild nuts and berries, but most of us now do these things only as hobbies or to supplement our diets. Societies that use hunting and gathering as their primary survival strategy are few in number today.

Recent history provides enough examples of such societies, however, that we can see the basic outlines of their food gathering strategies and other social characteristics. Plains Indians in the U.S. and Canada hunted bison as their primary source of food. Since the great bison herds moved in search of grass and water, the Indians moved with them rather than face starvation in permanent villages or cities. The teepee thus became the favored dwelling; it was quickly dismantled, moved, and reassembled whenever the need arose. The bison, especially the rare white bison, also took on religious significance. The Indian apologized to the spirit of the bison even as he took its life to sustain his own and that of his people. Hunting proceeded only until the need for food was met. Nothing was wasted. Hides provided robes and teepee covers. Bones were made into needles and serving spoons. To overhunt game for sheer sport was unthinkable, since it might jeopardize next year's food supply. Only during the Golden Age—after the Plains Indians had obtained horses and rifles, but before they were reduced to reservation status—was a relatively successful hunt assured, and then only after a herd had been located. Previous to that time, the chief hunting tactics had been to stampede the bison over a cliff or through a small opening in a preset prairie fire.

Since food and sometimes water are usually limited in the natural environment, they can quickly be exhausted. Hunting and gathering societies are thus forced to remain nomadic. Their size is limited to small bands for most of the year. They do not bother to build cities, as it would be impossible to sustain them. The family and clan are the primary groupings. Since survival may depend on sharing, little social inequality exists, other than that suggested by age and sex. Men typically do most of the hunting, especially that which involves extended travel and absence from home. Women typically care for home, hearth, and small children, and may in fact be pregnant or caring for children for most of their adult lives. Structural-functionalist sociologists and anthropologists suggest that such sex-segregated gender roles are more efficient—and thus increase the chance of survival—than a more egalitarian strategy. After all, before the invention of infant formula, what sense would it make to send pregnant women out on the hunt and ask fathers to stay at home and tend to infants?

PASTORAL SOCIETIES

> *The LORD is my shepherd, I shall not want;*
>
> *he makes me lie down in green pastures.*
>
> *He leads me beside still waters; he restores my soul.*
>
> *He leads me in paths of righteousness for his name's sake.*
>
> *Even though I walk through the valley of the shadow of death,*
>
> *I fear no evil; for thou art with me; thy rod and thy staff, they comfort me.*
>
> —Psalm 23:1-4, RSV

Several thousand years ago, humans learned to domesticate animals. Herding tame animals and depending on them for meat, milk, and wool is a more efficient survival strategy than hunting and gathering, since the tame animals do most of the work of finding forage and water and converting it into meat. Cattle, sheep, goats, yaks, reindeer, llamas, and others provide a sort of walking bank account that can be tapped whenever food is needed. Westerners often have norms against using blood for food, but some herders such as the East African Maasai and Boran occasionally extract blood to be used as food, and do so skillfully enough that the cow or goat so "tapped" rarely dies.

However, since grazing animals will eventually exhaust most supplies of food and water, pastoralists or herders still need to occasionally move their dwellings and encampments in search of water and greener pastures. While land is generally not considered private property, grazing rights may be. Feuds and battles may break out even between kinsmen, as they did between Abram and his nephew Lot in the Old Testament. (See Genesis 13:2-7.) Social inequalities become pronounced as some successful herders like Abram amass huge flocks and herds, while others may own no or few animals, forcing them to take employment as shepherds for others. Unmarried young men are also often assigned the herding job, as was David in the Old Testament before he became a king.

Families in pastoral societies are almost always male-dominated or patriarchal and patrilineal, tracing descent and passing on property through the father rather than the mother. The wealthiest men are often elevated to positions of highest status as chiefs, and sometimes allowed to take more than one wife, as has been common among African pastoralists.

The religion of pastoralists usually focuses on one supreme God (monotheism), as in Judaism, Islam, and Christianity. God and his priests may be called pastors (shepherds), an image found in the familiar and much loved Psalm 23. While few Americans, Canadians, or Australians still live as pastoralists, many of us still think of God and our religious leaders in these bygone pastoralist images.

HORTICULTURAL SOCIETIES

Horticultural or hand-gardening societies have been especially common in forested tropical areas of our world, such as Africa, Asia, and South and Central America. Where modern technology has not yet become dominant or has only recently appeared in these parts of the world (e.g., the Yanomano of the South American Amazon rain forest), horticulture remains the predominant survival strategy. Fire is often used to clear the forest during the pronounced dry season in order to plant crops such as corn, manioc, or yams just as the rainy season begins. Villages of thatched-roof dwellings become semipermanent, but may be moved if soil fertility declines or disease invades the village. The religion of such societies usually involves appeasing various spirits to insure good harvests and to avoid disease; thus, it is called spiritist religion.

The Anasazi and Hohokam peoples of the southwest desert in the United States were also originally horticultural, growing their crops of corn, beans, and squash in a very arid environment with the aid of irrigation, hand planting, and cultivation. Some of their descendants are still farmers. Since most use modern technology such as tractors, these descendants are no longer true horticulturists.

AGRICULTURAL SOCIETIES

The invention of the plow about 6,000 years ago provided another quantum leap in food production. Usually made of wood and pulled by draft animals such as oxen, horses, or water buffalo, the plow could uproot weeds, young trees, and shrubs, removing plant competition for the crop about to be planted. Plows also bring buried soil nutrients back up into the plant root zone and can incorporate animal manure back into the soil as natural fertilizer. Draft animals make it possible to cultivate much more land than is possible for horticulturists working by hand. This frees significant numbers of people from food production, allowing the construction of permanent cities composed of artisans, priests, merchants, and teachers. Animals must still be used to bring food to the city from the surrounding rural area, so most cities remain

Tractors would get the work done faster, but horses and hard work keep us closer to God.

Anonymous Amish bishop

fairly small by modern standards. Walled cities such as ancient Jericho provide safe shelter at night for farmers who may return to till their fields and harvest crops by day.

Today's remaining agricultural societies are most common in the small villages of Southeast Asia and the Indian subcontinent. The Amish are among the very few North Americans who still use horses for both farm work and for transportation. As such, their lifestyle is romanticized by journalists and tourists, who flock to see the Amish as a kind of living museum of how their ancestors used to live.

MODERN ECONOMIES

INDUSTRIAL SOCIETIES

While previous transitions had each provided improvements in subsistence, especially the development of animal-powered plow culture, no transition has been as revolutionary for the economy and for human society in general as the set of changes ushered in by the **Industrial Revolution**. This revolution began in the late 1700s in Great Britain, then spread to the rest of Western Europe and overseas to North America, Australia, and New Zealand, finally reaching most of the world. Because of the Industrial Revolution, machines were invented to do the work formerly done by humans or by animals. The steam engine was one of the first of these inventions. It used wood or coal to heat water to produce steam, the release of which powered the first steam locomotive trains, thrashed grain from straw, and plowed land. Eventually the internal combustion engine replaced the steam engine. Again, a quantum leap in food production was made possible. Tractors made it possible for one farmer or farm family to farm the same amount of land previously farmed by several horse-powered farm families. Scientific improvements in hybrid seeds and the development of synthetic fertilizers, herbicides, and pesticides further increased crop production. Today only 2 percent of North Americans are still needed to produce food for the entire populations of Canada and America, and much of the harvest can be exported. Modern agriculture is really industrial agriculture.

As happened on a much smaller scale with the development of animal-powered agriculture, the transition to machine-powered food production, transportation, and work generally set in motion a host of other changes. Displaced farmers flocked to cities, some of which grew to contain millions of people. These persons worked the factories that made Western Europe and North American societies truly industrial societies, as manufacturing became the engine of economic growth. The **assembly line**, pioneered by Henry Ford in the automobile industry, became a prototype for efficiency and speed in manufacturing.

Production became so efficient that manufacturing workers were displaced, creating crises in unemployment. In the formerly dangerous work of coal mining, huge mechanical augers bore through the earth to remove coal from the veins of the Appalachian region, putting miners out of work. The remaining manufacturing workers and miners gradually learned to exert greater collective power by organizing **labor unions** and voting for pro-union candidates for political office. They achieved remarkable gains in wages, working conditions, and fringe benefits, even as further mechanization made more of their jobs obsolete.

While work becomes easier and more productive in industrial societies, other changes are less clearly positive. Some sociologists of religion like Durkheim see the roots of secularization begin during the machine age, evidenced by a decline in religious faith and adherence, as well as the breakup of rural communities.[1] People are forced to become more mobile as they search for jobs wherever they may be found, but this tends to weaken family and com-

Chapter Fifteen: Economic Life

munity ties. Having machines do the work that people formerly did by hand is a mixed blessing. People benefit from the increased leisure time, but boredom and depression may actually increase as people have too little to do. Early retirement can lead to similar crises, especially for adult men who were socialized to value their lives in terms of the work they performed.

POSTINDUSTRIAL SOCIETIES

Some sociologists and philosophers now argue that the most highly developed societies of the modern world have been transformed again, this time to economies and societies called **postindustrial** or postmodern societies. Machines still do most of the work and manufacturing remains important. However, blue-collar work in **old economy** manufacturing jobs no longer forms the leading edge of economic growth. In the **new economy**, the processing and transfer of information and entertainment—through service occupations dependent on high-technology devices such as the computer, interfaced with other computers through the **Internet**—is now seen as the engine of growth. Computer literacy becomes essential in virtually every professional occupation. Journalists, teachers, managers, accountants, engineers—all become computer dependent. Their work is plunged into chaos by temporary power outages caused by electrical storms or the man-made rolling blackouts of California in 2001. Even manufacturing and agriculture become computerized.

Postindustrial communication advances make it possible for the whole world to view Olympic athletic competitions and World Cup soccer live from virtually anywhere in the world. Leisure time increases even more, especially for well-paid professionals in highly developed nations. "Couch potatoes" relax in their home entertainment centers, virtual home theaters. Health clubs and "fat farms" spring up to help the couch potatoes burn off the fat that results from lack of physical exercise. Increasing numbers of surgeons make their living providing facelifts, tummy tucks, and liposuction to affluent consumers who want to "make over" their appearance. Eating disorders such as anorexia and bulimia become commonplace among affluent young women.

Some trends begun in industrial society continue, such as the increase in the **division of labor** noted by Durkheim and others.[2] Assembly-line production techniques spread from the manufacturing sector to service industries, as demonstrated convincingly by George Ritzer in *The McDonaldization of Society*.[3] The McDonald's Corporation perfects the hyper-rational stress on efficiency, predictability, calculability, and control of humans by machines that Weber had noted much earlier. Many consumers come to expect and demand hyper-efficient service, not only from the fast-food industry, but also from automatic teller cash machines, multichannel cable television service, and even in McDonaldized religious services delivered through the electronic church. The idyllic close-knit fabric of village life in Redfield's **folk society**[4] and Tonnies' **gemeinschaft** supposedly gives way to an impersonal, fast-paced urban society that Tonnies called **gesellschaft**.[5] While this transition may have begun long ago, it reaches its apex in postmodern society. Durkheim's **collective conscience**[6] seems to have disappeared, leading to increased problems with social deviance, crime, suicide, and other signs of social malaise. While overall wealth and prosperity are at all-time highs, a permanent or semipermanent **underclass**, living in decaying inner-city cores and remote rural areas such as the Pine Ridge Indian reservation of South Dakota, seem unable to escape poverty and its associated problems.

However, postindustrial economies also offer positive benefits. Aside from the obvious expansion in personal choices for entertainment, education, health care, religion, and just about everything else available to those with money and Internet access, there is less need to uproot families in search of new jobs. It is possible for some **information industry** workers such as writers, data-entry operators, telemarketers, and software designers to work from the comfort of their homes in rustic rural settings in Idaho, Vermont, or Montana, as long as they have access to the Internet. One can work in the morning at the leading edge of postmodern society and hike in the mountains and fish for trout in the afternoon. In ideal situations such as these, professional men and women also can attend to the needs of small children without leaving home or giving up their jobs.

FEATURES OF MODERN ECONOMIES

SEPARATION OF HOME AND WORKPLACE

In spite of the advantages of some information industry workers, most workers in industrial and postindustrial societies need to leave home to bring home their bacon. The separation of home and workplace has become a taken-for-granted feature of modern society. Husband and wife often go off to separate workplaces, while Johnny goes to one elementary school, Susie to middle school in a different neighborhood, and Robert to high school in yet another neighborhood. Families scramble to keep in touch. Home becomes a station for sleeping and refueling. Even much of the refueling is done on the fly—grabbing a meal from McDonald's or another fast-food restaurant's drive-up window. Parents rush to ferry children to various school activities, retreating to the home only to recover for the next round of the same. Nurture and socialization of children, the quality of marriage and family life, and loyalty to local communities and churches often suffer as a result of this separation of home and workplace.

SEPARATION OF OWNERSHIP AND CONTROL

Preindustrial family farmers and cottage industry producers worked together in home-based, family-run economic activities that helped to unite them. These groups exerted a high degree of ownership and control over what they produced and how they produced it. However, the modern manufacturing sector (dominant in industrial society) and the information services sector (dominant in postindustrial society) are both centered in large, **joint-stock corporations**. These corporations—

owned not by one person or family, but by thousands of shareholders—are managed by paid professionals who may or may not own stock in the company. The managers decide what will be produced, how it will be produced, and how and to whom it will be marketed. As long as the company makes a considerable profit and stockholders receive dividends and capital gains on their investments, presumably everyone is happy. However, most owners of company stock exert little control over management decisions and few are able to attend annual shareholders' meetings. When they do, they are rarely able to force through shareholder initiatives to change the direction of management. Managers learn well the lesson that the bottom line is profit. If they fail at helping the firm realize a profit, they may be out of a job.

WOMEN'S ENTRY INTO THE LABOR FORCE

Many modern women have chosen to have fewer children than their mothers and grandmothers. Reasons for this include:

- Levels of education and prosperity have increased in modern societies.

- Children are no longer seen as an economic asset, but rather as a high-cost endeavor.

- Modern birth control makes reduced family size possible.

Some women choose not to marry and/or have any children. Even those who do have children spend an increased number of years without children at home. Many such women seek paid employment outside the home. Even those with young children at home often wish or feel compelled to work outside the home, either for reasons of economic necessity or self-fulfillment.

As late as the early to mid-twentieth century in North America, women in the paid labor force were a minority, and most of those were single women. In late modern and postmodern society, however, most women now have entered the paid labor force, rather than remain as stay-at-home moms. The result is that between 40 and 50 percent of the labor force of highly developed industrial and postindustrial societies is now comprised of women. In virtually all such societies, occupations formerly dominated by men—such as lawyers, doctors, college-level teachers, etc.—now contain significant numbers of women.

However, other occupations remain virtual pink-collar ghettos: secretaries, elementary school teachers, child-care workers, and cosmetologists, to name a few. Work performed primarily by women is still not compensated at levels commensurate with that performed primarily by men. Also, women remain much more likely than men to interrupt their careers for childbirth and child care, or to follow a spouse to a new location. Most women who work outside the home find that they have **dual careers**—one that is compensated monetarily and one that is not. While some men are making increased efforts to perform more housework and child care, women still perform the lion's share of such work.

GLOBALIZATION

As international trade increases and rapid, efficient communication and transportation seem to shrink the size of our world to a **global village**,[7] economies and nations of the world become inexorably linked in ways not previously foreseen. This is known as **globalization**. Such events as Marco Polo's historic journey and the era of European colonialism are examples of limited interaction in the past. But global linkage has become much more pervasive in industrial and postindustrial society. Free trade agreements first used with success in the European Economic Community (now called the **European Union)** are the pattern for the **North American Free Trade Association.** NAFTA may soon be extended to virtually the entire Western Hemisphere. Goods and services flow between nations at lightning speed, facilitated by the instant communication of the Internet and by the emergence of English as a **global language**. Almost without exception, the largest corporations of the modern and post-modern world do business in more than one nation, thus earning the description **multinational corporations**. Some have budgets larger than those of entire nations, and exert formidable political power in the nations in which they do business.

CAPITALISM VS. SOCIALISM

> *"The market price of every particular commodity is regulated by the proportion between the quantity which is actually brought to market, and the demand of those who are willing to pay the natural price of the commodity."*
>
> –Adam Smith, *The Wealth of Nations* (Chicago: Henry Regnery & Co., 1953).
>
> *"Every great town has one or more slum areas into which the working classes are packed . . . The streets themselves are usually unpaved and full of holes. They are filthy and strewn with animal and vegetable refuse. Since they have neither gutters nor drains the refuse accumulates in stagnant, stinking puddles. Ventilation in the slums is inadequate owing to the hopelessly unplanned nature of these areas."*
>
> –Friedrich Engels, *The Condition of the Working Class in England* (New York: Macmillan Publishing Co., 1958).

Some of the most heated arguments in modern times have been between the advocates and critics of classic free-market capitalism. Adam Smith and his latter-day disciples represent the advocates, while critics include Karl Marx and his latter-day disciples. In practice, few economic systems have approached the ideals held by either Smith or Marx.

CLASSIC FREE-MARKET CAPITALISM

The Scottish moral philosopher Adam Smith laid the blueprint for and argued the superiority of modern capitalism in 1776, the year the United States achieved its independence from Britain. Key features of capitalism begin with the free market, where at least in theory a nearly unlimited number of would-be producers and suppliers are free to offer goods and services for sale. An equally unlimited number of would-be buyers are then free to purchase or decline to purchase the same. Government is to keep its hands off this **laissez-faire** market in which an "invisible hand" will presumably operate in utilitarian fashion to see that the needs of both producers and consumers are met at fair prices determined by the free market and nothing else. The expectation of profit derived from such sales will presumably guide producers to maximize both production and quality of goods and services, since consumers will shop elsewhere if they are displeased. Property is to be privately owned, in order for property owners to profit from gainful use of their property, whether land, factories, or invested capital.

Considerable evidence supports that capitalist economic systems are not only productive and efficient, but result in producing high-quality goods and services. This observation has caused some enthusiasts to proclaim that capitalism is somehow God-ordained, or at least divinely approved. The observation that those who have most profited from capitalism are usually those most likely to consider it divinely approved does not escape sociologists, however! Nor does the observation that capitalism seems to "work" because it allows human selfishness free reign.

It is important to note that purely capitalist economic systems (as envisioned by Adam Smith) would include no local, regional, or national government attempts to ameliorate poverty, no unemployment or disability benefits, no government subsidized health care or education, and no social security programs for the elderly. Only those persons who could afford to purchase desired goods and services would be able to purchase them. In a purely capitalist economic system, the fear of poverty is thought to be sufficient to motivate people to work. While the private charity efforts of individuals and churches are acceptable, they are to be voluntary, not coerced indirectly through government taxation and redistribution to the poor.

While no known society has a purely capitalist system, those which can be termed capitalist permit individuals to own private property, encourage a free market to operate with a minimum of restrictions, and allow entrepreneurs to keep most of the profits they realize from the sales of goods and services. These include the economic systems of Canada, the United States, Western Europe, Australia, Japan, and those of less prosperous nations such as South Korea, Taiwan, Mexico, Brazil, and South Africa.

SOCIALISM AND THE MARXIAN CRITIQUE OF CAPITALISM

Karl Marx and his loyal benefactor and editor Friedrich Engels lived during the time that early industrial capitalism transformed Europe. While overall wealth may have been growing, Marx and Engels were deeply troubled by what appeared to them to be the wretched lot of those who worked in the grime and gloom of the English textile mills. The things we take for granted today—subsidized medical care, social security, workmen's compensation for injuries, and other fringe benefits—were unavailable under early industrial capitalism. Retreating down filthy streets to their dank basement hovels after work, the life of most workers was hardly attractive.[8]

Marx was convinced that the capitalist owners, or **bourgeoisie**, were becoming wealthy at the expense of their miserable workers, the **proletariat**. Since it would remain in the self-interest of the owners to pay their workers as little as possible, Marx saw continual and worsening impoverishment as the lot of workers under capitalism. He dreamed of a classless **socialist** society in which citizens would jointly own all property, work together for the common good, and where monetary and other rewards would be allocated on the basis of need, rather than on the basis of ownership of property.

Marx's insights into the degree to which economic divisions and economic self-interest cause human conflict are at the root of sociological conflict theory. He hoped that the abolition of class divisions would produce a classless and therefore largely conflict-free society.

While no known human society that has attempted to institute socialism has come close to achieving this utopian vision, socialist economic and political systems have clearly departed from the basic outlines of capitalism. In societies such as the People's Republic of China, the former Union of Soviet Socialist Republics, and Castro's Cuba, most private property was confiscated and placed under the ownership and control of the national government. While people were provided jobs, production and control remained in the hands of the state, and prices were fixed or commanded by the state. Therefore, such systems can also be referred to as command economies.

Socialist societies characterized by state ownership and control (rather than private ownership and control) lack free markets. Since they also offer minimal if any profit motive, they are often plagued by low economic productivity and shoddy workmanship. After all, if I know I will have a job provided for me and my wage does not depend on how hard I work, why work harder? Why pay attention to quality workmanship? When East Germany (a socialist satellite of the USSR) was about to be reunited with capitalist West Germany, many East Germans put their state-produced Trabant automobiles out for the garbage men to pick up. This indicated their disdain for the quality of socialist goods. The Soviet economy was also plagued with poor quality goods and low economic productivity.

However, socialist nations offer some positives in leveling the economic and social playing field. Income disparities between the highest paid and the lowest paid workers are significantly smaller than those in capitalist economies. In addition, many socialist societies—such as Castro's Cuba in the 1960s and Sandinista-controlled Nicaragua in the 1980s—realized significant gains in the distribution of health care and literacy education for those at the bottom of their societies. We can generalize here and state that socialist societies produce less than capitalist societies, but they spread what they produce more evenly among their citizens. They also tend to have oppressive governments that allow little freedom of political and sometimes religious expression, although these conditions have sometimes been present in capitalist nations as well.

DEMOCRATIC SOCIALISM AND THE WELFARE STATE

Many modern societies have attempted to combine the best of capitalist productivity and quality of workmanship with the greater economic and social equality of socialism, usually within the freedoms accorded by a Western democratic style of government. One such country is Sweden, which combines an essentially free market with high rates of taxation, while making government benefits in education and health care available to all its citizens. Sweden is an example of **democratic socialism**. Countries like the United States—which remain more heavily capitalist than socialist in providing significant but fewer guaranteed benefits to all, as well as lower rates of taxation—are more commonly called examples of the modern **welfare state**. Typically, such societies experience more and more political demands to increase government benefits to more and more persons. Witness, for example, social security, workmen's compensation, Medicare, and Medicaid programs in the United States.

However, recent experience in Sweden proves the difficulty of maintaining high levels of productivity in a socialist system under the equally high rates of taxation necessary to provide benefits to all citizens. High rates of taxation reduce the incentive to work and invest. Sweden has thus moved in recent years to lower its taxes, which can be seen as a slight pulling away from socialism and moving toward capitalism. Those U.S. presidents with a strong ideological or practical commitment to capitalism, such as Ronald Reagan and George W. Bush, also have moved to reduce marginal income tax rates, often arguing that if wealthy citizens prosper, all citizens will prosper. Notably, the United States has been unwilling to provide nationalized health care for all citizens as have Sweden, Great Britain, and Canada. This can be seen as an indication that the U.S. remains more clearly capitalist than many other Western democracies, even though social security and Medicare have proven so popular that they are almost certain to continue in some form.

At the same time that essentially capitalist societies such as the U.S. and Canada have incorporated increasing amounts of socialism, many socialist societies have attempted to incorporate some features of capitalism. The former Soviet Union is the best example here, but

China, Cuba, and Tanzania have also moved in this direction. Capitalist influence can be seen in such practices as allowing persons to garden private plots or run small cottage-industry activities, as well as profit from the sale of goods and services produced at home and sold in a free market. Such concessions provide greater profit motives and incentives to work than can be found in a purely socialist system. This trend—capitalist nations incorporating socialist features, and socialist or formerly socialist nations moving in a capitalist direction—can be termed **convergence**.

UNDERDEVELOPMENT, OVERDEVELOPMENT, AND MISDEVELOPMENT

Until recently, social scientists and the general public in the wealthy capitalist nations of the free world have assumed that poor nations remain poor because they are **underdeveloped**. The logical thinking is that these underdeveloped nations could escape poverty if they would follow the lead of the already wealthy nations of Western Europe and North America. For example, economist Walt Rostow argues that saving is the key to economic growth and a way that poor nations can escape poverty.[9]

However, other thinkers point out that the development of the wealthy capitalist nations has come at a high price. Such nations use incredible amounts of energy and natural resources—among them nonrenewable resources like petroleum. It is possible to argue that North American and European societies are thus **overdeveloped**, and that if poor nations would become wealthy and emulate their lifestyles, the world as a whole could not sustain such "development." Additionally, neo-Marxian thinkers like Immanuel Wallerstein argue that wealthy **core nations** at the center of a world capitalist system remain wealthy partly due to continued exploitation of the **periphery nations**—those on the margins of the world capitalist system.[10] Such nations export their raw materials at low prices to wealthy nations, and then buy back manufactured goods from those nations at much higher prices. They also remain indebted to banks in wealthy nations, and often spend all or most of their yearly income just to service the interest payments on their debts. Following this logic, the poor nations of the world may be described as **misdeveloped** rather than underdeveloped.

HOW CHRISTIANS CAN CHANGE THE WORLD

Take a few moments to consider how you and your friends could use economic actions and resources to change the world. You may be tempted to say, "I'm just a poor student, so I can't do anything." Not only would you be wrong, but you would also be "copping out."

All of us purchase goods and services as economic consumers. In 1955 African American Christians in Birmingham, Alabama, decided they could no longer support the city-run segregated public bus system. They organized a boycott of city buses and then walked or arranged alternative transportation at considerable personal sacrifice. City officials expected the boycott to die after a few days, but the boycotters persisted. They changed the world. They helped to end racial segregation and to promote racial equality in America and around the world. You too can join with fellow Christians to boycott products and services of companies that promote ungodly values.

If you feel that too many Americans are trapped in the "buy, buy, buy" mentality of our consumerist, materialistic society, simply buy less. Purchase only those goods and services that meet basic human needs and that do not harm fellow human beings or the environment. Simplify your life. Decide how much you realistically need to live on, and give the rest to Christian organizations and other worthwhile charitable groups.

If you happen to have the funds necessary to invest in such things as a retirement account, the purchase of a home, or your children's future education, invest those funds wisely and responsibly—in ways consistent with your Christian values. Social responsibility investing is rapidly gathering momentum and is affecting corporate boardroom production and marketing decisions. Wall Street is taking note. Get on board. Be a world changer.

overview

- The economy is that sector of society that manages the production, distribution, and consumption of goods and services. Modern societies use various forms of money as a medium of exchange, but some premodern societies lacked money and used barter to exchange goods and services.

- The primary sector of an economy is that which extracts products from nature. Premodern societies include hunting and gathering, pastoral, horticultural, and agrarian societies, all dominated by the primary sector.

- Modern societies include industrial and postindustrial societies. The secondary or manufacturing sector provides the engine of economic growth in early industrial society. The tertiary or services sector employs most workers and provides the engine of growth in late industrial and postindustrial societies.

- Key features of modern economies include the separation of home and workplace for most workers, separation of ownership and control in joint-stock corporations, increased entry of women into the paid labor force, and globalization of a world economy dominated by multinational corporations.

- Capitalist economies are those which allow individuals to own and profit from private property and economic activity in a free market. Socialist economies turn to government to own property and control economic production and distribution.

- While capitalist economies have proven more productive, socialism does a better job of reducing economic disparities. Some nations thus choose to combine features of both capitalism and socialism. Even societies that strongly espouse one ideology over the other tend to combine elements of both, a trend called convergence.

- Wealthy developed capitalist nations are often held up as models of development for poorer nations to emulate. However, it is also possible that poor nations are really misdeveloped rather than underdeveloped.

key concepts

assembly line
Highly automated and efficient production method pioneered in the auto industry by Henry Ford.

barter economy
An economy that lacks money and instead exchanges goods and services directly.

blue-collar workers
Wage laborers who work with their hands in manufacturing and service occupations and enjoy lower pay and benefits than white-collar workers.

bourgeoisie
Marx's term for the capitalist class of productive property owners.

boycott
An organized movement that attempts to achieve objectives by asking individual consumers to refuse to purchase certain goods and services.

capitalism
An economic system based on private ownership of productive property, the profit motive, and a free market.

collective conscience
Durkheim's term for the collectively held set of values, beliefs, norms, and sanctions tied to religion; these provide the basis for social order in preindustrial society but weaken in modern society.

Christian socialism
Attempts by small Christian communities such as the Hutterites to institute shared property ownership and economic production, distribution, and consumption.

core nations
Wallerstein's term for wealthy nations at the center of the world capitalist system which dominate poorer nations.

convergence
The trend for capitalist and socialist economic patterns to be combined in modern economies, regardless of ideological preferences.

democratic socialism
An attempt by some western European nations such as Sweden to incorporate income-leveling features of socialism with an essentially capitalist free-market economy.

division of labor
The variety of occupations associated with modern societies.

dual careers
The tendency for married women in modern societies to perform unpaid work at home along with paid work at their job outside the home.

European Union
An economic union of European nations that has removed barriers to free trade within Europe and is instituting a common currency called the *Euro*.

folk society
Redfield's term for highly stable rural preindustrial society.

gemeinschaft
Tonnies' term for the close, intimate community life characteristic of small rural preindustrial societies.

gesellschaft
Tonnies' term for the impersonal urban mass

society characteristic of large industrial societies.

global language
A language widely used throughout an interconnected world. Formerly Greek, Latin, and French played this role in the Western world; English has now become a global language uniting the entire world.

global village
McLuhan's term for the increasingly interconnected world of the information age.

globalization
The modern tendency for economic and social interaction to transcend national and political boundaries, tying persons and nations together as never before.

Hutterites
An Anabaptist Christian group which practices communal living and sharing of goods and services, mostly on the prairies of Canada and the United States.

Industrial Revolution
The movement beginning in western Europe in the eighteenth century to substitute machine power for human and animal power; marks the division between preindustrial and modern society.

information industry
The worldwide networking of information flows made possible by the computer and the Internet, resulting in the **information age** and marking the transition from industrial to postindustrial society.

Internet
The global networking of computers and information flows characteristic of postindustrial society.

joint-stock corporation
A business organization owned jointly by stockholders rather than by private individuals and managed by paid professional managers.

Jubilee
A current religious and political movement modeled on the Old Testament Jubilee; asks wealthy nations to forgive debts of poor nations.

kibbutz (pl. kibbutzim)
Hebrew word for Israeli collective farms and communities.

labor force
The sum total of persons employed in various occupations.

labor unions
Organizations of workers in various industries that attempt to bargain collectively for improved wages and working conditions.

laissez-faire
French term used by Adam Smith to express the capitalist conviction that economic activities should be free of government regulation and interference.

McDonaldization
Ritzer's term for efficient, practical, calculable, and machine-controlled rational economic activity in the modern and postmodern world.

misdevelopment
The conviction that poorer nations of the world may suffer development distorted by the domination of wealthy capitalist nations; preferred over the term underdeveloped as an explanation

for their continued poverty.

multinational corporations
Large business organizations doing business in several nations.

new economy
Economic activity in the highly technological information industries of postindustrial society.

North American Free Trade Association
An economic and political arrangement by which Canada, Mexico, and the United States have removed most tariffs and other trade barriers to encourage economic activity in the North American region.

old economy
Economic activity in manufacturing sectors which formed the engine of economic growth in industrial society and is still present in postindustrial society.

overdevelopment
Term used to imply that wealthy nations of the world owe their wealth to the exploitation of poorer nations and of world resources.

periphery nations
Poor nations on the margin of the world capitalist system and presumably exploited by wealthy core nations.

pink-collar workers
Workers in overwhelmingly female occupations, usually low-level service occupations.

postindustrial societies
Societies in which information and technology industries predominate.

preindustrial societies
Societies that do not use modern machines to produce food or do other work, but instead use human labor or that of animals.

primary sector
The sector of the economy that extracts products from nature.

proletariat
Marx's term for wage laborers under capitalism, especially those in manufacturing.

secondary sector
The sector of the economy which transforms raw materials into manufactured goods not already existing in nature.

social responsibility investing
A recent trend in which individual and institutional investors limit their investments to ethically responsible economic activity.

socialism
An economic system in which government owns productive property and controls economic production in the name of the people.

tertiary sector
The sector of the economy which provides services to others.

underclass
The semipermanent group of persons stuck at the bottom of modern society and seemingly unable to escape.

underdevelopment
Term which implies that poor nations could become wealthy if they would develop as modern nations have done.

welfare state
A nation such as the United States which has incorporated some elements of socialism into an essentially capitalist economy.

white-collar workers
Highly paid and respected workers in managerial and professional careers.

endnotes

1. Emile Durkheim, *The Elementary Forms of the Religious Life* (New York: Free Press, 1965).
2. ——————, *The Division of Labor in Society* (New York: Free Press, 1964).
3. George Ritzer, *The McDonaldization of Society* (Newbury Park, CA: Pine Forge Press, 1993).
4. Robert Redfield, *The Primitive World and Its Transformation* (Ithaca, NY: Cornell University Press, 1953).
5. Ferdinand Tonnies, *Community and Society* (East Lansing, MI: University of Michigan Press, 1957).
6. Durkheim, *The Division of Labor in Society*.
7. Marshall McLuhan and Quentin Fiore, *The Medium is the Message* (New York: Bantam Books, 1967).
8. Karl Marx and Friedrich Engels, "Manifesto of the Communist Party" in *Basic Writings on Politics and Philosophy* (Garden City, NJ: Anchor Books, 1959).
9. Walt W. Rostow, *The Stages of Economic Growth: A Non-Communist Manifesto* (Cambridge: Cambridge University Press, 1960).
10. Immanuel Wallerstein, *The Modern World System* (New York: Academic Press, 1974).

CHAPTER SIXTEEN

Politics and Government

chapter outline

I. Introduction: Does One Vote Count?
   A. The presidential election of 2000
   B. The common good

II. Authority and power
   A. Traditional authority
   B. Charismatic authority
   C. Legal-rational authority

III. Theoretical perspectives
   A. Structural-functionalism
      1. Functions of politics and government
   B. Conflict perspective
      1. Power elite model
      2. Pluralist model

IV. Religion and politics

V. How Christians can change the world
   A. Extending representation
   B. Peacemaking

biblical reflection

"Then the one who had received the five talents came forward, bringing five more talents, saying, 'Master, you handed over to me five talents; see, I have made five more talents.' His master said to him, 'Well done, good and trustworthy slave; you have been trustworthy in a few things, I will put you in charge of many things.'"

—Matthew 25: 20-21

DOES ONE VOTE COUNT?

The struggle for power and privilege can get particularly vicious.

THE PRESIDENTIAL ELECTION OF 2000

The presidential election of 2000 will not soon be forgotten. Historians for many years to come will cite this contest between George W. Bush and Al Gore as the closest election in American history. It is also one of the few in which the popular vote elected one candidate and the electoral college elected another. The adage "Every vote counts" literally came true. A few votes cast or counted differently in a few key places would have changed the outcome.

This election reveals so much about politics in America and is a rich sociological case study. In spite of the sharp differences of opinion both about the candidates and the process by which the final vote was determined, there was a peaceful transition of power. This is indeed remarkable. When the court decisions were handed down and the votes counted according to the guidelines, the defeated incumbents left office willingly and the new President and his staff took charge.

The election is an interesting window into American society. The process is based on legal and rational principles that have broad acceptance across all segments of society. Yet only about half of the eligible voters voted in the 2000 election and considerably fewer participated in other ways. It is clear that many people don't study political issues in depth and that trust in political institutions is declining.

In this pivotal election, polls were more numerous and more sophisticated than at any time in the past. Concepts usually reserved for social scientists—like random samples, focus groups, and margin of error—were used commonly, even in letters to the editor in small-town newspapers. Candidates crafted their speeches and their public positions after reading the latest polls. They focused on insignificant issues and ignored important ones because polls suggested one might get more votes than another. Exit poll reports after the election caused emotions to rise and fall as first one candidate and then the other was projected to win and the results were ultimately "too close to call."

The campaigns were also sophisticated exercises in impression management, driven by the important role TV played. Highly managed shows, the conventions were directed to the TV audience, not the participants. Travel schedules were arranged and audiences chosen—and ignored—for what they symbolized. Images were masterfully "managed" to impress particular segments of the population.

When all the votes that counted were counted, the election appeared to be a "dead heat." But a closer look shows what Robert J. Bresler in *USA Today* identified as a number of "fault lines" emerging in American society.[1] Men tended to vote Republican and women Democratic, with the largest differences between married men and single women. Fifty-eight percent of married men voted for Bush and 63 percent of single women voted for Gore. Fifty-seven percent of college-educated women voted for Gore, and 57 percent of college-educated men voted for Bush. Racial differences are even more pronounced: nearly 90 percent of Blacks voted for Gore, while 54 percent of the White vote went for Bush.

The election also revealed a cultural gap reflected by geographical and religious differences in voting patterns. The middle of the country voted strongly Republican. Gore carried most of the states in the Northeast and Pacific Coast area. Fifty-nine percent of people from small towns and rural areas voted for Bush, while 60 percent of those from cities voted for Gore. There are also religious differences. Eighty percent of conservative Christians voted for Bush, while 60 percent of those who rarely or never attend church voted for Gore. In what is a particularly significant observation, Bresler comments that in this election "the gap over culture, geography, race, and gender is deeper than that over income or education."[2]

However, the income gap did become important during the vote count when it was found that methods of voting differed widely across the country. Some areas used antiquated technology that some persons found to be confusing. Many of these areas were poor neighborhoods. In general, higher percentages of higher income people voted than lower income people.

THE COMMON GOOD

In every society there are those who are weak and who need the broader society to take care of them. Over and over in the Old Testament of the Bible, prophets strongly called for society to take care of strangers (i.e., people from other countries who were living in the area), the orphans, and the widows. Because these people's needs were often not taken care of by the "normal" operations of society, special attention was required.

Society must always find ways to regulate individual action in order to protect the legitimate rights of others. It must find ways to do things that serve the **common good**. It must control violence and the use of force. And it must find ways to care for people who are weak and in particular need of help.

The **political institution** is the organized set of beliefs and practices by which society works together to respond to these needs. It is society's way to make collective decisions.

Government is comprised of formal organizations that implement and carry out actions to serve the "common good." Taxation, laws and regulations, and governmental projects and programs are all formal embodiments of collective action. The way government is organized, the values on which it is built, the actions it takes, and the way it works vary in different communities and across cultures.

By looking at various systems of government and at how authority is developed, this chapter examines the foundations of political and governmental institutions. It examines how sociologists understand politics and government from functionalist and conflict theoretical perspectives. And it describes decision-making structures and the relationship between religion and politics, demonstrating how politics and government actually work in the United States.

AUTHORITY AND POWER

One of the fundamental questions of politics is how a particular individual or group gets its power to govern. Harold D. Lasswell defined politics as the study of "Who Gets What, When and How."[3] The political system needs to make decisions and implement them. It cannot please everyone all the time. Politics and government

 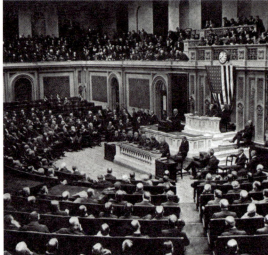

Military power is coercive because it relies on fear for compliance. In contrast, authority is perceived as legitimate since it relies on the consent of the people.

are related to decisions for the entire society. These decisions include how the resources of society are to be allocated and how actors, both individual and corporate, are controlled. Power is the currency of the political process.

Power may be legitimate or illegitimate, depending on the consent of the people over whom the power is being exercised. C. Wright Mills defines **power** in terms of persons being able "to realize their will, even if others resist it."[4] Others have defined power as the ability of A to get B to do what A wants. These two dimensions of power—the ability to get things done and the ability to get others to do things—point both to the important distinction between legitimate power and illegitimate power and the difference between force and authority.

Some governments maintain their power by coercion and force. Totalitarian governments in the world maintain control of a society through a powerful leader, who is usually backed by military strength and secret police. This sometimes involves brutal and inhumane methods of control without the involvement or consent of citizens. A group called Freedom House in Washington D. C. publishes an annual report that examines civil rights and political liberty around the world. In 1999 they suggested that 88 percent of the nations with 40 percent of the world's people offered extensive political and civil rights to their citizens. An additional fifty-three countries with 27 percent of the population were characterized as being partly free. The remaining fifty nations with 34 percent of the world's population were in a category described as not free. According to the definitions and analyses of Freedom House, democracy has made significant gains in recent years.

In addition to exacting a high cost from the people they govern, governments that maintain their power through coercion are often unstable. Effective and just political systems are based not on coercive power but on authority.

Authority is power that people perceive as legitimate. In contrast to force, which is imposed by a powerful person or group, authority involves some element of voluntary acceptance on the part of those involved. Max Weber identified three ideal types of authority—traditional, charismatic, and legal-rational.[5] These three types are also somewhat related to a society's level of development. Authority in modern societies rests more on rational calculations of citizens than it does in traditional societies. This rationality recognizes the need for authority and for the direction and control it includes. Elements of these different kinds of authority are of course present in all societies.

TRADITIONAL AUTHORITY

Traditional authority rests on long established patterns deeply rooted in the culture. People accept these to be appropriate primarily because they have lasted a long time. The society gives authority to persons and positions supported by tradition. Positions are often inherited, not earned. Until the middle of the twentieth century, Japan was ruled by an emperor who was treated much like a god and whose power had been passed from generation to generation for many years. The emperor's ability to govern rested on traditional authority, not on his qualifications or his selection by the people. The survival of the monarchy in some countries—even those where it is largely ceremonial, such as Britain—can be traced to the power of tradition.

Tradition is an important factor in establishing legitimacy for a particular kind of government and for the persons who hold positions within that government. Transmitted by socialization, traditions have been internalized to the extent that they often are not even recognized. Consequently they not only are taken for granted but are not seriously questioned. Tradition represents patterns that have survived over periods of time and have served society well. Tested and shown to "work," they are not easily abandoned.

On the other hand, following tradition merely because it has "always been that way" shows immunity from thoughtful analysis. This practice also resists adaptation to changing conditions and situations even when change would be beneficial. Functionalism provides a theoretical base for understanding the power and importance of tradition.

CHARISMATIC AUTHORITY

Where traditional authority is given legitimacy because "it has always been done that way," **charismatic authority** emerges from the personal characteristics of an individual who draws followers. These qualities inspire confidence, obedience, and devotion. Martin Luther King, Jr., John F. Kennedy, Joan of Arc, and Jesus are examples of persons who had great influence, partly because of their charisma. A charismatic leader who builds broad support for the movement through persuasive speeches and courageous acts often leads significant social movements. Many people who heard Martin Luther King's "I Have a Dream" speech were moved to change their ideas and attitudes and to fight racism in their own communities and churches. On the other hand, there are charismatic leaders whose impact has led to violence or to the maintenance of destructive social patterns. Hitler, Idi Amin, Jim Jones, and leaders of militias and hate groups have caused incredible harm and social unrest.

Because charismatic authority rests on one individual and the persuasiveness of that individual, it can be dangerous. Charismatic individuals are usually "lone rangers" who are not accountable to others and who do not have checks and balances on their ideas. These ideas can be constructive and based on credible evidence. They can also be destructive and based on unsubstantiated notions, some quite strange. Because persons are drawn to support charismatic leaders largely by spontaneous emotional reactions, careful thought or deep analysis does not always temper their actions. It is difficult to build a stable government or organization on a charismatic individual. These leaders emerge quickly and just as quickly disappear. Change must become institutionalized to survive.

The process by which spontaneous behaviors or organizations become predictable, patterned, and institutionalized is called the **routinization of charisma**. Programs initiated by charismatic leaders become part of the social fabric, often through a formal bureaucracy. Spontaneous actions become predictable, patterned, and organized. For example, Christianity began with Jesus, a charismatic leader. Over time Christianity became organized and institutionalized into various churches and highly complex religious organizations based on legal-rational principles. Specific symbols and practices also became patterned and predictable. The first time hands were raised in praise during a worship service was a charismatic, spontaneous event. Over time this practice has become "routinized." It is now possible to predict at which kinds of services hands will be raised, during which times of the service they will be raised, how they will be raised, and even who will raise their hands. In a similar manner, many of the revolutionary changes Martin Luther King, Jr. advocated have since become law.

LEGAL-RATIONAL AUTHORITY

Weber's third type of authority—**legal-rational authority**—is based on the legality of enacted rules based on rational choice, thought, and analysis. An example is a political system based on a constitution that spells out expectations and procedures. Those elevated to authority are given legitimacy by the rules and processes that bring them to authority and give them authority to govern. This implied social contract between the leader and followers is reflected in Abraham Lincoln's famous words from the Gettysburg Address: "That government of the people, by the people, for the people, shall not perish from the earth." A specific case of legal-rational authority is found in formal bureaucratic organizations.

In contrast to a worldview that attributes things to fate or magic, a rational worldview

TABLE 16:1
Kinds of Authority

Type of Authority	Characteristics	Strengths	Weaknesses
Traditional Authority	Based on "the way it has always been." Persons inherit roles that are based on ascribed statuses.	Tested by experience of the past. Stable. Inheritance is clear.	Resists change. Leaders may not be competent.
Charismatic Authority	Based on the personal characteristics of an individual.	Can inspire innovation, creativity, and change. Followers are intensely loyal and "obedient."	Rests in one individual who is not accountable. Difficult to maintain and continue. Can be abused.
Legal-Rational Authority	Based on a "social contract" and consent of the governed. Reflected in written rules and procedures. Persons earn roles based on competence.	Perceived as legitimate. Reflects the wishes of the people. Competent leaders. Stable over time.	Can become bureaucratic and unresponsive. Incumbents gather power. Change takes time. Loses legitimacy when people think government is not responsive. Assumes broad participation that may not happen.

consciously links results to causes and means to ends. This characterizes modern societies. While tradition and charisma play a part even in modern society, they are moderated by rational calculations, written laws and procedures, and formal structures. In a democratic society, these laws and procedures are established by mechanisms that reflect the best judgment of the people as to what leads to a good society. Officials hold office because the people choose them, presumably for their competence and suitability for the office. Authority rests in the office, not in the officeholder, and lasts only as long as the term of office.

This kind of authority and the responsiveness and stability resulting from it are often taken for granted. A democratic representational government based on legal-rational principles is a rather remarkable thing that needs to be nurtured and maintained.

THEORETICAL PERSPECTIVES

Structural-functionalist theory and conflict theory give different windows into understanding politics and government in the United States. These perspectives are useful in both a descriptive and normative way. Descriptively, these perspectives help us understand how politics and government really work. Viewing them in a normative way (i.e., suggesting how things ought to be) helps us make decisions and point policies and approaches in directions that lead to a good society.

STRUCTURAL-FUNCTIONALISM

A **functionalist** approach begins with the assumption that society's patterns and activities exist in the long run because they perform functions society needs and because they contribute to society's stability and survival. Every system has manifest functions, latent functions, and dysfunctions. Identifying these functions is one way of understanding politics and government.

FUNCTIONS OF POLITICS AND GOVERNMENT

Maintain a monopoly on legitimate force. According to Weber, the primary function of a political system is to maintain a monopoly on legitimate force and to use legitimate force both internally and externally to serve the common good.[6] It would be unthinkable in our society to have police forces and jails owned and maintained by businesses or powerful families. Nor would we think of multinational corporations having their own armies and navies to protect our country from attack and to protect their interests around the world. However, in some parts of the world, drug cartels and other powerful organizations have police forces and armies that compete with the country's legitimate policing forces.

In a country that works in the interests of the common good, the political and governmental system owns and controls police and military organizations. While these are allowed to use force in carrying out their duties, they tightly regulate the use of force by private citizens.

Preserve order and freedom. One of the functions of government is to preserve internal order so that life is predictable and secure. Rules are needed to guide behavior and to control people who choose to violate the interests of others. A simple illustration shows the importance of this function. It really doesn't matter on which side of the road vehicles travel, but it is quite important that everyone going in the same direction travel on the same side of the road. Acting for the "common good," government tells us where to drive. At first thought, it would seem that those laws limit freedom. After all, wouldn't we have more freedom if we could travel on whichever side of the road seems good at a particular time? Upon further reflection, however, we realize that freedom really comes from knowing that no one will come down the "wrong" side and cause a head-on collision.

The political and governmental system protects us from each other with criminal laws and regulates our behaviors with civil and regulatory laws. It not only provides internal protection, but also protects us from external threats.

Provide for the common welfare. Humans are fundamentally social in nature. While we carry out many responsibilities individually, many other things are best done together in collaborative ways. Politics is the institution and government is the organization through which collaborative things are done.

An increasing number of activities crucial for the smooth operation of society are best accomplished by an agency that represents the entire society. School systems now provide most of the education that families used to do. As economic systems become complex, regulations are needed to make sure individuals can have confidence that organizations like banks, businesses, and stock markets will act fairly and give honest, accurate reports. We rely on governments to assure us that medical doctors and social workers are competent and that restaurants are clean. Accrediting agencies guided by a government agency assure the quality of college education. Society benefits from a national system of roads and railroads. Children are safer because they are required to ride in car seats. Checkpoints help keep drunk drivers off the road. All of these things and many more are best accomplished by the political system that represents all the interests of society.

Maintain relationships with other countries. It is no longer possible for a country to exist as an isolated unit. As transportation and communication increase in efficiency, countries become increasingly interdependent. Every country relies on resources from other countries, such as raw materials, oil, and expertise. The government maintains diplomatic relations and develops trade policies to facilitate this interdependence. It also maintains a military force to protect itself and to maintain order in the world at large.

Provide for weak and marginalized members of society. An important moral responsibility of the political system is to take care of persons neglected or ignored by the other institutions and sectors of society. The rich and strong will be able to take care of themselves and make sure that society serves their interests. But others need help. As mentioned earlier, the prophets of the Bible constantly reminded kings and other leaders to show particular concern for the fatherless, the strangers, and the widows. Jesus announced that the sheep would be separated from the goats based on how well they had cared for people on the edge of society.

In our society particular groups need special care. These include persons disabled by physical or mental illness and persons isolated from families and communities. Approximately 11.8 percent of families have incomes below the poverty line and are marginalized by their poverty. One out of every six children lives in poverty. Areas of our country were left out of the economic boom of the last decade, persons who live in Appalachia and other pockets of rural poverty, in inner cities, and on Native American reservations. The political system has a special responsibility to look after and provide for people on the fringes. In the final analysis, a society will be judged not so much by how many opportunities it provides for the rich and strong, but by how well it cares for the poor and weak.

Collect taxes. All of the above activities take money in order to facilitate their functions. It would be nice if citizens would voluntarily make contributions to pay for all the benefits and services they receive and that they would do so somewhat in proportion to the benefits the society provides for them. However, that is unlikely. The sixth function of government is to collect and disburse taxes to pay for carrying out the other functions.

THE CONFLICT PERSPECTIVE

Where the functionalist perspective focuses on the emergence of societal patterns that serve the needs of society and contribute to the stability of society, the **conflict perspective** focuses on the conflicting groups and interests in society. It asks questions about how groups with conflicting interests and different levels of power are involved in political decision making and whether all segments in society have their interests represented adequately. The conflict perspective suggests both empirical questions and normative ones. The empirical questions ask *how decisions are actually made* and the normative questions ask *how decisions ought to be made*.

According to C. Wright Mills, General/President Eisenhower was an example of a power elite because he held power in both the military and government.

THE POWER ELITE MODEL

C. Wright Mills challenged the prevailing assumptions that our society was in fact representatively democratic.[7] He suggested that there are, in reality, three levels of power in the country that form a power pyramid. At the bottom are the unorganized powerless *masses* that believe in democracy because of education and socialization. According to Mills, they are often uninformed and easily manipulated by the media and by powerful politicians. In effect they have little impact on society's important decisions. In the middle is a group of competing *interest groups and politicians*. Mills suggested that these groups often are stalemated and essentially balance each other. At the top is the **power elite**, those who actually make the decisions for society. This elite is composed of the powerful leaders in the military, in business, and in the government. They not only control the decisions in their own organizations, they interact with each other to make sure that decisions reinforce one another.

A more recent study by G. William Dumhoff (1998) adds support to the power elite thesis.[8] He identified the power elite as consisting of a social upper class, a corporate community, and a set of policy formation organizations. The latter include labor unions, environmental organizations, liberal churches, universities, and some minority group organizations. While these groups overlap to some extent, they do become involved in different issues and disagree on specific issues.

Based on a series of "power structure" studies, evidence points to a power elite in cities and small communities. One of the better known studies was Floyd Hunter's study of Atlanta.[9] He concluded that a small group of conservative, cost-conscious business leaders in effect had the ability to control the decisions in that community. This study and others were criticized because they relied on perceptions and reputational reports of how decisions were made, rather than on more objective measures.

In a Principles of Sociology class a number of years ago, a first-year student challenged the professor's suggestion that the town in which the college was located was run by a power elite. With the full support and encouragement of the professor, he set out to prove the professor wrong. He collected the names of all the persons who served on elected and appointed commissions and boards of the town. He then identified their occupations to test his hypothesis that a wide range of people and occupations was represented in the formal decision-making structure. If the structure were pluralistic, decisions would reflect the interests of the entire community.

Fully 64 percent of the positions were filled by active or retired business executives, 13 percent by city officials, 11 percent by medical doctors, and 5 percent by educators. Working-class citizens filled the remaining 5 percent. Twelve of the twenty-one boards and commissions were controlled by businessmen but, in the opinion of the student, were not based on issues that affected business. Other than the biracial committee, only one Black held a position on any other board, and he was a member of two. Approximately half of the boards were appointed by the City Council. The student concluded that the formal decision-making structure of that community was dominated by a small segment of the community. Business interests had major influence, while the interests of working-class people and persons of color were not represented directly.[10]

Iron Law of Oligarchy. There is a tendency for organizations and political structures to shift toward "rule by a few." Robert Michels studied socialist parties and labor unions in Germany. He concluded that because of what he called **the iron law of oligarchy** even democratic parties working for progressive causes develop a power pyramid and degenerate into rule by a few.[11]

THE PLURALIST MODEL

While many sociologists suggest that power is concentrated at the top of a pyramid of power, others suggest that power is in reality widely diffused. The **pluralist model** suggests that many groups representing different interests influence decisions. These groups move in and out of the decision-making process depending on their level of interest in a particular decision. Pluralists argue that decisions are based on a changing set of decision-makers engaged in a process of coalition-building around issues in which they have a stake.

One of the strongest advocates of this position is Robert Dahl, who studied in New Haven, Connecticut.[12] He found that the unit of influence is a set of interest groups that talk to officials and politicians on specific issues. They lobby, make contributions to candidates and political parties, and use other means of persuasion to make sure their interests are protected. The presence of these groups—combined with the fact that legislators are accountable to their constituencies through voting—suggests that the decision-making structure is in fact pluralistic.

On the national scene, many groups work to influence government policy and action. Among the most powerful are individual industries and trade associations. They try to limit government regulation, influence trade policies, and encourage economic policies that are favorable to them. Powerful professional associations like the American Medical Association are particularly strong and effective in influencing health-care decisions that affect medical doctors. Educators, social workers, and many other professional groups make sure their voices are heard. Besides industry, trade, and professional organizations, other groups are formed around a variety of interests. The National Rifle Association, National Organization of Women, the Sierra Club, the National Association of Colored People, and right-to-life organizations all spend large sums of money to persuade decision-makers and to influence public opinion to support their points of view.

In recent years many **special interest groups** have formed **Political Action Committees** (PACS), organized to fund campaigns and to either support or oppose candidates. PACS have become increasingly important as the expenses for political campaigns increase and as campaign finance laws restrict direct contributions. A report from the Federal Election Commission indicates that for the eighteen months between January 1, 1999 and June 30, 2000, 4,393 PACS raised $430.6 million and contributed $167 million to federal candidates. Of this amount, incumbents received $133.4 million, challengers $14.3 million, and candidates for open seats $19.3 million. Republicans received $86.3 million and Democrats 80.3 million.

Some PACS represent public interest concerns, but the largest number of PACS responsible for most of the contributions are corporations, trade associations, and labor unions that are working for their own narrow interests.

The church makes its voice heard through national associations, denominations, and special interest groups, though its voice is rather weak in comparison to the others. Many churches have offices in Washington, D.C., and in state capitols. These offices are particularly concerned about decisions that relate to people in need and also to those decisions with implications for social justice. They keep the churches informed, and encourage churches and members to express their convictions to decision makers. They also position themselves as a voice for those who do not have a voice in the political decision-making process. Church related organizations are concerned about such issues as nuclear proliferation, the environment, hunger, abortion, the death penalty, persecuted Christians, human rights violations, and most other moral issues.

Pluralists point to the large number of special interest groups and PACS, as well as to the election process itself to suggest that decision making is in fact a reflection of a pluralistic structure of competing interests.

RELIGION AND POLITICS

Both American society and the church have been ambiguous about the relationship between religion and politics. In many ways the relationship is cozy and comfortable. But there is also a high level of mutual suspicion. It is quite common for recent presidents and presidential candidates to end speeches with "God bless you." Sessions in the Senate and House of Representatives begin with prayer and a new president is sworn into office with his hand on a Bible. Most people recognize the importance of a moral base for society and politics. Religion is a major source of moral values and a major motivator to live by them. Yet we are also afraid of religion. The Constitution forbids the establishment of religion and the Supreme Court has ruled against certain religious acts, such as prayer in public schools.

Churches have taken a wide variety of positions on the relationship between religion and politics—or church and state as it is often called. On one side are some, like Old Order Amish, who have traditionally emphasized a "two-kingdom" theology. They tend to emphasize the conflicts and differences between the Kingdom of God and the kingdom of the world. They do not expect the government to follow God's will because the government is secular. Nor do they expect the government to provide benefits such as social security or even education for them because they take care of their needs through the church. They do see the need for a government to maintain order in society, since most people are not members of the church. They do not try to tell the government what to do, and they prefer for the government to return the favor.

Those who believe in two-kingdom theology see many conflicts between church and state.

However, one of the most problematic areas is in the use of force. On the one hand, the Kingdom of God is based on love and mercy, even to the point of loving enemies and not resisting those who do harm. Political structures, on the other hand, rely on force—even the taking of life—to maintain internal order, as well as external order in war. As part of their loyalty to the Kingdom of God, people who hold a strong two-kingdom theology separate themselves from society in many ways, including not joining the military nor taking political offices that require the use of force. Many, but not all, choose not to vote because they would not want their vote to help elect someone who might later do something God says is wrong. For example, a vote for the president is a vote for the commander in chief of military forces. In that role he is expected to use war to protect the interests of the country. Thus, war would be seen as wrong since it uses violence and killing. During times when young men were required by law to serve in the military, a legal provision required persons who were conscientious objectors to serve an equivalent amount of time in social service programs in the United States and abroad.

On the other end of the continuum are Christians who, while recognizing the separation of church and state spelled out in the Constitution, in reality think of the United States as a Christian nation. They see little or no conflict between church and state, and have no problem being citizens of the Kingdom of God and citizens of the United States simultaneously. They expect the government to follow God's will and to even require religious activities like prayer for all students in public schools. They see no conflict in using the power of government to implement Christian agendas, nor do they see requiring certain Christian practices as a violation of the principle of separation of church and state.

An extreme of this latter position is found in some Islamic countries where church and government are united and the laws of the church are enforced by the government. Until recently, a law in Afghanistan required even visitors from other countries to follow religious practices during religious holidays. If they refused, they were forced to leave the country. Within the last forty years, many states in the United States had laws that required stores to be closed on Sundays.

Most Christians find themselves somewhere between these extreme positions. They recognize that the United States is based on freedom of religion. They understand that there is a difference between the church (which follows God's laws) and the state (which represents a consensus of the people). They also recognize the state's responsibility to protect the rights of individual citizens from what is sometimes called the "tyranny of the majority," the ability of a majority that thinks one way to impose its will and violate the rights of a minority that thinks differently.

Two recent studies are particularly noteworthy. One of the most interesting and controversial political movements in the past several decades has been the emergence of the so-called "Christian Right." In their book *Blinded by Might*, Cal Thomas and Ed Dobson reflect on that movement in which they were active participants.[13] They support the right and responsibility of Christians to influence politics and public policy from the perspectives of their Christian convictions. But they criticize the movement's agenda to reduce the Christian faith to a series of political positions and use political power to bring about a Christian society. Both, they say, are theological heresies.

Yale law professor Stephen Carter takes a broad and philosophical approach.[14] He points out what became clearly evident in the 2000 election. Religion is a powerful and major factor in American politics. For him there is no question that the society needs the moral insights and convictions of Christianity as a foundation for the political process. Christians bring concern for integrity and justice, which are foundational for a democratic system. They also bring a particular concern for the poor and marginalized segments of society, which is essential if the system is to work for the common good. Because they support values that are good for society, Christians have every right to raise their voices persuasively in the political arena. However, Carter also recognizes that taking on a political agenda can endanger the church by compromising its own identity and strength.

Commenting on the possible formation of a Christian political party, C. S. Lewis said: "If it were truly Christian, then it would preach the whole package of the Christian faith and thus, would be too demanding to succeed at the ballot box. But if it were truly a political party, it would be driven to make the kinds of compromises needed to win elections. Thus it would not be truly Christian."[15] This statement ably captures the ambiguities between Christianity and politics (or church and state).

One recent issue that has raised both hope and concern is the Bush administration's plan to make government support available to faith-based organizations for the purpose of doing social service work. Many faith-based groups are very efficient at performing quality social service. Churches often have deep roots in the community and are among the most authentic community organizations. The church provides power, motivation, and a supportive community—all necessary for persons to make long-lasting changes. So there are many reasons for the government to choose to work through churches and other faith-based groups in fostering community change and providing needed services.

On the other hand, both the government and the church are concerned about too close a relationship. Churches fear that if they receive money from the government, "strings" will be attached that will restrict the freedom of the churches to act in ways they think are best. They particularly fear that added bureaucracy will divert attention and resources from direct service. Some also fear that churches will use government money to proselytize in ways that are inappropriate, and that churches will restrict services to members of the church rather than serve the whole community.

HOW CHRISTIANS CAN CHANGE THE WORLD

EXTENDING REPRESENTATION

Clearly God calls us to become involved in the process of providing for the welfare of the community. Jesus affirmed the authority of government when He commanded, "Render therefore unto Caesar the things which are Caesar's; and unto God the things that are God's" (Matt. 22:21 KJV). Given the ideal of democracy that guides our society and the concern for justice that is shared by most people, it is important to: 1) intentionally work to include the interests of underrepresented groups in the decision-making structure, and 2) to make sure the "common good" has a strong voice.

Various strategies work effectively when it comes to increasing representation. Voter registration drives broaden involvement in elections. Community organization efforts can be directed toward organizing interest groups around issues that are of particular concern. A number of welfare rights organizations scattered around the country have become important voices for the needs of poor people. Through AARP (formerly known as the American Association of Retired People), older people have become very influential politically. Communities can organize to represent their interests and needs. Other groups speak for people who cannot speak for themselves, such as children, persons in prison or on death row, illegal immigrants, and disabled people. Churches can be particularly important because they speak with moral authority and represent concerns for justice rather than mere self-interest.

While men and women vote at nearly the same rate, other groups of people have significant differences in voting rates. According to the Federal Election Commission, people over the age of sixty-four vote at twice the rate of people under the age of twenty-four. White people are more likely to vote than Black or Hispanic people. People with higher incomes vote in greater proportions than people with lower incomes. This discrepancy is also seen in the ratio of Black to White officeholders.[16] In 1970, 1,469 Black officials held elected positions in the country. In 1998, there were 8,868, a sixfold increase. Even so, Blacks are still significantly underrepresented. Only 2 percent of all elected officials in 1999 were Black. In general, people who are more involved in society, who have higher confidence in social and political institutions, and who are in positions to influence society in other ways vote in higher percentages.

The voting rates of young people are low and declining. This decline reflects a general disengagement from politics and the political process. Each year a survey is given to several hundred thousand college freshmen from all kinds of colleges and universities.[17] In 1998, 25.9 percent reported that it is important for them to keep up-to-date with political affairs. This is a drop from 57.8 percent in 1966. In the same year, only 14 percent said that they frequently discuss politics with their friends, a drop from 30 percent in 1968. The decline in political participation by younger people means that politicians may not take their concerns seriously.

Why are people less involved in their communities? In his intriguing book, *Bowling Alone*, Robert Putnam observed that in the past people bowled together in leagues; however, now most bowl alone.[18] He examined masses of survey data from major national polls. *Bowling Alone* is only one symbol of a broad general decline in individual American participation in the organizations and activities that nurture civic life.

Putnam uses the term **social capital** to describe the social fabric that supports and nurtures civic life.[19] The idea of physical and human capital is familiar. People need tools, skills, the proper environment, infrastructure, and training to be productive. Social capital works in the same way. "Social capital refers to connections among individuals—social networks and the norms of reciprocity and trustworthiness that arise from them."[20] It is related to what others have called civic virtue, civic culture, or civic responsibility. The trust and connections that are part of social capital are what allow people to know the needs of others and to act for the common good.

Putnam cites many indications of this decline in the general social structure, things such as a decline of participation in community organizations, growing individualism, declining church attendance, less letter writing, and declining trust in social institutions and neighbors. The effect on civic participation is reflected in a

People are less involved in community events. More and more people bowl alone instead of in a league.

decline in voting, growing distrust of the government, declining party mobilization, decreasing interest in following public affairs, declining participation in political campaigns, fewer people signing petitions and writing letters to congressmen and newspapers, and fewer people running for political office.

He concludes, "The frequency of virtually every form of community involvement measured in the Roper polls declined significantly, from the most common—petition signing—to the least common—running for office. Americans are playing virtually every aspect of the civic game less frequently today than we did two decades ago."[21]

PEACEMAKING

Jesus said, "Blessed are the peacemakers, for they will be called the children of God" (Matt. 5:9). Christians need to become more involved in peacemaking. At almost any time there are a number of violent conflicts going on somewhere in the world. The cumulative loss of life and the damage done by war is impossible to calculate. War is as old as the human race, yet understanding ways to prevent and resolve conflicts is one of the great challenges for the twenty-first century. A war waged with bows and arrows hardly compares to one that includes nuclear bombs. The potential now exists to completely destroy the world if a nuclear war gets out of control.

Military expenditures in the United States take up a large proportion of the federal budget. The percentage is even greater in some third-world countries. In 1999 the United States spent $277 billion or 16 percent of all federal spending on direct expenses for defense. This amounted to more than $1,000 for each man, woman, and child in the country. If we include interest on the federal deficit (incurred because of defense expenses and defense related expenses hidden in other programs such as foreign aid), the number increases dramatically. In 1997 the United States exported $31,800,000 worth of arms to other countries.

But war itself is not the only concern of sociologists. They have identified **militarism** as a societal focus on preparedness for war that results in pervasive military symbols and ideology in the culture. Values such as extreme patriotism, uncritical faith in authority, and unquestioning obedience support militarism. Cynthia Enloe described the effects of militarism:[22]

> *Military expenditures, militaristic values, and military authority now influence the flow of foreign trade and determine which countries will or will not receive agricultural assistance. They shape the design and marketing of children's toys and games and of adult fashions and entertainment. Military definitions of progress and security dominate the economic fate of entire geographic regions. The military's way of doing business opens or shuts access to information and technology for entire social groups. Finally, military mythologies of valor and safety influence the sense of self-esteem and well-being of millions of people.*

The ideology of militarism has contributed to the growth in the number of militia and paramilitary groups in recent years, as well as other groups and individuals who choose to use violence. People who have low self-esteem, are experiencing difficulty reaching their goals, feel bullied by individuals or the system, or are marginalized or disenfranchised in other ways sometimes resort to militaristic actions to achieve status, express frustration, or fight a system from which they have become isolated.

A particularly relevant and challenging opportunity for Christians to use sociology for social change is in the area of peacemaking, reconciliation, and conflict resolution. Sociologists have been active in recent years in some of the tension areas of the world. These include

People becoming involved in the political process can change the world!

Nicaragua after the Somoza regime was deposed, Northern Ireland, Somalia, South Africa, Yugoslavia, and the Middle East. The U. S. State Department and U. S. Institute of Peace incorporate sociological insights into their work. In recent years, religion and culture-based approaches to conflict resolution have been implemented both internationally and domestically.[23]

overview

- Politics is the institution that determines and implements the goals and collective actions of a group. Government is the set of formal organizations that carry out actions. Sociologists study the interaction between the political system and other aspects of society.

- Power is the currency of political systems, the power to get things done, and the power to get others to do things. Force is illegitimate power. Legitimate power or authority can be understood by three ideal types: traditional, charismatic, and legal-rational. Traditional power rests in deeply held traditions. Charismatic power rests in the personal characteristics of a leader. And legal-rational power rests in laws and rational principles and procedures.

- Two theoretical perspectives are used as windows into understanding politics and government. The structural-functionalist perspective focuses on functions that contribute to the stability and survival of society. The conflict perspective focuses on competing interests and competition of groups.

Sociology: A Christian Approach for Changing the World

- Sociologists try to understand how political decisions are made. There is a tendency for democratic organizations to degenerate into "rule by a few." Michels called this the "iron law of oligarchy." This supports the Power Elite model, which suggests that power is organized in a pyramid with a group of powerful social, corporate, and government leaders at the top.

- In contrast, others argue that power is organized in a pluralism of groups that organize around particular issues to influence political decision making.

- Participation in civic society has declined in recent years. This is true if participation is measured by such things as voting records, citizens helping with campaigns, or people keeping up with and discussing issues. Robert Putnam argues that "social capital" is declining. Included in social capital are the social networks and norms of reciprocity and trustworthiness needed to maintain a political system based on the participation of its members.

- Militarism, a way of thinking which focuses on preparedness for war and results in pervasive military symbols, ideology, and values, has significant impact on society, influences the allocation of resources, and gives rise to militias and other groups in society.

- A particular contribution sociology makes is its understanding of peacemaking, reconciliation, and conflict resolution.

- Religion and politics are intertwined in complex ways. In many respects the relationship is cozy and comfortable. In other ways it is conflictual. Society needs the moral vision and principles that religion provides. Yet, there is danger—both to a democratic political system if it allies itself too closely with a particular religion, and to religion if it becomes a series of political positions and uses political power to bring about its mission.

- Ultimately a society and its political system will not be judged by how many opportunities it provides for the rich and powerful. It will be judged by how well it cares for the poor, the weak, and the marginalized, how well it incorporates the legitimate interests of all of its citizens, and how well it protects the rights and interests of minority groups.

key concepts

authority
Power that people perceive as legitimate.

charismatic authority
Authority that rests on the personal characteristics of an individual who inspires loyalty.

common good
Those actions and patterns that benefit society as a whole.

conflict perspective
A theoretical perspective that focuses on the role of conflict and power in society and on the existence of competing interests between groups.

functionalist perspective
A theoretical perspective that focuses on the ways social structures and patterns contribute to the maintenance of social order.

iron law of oligarchy
The process by which organizations and political systems shift toward "rule by a few."

legal-rational authority
Authority based on law and rational principles.

militarism
A way of thinking that focuses on preparedness for war and results in pervasive military symbols, ideology, and values in society.

political action committees (PACS)
Special interest groups organized to influence policy by contributing to candidates and campaigns.

pluralist model
A type of political structure characterized by a plurality of competing interests that influence decision making.

political institution
The social institution that determines and implements the goals and collective actions of a group.

power
The ability to get things done and/or to control others even against their will.

power elite model
A type of political structure characterized by a social, economic, and political elite who control decisions.

routinization of charisma
The process by which spontaneous acts become predictable, patterned, and organized.

social capital
The social networks and norms of reciprocity and trustworthiness that support and nurture civic life.

special interest groups
Groups that advocate on behalf of a particular interest.

traditional authority
Authority that rests on tradition.

endnotes

1. Robert J. Bresler, "The Muddled Meaning of the 2000 Election," *USA Today* (Jan. 1, 2001).
2. Ibid.
3. Harold D. Lasswell, "Politics: Who Gets What, When and How," in *The Political Writings of Harold D. Lasswell* (New York: Free Press, 1951).
4. C. Wright Mills, *The Power Elite* (Oxford: Oxford University Press, 1959), 9.
5. Max Weber, *The Theory of Social and Economic Organization*, trans. Talcott Parsons (New York: Free Press, 1947).
6. Ibid.
7. Mills, *The Power Elite*.
8. G. William Dumhoff, *Who Rules America* (Mountain View, CA: Mayfield Publishers, 1998).
9. Floyd Hunter, *Community Power Structure: A Study of Decision Makers* (Chapel Hill: University of North Carolina Press, 1953).
10. C. Martin, unpublished paper (Harrisonburg, VA: Eastern Mennonite College, 1971).
11. Robert Michels, *Political Parties* (Glencoe, IL: Free Press, 1915).
12. Robert Dahl, *Who Governs?* (New Haven, CT: Yale University Press, 1961).
13. Cal Thomas and Ed Dobson, *Blinded by Might* (Grand Rapids: MI: Zondervan, 1999).
14. Stephen L. Carter, *God's Name in Vain: The Wrongs and Rights of Religion in Politics* (New York: Basic Books, 2000).
15. C. S. Lewis, "Meditation on the Third Commandment," in *The Quotable Lewis*, ed. Wayne Martindale and Jerry Root (Wheaton, IL: Tyndale House Publishers, 1989).
16. T. Caplow, L. Hicks, and B. J. Wattenberg, *The First Measured Century: An Illustrated Guide to Trends in America, 1900-2000* (Washington, D.C.: The AEI Press, 2001), 186.
17. L. Sax, "Citizenship and the American College Student," in *Civic Responsibility and Higher Education*, ed. T. Ehrlich (Phoenix: Oryx Press, 2000), 3-18.
18. Robert D. Putnam, *Bowling Alone: The Collapse and Revival of American Community* (New York: Simon and Schuster, 2000).
19. ————, "Bowling Alone: America's Declining Social Capital," *Journal of Democracy* 6, no. 1 (1995): 65-78.
20. Putnam, *Bowling Alone*, 19.
21. Ibid, 41.
22. Cynthia Enloe, "Feminists Thinking About War, Militarism and Peace," in *Analyzing Gender: A Handbook of Social Science Research*, ed. B. H. Hess and M. Feree (Newberry Park, CA: Sage Publications, 1987), 542-43.
23. J. P. Lederach, *Preparing for Peace: Conflict Transformation Across Cultures* (Syracuse, NY: Syracuse University Press, 1995); and C. Sampson and J. P. Lederach, *From the Ground Up* (New York: Oxford University Press, 2000).

additional sources

W. Bennett, *The Index of Leading Cultural Indicators* (New York: Broadway Books, 1999).

J. Denis and I. Derbyshire, *Political Systems of the World* (New York: St. Martin's Press, 1996).

D. D. Eisenhower, "President Eisenhower's Farewell to the Nation," in *Making War, Making Peace: Social Foundations of Violent Conflict*, ed. F. M. Cancian and J. W. Gibson (Belmont, CA: Wadsworth Publishing Co., 1990).

J. R. Feagin and C. B. Feagin, *Social Problems: A Critical Power-Conflict Approach* (Englewood Cliffs, NJ: Prentice-Hall, 1986).

CHAPTER SEVENTEEN

Collective Behavior and Social Movements

chapter outline

I. Collective behavior and social movements defined
   A. Collective behavior
   B. Social movements

II. Types of collective behavior
   A. Four dimensions of collective behavior
   B. Panic
   C. Publics and public opinion
   D. Expressive crowds and issueless riots
   E. Acting crowds and unorganized protests
   F. Crazes
   G. Protests and social movements

III. Causes of collective behavior and social movements

IV. Structure and process

V. A Christian perspective on collective behavior and social movements

biblical reflection

"Let justice roll down like waters, and righteousness like an ever-flowing stream."

—Amos 5:24

(The inscription on the fountain in front of the Southern Poverty Law Center, Montgomery, Alabama—an organization that evolved from the Civil Rights Movement.)

The study of collective behavior and social movements is a fascinating area within sociology. **Crowd** behavior, the response of individuals and organizations to disasters, rumors, popular fashion and fads, and organized attempts to change the way in which almost any aspect of social life is conducted—all are studied under the categories of collective behavior/social movements. This chapter is organized around the following questions and includes brief examples to clarify points under each. These questions are:

1. What is collective behavior as opposed to individual behavior?

2. How does the sociological approach differ from the psychological approach when studying collective behavior and social movements?

3. What different types of collective behavior and social movements have been identified?

4. What causes collective behavior and social movements to appear?

5. What structural characteristics describe episodes of collective behavior and social movements?

6. How should Christians use the principles of collective behavior and social movements to change the world?

COLLECTIVE BEHAVIOR AND SOCIAL MOVEMENTS DEFINED

Why should we consider collective behavior and social movements an area of sociological investigation? Collective behavior has in common the study of situations in which the social bond has become problematic. Many scholars have proposed different ways in which the individuals involved in an incident of collective behavior—such as a crowd, a protest, a fad, a social movement organization—are linked together. Herbert Blumer suggests that a special form of communication occurs in such settings. He refers to such communication as **circular reaction**, by which he means the direct transfer of an emotional state from one individual to another.[1] Early scholars such as Robert Park and Ernest W. Burgess called to mind the image of a stampede of cattle.[2] A founder of the field of collective behavior, Gustave Le Bon, referred to such communication as "contagion."[3]

COLLECTIVE BEHAVIOR

Collective behavior is a situation in which a direct transfer of emotional states (hostility, joy, fear) occurs without thought between individuals in a given situation. This kind of communication contrasts with everyday communication in which an individual interprets the behavior of another before responding to it.

A number of related concepts appear in sociological and social psychological literature to explain similarity of behavior in persons who are gathered in one place. Imitation, identification, sympathy, and empathy are all terms that are used by collective behavior scholars in association with similarity in behavior.

Another theorist, Neil Smelser, suggests that collective behavior is defined by a belief about something that is shared by the individual members of the group. The *generalized belief* shared by individual members of a collectivity is the key to what separates collective behavior from group behavior.[4] The difference between collective behavior and other group behavior is that the shared belief contains elements that represent delusions or misperceptions about appropriate behavior in response to a given set of stress-

Crowds at a sporting event frequently experience emergent norms. Do you see some behaviors in this crowd that individuals probably would not do, except for the others around them?

ful conditions. An example is the attempt to escape from a common threat in a confined place. The fire in the Cocoanut Grove nightclub may have precipitated such great fear that those inside trampled each other to death trying to get out the front doors rather than seeking other alternatives.

Ralph Turner and Lewis Killian have observed that people who engage in collective behavior act in similar ways. They define the distinguishing characteristic of collective behavior as **emergent norms**.[5] In response to the stressful or ambiguous conditions that give rise to rumors, panics, crowds, and related phenomena, new sets of expectations for behavior are generated. These norms are treated as binding in the particular situation or group. So, for example, the lynch mob expects those present to go along with the hanging of the prisoner. These norms are a much more specific kind of statement about expected behavior than generalized beliefs.

All of the above definitions rely on concepts that cannot be directly observed. Clark McPhail offers a definition of collective behavior that focuses specifically on observable behavior—for example, a group of people marching in a common direction to a song they are singing in unison. His definition of collective behavior includes these elements: "two or more persons; engaged in one or more behaviors; judged common or concerted; on one or more dimensions."[6] Clearly this is a different way to define collective behavior. The criterion here is *common behavior*.

Four elements, then, define what makes collective behavior a form of group behavior as opposed to the simply convergent behaviors of individuals. These elements are specialized communication, shared beliefs, shared norms, and patterned behavior all within a collectivity.

SOCIAL MOVEMENTS

Collective behavior—such as a lynch mob, a crowd at a soccer match, a group discussing rumors about sickness in a factory, and a protest around a nuclear plant—is transitory. **Social movements** are interpreted as groups with a particular interest in bringing about change in some aspect of the social order. Joseph Gusfield defines social movements as "socially shared activities and beliefs directed toward the demand for change in some aspect of the social order."[7] This definition makes both "common interest" and "activities" central to defining the boundaries of this social behavior.

TYPES OF COLLECTIVE BEHAVIOR

Collective behavior is characterized by many events and episodes that seem to be unusual or strange. Because these behaviors seem bizarre, they catch our attention. How can we accurately

TABLE 17:1

The Types and Dimensions of Collective Behavior

TYPE	CONSCIOUSNESS OF KIND	SOCIAL INTERACTION	FORMAL, WRITTEN RULES	POLARIZATION
The panic	Not necessary	Not necessary	Not necessary	Always present
The public	Always present	Not necessary	Not necessary	Always present
The expressive crowd and issueless riots	Always present	Always present	Not necessary	People focus on the activity of the collective
The acting crowd and unorganized protests	Always present	Always present	Not necessary	Always present
The craze	Always present	Always present	Rules governing apply generally to institutional area of the activity	Always present
The social movement	Always present	Always present	Always present	Always present

describe all these different forms? Which ones should be grouped together? What aspects of the behavior should we concentrate on as we write our descriptions? These questions are a continuing source of controversy in the field of collective behavior and social movements. Table 17:1 presents a typology of collective behavior developed over the last twenty years.

FOUR DIMENSIONS OF COLLECTIVE BEHAVIOR

The typology starts with the assumption that collective behavior is group behavior. Robert Bierstedt suggested four different observable dimensions of group behavior.[8]

1. The first dimension is that members of a group identify with each other. They share a "consciousness of kind." **Consciousness of kind** was a concept introduced by an early sociologist, Franklin Giddings.[9] The concept refers to the idea that animals or people with similarities recognize those similarities as meaningful. Sharing the same language, the same skin color or other body characteristics, the same customs, or the same gender may make us feel closer to persons in a group.

2. The second dimension is *social interaction*. This refers to people's presence and how people in the collectivity exchange conversation or gesture to one another. Face-to-face interaction occurs within the collectivities studied.

3. The third dimension refers to the presence of *formal, written rules for behavior*. Formal organizations of all sizes expect certain behaviors from their employees, clients, and members. Whether the organization is a small private business like a used clothing store, a public institution such as a community high school or post office, or a voluntary

association like the Rotary Club or Kiwanis Club with chapters all over the country, the formal rules help structure interactive behavior. Compared to informal groups (one's friends at school), the rules in these organizations are written down and remain relatively stable over time.

4. The fourth dimension is **polarization**. Clark McPhail, Roger Brown, Stanley Milgram, and Hans Toch all note the tendency of collectivities to focus on a limited number of points.[10] This is known as the polarization of a collectivity. Often a single person or pattern of behavior will become fixed in the attention of all members of a crowd or audience. This can be observed rather easily if a picture is taken of the collective group.

A student at the University of Tennessee, Michael Worthington, observed that festival seating at a rock concert gives the opportunity for different points of focus to develop among members of the audience. Near the stage a large group of persons will gather to watch the band perform and perhaps clap or dance during the performance. Farther from the bandstand, a small group of ten or so persons may be sitting in a circle passing a burning, hand-rolled cigarette from one to another. These are examples of different points of focus in the audience as a whole. In a lynch mob, those near the center of the activity may be focused on the leaders or on the person to be hanged, while those on the fringes may be focused on the crowd itself.

PANIC

Panic is a response of a group of individuals to a threatening situation. Another term found in the literature that describes the phenomenon more accurately from a sociological rather than a psychological point of view is **hysterical contagion**. Here the members of a particular community or group share the same fear or same perception of a threat. Sometimes the threat is real, as in the case of a disaster. Sometimes the threat is imaginary, as in the case of mass hysteria.

An example of mass hysteria is the case of the "phantom gasses" of Mattoon, Illinois, documented by Donald Johnson during the 1940s.[11] In *The June Bug*, Kerckhoff and Back document another example of hysterical contagion related to a nonexistent insect thought to cause nausea and other sickness.[12] In each of these instances, people experienced symptoms of illness or sleepiness because they "thought" they had been gassed or bitten. In neither case could authorities find evidence to support what the affected individuals believed to be the source of their illnesses.

PUBLICS AND PUBLIC OPINION

The *public*, a category of people having common interests or characteristics, is important in the field of collective behavior and social movements because it gathers around a particular issue. Various publics divide over such things as the welfare policy in the United States, the role of organized labor in negotiating with the government, the place of prayer in the schools, and the legitimacy of abortion.

This field of collective behavior is now a separate focus of study in the academic world and is found in Departments of Political Science, Colleges of Communication, and Schools of Journalism. Scholars in this area study such issues as the influence of various mass media on public opinion and the importance of public opinion in determining how people will vote. An excellent review of definitions of public opinion appears in *The Spiral of Silence* by Elizabeth Noelle-Neuman.

Many commercial research firms have developed ways to measure public opinion. Three of the largest and most well known are Gallup, Harris, and Roper. Because public opinion shifts and provides an indicator of how society and its institutions may be changing, scholars continue to be interested in studying its implications.

EXPRESSIVE CROWDS AND ISSUELESS RIOTS

The **expressive crowd** is an older term Blumer used to refer to groups of people that appear to be simply having a good time or to be focused on the activities of the crowd. In this situation, there is no apparent objective in mind other than the activity of the crowd itself.[13]

Gary Marx formulated the term **issueless riot** to refer to a crowd that seems out of control. Examples include crowds that destroy private and public property following a World Series victory.[14] Since such crowds or assemblies of people do exist, we mention them here. However, such behavior does not fit well with interpretations of collective or group behavior that want to see all behavior as somehow directed toward achieving some goal for the group. In this case, the goal seems to be emotional release; the activity of the crowd provides that discharge of emotions.

ACTING CROWDS AND UNORGANIZED PROTESTS

Acting crowds and unorganized protests have a clear point of focus. Smelser describes this activity as the *hostile outburst*.[15] The lynch mob is the most widely studied example of a crowd that appears in a relatively spontaneous manner. Here the focus is on the prisoner or person accused of some crime or act that the local population is not willing to tolerate.

In both the Los Angeles riot of 1992 (following the first trial of police officers involved in the beating of African American Rodney King) and the Miami riot of 1980, crowds beat white motorists who were passing by. As part of the larger collective action, these small groups illustrate an aggregate of people in a stress situation who come together, select a target, and attack.

Scholars such as Enrico Quarantelli and Russell Dynes point out that crowds in a civil disturbance and crowds in a disaster often act in very different ways, although both may have a point of focus.[16] In a disaster, a group may assemble during the recovery period for the purpose of working together to clean up or help the injured. In a civil disturbance, a crowd may assemble to break into and to loot businesses of persons thought to be on the opposing side of the issue. At times, hostile crowds have been controlled by providing multiple points of focus, thereby splitting the group or preventing it from reaching agreement on a single objective.

CRAZES

One of the most theoretically sophisticated and differentiated classifications of the craze appears in Neil Smelser's *Theory of Collective Behavior*.[17] He characterizes the **craze** as a positive impression that the activity engaged in by the collectivity will have a beneficial outcome. Smelser identifies four types of crazes, depending on the institutional area of the society in which they are found.

1. *Economic crazes:* Stock market booms are an example of a craze in the area of the economy.

2. *Religious crazes:* Revivals are an example of a craze in the area of religion.

3. *Political crazes:* Convention activities and the developing enthusiasm for a can-

didate serve to exemplify a craze in the area of political institutions.

4. *Social crazes:* **Fashion**—particularly fashions in clothing, hairstyles, use of make up, style of music—fall into the area of the craze in sociability institutions.

PROTESTS AND SOCIAL MOVEMENTS

Most social movements work within a specific institutional area or target specific laws, practices, or traditions within the society. For example, various groups have advocated equal civil rights for minorities within society. These minorities include racial and ethnic groups, groups with different sexual orientations or practices, and sometimes groups that simply see the government as infringing on their rights as human beings.

Most social movements use nonviolent and even institutionalized means or tactics to achieve change in the society. For instance, labor unions in this country have succeeded in getting much labor legislation passed to legitimate their collective bargaining procedures. Binding arbitration mediated by the government can be used to settle long-term disputes between management and labor. Of course, counter movements in the labor area also exist, such as those advocating the passage of "right to work" laws in various states.

Other groups such as the Ku Klux Klan have used violent means in the past (lynching, shooting, or terrorizing groups) to oppose social change. Vigilante groups, insurgent groups, transnational groups, and even the state may use terrorist tactics to promote or oppose social change. Gurr defines terrorism as "the use of unexpected violence to intimidate or coerce people in the pursuit of political or social objectives."[18] Historians have noted that the Ku Klux Klan is recognized throughout the world as a cultural symbol of terror and violence associated with racism.[19] Other examples of terrorist acts are the 1995 bombing of the Federal Building in Oklahoma City and the 2001 terrorist attacks of the World Trade Center and the Pentagon. These actions have caused the loss of many innocent lives and drawn attention to the causes espoused by terrorists. Although associated with large social movements, individual terrorists may be organized in small cells that have little contact with and know little about the plans and behavior of the other cell groups.

Most social movements use nonviolent means to bring about change in society.

Chapter Seventeen: Collective Behavior and Social Movements

CAUSES OF COLLECTIVE BEHAVIOR AND SOCIAL MOVEMENTS

Different forms of collective behavior and social movements emerge when the existing institutionalized social relationships and norms are under pressure or stress. Some scholars interpret collective behavior as arising when existing institutions or patterns of behavior seem inadequate for dealing with the challenge of some specific situation. In disaster situations, an official with the mayor's office may not know to which of a number of community emergencies to respond first. This will be particularly problematic unless there is a disaster plan. Stress can occur as well when existing social ties or bonds are threatened. Riots and disasters often destroy material items such as mementos that have special significance to individuals.

Theorists talk about the *causes* of collective behavior and social movements in a variety of ways, but a common theme is ambiguity or uncertainty about expected behavior and the consequences of particular behavior. The uncertainty about what to do to escape a fire in a movie theater with a seemingly limited number of exits can create the need for an emergent norm to control panic flight. In social movement theory, people may look for an underlying grievance as a basic cause for protest activity. The long-term differential between what women and men are paid for the same work is one example of a grievance. The failure of an employer to bring working conditions up to safety standards is another example of a grievance.

In the area of social movements, several scholars have argued that there are enough grievances to produce many movements and that ideologies are easily crafted to define existing social arrangements as grievances. From the standpoint of these individuals, a crucial component in the emergence of a social movement is adequate leadership and the material resources both to organize and advance the goals of the movement. In these cases, strategy and tactics must include securing resources above and beyond those provided by the beneficiaries of the movement's success. Finding people with funds who are willing to contribute to attaining the movement's goals is essential. Leaders skilled in mobilizing and organizing existing participants and helping to craft a plan of action are essential to these theories.

The **resource mobilization** approach has provided a valuable corrective to the view that the only persons concerned with a movement's success in achieving its goals are the people within the movement. This approach also draws upon organizational theory, calling attention to the fact that many of a movement's goals can be obtained without the activity of every movement member. These members still benefit from the achievement of a movement's goal, such as a safer workplace, the vote for women, or a cleaner environment. The organization or movement needs to avoid having too many of these individual members or a "free-rider problem" will result.

STRUCTURE AND PROCESS

What does a crowd look like? Is it possible to describe different parts of a crowd or audience? What different positions can one find in a movement's organization? Is there an identifiable pattern of relationships or sets of actions in a panic situation or state of hysterical contagion? Do rumors flow along established channels of communication or do the messages in an episode of collective behavior or in a social movement create new channels? When sociologists examine an assembly of people who are conducting a protest against abortion clinics or nuclear plants, they can identify three or four clearly distinguishable positions:

1. *Leaders* are directing the action and providing examples for the group.

2. A *core* of persons who may have accompanied the leader to the demonstration are singing, carrying signs, or shouting encouragement to the leaders who are blocking the entrance to the clinic or to the nuclear plant.

3. Also present may be *agents of social control*, such as the police, who are arresting the persons blocking entrance to the clinic and/or attempting to keep picketers or other demonstrators the required distance away from the target of the demonstration.

4. A final group may be a crowd of *interested bystanders* who have gathered to observe the demonstration and the action being taken against it.

Process in collective behavior and social movements refers to the way in which communication takes place in a group and the way in which new expectations for appropriate behavior emerge. Communication may flow along established channels as specified in the organization chart. Communication may flow along friendship lines. Rumors arise to help define what behavior is appropriate in new situations, such as disaster response or protest actions. The messages spread more widely among acquaintances than among close friends. Close friends communicate with each other in their social circle, thus limiting unverified information such as gossip. The process of communicating a message from one person to another may result in the elimination of details, the organization of the message around a central theme, and making the message agree with the cultural and personal biases of the person passing the message to another.

Keynoting and identification are processes observed in explaining the way followers relate to leaders in groups. In **keynoting**, the follower takes the action of a leader as a model for his or her own behavior. Imitation or similar behavior occurs. In **identification**, the follower not only takes the actions as a model, but identifies with the leader to the extent of modeling his or her own identity on the one the leader projects. Charismatic leaders like Gandhi, Hitler, and Martin Luther King, Jr. have had this effect on people.

A CHRISTIAN PERSPECTIVE ON COLLECTIVE BEHAVIOR AND SOCIAL MOVEMENTS

Christians have founded and supported social movements and have engaged in many forms of collective action. Rodney Stark's *The Rise of Christianity* suggests that the movement centered on Jesus is an example of a very successful social movement.[20] When you examine Gusfield's definition of social movement, the emphasis is on change in some aspect of the social order.[21] Christianity attempts to achieve this change by converting individuals who in turn work to change the social order.

Christ spoke of the last judgment in Matthew 25:31-46. The last judgment focused on actions taken to feed the hungry, give drink to the thirsty, visit the prisoner, take in the stranger, clothe the naked, and help the sick. All of these people are outside the mainstream of society. Christianity demands that provision be made for all, including those that the well-cared-for members of society have forgotten.

Christianity demands a deeper fulfillment of existing norms and values as well. Take a look at the Sermon on the Mount in Matthew 5.

Jesus calls for a radical reformation of the social order.

> "You have learned that it was said to those of ancient times, 'You shall not murder'; and 'whoever murders shall be liable to judgment.' But I say to you that if you are angry with a brother or sister, you will be liable to judgment; and if you insult a brother or sister, you will be liable to the council; and if you say, 'You fool,' you will be liable to the hell of fire" (5:21-22).

Or consider the problem of infidelity and its effect on the family in contemporary America. "You have heard that it was said, 'You shall not commit adultery,' But I say to you that everyone who looks at a woman with lust has already committed adultery with her in his heart" (5:27-28).

Christians have learned how to embody these values and put them into action to change society using the direct action tactics of protest and boycott. Some Christian groups supported a boycott of table grapes to force California growers to allow field workers to organize. Other Christians gather at execution sites to hold vigils and carry signs protesting capital punishment. Ministers marched in the South to secure voting rights for African Americans. Christians organized and participated in movements for civil rights and putting an end to drunk driving. Lyle Schaller's book, *The Change Agent* provides a Christian perspective for those individuals who want to bring about change in the social order.[22] Christians change the world by putting the values and behavior taught in the New Testament into practice.

overview

- The study of collective behavior and social movements as a field of study within sociology contains some of the scholar's most intriguing puzzles and fascinating subjects.

- Fads, fashion, opinion, hysterical contagion, response to disaster, riots, and social movements are not simply the result of a bunch of crazy or out-of-control individuals. Instead, they represent a collective response generated by group processes.

- How do we start to separate the individual characteristics that influence behavior from the impact of social conditions? What is the nature of the social bond that holds us together in groups? This chapter has provided you with a series of key questions to ask about incidents and groups in the area of collective behavior and social movements. You may use these to determine your own interpretation of the ferment, the unrest, and the movement toward change that seem to characterize daily existence.

key concepts

acting crowd
As described by Blumer and others, this group of people has a selected objective; the energy of the crowd is directed toward accomplishing this objective; often the objective is of a hostile or destructive nature; in disasters, groups may assemble without prior organization to provide aid.

circular reaction
According to Blumer, the direct transfer of emotional states between individuals in a crowd.

collective behavior
An aggregate or collectivity of people involved in spontaneous, unplanned, and unstructured behavior.

consciousness of kind
A common feeling or identity that is shared among people of the same race/ethnicity, nationality, gender, communal or religious collectivity.

craze
A form of collective behavior that varies with the institutional area in which it emerges—economic, political, social, or religious.

crowd
A collectivity of people gathered in one particular place; may or may not have any common bonds or interaction.

emergent norm
Expectations for behavior that emerge within a particular and usually temporary situation; understood by those present as defining what is and is not appropriate behavior under the circumstances.

expressive crowd
A group of people directing all of their energy toward the crowd itself with no apparent objective in mind outside the activity of the crowd; contrasts with the **acting crowd** which has a point of focus and a targeted action outside the crowd.

fashion
The prevailing norms of dress for a particular time and place.

identification
When the follower in a group not only takes the actions of the leader as a model, but identifies with the leader to the extent of modeling his or her own identity on the one the leader projects.

issueless riot
According to Gary Marx, relatively spontaneous illegitimate group violence contrary to traditional norms, which neither serves as a means to an end nor is characterized by a group-shared generalized belief.

keynoting
When the follower in a group takes the action of a leader as a model for his or her own behavior, resulting in imitation or similar behavior.

panic/hysterical contagion
A shared belief that often leads to irrational action and may be accompanied by a heightened and fear-filled emotional state; the spread of panic through a group often appears when escape from the source of the fear seems limited.

polarization
A phenomenon noted in audiences (or other situations where more than two persons are present) when the majority of the group or aggregate shares a common point of attention.

process
In collective behavior and social movements, process refers to the way in which communication takes place in a group and the way in which new expectations for appropriate behavior emerge.

resource mobilization
An approach to the study of social movements that emphasizes the existence of experienced leadership and adequate resources (e.g., money, facilities, social networks) in interpreting the rise of a social movement; contrasts with shared grievances which motivate the aggrieved to act.

social movement
According to Gusfield, socially shared activities and beliefs directed toward the demand for change in some aspect of the social order.

endnotes

1. Herbert Blumer, "Collective Behavior," in *Principles of Sociology*, 2nd ed., ed. Alfred McClung Lee (New York: Barnes and Noble Publishing, 1955).
2. Robert Park and Ernest Burgess, *Introduction to the Science of Sociology* (Chicago: University of Chicago Press, 1921).
3. Gustave Le Bon, *The Crowd: A Study of the Popular Mind* (New York: The Macmillan Co., 1896).
4. Neil J. Smelser, *Theory of Collective Behavior* (New York: Free Press, 1963).
5. Ralph Turner and Lewis Killian, *Collective Behavior*, 2nd ed. (Englewood Cliffs, NJ: Prentice-Hall, 1987).
6. Clark McPhail, *The Myth of the Madding Crowd* (New York: Aldine de Gruyter Publishing, 1991).
7. Joseph R. Gusfield, *Protest, Reform and Revolt: A Reader in Social Movements* (New York: John Wiley and Sons, 1970).
8. Robert Bierstedt, *The Social Order* (New York: Basic Books, 1957).
9. Franklin H. Giddings, *The Elements of Sociology* (New York: The Macmillan Co., 1898).
10. Clark McPhail, *The Myth of the Madding Crowd*; Roger Brown, "Mass Phenomena," in *Handbook of Social Psychology*, vol. 2, ed. Gardner Lindsey (Reading, MA: Addison-Wesley, 1954); Stanley Milgram and Hans Toch, "Collective Behavior, Crowds, and Social Movements," in *Handbook of Social Psychology*, 2nd ed., ed. Gardner Lindsey and Elliot Aronson (Reading, MA: Addison-Wesley, 1969), 507-610.
11. Donald Johnson, "The Phantom Anesthetist of Mattoon: A Field Study of Mass Hysteria," *The Journal of Abnormal and Social Psychology* XL (April 1945): 175-86.
12. Alan Kerckhoff and Kurt W. Back, *The June Bug: A Study of Hysterical Contagion* (New York: Appleton-Century Crofts, 1968).
13. Blumer, "Collective Behavior."
14. Gary Marx, "Issueless Riots," *Annals of the American Academy of Political and Social Science* 391 (Sept. 1970): 21-33.
15. Smelser, *Theory of Collective Behavior*.
16. Russell R. Dynes and E. L. Quarantelli, "Effects of Disaster on Community Life, and Function of an Organization under Stress," in *Proceedings of Seminar on Family Agencies' Role in Disaster* (Canadian Department of National Health and Welfare, November 14-17, 1966).
17. Ibid.
18. Ted Robert Gurr, "Political Terrorism: Historical Antecedents and Contemporary Trends," in *Violence in America: Protest, Rebellion, Reform*, vol. 2, ed. T. R. Gurr (Newbury Park, CA: Sage Publications, 1989), 201-230.
19. Steven E. Barkan and Lynne L. Snowden, *Collective Violence* (Boston: Allyn & Bacon, 2001).
20. Rodney Stark, *The Rise of Christianity: A Sociologist Reconsiders History* (Princeton: Princeton University Press, 1999).
21. Gusfield, *Protest, Reform, and Revolt*.
22. Lyle E. Schaller, *The Change Agent* (Nashville: Abingdon Press, 1972).

additional source

Elizabeth Noelle-Neuman, *The Spiral of Silence: Public Opinion, Our Social Skin* (Chicago: University of Chicago Press, 1986).

CHAPTER EIGHTEEN

Social Change

chapter outline

I. Change is inevitable
   A. Change must be managed
   B. Sources of social change
II. Theories of change
III. Making a difference
IV. A personal example

biblical reflection

"For our struggle is not against enemies of blood and flesh, but against the rulers, against the authorities, against the cosmic powers of this present darkness, against the spiritual forces of evil in the heavenly places. Therefore take up the whole armor of God, so that you may be able to withstand on that evil day, and having done everything, to stand firm."

—Ephesians 6: 12-13

In this text we have talked about many social problems. Often we just want to throw our hands up and say, "That's just the way it is. Things will never change." Other times we have sought to point a finger at the person causing the problem and declare, "*You* must change." But in this text we have also given you strategies to analyze and solve social problems. Instead of blaming others, Paul is exhorting us in this passage to look past "flesh and blood" and analyze the "rulers" and "authorities." It is often easier and more effective to change an institution than to change an individual. This chapter will give direction to "take the whole armor of God" and promote effective social change. It takes courage, though. We must beware of those "spiritual hosts of wickedness in the heavenly places": those ill-directed church people, public officials, and others in whom we place too much trust.

God intends for you to be a change agent. Perhaps God has not called you to make a little change in millions of lives, but you can make a big change in the lives of a few people. Start with your family, your workplace, and your church. God commands us to make a difference; sociology can tell us where and how.

CHANGE IS INEVITABLE

Think of all the changes that have taken place within your lifetime: computers, the World Wide Web, cell phones, rap music, the breakup of the Communist Bloc, and the thawing of the Cold War. These have all made a profound impact on the way you see your world. The nature of your personal interactions has been forever altered.

You view some of these changes as very positive, while you lament other changes. Each change has a ripple effect that impacts other changes. For example, e-mailing means less face-to-face and voice-to-voice interaction. The World Wide Web has impacted commerce, creating a whole new way to shop.

Change is accelerating. We are already in the midst of spiraling social change at a rate unsurpassed in human history. The world is changing at a dizzying pace, leaving many of us perplexed. Cultures with limited access to new technology are becoming more and more isolated. A new form of illiteracy—computer illiteracy—creates a new form of world poverty. The struggle between the "haves" and "have nots" is now a clash between the computer literate and

Changing technology has resulted in a large gap between the "haves" and the "have nots."

illiterate. Nations with access to computer technology are far outpacing less developed nations.

CHANGE MUST BE MANAGED

If people are not able to manage the change around them, they will be swept away by its impact. Change will happen—it is inevitable. Unmanaged change can be devastating. For example, uncontrolled development of ocean-front property on the bluffs of the Pacific Ocean has led to mud slides and devastation.

Sociology gives us the insight to plan effectively so that change will have a positive impact on the world, rather than create instability. The ability to lead positive change starts with an understanding of the social world around us.

SOURCES OF SOCIAL CHANGE

By becoming aware of social change, its characteristics and causes, one can better plan to lead productive change. *Discovery* and *invention* precipitate most contemporary social change. Inventions such as the computer can be the source of great cultural conflict. Many people were reluctant to give up their typewriters and learn a new way of producing documents. However, as costs came down and technology became more "user-friendly," more and more people took the plunge into the computer age. Thus, the new technology produced **diffusion** as ordinary people slowly embraced new products until they became a regular part of the culture. We find it hard today to understand the old stalwarts who do not receive E-mail and insist on using a typewriter.

This process of cultural diffusion creates a *culture gap* between those cultures that regularly use the new technology and those cultures that are left behind with outdated methods of doing business. In his book *Powershift*, Toffler points outs that technology creates new sources of knowledge.[1] The people who control this knowledge become the new power brokers. The future will see new sources of wealth, new symbolic knowledge, and new military powers. The United States and Europe will no longer dominate the world. Traditional power structures will fade as we see new global power bases that

Though we take technology for granted, most of the world has never seen a computer.

Chapter Eighteen: Social Change

have no geographic boundaries.

Diffusion occurs with ideas, as well as with new products. However, things are more quickly diffused than ideas. American culture was fairly swift to embrace the new technology that made organ transplants possible. However, resolution of the ethical dilemmas surrounding the selling of body parts has been slow in coming. Likewise, while we have eagerly embraced cell phones, we have been less willing to yield to warnings concerning their use when we drive.

Changing *demographics* also precipitate social change. As the population has moved away from industrial cities of the northern United States to the sunshine of Silicon Valley, tremendous social changes have resulted. Miles of abandoned factories in the North become trendy, upscale townhouses for young urban professionals ("yuppies") or ghettos for a new generation of immigrants from the Southwest. Many social changes have occurred because nonwhites now outnumber Whites in most urban areas.

Sometimes we will want to change already existing norms or laws so that a change can benefit society. Such a movement is called a **reform**. An example would be Civil Rights legislation, which makes it illegal to discriminate against people on the basis of race, religion, gender, age, or sexual orientation. Even though we cannot legislate how people see or define situations (we can't make *prejudice* illegal), by creating a system whereby we are less likely to see the consequences of prejudice (discrimination), we will eventually change the way people see the world.

Legal reform is the most common way people change their society in North America. But what if the legal system itself is so corrupt that one cannot work within the system to reform the system? In that case a **revolution** may be necessary. This involves abolishing one system and replacing it with another. Usually violence and bloodshed ensue.

The difference between reform and revolution can be seen in this way: You are cooking a stew and upon tasting it are disappointed in its flavor. You may choose to add a little salt (reform) to improve the taste. But suppose the top of the saltshaker comes off and the entire contents spill into the stew. In this case the stew may be so salty that there is no other alternative but to throw it out and start again (revolution). Certainly the former is preferable. It is much easier to reform the world than to initiate a revolution. But sometimes revolution is necessary to put the society on its rightful track. You decide.

In the gemeinschaft community, everyone knows and trusts one another. In a gesellschaft society, people are more impersonal and governed by formal rules.

THEORIES OF CHANGE

How does the process of social change occur? In this section we will revisit (for one last time) two of the major theoretical perspectives to look at their insights on social change. First, however, we will consider large-scale explanations of modern society.

German sociologist **Ferdinand Tonnies** sought to account for the loss of community brought about by the Industrial Revolution.[2] He theorized that traditional society (what he termed gemeinschaft) was characterized by face-to-face interaction united by a spirit of community. This small town or village mentality still exists in small communities today. Generally, however, increasing population and diversity have fueled a move to secondary relations. In this gesellschaft, people become depersonalized and are only marginally involved with their world. Trust deteriorates and is replaced by a legal system that prescribes behavior.

French sociologist **Emile Durkheim** posited a similar theory.[3] Also interested in the social impact of the Industrial Revolution on modern society, he focused on changes in social integration and solidarity with the advent of economic changes. In a traditional society, one craftsman would build and sell an entire product. Such a society is characterized by *mechanical solidarity*—people held together by moral agreements about what is good and right. With industrialization comes the division of labor, so that a product is built by many individuals, all of whom contribute a highly specialized task. Thus, the worker becomes fragmented and not as personally invested in the product. Such a society requires *organic solidarity*, characterized by bureaucratic rules proscribing normative behavior. When those rules are not present, Durkheim predicted that society would suffer in a state of *anomie*, or normlessness.

We can see evidence of the tensions of modernity as we observe the world around us. The gesellschaft nature of our society means that as we become more diverse and highly specialized, we lose a collective moral sense (what Durkheim called *collective conscience*) about what is right and wrong. Traditionalists will hang on to the gemeinschaft agreements about moral behavior. As society becomes more diverse, there will be tensions and few agreements about moral values. Thus, modern society celebrates the individuality of people to "do their own thing." Durkheim was optimistic that a society governed by bureaucratic rules would maintain stability. However, we see many instances in which the rules are unclear (anomie) and society is in tension.

A *structural-functional perspective* on social change would see the society as a well-oiled machine functioning to promote stability. Talcott Parsons said that as external changes (discoveries and inventions, for example) confront the existing system, adaptations and adjustments will be made to maintain order.[4] Changes in the social system occur very slowly, maintaining the equilibrium of the system as a whole. This *dynamic equilibrium* enables social change to occur without creating constant tension and conflict.

According to the structural-functional perspective, the system works to maintain order and needs little change. Individuals within society may create problems threatening the stability of the social system. Therefore, since individuals are the source of the problem, change must be done on an individual basis. For example, illegal drug distribution and use threatens the social order, so the individuals distributing and using illegal drugs must be tracked down and reformed. This assumes the system works and the individuals are at fault. It puts responsibility of social change on the shoulders of individuals in need of change.

In contrast, the *conflict perspective* would look at ways in which the social system itself creates conflict and tension and is in need of change. From this perspective, individuals are dehumanized and exploited by a deficient social system. Instead of focusing on individual change, the conflict perspective would look at ways in which the social structure can be reformed to make it more amenable to the needs of the individual. For example, rather than seeing the problem of illegal drug use and distribution as solely a product of individual deficiency, the conflict perspective would have us look at ways in which the society encourages and glamorizes drug use. They might also examine a law enforcement system that inadequately blocks the entry of illegal drugs into the country.

In political speeches and in the popular media, we hear a lot about how individuals have to change. But we hear little about the need to change social structures. It is more fashionable to blame other people for problems. It gets us "off the hook" for the social ills around us. Yet the verses in Ephesians cited at the beginning of this chapter remind us we should look beyond "flesh and blood" explanations and look to the "powers"—the social structure—as the source of social problems.

Both the structural-functional and conflict perspectives are plausible explanations of social

People who seek social change are often rejected by people in power. These students found their school paper censored when they printed articles critical of the administration.

change. Taken together they give a more complete view of the world. For example, suppose you have a "problem" of being late to class. A structural-functionalist would suggest that this is the fault of the individual. You need to take personal responsibility for getting to class on time. However, the conflict perspective would add that there might be structural deficiencies that create barriers to punctuality. Perhaps the traffic in your town creates barriers for you. Perhaps the institution fails to provide adequate and convenient parking. Perhaps a professor kept you late in your previous class. Perhaps your employer prevented you from leaving work on time. Certainly you need to take personal responsibility to do all you can to get to class on time. However, there are probably social structural changes that could aid your punctuality. We need to look at social problems from both perspectives.

MAKING A DIFFERENCE

> *I shall be telling this with a sigh*
> *Somewhere ages and ages hence:*
> *Two roads diverged in a wood, and I –*
> *I took the one less traveled by,*
> *And that has made all the difference.*
>
> —Robert Frost,
> "The Road Not Taken"

God calls us to make a difference in the world. We change the world a little each day by each word we speak and by each act of love or hate we generate. It starts with a plan of the heart. What is important to you? What is your vision for the future? What changes will it take to get there? By working with other people, you can take a step toward the world God intends for you.

Examine your motivations for change. Many short-lived social reforms are rooted in self-interest. The "hippies" of the 1960s were largely upper-middle-class youths who sought attention and thrills. There are still plenty of guilt-ridden affluent Americans who become "do-gooders" to appease their consciences. There are also narrow-minded religious fanatics who want to justify their beliefs by converting everyone to their way of thinking. Be careful of these people. Their fire for change will soon burn out. They will become disenchanted when the changes they seek are not easily won.

You can expect some resistance. Do not lose patience. You may never see the fruition of your labors for social change. Remember the women of the first Women's Rights Convention in 1848. There, Elizabeth Cady Stanton, Lucretia Mott, and three hundred others first proposed that women be given the right to vote. The nineteenth amendment to the Constitution was finally ratified in 1920, giving women the right to vote. Accomplishing this took seventy-two years of constant pressure—marching, bargaining, compromising, and public demonstrations. None of the original leaders ever got the opportunity to vote. Yet they were the torchbearers for generations of women who now hold positions of power in practically every social institution.

In his analysis of collective behavior, **Neil Smelser** has observed five conditions that must be present for a social change movement to occur.[5] It is helpful to think about these conditions when planning to make a difference in the world. Think about how to apply them to the change God is calling you to make. We will use the Christian church as our example to illustrate how these conditions work.

1. In order for social change to occur, ***the social structure must be conducive to change***. It is nearly impossible to effect lasting social change within a structure that is extremely tight and inflexible. The social conditions must be ripe for change and windows of opportunity must exist within which change agents can operate. For example, in the "fullness of time" God sent Jesus. Bethlehem was far from

This Australian Aborigine protest seeks an end to an oppressive social structure.

the center of power. The social structure there was flexible enough to allow a Messiah to operate.

2. There must also be **structural strain** or else no one will perceive a need for change. People have to sense that there is something amiss in the social environment. People will seldom wish to change when things appear to be going well for them. But when pocketbooks are empty or personal relationships are in tatters, people will look for someone or something to lead them to change. For example, at the time Jesus was born there was considerable political unrest. Tensions between the rule of Rome and local authority found the Jewish community sandwiched in turmoil. The time was right for a Messiah.

3. When these conditions are present, the time is ripe for the ***growth and spread of a generalized belief***. People will be looking for some explanation for their stress and are ready to act on a possible solution to their plight. In Jesus' time, John the Baptist got people to think about a coming Messiah. When Jesus started preaching that the poor were blessed and would inherit the Kingdom of Heaven, people were ready to listen and accept Him as their Savior. It is important to note that Jesus enlisted the help of disciples to spread the word. It is necessary to work with others to educate people about social conditions. This is the idea phase. But to really work, we must move on into the action phase.

4. A ***precipitating event or events*** is the spark that is necessary to move people from ideas to action. This triggering event may be natural or human-made. It helps if this event is widely publicized. It inflames the passions of people to action. The very public crucifixion of Jesus may have been intended to squelch a coming rebellion, but it turned out to be a precipitating event for Christians. Likewise, Pentecost might be seen as a precipitating event that sparked the birth of Christianity as a world religion.

5. An important part of any social change is the ***mobilization of participants***. One person is rather limited in effecting lasting social change. To make a difference in the world, people must work together. The participants are the hands and feet to bring the ideology to life. These participants must be educated about the reasons behind the change, but must also be trained to act to change. Jesus showed

people by example how to challenge the existing social structures of the day. After His death and resurrection, His disciples became active participants in a radical social change movement. They effectively mobilized more and more participants who went from being "hearers of the Word" to "doers of the Word."

6. Finally, you must be prepared for *mechanisms of social control*. For every social change there will be conservatives who feel threatened and will do all they can to oppose the change. When conservatives hold key seats of power, the opposition will be intense. These are people for whom the current structure is very rewarding, so they do not understand the need for change. To overcome such control, one might utilize the educational institutions to appeal to reason. The Christian church has periodically overcome social opposition by having Christians become active leaders in the social institutions. By working within the system, Christians can effectively overcome social control and thus change the system.

As you plan to make a difference, consider these conditions and do all you can to create lasting change. It all starts with a changed individual who clearly examines his/her heart for the right motivations for change. Change is not about self-glory. Do not expect a trophy or your name in the paper. Quite likely, many people will despise you for upsetting their world. Recall that Jesus was also despised. At least you probably will not be condemned to die on a cross for trying to make the world a better place.

Remember that you must work with other people and build a team to garner lasting change. This is where the church comes in. True change only occurs when values are affected; therefore, any change agent will have to work with the religious institutions. The church is

As you work toward social change, you can expect the exercise of social control by authorities in power.

often a conservative or reactionary force as it transmits the traditional values of the past. But the church can be a vehicle for social change. Examples are the Civil Rights Movement, which began in the Black churches of the South, or the Socialist revolutions of Central America. Reformers can use the power of the churches to change the hearts of the people and thus begin a grass roots revolution.

A PERSONAL EXAMPLE

-Cynthia B. Tweedell, General Editor

In the 1970s, I attended a small private college that was struggling with its church affiliation. To the outside observer, the students on this campus closely resembled those at secular institutions. Fraternities and sororities dominated the social life of the campus. Drinking, drug use, and premarital sex were common. I came to the campus as a newly dedicated Christian, knowing that God intended for me to make a difference in the world, but unsure where to start. At fall orientation, I asked my student leader where I might find Christian fellowship on campus. It so happened that she and a few others had recently discovered a tiny room marked "Chapel" on the second floor of the Student Center. It was overrun by storage boxes, but these students spent some time clearing the clutter and found an altar, a prayer rail, a metal cross, and a tiny stained glass window. They had begun meeting there during spring semester and were planning to have a regular prayer meeting at 12:30 each weekday afternoon. She invited me to attend.

I shared the "secret" about the prayer group meeting in the chapel with my roommate. I had seen the Bible strategically placed next to her bed, so I thought it might be "safe" to suggest we attend the meeting together. The next day we excused ourselves early from lunch with some other freshmen women, saying we were "going to meet with some people." When we got to the chapel we were surprised to see about ten people there: five were the sophomores who started the meeting the year before, and five were new freshmen. The room only had six chairs, so we sat on the carpet and held hands, praying for social change on our secular campus.

Each day the numbers in the prayer meeting grew. By the end of the second week of school, fifty of us overflowed into the conference room next door. We began to subdivide into small groups of five to handle all the prayer requests. The top request was always "social change on our campus."

The college began to take notice. Officials said we could not utilize the conference room unless we were an official student organization that reserved the space in advance. We had no leadership, no faculty advisor, and no formal recognition by the college. In fact, we began to target the existing religion faculty and official college "Religious Life Committee" as part of the problem on the campus. We sought out pastoral leadership from some of the local churches, but they were reluctant to send a pastor to shepherd a group of Christians who challenged the official leadership of the college.

God was answering our prayers. But without leadership and organization, the group floundered. Using a democratic style of leadership, we managed to organize some activities, such as retreats and nursing home visitations. We tried to revive an overgrown "Bible Garden" we found hidden on campus, but received resistance from the college personnel for "unauthorized planting of flowers."

We struggled with the integration of our Christian ideals with our academic activities. We found little support for our Christian beliefs from our faculty and often felt pressured to keep quiet about our faith in our academic discussions. When I confessed to the prayer group that I felt God had called me into sociology as a profession, one fellow Christian was very serious when she said, "You can't be a Christian and be a sociologist. They're all atheists." I felt challenged to prove her wrong, but was quite confused about the connection between my faith and my future profession. Like the others in the group, I began to separate my faith from my daily academic life. We began to compartmentalize our faith and our professions, because we lacked the intellectual support we needed to integrate faith and life. As we became more involved in our academic majors, we became less active in our Christian fellowship activities. By my junior year, the prayer group had become fragmented over issues like speaking in tongues and healing. What little power we had gained through our unity became lost in our disunity over the manner in which we should pray.

Today such splits seem ludicrous, but this was a typical struggle for Christians in 1975. As the Jesus Movement of the 1970s matured, it also splintered into progressive and conservative factions. Perhaps this was a cleansing that needed to take place before Christians would finally begin to unite into a highly organized activist group in the 1990s.

We can use some of the concepts from my story to analyze the college social change group. It appears we had participants, but lacked organization and leadership. We lacked a unified ideology and had no clear goal. But the college and the larger society were in a state of structural strain and were conducive to change. So it was inevitable that conservative and more liberal Christians would clash on campus over which form the religious activities should take at this college.

But the most important thing we had was prayer: consistent, fervent, persistent prayer. We were often unsure for what we ought to pray or how we ought to pray. Yet we continued to pray.

And despite our bumbling, God answered those prayers. The college began to change. When I returned five years after graduation, I found an "official" Bible Garden creatively planted with shrubs and flowers. Ten years after graduation, I returned to find a real chapel—a beautiful building with many rows of pews and lovely windows.

And God answered my personal prayers of confusion over whether a Christian could be a sociologist. I eventually began to understand how to integrate my sociology with my faith. God led me into sociology so that I could make a difference in the lives of thousands of students and even in the structure of higher education itself.

We have ended on a positive note. We are not merely puppets on a string pulled around by the whims of conservative social institutions. We can look up and ask, "Who's pulling those strings?" Through understanding the social structures, we can resist becoming victims of those structures and can occasionally tug back and control some of the movements of the puppeteer (society).

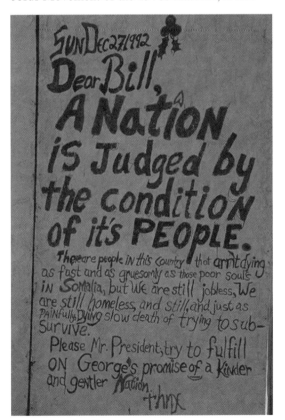

Your efforts for Christ are never in vain.

overview

- Social change is inevitable. We cannot choose to avoid change, but we can choose how to respond to change. By productively managing social change, we avoid getting swept away by it.

- Social change can come from many sources. Most often, new technology sparks social change. New inventions and ideas become diffused so that they permeate all of society.

- Sometimes society is in need of reform, a change in the norms or laws to accommodate new inventions or technology. Sometimes a revolution is required to replace a defunct system of control with a whole new way of seeing the world.

- Tonnies and Durkheim theorized that social relations become more complex as a small community changes into a large society. As a society becomes more diverse, there are fewer common agreements about moral values.

- A structural-functional perspective on social change sees change as gradual and systematic.

- A conflict perspective on social change sees change as a product of tensions and power struggles.

- Smelser analyzed social change movements in terms of the stages through which they move and the factors necessary for success.

- God calls each of us to be change agents. Not everyone will be a Martin Luther King, Jr., but each of us can make a difference in our little corner of the world.

key concepts

diffusion
The process by which an invention or idea becomes widely accepted by a society.

reform movement
A social change movement that addresses one aspect of society; the usual result is a change in a single norm, value, or law.

revolutionary movement
A social change movement that produces sweeping changes in a social system; often requires violent tactics.

Tonnies, Ferdinand
German sociologist who analyzed social change during industrialization in terms of the loss of community. His term *gemeinschaft* referred to a community characterized by a common set of values and face-to-face interaction. As a society modernized, it became a *gesellschaft,* characterized by impersonal relationships.

Durkheim, Emile
French sociologist who was interested in how society achieved social integration and stability as it became more complex. He theorized that societies moved from *mechanical solidarity* to *organic solidarity*.

Smelser, Neil
Twentieth-century American sociologist who analyzed the stages of social movements. He theorized that certain conditions were necessary for a social movement to occur and succeed.

endnotes

1. A. Toffler, *Powershift: Knowledge, Wealth, and Violence at the Edge of the 21st Century* (New York: Bantam Books, 1990).
2. Ferdinand Tonnies, *Community and Society (Gemeinschaft und Gesellschaft)* (New York: Harper & Row, Publishers, 1963; orig. 1887).
3. Emile Durkheim, *The Division of Labor in Society* (New York: Free Press, 1964; orig. 1895).
4. Talcott Parsons, *The Social System* (New York: Free Press, 1951).
5. Neil Smelser, *Theory of Collective Behavior* (New York: Free Press, 1962).

glossary

achieved status
Social position that is acquired because of one's ability to alter one's ascribed status.

acting crowd
As described by Blumer and others, this group of people has a selected objective; the energy of the crowd is directed toward accomplishing this objective; often the objective is of a hostile or destructive nature; in disasters, groups may assemble without prior organization to provide aid.

activity theory
Organized set of hypotheses viewing social activity as beneficial to the well-being of older adults.

age norms
Shared expectations of appropriate behavior for people at a given life stage.

age stratification
An unequal distribution of social resources based on chronological age. Age is one of several overlapping systems of stratification.

ageism
Negative attitudes and behaviors toward older people based on their chronological age.

aggregate
Social position that is acquired because of one's ability to alter one's ascribed status.

aging
A life-course process of growing older from birth to death and passing through a set of social positions and roles.

androgyny
Having the characteristics of both male and female; being neither distinctively masculine nor feminine.

anomie
The gap between society's success goal and the legitimate means for achieving that goal.

asceticism
Self-denial in the interest of showing religious devotion.

ascribed status
Social position that is acquired by persons at birth, according to their family background.

assembly line
Highly automated and efficient production method pioneered in the auto industry by Henry Ford.

assimilation
The fusion of formerly distinctive groups, resulting in the disappearance of any differences that serve as the basis for prejudice and discrimination.

authority
Power which people perceive as legitimate.

barter economy
An economy that lacks money and instead exchanges goods and services directly.

beliefs
The general agreement by the members of a society that a certain body of knowledge is true or valid.

blue-collar workers
Wage laborers who work with their hands in manufacturing and service occupations and enjoy lower pay and benefits than white-collar workers.

bourgeoisie
Marx's term for the capitalist class of productive property owners.

boycott
An organized movement that attempts to achieve objectives by asking individual consumers to refuse to purchase certain goods and services.

bureaucracy
A formal or complex organization characterized by centralization of authority, hierarchical chain of command, and emphasis on rationality, discipline, and technical knowledge.

Calvinists
Believe human beings can do nothing about their eternal destiny (predestination).

capitalism
An economic system based on private ownership of productive property, the profit motive, and a free market.

charismatic authority
Authority that rests on the personal characteristics of an individual who inspires loyalty.

Christian socialism
Attempts by small Christian communities such as the Hutterites to institute shared property ownership and economic production, distribution, and consumption.

church
Religious group that seeks merger with the secular world, expects loyalty from all persons in a given area (inclusive membership), and generally takes a conservative position regarding doctrine and ethics.

circular reaction
According to Blumer, the direct transfer of emotional states between individuals in a crowd.

cohort
A set of people born (or experiencing an event) during a given period of time, typically one or ten years.

collective behavior
An aggregate or collectivity of people involved in spontaneous, unplanned, and unstructured behavior.

collective conscience
Durkheim's term for the collectively held set of values, beliefs, norms, and sanctions tied to religion; these provide the basis for social order in preindustrial society but weaken in modern society.

common good
Those actions and patterns which benefit society as a whole.

Comte, Auguste
Nineteenth-century French social philosopher who is seen as the "father of sociology."

conflict perspective
A theoretical perspective that focuses on the role of conflict and power in society and on the existence of competing interests between groups.

conflict theory
Stratification theory that conceives of society as a system of conflicting interest groups; suggests that social order is based on organized coercion.

consciousness of kind
A common feeling or identity that is shared among people of the same race/ethnicity nationality, gender, communal or religious collectivity.

conservation
Efforts made by a group or organization that have the goal of self-perpetuation of the organization, as well as related programs and activities.

convergence
The trend for capitalist and socialist economic patterns to be combined in modern economies, regardless of ideological preferences.

Cooley, Charles H.
Social psychologist at University of Michigan; author of "looking-glass self" concept.

core nations
Wallerstein's term for wealthy nations at the center of the world capitalist system which dominate poorer nations.

counterculture
A group's way of thinking and acting that is an alternative to or in opposition to the norms and values of the larger society.

craze
A form of collective behavior that varies with the institutional area in which it emerges—economic, political, social, or religious.

crime
A violation of a law in a given society.

cross-sectional analysis
Research that collects data at one point in time.

crowd
A collectivity of people gathered in one particular place; may or may not have any common bonds or interaction.

cult
Small, loosely organized religious group that takes an eclectic approach to doctrine, tends to have poorly defined membership standards, and is held together by the force of the leader's personality.

cultural material
Tangible objects that facilitate and express cultural ideas and norms: for example, musical instruments, works of art, religious paraphernalia, currencies, shelter, and clothing.

cultural pluralism
A minority group's retention or preservation of cultural differences without prejudice or discrimination; difference with respect and equality.

cultural relativistic perspective
A view that acknowledges that every culture should be analyzed in its own context and by its own standards; an orientation that supports rational, empirical, and comparative analysis of cultures and rejects an ethnocentric view.

cultural universals
Cultural elements that are present in all human societies.

culture
A society's way of life, consisting of beliefs, values, norms, and symbols.

custodial care of the young
A latent function of education in which schools keep children out of harm's way until they are contributing members of the society.

death anxiety
Diffuse form of fear related to the termination of one's life.

democratic socialism
An attempt by some western European nations such as Sweden to incorporate income-leveling features of socialism with an essentially capitalist free-market economy.

dependency theory
An explanation of global poverty that says nations become poor when they are denied access to self-development strategies because of colonialism and economic dominance by well-developed nations

dependent variable
A variable that is influenced by another (independent) variable.

deviant behavior (social deviance)
Behavior that violates the norms of a society.

differential association
Developed by Edwin Sutherland, this theory states that people learn to be criminal when they have had an excess of experiences favoring law violation. They usually have these in primary groups.

diffusion
The process by which an invention or idea becomes widely accepted by a society

discrimination
Behavior in relation to a particular group or group member that is determined or influenced by perceived racial or cultural differences in that group; it may be positive or negative.

disease
A biologically defined disorder of an organism that impairs its ability to function.

disengagement theory
Perspective which presumes that age is accompanied by an inevitable and mutual withdrawal in social life.

division of labor
The variety of occupations associated with modern societies.

dominant group
The group in power and the one which other groups are expected to imitate in order to gain acceptance; the dominant group in America is White, Anglo-Saxon, and Protestant.

dual careers
The tendency for married women in modern societies to perform unpaid work at home along with paid work at their job outside the home.

Durkheim, Emile
Nineteenth-century French sociologist who sought to understand how social elements function to promote social stability.

dysfunction
When a group or organization functions in a manner that hinders the likelihood of accomplishing its original purpose; primarily due to excessive concern for perpetuating the organization and its associated programs and activities.

ego
The person we see ourselves as being; it attempts to reconcile the pressures between the raw drives of the id and the conforming demands of the superego.

emergent norm
Expectations for behavior that emerge within a particular and usually temporary situation; understood by those present as defining what is and is not appropriate behavior under the circumstances.

epidemiology
A systematic study of how diseases are distributed within a culture or society.

ethnic groups
Groups that share certain cultural differences which set them apart from the dominant group. National origin, language, religion, or general lifestyle offer the most common evidence of a group's ethnicity.

ethnocentrism
Attitudes which support beliefs that values and norms of one's culture are superior to those of another.

European Union
An economic union of European nations that has removed barriers to free trade within Europe and is instituting a common currency called the Euro.

expressive crowd
A group of people directing all of their energy toward the crowd itself with no apparent objective in mind outside the activity of the crowd.

extended family
Parents, dependent children, and other relatives.

family
Two or more people who are committed to each other over time, sharing intimacy, resources, values, and decision-making responsibilities, as well as assuming responsibility for the care of children.

fashion
The prevailing norms of dress for a particular time and place.

felony
A crime that is usually punishable by at least one year or more in a state or federal prison.

feminism
A reaction to sexist attitudes in society; the belief that women have been subordinated and must be given equal opportunities and status in all areas and institutions of society.

focal concerns
Walter Miller states that lower-class youth have certain focal concerns—trouble, toughness, fate, autonomy, smartness, excitement—that lend themselves to criminal/delinquent behavior.

folk society
Redfield's term for highly stable rural preindustrial society.

folkways
The customary ways people do things.

formal organization
A secondary group particularly organized to carry out explicit objectives, impersonal goals, and defined roles.

Freud, Sigmund
Credited with the development of psychoanalysis.

functional base
The original need or set of needs a group or organization is intended to address.

functionalist perspective
A theoretical perspective that focuses on the ways social structures and patterns contribute to the maintenance of social order.

gemeinschaft
Tonnies' term for the close, intimate community life characteristic of small rural preindustrial societies.

gender
The characteristics a society considers appropriate for males and females.

generalized others
Third developmental stage proposed by Mead in which a child moves from taking the role of "significant others" to a view of society's role in general; internalizing broad social expectations.

gerontology
Scientific study of aging.

gesellschaft
Tonnies' term for the impersonal urban mass society characteristic of large industrial societies.

global language
A language widely used throughout an interconnected world. Formerly Greek, Latin, and French played this role in the Western world; English has now become a global language uniting the entire world.

global village
McLuhan's term for the increasingly interconnected world of the information age.

globalization
The modern tendency for economic and social interaction to transcend national and political boundaries, tying persons and nations together as never before.

health
A state of complete physical, mental, and social well-being, not merely the absence of disease.

horizontal mobility
Movement within a particular social stratum.

Hutterites
An Anabaptist Christian group who practice communal living and sharing of goods and services, mostly on the prairies of Canada and the United States.

hypothesis
A statement about how two or more variables are related to each other.

"I"
George H. Mead's concept of an individual's view of her/himself as a total person; only one "I".

id
The total "raw" traits of a human; instinctual and compelling desires (Freud).

ideational definition of culture
Knowledge of cultural standards to which a person's behavior may or may not correspond.

identification
When the follower in a group not only takes the actions of the leader as a model, but identifies with the leader to the extent of modeling his or her own identity on the one the leader projects.

illness
An individual's awareness of the presence of disease in the body.

incidence
The number of new cases of a disease which occur in a population over a specific period of time (usually a particular year).

independent variable
A variable that causes change in another (dependent) variable.

Industrial Revolution
The movement beginning in western Europe in the eighteenth century to substitute machine power for human and animal power; marks the division between preindustrial and modern society.

industrialized society
Society that emphasizes manufacturing jobs.

infant mortality rate
The number of infants who, after having been born alive, die before their first birthday.

informal organization
The social structure that results when individuals interact within formal organizations.

information industry
The worldwide networking of information flows made possible by the computer and the Internet, resulting in the information age and marking the transition from industrial to postindustrial society.

institutional sexism
Practices within a social organization that systematically discriminate against men or women, making it more difficult for them to achieve.

interactionist theory
A micro-theory that focuses on the meanings created by the interpersonal exchange of symbols such as words, gestures, and other actions.

Internet
The global networking of computers and information flows characteristic of postindustrial society.

iron law of oligarchy
The process by which organizations and political systems shift toward "rule by a few."

issueless riot
According to Gary Marx, relatively spontaneous illegitimate group violence contrary to traditional norms, which neither serves as a means to an end nor is characterized by a group-shared generalized belief.

joint-stock corporation
A business organization owned jointly by stockholders rather than by private individuals and managed by paid professional managers.

Jubilee
A current religious and political movement modeled on the Old Testament Jubilee; asks wealthy nations to forgive debts of poor nations.

keynoting
When the follower in a group takes the actions of the leader as a model for his or her own behavior, resulting in imitation or similar behavior.

kibbutz (pl. kibbutzim)
Hebrew word for Israeli collective farms and communities.

kinship
Family ties established through marriage or lines of descent.

labeling theory
A theory associated with Howard Becker and Edward Lemert that contends deviance is not a quality of the act committed, but a consequence of others' defining the act as deviant; the person who moves from "primary" to "secondary" deviance accepts the label and embarks on a career as a delinquent or criminal.

labor force
The sum total of persons employed in various occupations.

labor unions
Organizations of workers in various industries that attempt to bargain collectively for improved wages and working conditions.

laissez-faire
French term used by Adam Smith to express the capitalist conviction that economic activities should be free of government regulation and interference.

language
The means of communication practiced by humans.

latent function
An unintended function of education; custodial child care is a latent function.

law
A type of social control exemplified by intention, authority, obligation, and sanctions; a systematic rule enacted by political authority that involves formal penalties for violations.

legal-rational authority
Authority based on law and rational principles.

liberal
Religious orientation that emphasizes the symbolic nature of religious truth, accepts a variety of interpretations of Scripture, and believes in a continuing unfolding of revelation from a variety of sources. True liberals disdain fundamentalism.

life expectancy
Number of years remaining in life, often calculated at birth or at key ages.

life-course perspective
View of aging that emphasizes the relatedness of an individual's thought and behavior at given life stages to previous life stages.

longitudinal design
Research collecting data at two or more points in time.

long-term care
Sustained provision of one or more services to enable people with chronically impaired functioning to maintain their maximum levels of performance.

looking-glass
Self-concept used by Charles Cooley to describe the process by which we estimate others' reactions to our behavior and feel corresponding feeling-states such as pride, embarrassment, or inadequacy in ourselves.

macro-level theory
Large-scale analysis of society such as structural-functional theory or conflict theory.

manifest function
An intended function of education; sorting students by ability and creating knowledge are two manifest functions.

marriage
The socially acknowledged and approved union of a man and a woman for the purpose of founding and maintaining a family.

masculinity/femininity
The social image of being male and female as determined and taught by society.

McDonaldization
Ritzer's term for efficient, practical, calculable, and machine-controlled rational economic activity in the modern and postmodern world.

Mead, George Herbert
Social psychologist at the University of Chicago who developed theories of mind, self, and society; stressed the impact of "generalized other" on the development of self.

measure of central tendency
A single typical value that characterizes a distribution of values. Three types of such a measure are mean, median, and mode.

melting pot
An idealistic version of how diverse races and ethnic groups fused into one, creating the amalgam which is America.

Merton, Robert
Twentieth-century American sociologist who analyzed social structures in terms of manifest and latent functions or consequences.

micro-level theory
Small-scale analysis of interpersonal social behavior such as interactionist theory.

militarism
A way of thinking that focuses on preparedness for war and results in pervasive military symbols, ideology, and values in society.

minority group
A group sharing certain identifiable differences in appearance, culture, or behavior, and for

whom these differences mean unequal treatment, restricted life choices, and limited rewards and/or achievements.

misdemeanor
Offense punishable by not more than a year in a county jail.

misdevelopment
The conviction that poorer nations of the world may suffer development distorted by the domination of wealthy capitalist nations; preferred over the term underdeveloped as an explanation for their continued poverty.

modernization theory
An explanation of global poverty that says nations are poor because they have not "modernized" by adopting Western economic systems and technology.

monogamy
Marriage to one spouse at a time.

morbidity rate
The incidence of disease in a population.

mores
Cultural rules that are essential for societal survival and have been codified into moral and civil laws.

mortality rate
The incidence of death in a population.

multinational corporations
Large business organizations doing business in several nations.

new economy
Economic activity in the highly technological information industries of postindustrial society.

nonempirical referent
Experience not directly verifiable through the physical senses.

normal aging
Naturally developmental processes of growing older as distinct from pathological processes which are more likely attributable to disease.

norms
The social behavior expected of people within a culture.

North American Free Trade Association
An economic and political arrangement by which Canada, Mexico, and the United States have removed most tariffs and other trade barriers to encourage economic activity in the North American region.

nuclear family
One or two parents and their children.

old economy
Economic activity in manufacturing sectors that formed the engine of economic growth in industrial society and is still present in postindustrial society.

other
Counterpart of "self" in a social situation; our view of the person in a dyadic relationship.

overdevelopment
Term used to imply that wealthy nations of the world owe their wealth to the exploitation of poorer nations and of world resources.

panic/hysterical contagion
A shared belief that often leads to irrational action and may be accompanied by a heightened and fear-filled emotional state; the spread of panic through a group often appears when escape from the source of fear seems limited.

Parsons, Talcott
Twentieth-century American sociologist whose

writings form the basis for structural-functional theory.

participant observation
A data collection method in which the researcher observes subject behavior while interacting with the subject(s) and making his or her identity as a researcher known.

periphery nations
Poor nations on the margin of the world capitalist system and presumably exploited by wealthy core nations.

Piaget, Jean
Swiss biologist and psychologist who stated that humans pass through inevitable growth stages in reasoning and are active participants in their social development.

pink-collar workers
Workers in overwhelmingly female occupations, usually low-level service occupations.

pluralist model
A type of political structure characterized by a plurality of competing interests that influence decision making.

polarization
A phenomenon noted in audiences (or other situations where more than two persons are present) when the majority of the group or aggregate shares a common point of attention.

political action committees (PACS)
Special interest groups organized to influence policy by contributing to candidates and campaigns.

political system
The social institution that determines and implements the goals and collective actions of a group.

polyandry
Marriage to more than one husband.

polygamy
Marriage to more than one spouse at a time.

polygyny
Marriage to more than one wife.

postindustrial societies
Societies in which information and technology industries predominate.

postindustrial society
Society in which most of the jobs deal with information instead of agriculture or manufacturing.

power
The ability to get things done and/or to control others even against their will.

power elite model
A type of political structure characterized by a social, economic, and political elite who control decisions.

preindustrial societies
Societies which do not use modern machines to produce food or do other work, but instead use human labor or that of animals.

prejudice
Negative feelings, beliefs, and tendencies to act against certain people because of their race, ethnic background, or behavior.

prevalence
The total number of cases present in a population at any given time; includes new cases as well as all previously existing cases.

primary group
A small number of people who regularly interact with one another in an intimate, face-to-face,

largely cooperative manner.

primary sector
The sector of the economy that extracts products from nature.

process
In collective behavior and social movements, process refers to the way in which communication takes place in a group and the way in which new expectations for appropriate behavior emerge.

profane
Common, everyday attitude toward behavior or objects; things that demand no special treatment.

proletariat
Marx's term for wage laborers under capitalism, especially those in manufacturing.

prophetic activity
A set of values and exceptions that can be used to evaluate social practices and advocate social changes.

proxemics
The physical space between people which is given sociocultural meaning.

race
A population sharing genetically or biologically inherited characteristics.

recidivism
Repetition of criminal or delinquent behavior; usually referred to as recidivism rate.

reform movement
A social change movement that addresses one aspect of society; the usual result is a change in a single norm, value, or law.

reliability
The consistency with which a measure can be reproduced.

religion
A group of people who meet together on some regular basis, who share similar beliefs, and who practice similar rituals regarding their notion of the sacred.

religiosity
Ways of expressing religious commitment.

religious dysfunction
Harmful effects of religion upon society.

religious function
Beneficial effects of religion upon society.

resource mobilization
An approach to the study of social movements that emphasizes the existence of experienced leadership and adequate resources (e.g., money, facilities, social networks) in interpreting the rise of a social movement; contrasts with shared grievances, which motivate the aggrieved to act.

Riley, Matilda White
Sociologist and major architect of age stratification theory.

ritual
Ways of relating to sacred things; stereotyped ways of acting toward the sacred.

role
The cluster of behavior norms or rules expected of a person occupying a particular social status or position.

role conflict
What results when two or more roles are contradictory or incompatible.

role strain
What often occurs when a role involves differing, inconsistent expectations.

routinization of charisma
The process by which spontaneous acts become predictable, patterned, and organized.

sacred
Things set apart for special consideration; that which is holy.

sanction
A means of encouraging conformity and discouraging deviance; refers to either positive or negative sanctions or approving or disapproving behavior.

sanctions
Positive and negative behaviors used to enforce a norm.

sanctions (negative)
Punishments used for violations of cultural rules.

sanctions (positive)
Rewards used for compliance with cultural rules.

secondary data
Information used by a researcher after it has been collected by another researcher.

secondary group
A medium-sized or large number of people who interact in an impersonal, formal, unemotional, partial, and nonpermanent manner.

secondary sector
The sector of the economy that transforms raw materials into manufactured goods not already existing in nature.

sect
Religious group that stands apart from the secular world, requires conversion to become a member, tends toward literal interpretation of Scripture, and emphasizes otherworldly rewards.

secularization
The decline of religious influence, or participation, or both.

self
The composite of one's perception, attitudes, and beliefs about himself or herself.

self-fulfilling prophecy
Robert K. Merton's theory of the process of becoming what you are predicted to be; the prediction becomes a causal factor in the learning process.

sex
The biological characteristics of being male or female; manifested in several ways: the chromosomes, the internal reproductive system, the gonads, the hormones, and the external genitals.

sexism
The belief that one sex is superior to the other and thereby entitled to exploit the other sex through stereotyping, work discrimination, laws, family, and other systems.

sickness
One's awareness of the presence of a disease in someone else which then causes that person to change his or her behavior toward the sick individual; behavior that violates the norms of a society.

significant others
Persons who are most influential in helping to determine the behavior of the individual.

simple random sample
A sample in which every combination of elements in a population has an equal chance of being selected.

Smelser
Twentieth-century American sociologist who analyzed the stages of social movements. He theorized that certain conditions were necessary for a social movement to occur and succeed.

social capital
The social networks and norms of reciprocity and trustworthiness that support and nurture civic life.

social class
An economic interest group that has both social recognition and a sense of in-group awareness.

social control
Ways in which individual behavior is directed toward socially acceptable standards.

social control
Theories associated with Walter Reckless and Travis Hirschi that suggest that weak social control mechanisms explain deviant behavior; either a formal or informal attempt to enforce conformity to society's norms.

social differentiation
The separation of social categories such as race, gender, or age.

social movement
According to Gusfield, socially shared activities and beliefs directed toward the demand for change in some aspect of the social order.

social responsibility investing
A recent trend in which individual and institutional investors limit their investments to ethically responsible economic activity.

social sin
Social structures and institutions which are built on individual sin.

social status
The social position of an individual in his or her society or smaller group. Groups also possess social status.

social stratification
The institutionalization or stabilization of status differences into hierarchical arrangements.

social structure
The ordered, patterned ways in which persons conduct themselves in social situations and how this organization of behavior relates to the rest of their society.

socialism
An economic system in which government owns productive property and controls economic production in the name of the people.

socialization
A manifest function of education in which the school teaches members of a society how to fit in.

society
A distinct group of people who occupy a common territory and live together long enough to organize themselves into a unit different from other similar groups.

sociological imagination
The ability to take a second look at the "world taken for granted," enabling an individual to see him/herself within a social context.

sociology
The scientific study of society that explores the antecedents and consequences of social behavior.

special interest groups
Groups that advocate on behalf of a particular interest.

status inconsistency
The incompatibility of one status with another.

stereotype
An idea about an individual based on preconceived, standardized characteristics alleged to a whole category of people.

strain theory
A theory (e.g., Merton's anomie theory) that suggests deviance may result when people are frustrated in their attempts to achieve a goal.

structure functionalism
A macro-theory that views society as a system of interconnected parts that depend on each other for proper functioning to maintain stability and equilibrium.

subculture
A portion of the population having distinctive norms, values, and traits.

superego
Freud's concept that refers to that part of the self which has internalized social norms and attitudes; corresponds to Mead's concept of "me" and is popularly known as one's conscience.

survey
A data collection method that elicits information by way of an interview or questionnaire.

symbols
Anything—object, gesture, word—that is given arbitrary meaning and about which members of a culture generally agree.

systematic sample
A sample in which every kth element is selected from a list after a start in which a random number between 1 and k is chosen.

tertiary sector
The sector of the economy that provides services to others.

the "elect"
Those destined for salvation.

Tonnies, Ferdinand
German sociologist who analyzed social change during industrialization in terms of the loss of community.

traditional authority
Authority that rests on tradition.

transmission of knowledge
A manifest function of education wherein schools teach students what they need to know to be successful members of the society.

Trekkies
Star Trek fans guided by beliefs in progress, discovery, science, and egalitarianism.

"2020 vision"
Recognition of the major demographic and social changes occurring about the year 2020.

underclass
The semipermanent group of persons stuck at the bottom of modern society and seemingly unable to escape.

underdevelopment
Term which implies that poor nations could become wealthy if they would develop as modern nations have done.

validity
The degree to which a measurement of a variable accurately reflects what it claims to measure.

values
Shared ideas of things members of a culture think are good and desirable.

vertical mobility
Movement up or down the class scale.

Weber, Max
Nineteenth-century German sociologist who sought to understand social structure.

welfare state
A nation such as the United States that has incorporated some elements of socialism into an essentially capitalist economy.

white collar crime (elite deviance)
Persons of high respectability and high social status who commit crime in the course of their occupation, amounting to billions more than "street" or "blue collar crime."

white-collar workers
Highly paid and respected workers in managerial and professional careers.

worldview
A comprehensible body of beliefs about how the world is organized as represented in a culture's myths, religious ceremonies, social behavior, and value system.

index

A

achieved status 53, 59, 138, 150

achievement motivation 114

acting crowds 292

activity theory 162, 172

African Americans 39, 41, 125-126, 133, 182, 184, 240, 243-244, 248, 296

age norms 156-158, 171-172

age stratification 157-158, 162, 172

ageism 157, 170, 172

agents of socialization 72, 74-76, 78, 140-141

aggregate 50-51, 59, 292, 297

androgynous 139, 151

anomie 65-66, 86, 96, 99, 303-304

anticipatory socialization 73, 75, 77

apartheid 123-124

asceticism 203, 211

ascribed status 53, 59, 122, 138, 150

Asian Americans 93, 161, 183, 192

assembly line 253

assimilation 129-130, 135

authoritarian personalities 128

authority 24, 35-36, 44, 48-49, 55, 57-59, 74, 85, 99, 114, 188, 206, 269-273, 279, 281-284, 306

B

Bailey, Garrick 29, 45

Balswick, Jack O. and Judith K. Balswick 191, 193

barter economy 248-249

Becker, Howard 89, 99-100, 206, 212

beliefs 12-13, 21, 28-29, 32, 35, 38-39, 41, 43-45

Berger, Peter L. 10, 46, 212

biculturalism 130

Bierstedt, Robert 290, 298

bilingualism 130, 133

Blau, Peter M. 119

blue-collar workers 249

Blumer, Herbert 45, 238, 246, 288, 292, 298

bourgeoisie 14, 258, 262

Brazil 217-218, 226, 230, 258

bureaucracy 57, 59, 189, 272, 279

Burgess, Ernest W. 288

bus boycott 248

C

Calvinist 114, 202-203

Campolo, Tony 56

capitalist 39, 202, 248, 257-260

charismatic authority 271, 283

China 30, 42, 160, 217-218, 226, 230, 258-259

Chomsky, Noam 33, 45

chronic illness 164-167, 171

church 2-3, 8, 13-16, 18, 21, 30, 38-40, 42, 51-53, 55-59, 64, 69, 72, 76-77, 96, 123, 134, 147, 149-150, 170, 172, 179, 189, 196, 198, 202-208, 210-211, 234, 243-244, 255, 269, 277-280, 300, 305, 307-308

circular reaction 288, 297

civil laws 44, 90

class 39-40, 48-49, 53, 55, 74, 85-87, 92-99, 106-111, 115-117, 127, 141, 164, 178, 181-182, 202-203, 225-226, 234-235, 239-240, 244, 249, 257-258, 275-276, 304-305

coercion 106, 117, 179, 270

cognitive development 71, 78

Cohen, Morris 197

Coleman, James S. 231

collective behavior 287-298, 305

collective conscience 13, 303

Collins, Randall 226, 231

common good 258, 269, 273, 279-280, 283

comparable worth 148

Comte, Auguste 3, 9

conceptual definition 18

conflict 14-16, 25, 36, 38-39, 49, 54-57, 69-70, 74, 84, 98, 105-108, 111, 113-114, 116-117, 127, 140, 150, 157, 177-179, 183, 190, 203-204, 210, 223, 225, 229, 237, 239-241, 245, 258, 269, 273, 275, 278, 281-283, 301, 304, 310

consciousness of kind 290, 297

containment theory 89

content analysis 20, 75

Cooley, Charles 50, 61, 67, 79

core nations 260, 262

corporate deviance 95

countercultures 39, 43

craze 292-293, 297

crime 3-4, 19, 83-85, 87, 89-95, 98-99, 127, 255, 292

criminal laws 90, 274

cross-sectional analysis 168, 172

cult 206, 210-211

cultural material 37, 44

cultural pluralism 129-130, 135

cultural relativistic perspective 41, 44

cultural universals 30-31, 44

culture 8, 27-45, 58, 64-66, 68-72, 74-78, 82, 92, 116, 127, 129, 134-135, 138, 144, 149, 156, 160, 177, 180-181, 188, 209, 222, 224, 235, 243-245, 269, 271, 280-282, 301-302

culture gap 301

D

Dahl, Robert 276, 285

David McClelland 114, 118

Davis, Kingsley 65, 80, 105, 118

death anxiety 170, 172

democratic socialism 259

demography 158

dependency theory 114-115, 117

dependent variable 18, 23, 25

deviance 5, 16, 81-101, 255

differential association 86, 97, 99

diffusion 114, 301-302, 311

discrimination 86, 125, 127-128, 133-135, 139, 146, 151, 179, 202, 228, 244, 302

disease 76, 127, 162-163, 167-169, 234-235, 238-239, 241-243, 245, 252

disengagement theory 162, 172

division of labor 26, 57, 149, 254, 262, 303

Dobson, Ed 278, 285

dominant group 125-131, 134-135

Doyle and Paludi 148, 151-152

Dumhoff, G. William 275, 285

Duncan, Otis Dudley 119

dynamic equilibrium 304

dysfunction 5, 49, 56-57, 59-60, 200-202, 211, 242

E

Edge, Findley 204, 212

education 13, 33, 35-36, 48, 58, 72, 74, 94, 96-97, 104, 106, 109-110, 116, 123, 125-126, 128, 139, 142, 147, 183, 185, 189, 202, 215-231, 234, 239-240, 244, 250, 255-256, 258-259, 261, 269, 274-275, 277, 307

elite deviance 92-95, 99

emergent norms 289

empirical 4, 31, 44, 123, 164, 201, 275

epidemiology 235, 239, 245

Erikson, Erik 70, 78, 80

ethical principles 24, 72

ethnic groups 124-127, 134-135, 182-183, 293

ethnocentrism 39-40, 44, 129, 133

expressive crowd 292, 297

extended families 177, 183, 190

F

family 2, 7-8, 15, 16, 28, 30, 35, 42-43, 50-51, 53, 55, 59, 64, 66-67, 71-74, 76, 82-83, 85, 89, 92, 97, 106-111, 129, 132, 139, 141-142, 145, 147, 149-153, 149-151, 160, 168-169, 175-190

family of orientation 177

family of procreation 177

felony 90, 94, 99

feminism 147-148, 150-151, 187-188

focal concerns 85, 99

folk society 255, 262

formal organization 57, 60

Freud, Sigmund 70, 79

Friedan, Betty 147-148

functions 13-14, 24, 26, 35, 37, 48, 60, 72, 94, 105, 126, 139-140, 150, 176, 190, 197, 200-201, 210, 224-225, 229, 237, 273-275, 282

G

gemeinschaft 255, 262, 303

gender 14, 18, 20, 42, 73, 75-76, 117, 136-153, 171, 176, 178-179, 183, 187-188, 234-235, 239-244, 250, 269, 290, 297, 302

gender stratification 139-140, 150

generalized others 15, 68

George Ritzer 58, 61, 254, 265

Germany 41, 126, 217-219, 230, 259, 276

gerontology 156, 172

gesellschaft 255, 262-263, 303

Giddings, Franklin 290, 298

Glaser, Daniel 86, 212

global village 256, 263

Glock, Charles 204

Goffman, Erving 69, 78, 80

government 2, 20, 30, 57, 83, 90, 95, 130-132, 139, 187, 189, 216, 218, 222, 234, 250, 257-259, 261, 269, 271-283, 291, 293

H

health care 112, 167-168, 187, 189, 234, 237, 240-241, 243-245, 255, 258-259

hierarchy 57-58, 114

Hirschi 88, 97, 99-100

horizontal mobility 111, 117

horticultural societies 251-252

hunting and gathering societies 216, 250

hypothesis 18, 21, 23, 25, 210, 276

hysterical contagion 291, 294, 296-297

I

"I" 69, 79

ideational 29-30, 44

ideology 41, 126, 281, 283-284, 306, 309

illness 110, 163-168, 171, 234, 236-239, 242, 245-246, 274, 291

in-group 50, 117, 126

independent variable 18, 23, 25

India 53, 159, 181, 198, 203, 217, 219-220, 226, 230

individual sin 6, 9, 133

Industrial Revolution 3, 9, 13, 253, 303

industrialized societies 216, 229

inequality 96, 105-106, 111-113, 116, 133-134, 138-140, 150, 178-179, 202, 225-226, 229, 237, 245, 250

informal organizations 51, 59-60

information industry 255, 263

institutional racism 127, 133

institutional sexism 140, 150-151

interactionist perspective 15-16, 25, 38, 49, 66, 140, 179, 190, 239, 245

interviews 19, 22

issueless riot 292, 297

J

Japan 159, 185, 217, 220, 222, 230, 241, 249, 258, 271

K

Kanter, Rosabeth 205, 212
Kelley, Dean M. 207, 213
kibbutz(im) 181, 248, 263
Killian, Lewis 289, 298
kinship 177, 182-183, 190
Kohlberg, Lawrence 71-72, 78, 80
Ku Klux Klan 133, 293

L

labeling theorists 89-90, 98-99
labor unions 57, 253, 263, 275-277, 293
laissez-faire 257, 263
language 15-16, 29-31, 33-34, 39-40, 44, 66, 68, 76, 110, 124-125, 129, 134-135, 141, 145-146, 178, 257, 263, 290
Lasswell, Harold D. 269, 285
latent 13-14, 48, 74, 224-225, 229, 273
latent functions 48, 225, 229, 273
Latinos 125, 182-183
law 36, 44, 83, 88, 90-91, 95-97, 99, 109, 130, 157, 181, 190, 272, 276, 278, 283-284, 304
laws 36, 44, 90, 123, 186, 269, 273-274, 277-278, 282, 293, 302, 310
Le Bon, Gustave 288, 298
legal-rational authority 272, 284
Lemert 90, 98-100
Lenski, Gerhard E. 119
Lewis, C. S. 279, 285
life expectancy 110, 159, 161, 169, 172, 235, 240-241, 245
life-course perspective 163, 171-172
Lippmann, Walter 40, 45
long-term care 155, 165, 168-169, 171-172
longitudinal research 165, 172
longitudinal study 23
looking-glass self 67, 78-79
lower-class 40, 53, 85-87, 92-94, 97-99, 107, 110-111

M

manifest 13-14, 26, 48, 57, 161-162, 204, 209, 224-225, 229, 273
manifest function 48, 224-225, 229, 273
marriage 36, 38-39, 73, 110-111, 176-179, 181-190, 199, 201-202, 255
marriage rate 184
Marx, Karl 14, 202, 258
mass media 40-41, 72, 75-76, 78, 89, 130, 156, 291
Matza and Sykes 86, 100
McDonaldization 58-59, 254, 263
McKenna, David 58, 61
McPhail, Clark 289, 291, 298
"me" 69, 79
Mead, George Herbert 15, 66-69, 74, 78-79
mean 23, 25
measure of central tendency 23, 25
mechanical solidarity 303, 311
median 23, 25, 109, 148, 182, 185
melting-pot 129, 135
Merton, Robert 12-13, 26, 86, 100, 139, 151
middle class 95, 110
Milgram, Stanley 291, 298
Miller, Walter 85, 98
Mills, C. Wright 10, 270, 275, 285
minority 42, 89, 112, 125-126, 128-132, 134-135, 143, 182, 228, 237, 256, 275, 278, 283,
misdemeanors 90, 99

Moberg, David 56, 61

mode 23, 25

modernization theory 113-115, 117

monogamy 177, 190

Montague, Ashley 123

Moore, Wilbert 105, 118

morbidity 165, 235, 239, 241, 243, 245,

mores 36, 43-44, 83, 90

mortality rate 235, 241, 245-246

N

Native Americans 35, 40, 124, 126, 130-133

negative sanctions 37, 83, 99

Niebuhr, H. Richard 206, 212

nonempirical referent 201, 211

normal aging 161-163, 173

normative culture 36

norms 7, 9, 18, 20, 36-37, 39-40, 42-45, 54, 60, 68, 70, 72, 74-77, 79, 82-90, 95-99, 127, 156-158, 171-172, 178, 183, 185, 201-202, 210, 251, 280, 283-284, 289, 294-295, 297, 302

North American Free Trade Association 257, 264

nuclear families 177, 181

O

O'Dea and Aviad 200-201, 210, 212

occupation 99, 106-110, 116, 149, 254

occupational prestige 108, 110

operational definition 18

organic solidarity 303

out-group 50, 126, 128

P

panic 291, 294, 297

Park, Robert 288, 298

Parsons, Talcott 12, 26, 113, 118, 173, 191, 236, 246, 285, 304, 312

participant observation 20, 26

pastoral societies 251

peer group 72, 74-75

peers 37, 68-70, 78, 83, 88-89, 137, 141, 143-144, 150, 224

Peoples, James 29, 45

periphery nations 260, 264

Peter Principle 58-59, 61

Piaget, Jean 71, 78, 79, 80

pink-collar workers 249

pluralist model 276-277, 284

polarization 291, 297

Political Action Committees 277, 284

political institution 269, 284

polyandry 177, 181, 190

polygamy 177, 191

polygyny 177, 191

positive sanctions 26-37, 83-84

Positivists 84

postindustrial 216, 219-220, 222, 225, 229, 254-257

postindustrial societies 216, 254-257

power 4, 6, 14, 16, 40, 48, 53, 58, 64, 72, 76, 84-85, 90, 95, 104-107, 111, 115, 122, 125-127, 135, 145, 165, 178-179, 182, 190, 202, 237-238, 248-249, 253, 257, 267-271, 275-276, 278-279, 282-284, 301, 304, 307-310

power elite 275-276, 283-284

preindustrial 249, 255, 264

prejudice 40-41, 92-93, 125, 127-130, 133-135, 228, 302

premodern economies 250-252

primary deviance 90

primary group 50-53, 60, 68

primary sector 249, 264

prisons 49, 77, 83, 94

profane 198-199, 211

proletariat 14, 258, 264

prophetic activity 202, 211

proxemics 33, 44

psychology 4, 9, 186, 189

public 6, 21, 36-38, 52, 65, 90, 94-95, 97, 125, 129, 135, 143, 158-161, 169, 176, 186, 188, 203, 205, 216, 226, 228, 234, 260, 268, 277-278, 281, 290-292, 300, 305-306

Putnam 193, 280, 283, 285

Q

questionnaires 19, 22

R

race 55, 73, 96, 117, 121-136, 157, 171, 182-183, 190, 233-235, 239-240, 244, 250, 269, 281, 302

racial and ethnic stratification 122, 126-128

Ratcliff, Donald 48-49, 54, 57, 61

real self 16, 69

recidivism 94, 99

Reckless, Walter 88-89, 99-100

reform 77, 94, 302, 310-311

reliability 18, 26

religion 3, 16, 30, 35, 38, 72, 76, 78, 111, 124-125, 131, 134-135, 139, 141, 145, 165, 170, 178, 186, 195-213, 234, 243-244, 245, 250-253, 255, 269, 277-278, 282-283, 292, 302, 306, 308

religiosity 204, 210-211, 243

Renzetti and Curran 145, 151-152

resocialization 77, 96, 98

resource mobilization 294, 298

response rates 22

retirement 123-124, 157, 162-165, 171, 254, 261

Riessman, Catherine Kohler 237-238

Riley, Matilda 158, 173

ritual 29, 33, 36, 38, 76, 199, 200-201, 204-205, 210-211

role 3-4, 54-55, 59-60, 66, 68-76, 78-79, 82, 89, 93, 96, 126, 139, 141-147, 158, 162, 164, 171-172, 181, 184, 186-189, 196, 202, 222, 224-225, 236-237, 243, 268, 278, 283, 291

role conflict 54-55, 59-60

role distance 69

role strain 54, 59-60

role-playing 66, 69, 75

Rosenthal, R. and L. Jacobson 227, 231

S

sacred 4, 29, 33, 76, 145-146, 196, 198-202, 204, 210-211

sanctions 7, 9, 36-37, 43-44, 83-84, 95-96, 99

school 2-3, 7-8, 13, 18, 37, 48-49, 52-54, 64, 66, 69, 71-75, 77, 89, 108, 111, 123, 133, 141-144, 147, 150, 160, 176, 178, 181, 189, 201, 216-222, 224-229, 255-256, 274, 290-291, 304, 308

science 2-4, 9, 19, 24, 35, 110, 112, 142-143, 197, 211

secondary data 19-20, 25-26

secondary deviance 90, 98

secondary group 50-53, 57, 60

sect 111, 205-207, 210-211

secularization 208-209, 211, 253

segregation 14, 127-128, 130-131, 133-135, 149, 172, 260

self-concept 16, 64, 66, 68-69, 89-90, 229

self-fulfilling prophecy 90, 142, 151

sex 33, 41-43, 92, 95, 104-105, 127, 138-139, 141-145, 147, 150-151, 157, 176, 183-185, 188-189, 242, 250, 308

sexism 140, 142, 145-146, 150-151

significant others 15, 68, 74, 79, 142

simple random sample 21, 26

situational isolation 65-66

Smelser, Neil 288, 292, 305, 311

Smith, Adam 257-258, 263

social bond theory 88-89

social capital 280, 283-284

social conflict perspective 14-15, 25, 106, 140

social construction of reality 55

social control 36, 44, 83-85, 88-89, 91, 94, 97, 99, 202, 237, 295, 307

social differentiation 104, 117

social exclusion 90

social interaction 2, 8, 29, 78, 290

social mobility 111, 177

social movements 157, 271, 287-291, 293-298, 311

social psychology 4

social sin 6, 9, 96, 105, 107, 122, 133-134, 138

social status 53, 55, 59-60, 74, 84, 99, 104, 108, 178

social stratification 103-119, 125-126, 138, 157

social structure 8, 13-14, 26, 48-49, 59-60, 68, 96, 127, 140, 150, 179, 280, 304-306

socialism 4, 248, 257-262, 264

socialization 40, 63-80, 87, 138, 140-141, 145, 150, 171, 178, 181, 224-227, 229, 255, 271, 275

sociological imagination 5, 9

Stark, Rodney 136, 204, 212-213, 295, 298

status inconsistency 53, 59-60

stereotype 40-41, 44

stereotypes 20, 40-42, 44, 126, 128, 143-144, 182-183, 190

strain theories 86-88

structural-functional perspective 12-14, 24, 26, 37-38, 48-49, 83-84, 105-106, 116-117, 126-127, 139-140, 150, 178, 190, 197, 224-225, 229, 236-237, 245, 273-274, 282, 283, 304, 310

subculture 39-40, 42, 45

subjectivists 84

substantive method 197

Sumner, William Graham 36, 45, 100

Sutherland, Edwin 85-86, 98, 100-101

surveys 4, 19, 21, 25-26, 108

symbolic interactionist theory 179, 226-227, 238-239

symbols 15-16, 25, 31-33, 39, 43-44, 49, 53, 56, 67-68, 86, 141, 179, 198, 272, 281, 283-284

systematic sampling 21, 26

T

tertiary sector 249, 261, 264

Thomas, Cal 278, 285

Thomas, W.I. 238, 246

Toch, Hans 291, 298

Toffler 301, 312

traditional authority 271, 284

Troeltsch, Ernest 205, 212

Turner, Ralph 289, 298

U

underclass 131, 255, 264

United Kingdom 217, 221-222

V

validity 18, 26, 88

values 12, 18, 25, 28-29, 31, 35-36, 38-40, 42-45, 49, 55, 58, 64, 72, 74-78, 82, 85, 89-90, 92-93, 95-98, 106, 109, 114, 116, 127, 143-144, 156, 176, 178-179, 183, 190, 201-202, 210-211, 260-261, 269, 277, 279, 281, 283-284, 295-296, 304, 307, 310-311

vertical mobility 111, 117

virtual self 69

W

Weber, Max 12-13, 26, 57, 61, 114, 202, 212, 270, 285

welfare 23, 43, 72, 105, 180, 190, 274, 279

welfare (system) 19, 57, 125, 182, 259-260, 291

white-collar crime 94-95, 99, 101

white-collar workers 108, 249, 264

Williams, Robin 35, 45

worldview 34, 39, 43, 45, 113, 116, 272

Wuthnow, Robert 209, 213

Y

Yinger, J. Milton 136, 196, 212